Ultimate React Native for Cross Platform App Development

Turn Your Ideas into Scalable, Production-Ready Cross-Platform React Native Mobile Applications for iOS and Android

Felipe Becker Nunes

www.orangeava.com

First Published: April 2026

Published By: Orange Education Pvt Ltd, AVA®

Address: 9, Daryaganj, Delhi, 110002, India

275 New North Road Islington Suite 1314 London,
N1 7AA, United Kingdom

ISBN (PBK): 978-93-49887-46-6

ISBN (E-BOOK): 978-93-49887-37-4

Scan the QR code to explore our entire catalogue

www.orangeava.com

Get a Free eBook

We hope you're enjoying your recent book purchase! Your feedback is incredibly valuable to us and helps other readers discover books that truly make a difference.

If you found this book useful or enjoyable, we'd greatly appreciate it if you could leave a short review with a 5-star rating on Amazon. Your review supports our work and allows us to reach more learners worldwide.

As a thank-you, we're happy to offer you a **free digital copy of this book** plus a **30% discount code** for your next purchase on our official websites:

www.orangeava.com

www.orangeava.in (For the Indian Subcontinent).

☑**How it works:**

Leave your review on Amazon, take a screenshot of the confirmation or use the following link to submit the claim and email it to **info@orangeava.com.** Once received the required detail, we will send your rewards within 24 hours, **along with one month free subcription to the book on AVA SkillShelf!**

Claim Form
https://rebrand.ly/4d2477

Thank you for your support—it truly means a lot to us.

Enjoy 1 Month of Free Access to AVA SkillShelf!

The future belongs to lifelong learners. With AVA SkillShelf, you go beyond reading books and start building real, job-ready skills curated by industry experts.

Your membership unlocks **200+ learning products** covering AI, Cloud, Python, Cybersecurity, Data Science, DevOps, and more—all in one platform. Our bestselling technical books are transformed into structured courses designed for practical, real-world application.

Learn directly from experienced professionals and published authors, with no filler—just actionable insights. Earn **verified digital certifications** to strengthen your CV, LinkedIn profile, and professional credibility.

Learn anytime, anywhere, on any device, at your own pace. Ideal for students, professionals, career switchers, and tech leaders.

For full access to all current and future courses, choose our **Annual Membership**. Simply scan the QR to get started!

For 1 month Free access, simply refer to the steps on the previous page titled: Get a Free ebook!

https://www.avaskillshelf.com/

Downloading the code bundles and colored images

Please follow the links or scan the QR codes to download the
Code Bundles and Images of the book:

https://github.com/ava-orange-education/Ultimate-React-Native-for-Cross-Platform-App-Development

The code bundles and images of the book are also hosted on
https://rebrand.ly/fdab3a

In case there's an update to the code, it will be updated on the existing GitHub repository.

Errata

We take immense pride in our work at **Orange Education Pvt Ltd,** and follow best practices to ensure the accuracy of our content to provide an indulging reading experience to our subscribers. Our readers are our mirrors, and we use their inputs to reflect and improve upon human errors, if any, that may have occurred during the publishing processes involved. To let us maintain the quality and help us reach out to any readers who might be having difficulties due to any unforeseen errors, please write to us at :

errata@orangeava.com

Your support, suggestions, and feedback are highly appreciated.

Dedicated to

My Beloved Parents:
Paulo Ubirajara Timler Nunes,
Geni Becker Nunes.
And
My Wife, Letânia Mireski.

About the Author

Felipe Becker Nunes is a software engineer and educator whose career bridges two complementary paths: building production-ready systems and teaching others how to build them well. With over five years of hands-on experience in software development, he works across the full stack using JavaScript and TypeScript, with strong expertise in Node.js, React, React Native, databases, and core software engineering practices.

Professionally, Felipe has designed and implemented end-to-end solutions spanning frontend and backend. On the frontend, he has delivered applications using React and Next.js with TypeScript, applying state-management patterns such as Context and Redux, and emphasizing maintainable, scalable component architectures. On the backend, he has built services with Node.js and TypeORM, integrating both SQL and NoSQL databases, and supporting deployments through Docker, CI/CD pipelines, and AWS infrastructure.

He has taught programming, web development, databases, and innovation across multiple academic levels and instructional modalities, consistently prioritizing active-learning methods and hands-on outcomes. Currently, Felipe teaches in a Systems Information program, mentors capstone projects, and develops frontend and backend solutions for institutional initiatives.

Felipe's academic background includes a Bachelor's degree in Information Systems, a Master's in Computer Science, formal teacher training, and a PhD in Informatics in Education. His interests lie at the intersection of software craftsmanship, learning design, and emerging technologies, with a recurring focus on empowering people to learn, ship, and grow.

About the Technical Reviewer

Padam Sandhu is a Lead Engineer at PayPal, where he builds end-to-end customer experiences across modern web platforms and backend services. He specializes in scalable UI architecture with React and TypeScript, and in integrating data-rich products using GraphQL to deliver fast, reliable, and accessible user journeys.

Known for balancing product impact with engineering excellence, Padam partners closely with product, design, and platform teams to turn complex requirements into clean, maintainable systems. With a full-stack mindset and a strong focus on performance and developer productivity, he enjoys creating solutions that scale for both customers, and the teams that build for them.

Acknowledgments

Writing a book is never a solo effort. Even when the work happens in quiet hours, it is carried by a whole network of people who encourage you, challenge you, and make it possible for you to keep showing up.

First, I am deeply grateful to my family. To my parents: thank you for the foundation you gave me as your guidance, patience, and constant support shaped the way I learn, work, and persist. To my wife: thank you for the daily encouragement, for believing in this project even on the days I doubted it, and for giving me the time and space to focus when it mattered the most. And to my wider family: thank you for cheering me up; understanding the long stretches of "I'm almost done," and celebrating every small milestone along the way.

I also want to thank everyone who helped turn this manuscript into a real book: editors, reviewers, and the publishing team, whose feedback, structure, and attention to detail made the material clearer and stronger. Your work raised the quality of every chapter.

To the developers, educators, and open-source maintainers in the React Native ecosystem: thank you for building tools, writing documentation, sharing examples, and answering questions in public. This book stands on that collective effort.

Finally, a big thank you to the readers! If you are holding this book, you are investing your time and attention into learning and building. I hope these pages help you ship apps with confidence, and also, you enjoy the learning process as much as I did writing it.

Preface

React Native has changed what it means to build mobile apps. Today, teams are expected to ship experiences that feel native, move fast, scale cleanly, and reach users on both iOS and Android often with a single codebase. That promise is exciting, but anyone who has tried to deliver a real product knows the full story: navigation edge cases, performance bottlenecks, offline behavior, app-store requirements, CI/CD pipelines, testing, and release workflows can quickly turn "Hello World" confidence into production anxiety. This book is written to bridge that gap.

It focuses on the parts of React Native that matter when you are building an app you intend to ship. It explains not only how to implement features, but why certain choices hold up better in real-world projects. Along the way, we will cover the fundamentals that make you productive (components, hooks, state, styling, and navigation), and we shall also steadily move into the realities of production engineering, authentication, data fetching, storage, offline-first patterns, performance profiling, architecture decisions, testing strategy, and deployment.

The approach is practical by design. You can learn through guided implementations, patterns that are widely used in modern mobile teams, and a consistent emphasis on maintainability that includes code organization, predictable state flows, reusable UI, and debugging techniques which help you move quickly without accumulating chaos.

This book is divided into 16 chapters, progressing from setup and core concepts to advanced topics and publishing. The details are outlined as follows:

Chapter 1 introduces React Native as a cross-platform framework, and helps you to understand where it fits compared to native development and other cross-platform approaches. You will also set expectations about performance, developer experience, and the trade-offs you are making, when you choose React Native.

Chapter 2 covers environment setup and project creation, including the practical differences between Expo and the React Native CLI. You shall also build a clean foundation so that you can iterate confidently, and avoid the most common setup pitfalls.

Chapter 3 focuses on React fundamentals in a mobile context such as components, props, state, hooks, rendering behavior, and the mental model, you need to reason about UI updates. You will also learn how to structure small features in a way that scales.

Chapter 4 dives into UI building blocks and layout styling, Flexbox, responsive design, theming, reusable components, and accessibility basics. You will also learn how to create interfaces that look consistent across devices, and feel polished.

Chapter 5 introduces navigation in real apps: stacks, tabs, deep links, guarded routes, and patterns for passing data safely between screens. You shall also learn how to design navigation flows that do not become fragile over time.

Chapter 6 covers state management and data flow starting from local state and Context, then moving into scalable patterns. You shall also learn when global state is helpful, when it is harmful, and how to keep logic testable.

Chapter 7 explores data fetching and API integration such as HTTP basics, error handling, caching strategies, pagination, and practical patterns for separating networking from UI. The goal is resilient data flows that behave well under real network conditions.

Chapter 8 focuses on authentication and security-minded design which includes session handling, token storage considerations, protecting screens, and common mobile security pitfalls. You will also be able to implement auth flows with a clear understanding of the trade-offs involved.

Chapter 9 introduces persistence and offline-first behavior local storage, structured caching, syncing strategies, and conflict considerations. You will also learn how to build experiences that remain useful, when connectivity is unreliable.

Chapter 10 addresses device capabilities and integrations such as notifications, camera or media access (where applicable), permissions, and platform-specific behavior. You shall also learn how to handle differences between iOS and Android without duplicating your whole app.

Chapter 11 is about performance which includes measuring, profiling, and improving. You will also learn how to think about rendering cost, list performance, memoization, and common bottlenecks, and how to fix them without premature optimization.

Chapter 12 covers architecture and maintainability such as folder structure, feature-based organization, separation of concerns, dependency boundaries, and patterns that keep your codebase evolvable.

Chapter 13 focuses on testing strategies: what to test, where to test it, and how to keep tests valuable, instead of brittle. You will cover unit tests, component tests, and practical guidance for end-to-end coverage.

Chapter 14 explains build and release workflows, including versioning, environment configuration, and automation. You shall also learn how teams typically manage dev/staging/production builds, and keep releases predictable.

Chapter 15 walks through deployment and publishing that includes store requirements, signing, app metadata, review pitfalls, release channels, and post-release monitoring considerations, so that you can go from "works on my phone" to "available in the store."

Chapter 16 or the final chapter of the book closes with advanced practices and next steps which includes keeping up with the ecosystem, evaluating libraries, planning upgrades, and making technology decisions that stay stable, as your app and team grow.

Who is this book for?

This book is for:

- Developers with JavaScript/TypeScript and React experience moving into mobile.
- Native developers who want to understand the React Native approach without hand-wavy explanations.
- Teams building real cross-platform apps, and wanting a clean, production-ready path.

Thus to sum up, if you code along and build the exercises, you will finish with not only a stronger understanding of React Native, but also the practical confidence to design, build, test, and ship cross-platform applications with a professional workflow.

DID YOU KNOW

Did you know that Orange Education Pvt Ltd offers eBook versions of every book published, with PDF and ePub files available? You can upgrade to the eBook version at **www.orangeava.com** and as a print book customer, you are entitled to a discount on the eBook copy. Get in touch with us at: **info@orangeava.com** for more details.

At **www.orangeava.com**, you can also read a collection of free technical articles, sign up for a range of free newsletters, and receive exclusive discounts and offers on Print Books and eBooks.

PIRACY

If you come across any illegal copies of our works in any form on the internet, we would be grateful if you would provide us with the location address or website name. Please contact us at **info@orangeava.com** with a link to the material.

ARE YOU INTERESTED IN AUTHORING WITH US?

If there is a topic that you have expertise in, and you are interested in either writing or contributing to a book, please write to us at **business@orangeava.com**. We are on a journey to help developers and tech professionals to gain insights on the present technological advancements and innovations happening across the globe and build a community that believes Knowledge is best acquired by sharing and learning with others. Please reach out to us to learn what our audience demands and how you can be part of this educational reform. We also welcome ideas from tech experts and help them build learning and development content for their domains.

REVIEWS

Please leave a review. Once you have read and used this book, why not leave a review on the site that you purchased it from? Potential readers can then see and use your unbiased opinion to make purchase decisions. We at Orange Education would love to know what you think about our products, and our authors can learn from your feedback. Thank you!

For more information about Orange Education, please visit **www.orangeava.com**.

Table of Contents

CHAPTER 1
Introduction and Environment

Introduction

In this chapter, we will discuss the fundamental pillars of **React Native**, a **framework** that enables the development of mobile applications for different platforms from a single codebase. We will begin by revisiting the context in which React Native had emerged, and will proceed to exploring its history and evolution. Next, we will highlight how its internal architecture, based on a "**bridge**" that connects **JavaScript** to **native code**, has revolutionized the way mobile interfaces are created. We will also cover advantages, challenges, and real-world use cases, illustrating how companies from various industries have benefited from the framework. Finally, we will present best practices, integrations with other technologies, and future trends, providing a comprehensive overview of everything React Native offers for modern mobile development.

Structure

In this chapter, we will cover the following topics:

- The Origin of React Native and Its Historical Context
- Expansion and Market Adoption
- Architecture
- React Native 0.83.1 and React 19 Integration
- Advancing towards a More Dynamic Architecture
- Integration with Modern Technologies
- Monitoring and Debugging
- Enhancing React Native Development
- Use Cases
- Benefits and Challenges of React Native
- Expo CLI versus React Native CLI: Understanding the Two Approaches
- JavaScript XML
- Setting Up the Development Environment

- Creating Your First React Native Project
- Project Structure
- Best Practices
- Trends and Future

The Origin of React Native and Its Historical Context

The development of mobile applications gained significant momentum starting in the 2000s, becoming an essential part of our daily lives. Today, practically all aspects of life—education, entertainment, communication, banking services, healthcare, shopping, and transportation—can be mediated through mobile devices.

To keep up with this trend, the **official React Native documentation (https://reactnative.dev/)** and various studies on cross-platform applications report that different solutions emerged for app development, with React Native standing out as one of the most effective and influential options.

Originally released by **Facebook (now Meta)** in 2015, React Native aimed to solve one of the main challenges of mobile development: maintaining separate codes for Android and iOS. By leveraging the power of JavaScript and React, the technology significantly reduced redundant work, delivering applications that run on multiple platforms without sacrificing native features.

However, it is important to understand the landscape before React Native: in the mid-2000s, smartphones became widely adopted, with **iOS (Apple) and Android (Google)** emerging as the dominant mobile operating systems. Each ecosystem used its own language and tools—**Objective-C (later Swift) for iOS and Java (later Kotlin) for Android**—forcing companies that wanted to reach both platforms to duplicate efforts and maintain separate development teams.

To overcome these difficulties, hybrid solutions emerged, promising "*write once, run anywhere*" by using technologies such as **HTML, CSS, and JavaScript**. Tools such as **PhoneGap and Ionic** encapsulated web content within webviews, but they often failed to deliver the expected native performance, especially in animations and interactions.

According to accounts from the **Facebook development team**, the success of the React library on the web inspired the idea of applying it to mobile development. This led to the creation of a **communication bridge** that allowed JavaScript to interact with native system APIs, generating truly native components rather than just web pages disguised as apps.

It was in this context that **React Native was born**, introducing a **new way to build cross-platform applications**. Now that we have an understanding of the initial context, let us explore how React Native gained widespread adoption in the market.

Expansion and Market Adoption

After a period of internal development and a hackathon, Facebook officially introduced React Native to the public in 2015. The first demonstration took place in January of that year at the **React.js conference**, and by March, the framework was released as an **open-source project on GitHub**. Initially focused on **iOS**, React Native quickly expanded to support **Android** later that same year, allowing developers to build native applications for both platforms from a single JavaScript codebase.

From that point forward, major companies including **Instagram, Skype, Bloomberg, Tesla, and Pinterest** began integrating React Native into parts or even the entirety of their applications. The relatively smooth learning curve for JavaScript developers and the fast release cycle of new features contributed to the rise of the framework as a preferred choice for many development teams.

In 2016, there were plans to extend React Native beyond iOS and Android, with Microsoft collaborating to introduce support for **Windows** and Samsung exploring its use for **Tizen**. By 2017, the React Native community had grown significantly, despite occasional setbacks, such as temporary app store rejections—which, according to reports, were traced to third-party libraries rather than the framework itself. Nonetheless, the ecosystem continued to expand, attracting thousands of contributors and a vast repository of packages and libraries.

Over the following years, the framework underwent continuous improvements. In 2018, the React Native team announced a **major architectural overhaul (New Architecture)** aimed at optimizing rendering and reducing communication bottlenecks between JavaScript and native code. This effort led to the creation of **Fabric** (a new rendering engine) and **Turbo Modules**, both designed to improve performance and responsiveness.

Meanwhile, in 2019, Facebook (now Meta) introduced **Hermes**, a JavaScript engine optimized for mobile devices, initially targeting **Android**. Hermes reduced startup time, memory usage, and even the binary size. Later, with support for **iOS (starting from React Native 0.64)**, reports indicated a 40% decrease in startup time on iPhones.

These initiatives demonstrate the ongoing commitment of Meta in improving React Native. Recent versions (0.70 and beyond) have adopted Hermes as the default JavaScript engine and integrated optional elements of the **new architecture**, ensuring that the framework remains up-to-date with the latest iOS and Android releases.

Today, React Native is firmly established as one of the leading mobile development tools, evolving with a focus on performance, developer experience, and platform versatility. With this foundation in mind, let us now delve into the architecture that underpins React Native and discover how it achieves native-like performance across multiple platforms.

Architecture

React Native renders real native UI on each platform (for example, **`UIView`** on iOS and **`ViewGroup`** on Android), rather than relying on webviews for the interface layer. JS-native communication has evolved from the legacy, batched asynchronous **Bridge** to the **New Architecture**, which removes the asynchronous Bridge and uses **JSI**, along with **TurboModules** and **Fabric**—often described as "bridgeless."

This approach allows developers to achieve performance comparable to applications built in Swift/Objective-C or Kotlin/Java, without relying on web-views for the interface layer. In the current React Native release line (0.83.x), the modern systems underpinning React Native are the **New Architecture** pillars—**JSI**, **TurboModules**, and **Fabric**—which replace the legacy Bridge-based model.

New Architecture (JSI, TurboModules, and Fabric)

- **JavaScript Interface (JSI):** The New Architecture removes the asynchronous **Bridge** and replaces it with **JSI**, which enables direct JS-native interaction via shared references and avoids Bridge serialization overhead; it can also support synchronous calls where appropriate.
- **TurboModules:** The native module system of the New Architecture, designed to modernize and streamline native-module integration and access patterns under the JSI-based model.
- **Fabric:** The New Architecture renderer that redesigns how native views are created and updated, improving rendering consistency and enabling closer alignment with modern React rendering capabilities.

Hermes as the Default JavaScript Engine

Hermes is used by default by React Native, and no additional configuration is required to enable it. For many apps, Hermes improves start-up time and reduces memory usage compared to JavaScriptCore; React Native also ships a Hermes build bundled to match each React Native release.

Improvements for iOS and Android

- **iOS Updates:** Recent versions of React Native improve compatibility with **iOS 15+** and support advanced system features (such as **Swift Concurrency**) while still maintaining compatibility with older versions.
- **Android Enhancements:** React Native now integrates better with **modern Gradle configurations** and Android libraries, reducing manual setup for projects using the CLI.

Interoperability with React

- **Concurrent Rendering:** The new architecture, along with Fabric, enables the use of the concurrent rendering features of React, thereby, improving UI responsiveness by allowing processes to pause and resume rendering when necessary, preventing noticeable blocking.
- **Suspense:** This feature simplifies asynchronous loading, allowing developers to display placeholders or loading states in a more declarative way.

Improvements in Developer Experience

- **Revised CLI:** The React Native team has refined the **official CLI**, making it easier to configure projects from scratch, especially for developers working with **native modules**.
- **Updated Documentation and Examples:** The official site receives frequent updates, providing clear guides on the **New Architecture**, along with step-by-step instructions for enabling **Fabric** and **TurboModules**.

Even as the platform evolves, the core ideas of React Native remain consistent:

1. **Native UI Rendering:** React Native renders real native UI on each platform (rather than running the interface in a webview).
2. **JS-Native Interoperability:** React Native coordinates JavaScript and native code so that UI and native capabilities can be updated in response to React state. *(Historically this used the "Bridge"; modern React Native emphasizes the New Architecture and a more direct, "bridgeless" model.)*
3. **Fast Refresh:** Code changes are reflected quickly on device or emulator to speed up UI iteration during development.

React Native 0.83.1 and React 19.2 Integration

At the time of writing, React Native **0.83** ships with **React 19.2**. In practice, this means you can use the React 19 feature set in mobile projects while also benefiting from the React 19.2 additions that React Native highlights for this release—most notably `<Activity>` and `useEffectEvent`. Key React 19 / 19.2 capabilities relevant to mobile are as follows:

- **`Actions` (Async Transitions):** React 19 adds support for using async functions in transitions ("`Actions`") to handle pending states, errors, and optimistic updates more ergonomically.
- **`useActionState`:** A hook for managing state derived from an Action result, including a built-in pending flag.
- **`useOptimistic`:** A hook for optimistic UI updates while an async action is in flight.

- **`use`:** A new API for reading promises or context during rendering; React can suspend while a promise resolves.
- **`ref` as a prop:** In React 19, function components can access `ref` as a regular prop, reducing reliance on `forwardRef`.

React 19 also introduces **React Compiler**, an optimization feature that enables **automatic memoization**, following the best practices of React for performance improvements. With **React Native 0.83**, React Compiler setup is simplified; developers only need to install the compiler and configure a **Babel plugin** in Metro, eliminating the need for multiple separate packages.

Other Notable Changes and Platform Updates in the 0.83.x Line

- **Developer tooling improvements (0.83):** React Native 0.83 introduces significant enhancements to React Native DevTools, including Network inspection and Performance tracing panels.
- **Web API support (0.83):** React Native 0.83 adds Web Performance APIs as stable and introduces `IntersectionObserver` support in Canary.

Advancing towards a More Dynamic Architecture

With React 19 integration, Hermes as the default engine, and the migration to JSI, TurboModules, and Fabric, React Native continues evolving toward a more dynamic and optimized architecture. The latest versions focus on:

- **Lower Complexity:** Shorter release cycles, fewer breaking changes, and easier adoption of new features.
- **Better Performance:** Support for **vector drawables**, improvements in rendering speed, and faster build times.
- **Enhanced Developer Experience:** Improved **debugging tools**, optional JavaScript logs, **React Compiler integration**, and better support for brownfield iOS apps.

Overall, with each new version, React Native reinforces its status as a powerful cross-platform development framework, combining high performance with native flexibility. For developers looking to migrate or start projects, **Upgrade Helper** provides detailed instructions for smoothly adopting new features across versions.

Having explored how React Native keeps evolving and improving, let us now examine the modern technologies and services that integrate seamlessly with it, enhancing both development efficiency and application capabilities.

Integration with Modern Technologies

The **React Native ecosystem** benefits from various tools and services that facilitate the development of robust mobile applications. Some of the most common integrations are as follows:

- **TypeScript:** The use of **TypeScript** has become almost a standard in many React Native projects, providing static typing and productivity enhancements such as auto-completion and safer refactoring. Adopting TypeScript is simple—developers only need to **add a `tsconfig.json` file** and use **`.tsx`** extensions for components. Many popular libraries already include TypeScript definitions, ensuring smooth integration. As a result, TypeScript helps prevent common runtime errors in JavaScript and promotes a clearer and a more reliable code.

- **GraphQL with Apollo or Relay:** React Native does not impose limitations on **API consumption**—both **REST** and **GraphQL** are supported. However, many developers prefer **GraphQL** due to its ability to fetch only the required data for each screen, reducing network overhead.

  Tools such as **Apollo Client** work in React Native the same way they do in web applications—by installing the client and configuring hooks such as `useQuery` and `useMutation`. This setup even allows developers to share query logic across web and mobile apps. Large companies using React Native often adopt GraphQL with Apollo or Relay, leveraging a unified data management approach across multiple platforms.

- **Firebase:** For those looking for a scalable backend solution, **Firebase** offers authentication, real-time databases, storage, and notifications. The **React Native Firebase** project (community-maintained with official Google support) provides specific packages for each service, including **Analytics, Cloud Firestore, Cloud Functions, and Crashlytics.**

  With Firebase, developers can integrate backend functionalities without setting up their own servers. For example, installing `@react-native-firebase/auth` enables **authentication methods** (email, Google, Apple, and so on), leveraging **native SDKs** already integrated into Firebase.

  Additionally, Firebase provides push notifications via **Firebase Cloud Messaging (FCM)** for both Android and iOS, accelerating the development of advanced features.

Monitoring and Debugging

To effectively monitor, debug, and maintain a React Native app, developers typically combine production monitoring with modern local debugging tools:

- **Crashlytics and Sentry (production monitoring):** React Native apps commonly integrate Crashlytics (Firebase) and/or Sentry to capture JavaScript exceptions and native crashes, helping teams triage and fix issues before they affect more users.
- **React Native DevTools (current default debugger):** For local development, the recommended, built-in debugger of React Native is **React Native DevTools**. It replaces older debugging frontends such as the Flipper-based React Native plugin flow and prior debugger approaches, and provides integrated React DevTools capabilities plus dedicated panels for debugging.
- **Network and performance inspection (today):** In the 0.83 release line, React Native DevTools includes first-class **Network inspection** and **Performance tracing** panels. Network inspection captures calls from `fetch()`, `XMLHttpRequest`, and `<Image>`, and can show where a request originated; performance tracing provides a unified timeline view to diagnose runtime slowdowns.
- **Flipper (legacy / older codebases):** You may still encounter Flipper in older React Native projects or legacy setups. However, React Native removed native Flipper libraries/setup from **new projects** and the React Native Flipper plugin flow is **unsupported** for React Native-specific inspection features. Treat Flipper as a legacy tool you might need to understand when maintaining older apps, not the primary recommended debugger for modern projects.
- **Logging best practices:** Keep structured logs (locally and/or in a centralized sink) to investigate user-reported issues. Apply privacy and security best practices to avoid logging sensitive data.

Enhancing React Native Development

By integrating these technologies—whether for static typing, data consumption, backend integration, monitoring, or debugging—React Native becomes an even more comprehensive solution for modern mobile development.

Together, these tools create an ecosystem that supports:

- Faster development cycles.
- Greater reliability.
- Cloud and analytics support for production apps.

This enables a continuous cycle of development and improvement, making React Native a powerful choice for building scalable, high-performance mobile applications. Let us now explore how companies of various sizes—from startups to large corporations—are putting React Native into practice, illustrating its capabilities and versatility in real-world scenarios.

Use Cases

React Native, due to its maturity and popularity, has been adopted by companies of all sizes; from startups to large corporations, for large-scale applications. The following are some key examples that illustrate this adoption:

- **Meta (Facebook):** As the **original creator** of React Native, Meta integrates the framework into **strategic parts** of its ecosystem. It is used in products such as **Marketplace, Oculus VR applications, and Ad Managers**.

  Instagram, also owned by Meta, implemented React Native to launch features simultaneously on Android and iOS, demonstrating productivity gains and improved performance in specific modules.

- **Microsoft:** A major supporter of React Native, Microsoft maintains official versions for Windows and macOS and has migrated sections of its apps (such as **Office, Outlook, Teams, and Skype**) to React Native.

  This adoption allows Microsoft to synchronize updates across platforms while leveraging tools such as CodePush for **automated over-the-air (OTA) deployments**, accelerating the development cycle.

- **Tesla:** The mobile app of Tesla demonstrates how React Native can deliver near real-time responsive interfaces.

  The app provides remote control for vehicle functions (**locks, climate control**) and charging status, with simultaneous releases for iOS and Android. This approach reduced development efforts, while maintaining a consistent user experience.

Other Notable Examples

Many well-known apps rely on React Native, including:

- **Discord:** Voice and text communication.
- **Pinterest:** Image-sharing platform.
- **Uber Eats:** Restaurant management panel.
- **Shopify:** E-commerce platform.

React Native is also gaining traction in **finance (Coinbase, Bloomberg)** and is being integrated into high-demand services across various industries.

The versatility of React Native is evident in the wide range of companies that use it—from prototypes to complex applications.

Its ability to deliver cross-platform solutions quickly streamline product evolution that makes it a solid choice, even for large-scale implementations. Now, let us delve into the benefits and challenges of React Native. In the following section, we shall explore the key advantages that make React Native so appealing, as well as the challenges one needs to address when adopting this approach.

Benefits and Challenges of React Native

React Native bridges the productivity of web development with the performance of native applications. The technology allows developers to build apps for **both Android and iOS** using a shared JavaScript/React codebase while maintaining a high level of adherence to native interfaces. Let us now discuss the advantages that make React Native so appealing and the key challenges that may require attention when adopting this approach.

Benefits of React Native

React Native has become a popular choice for mobile development because it enables teams to build cross-platform applications with a shared codebase while still delivering a near-native user experience. It helps reduce development time, improve code reuse, and streamline maintenance across iOS and Android. These advantages make it especially valuable for projects that need faster delivery without sacrificing performance and usability.

Cross-Platform Development with a Single Codebase

- **Write once, run anywhere:** React Native enables developers to write screens and functionalities **only once**, significantly reducing the effort required to adapt the app for each platform.
- **Faster feature releases:** A single development team can build features for both Android and iOS, accelerating the release cycle.
- **Simplified maintenance:** Managing a single codebase reduces complexity compared to maintaining separate native apps.

Optimized Costs and Maintenance

- **Code reusability:** The same bug fixes and improvements apply to both platforms, reducing development costs and preventing inconsistencies between versions.
- **Time and resource savings:** Companies can launch products faster without compromising quality, making React Native a cost-effective solution.

Rapid Prototyping and MVP Development

- **Inspired by the web development model:** React Native allows developers to build **Minimum Viable Products (MVPs)** quickly, making it an excellent choice for startups and large enterprises looking to test market hypotheses before committing to full-scale app development.

Vibrant Ecosystem and Community Support

- **Extensive library support:** The popularity of React Native has led to a vast selection of open-source libraries and tools, making it easier to implement features such as maps, payments, and notifications.
- **Active community:** Developers benefit from a strong support network, including forums, groups, and extensive documentation.

Web Developer Productivity

- Developers familiar with React will find React Native easy to learn since it shares the same component-based and declarative state management approach.
- Web development tools such as VS Code, ESLint, Prettier, and package managers (npm/yarn) work similarly in React Native, ensuring a smooth workflow.

Seamless Integration with External Libraries

- **Firebase integration:** React Native works well with **Firebase** for authentication, real-time databases, and push notifications.
- **State management:** Redux and other state management solutions work without major complications.
- **Error tracking:** Services such as **Sentry and Crashlytics** help monitor and debug issues efficiently.

Challenges and Limitations of React Native

Despite its advantages, React Native also comes with trade-offs that teams should evaluate carefully before adoption. Some limitations arise from dependency on third-party libraries, differences in platform-specific behavior, and occasional need for native code integration. Understanding these challenges helps set realistic expectations and supports better architectural and planning decisions.

Performance Limitations for Graphically Intensive Applications

- **Almost-native performance:** React Native delivers near-native performance for everyday apps.
- **Limitations in 3D rendering and complex animations:** Apps that rely heavily on 3D graphics, physics calculations, or high-performance animations may experience delays due to the JavaScript-native bridge.
- Workarounds exist, but some projects opt for native development when high-performance graphics are essential.

Frequent Version Updates and Compatibility Maintenance

- **Rapid evolution of React Native:** The framework and its dependencies are frequently updated, requiring constant version upgrades to maintain compatibility with iOS and Android updates.
- **Potential for breaking changes:** Developers must regularly test and update dependencies to avoid compatibility issues.

Working with Native Modules

- **Accessing advanced native features (For Example, Cryptography, High-Performance Audio, Specialized Hardware):** These may require developers to write native code (Swift/Objective-C for iOS, Java/Kotlin for Android).
- **Additional expertise required:** Although React Native eliminates the need for separate native apps, teams may still need some native development knowledge.

App Size Considerations

- React Native apps tend to be slightly larger than fully native apps because they include JavaScript runtime and framework libraries.
- Optimization efforts are ongoing, but for projects where app size is a critical factor, this overhead may require consideration.

Library Fragmentation and Maintenance

- **Open-source dependencies:** While the ecosystem is rich, some third-party libraries may become outdated or lag behind React Native updates.
- Testing and manual fixes may be necessary to maintain stability.

Balancing Pros and Cons

Overall, React Native occupies an attractive middle ground:

- It delivers near-native performance for most use cases without sacrificing productivity.
- It outperforms hybrid solutions (such as webview-based apps) by rendering truly native components.
- It simplifies app maintenance and evolution, as both iOS and Android versions share a single codebase.

For business, consumer, or general-use applications, React Native delivers excellent results.

However, for projects requiring high-performance graphics, intensive native integrations, or extremely optimized applications, native development or alternative solutions may be more appropriate.

Even so, React Native remains a proven and powerful tool for:

- Reducing costs.
- Accelerating app launches.
- Maintaining a sustainable development workflow.

Building on these strengths, the ecosystem offers two primary approaches for initiating and managing projects: **Expo CLI** and **React Native CLI**. Let us explore each option in detail to help you decide which approach best meets your project requirements.

Expo CLI versus React Native CLI: Understanding the Two Approaches

The **React Native ecosystem** essentially offers two main approaches for starting and managing projects: **Expo CLI** and **React Native CLI**. This duality exists because, while some teams prioritize fast setup and abstraction of native configurations, others need full control over platform-specific details. **Expo CLI** provides a simplified experience—ideal for beginners or quick prototyping—whereas **React Native CLI** offers maximum flexibility for those who require advanced features and deep integrations with Android or iOS.

Expo CLI

- **Ease of Use and Speed:** Expo abstracts much of the Gradle (Android) and CocoaPods (iOS) configurations, speeding up project setup. It is particularly beneficial for new developers or teams looking to create prototypes without dealing with native code details.
- **Prebuilt Modules:** The Expo SDK includes built-in functionalities such as camera, location, notifications, and sensors. This allows developers to add features without installing extra libraries or manually configuring native code.
- **Build and Deployment:** Expo provides cloud-based services (EAS) for building Android/iOS apps, eliminating the need for local machines with native tools installed. It also supports Over-the-Air (OTA) updates, enabling bug fixes and feature updates without resubmitting the app to app stores.

About the limitations, some native modules may not be compatible or require **config plugins** when using the **bare workflow**. In such cases, developers can migrate to React Native CLI or use the bare workflow within Expo, ensuring greater customization flexibility.

React Native CLI

- **Full Flexibility:** Allows direct editing of native configuration files; Gradle for Android or `.plist/Info.plist` for iOS. This enables detailed customizations and the addition of specific functionalities in brownfield applications, or when integrating SDKs and advanced hardware resources.
- **Deep Integration:** If a project requires advanced encryption libraries, proprietary APIs, or the latest native technologies, React Native CLI provides greater control. This level of customization is often essential for enterprise environments or solutions that demand high performance and security.
- **More Complex Setup:** Developers must manually install Android Studio (SDKs) and Xcode, along with additional configurations for each platform. Teams unfamiliar with native development may find the setup more time-consuming.

Table 1.1 shows the differences and main points in each approach:

Capability / Constraint	Expo Go	Expo Dev Build (Custom Dev Client)	Bare React Native CLI
Custom native modules?	No (limited to what is bundled in Expo Go + supported JS-only libraries)	Yes (add native code via config plugins and/or custom native projects)	Yes (full native freedom)
Third-party SDK constraints?	High (must be compatible with the runtime of Expo Go; many native SDKs will not work)	Medium/Low (most SDKs work; may require config plugins or native edits)	Low (direct integration of any SDK)
App Store builds?	Yes, but not using Expo Go itself; you build a standalone app	Yes (common/recommended for production in Expo workflows)	Yes (standard native build pipelines)
CI/CD?	Yes (commonly via EAS Build / EAS Submit)	Yes (commonly via EAS; also possible self-hosted)	Yes (Fastlane, GitHub Actions, Bitrise, CircleCI, and the like)
OTA updates?	Yes (via Expo Updates; subject to platform policy and architectural constraints)	Yes (same model as Expo Go—works with Expo Updates)	Optional (not built-in; you add something like CodePush or a custom solution)
Best for	Learning, quick prototyping, demos	Production apps needing native SDKs while keeping Expo tooling	Full native control, complex native requirements, brownfield/embedded RN
Typical "switch" trigger	You need a native SDK / custom native module	You need deeper native customization than config plugins allow	You are already fully native, or requirements demand direct native control

Table 1.1: *Main Points in Each Approach*

In practice, "Expo" can mean two different local-development experiences: **Expo Go** (the standard shared client) and **Expo Development Builds** (a custom dev client compiled with your native dependencies). Teams typically start with Expo Go for speed, move to a Dev Build when they need native SDKs/modules, and choose Bare React Native CLI when they require full native control or are integrating into the existing native apps.

Approach to be Chosen

- **For Learning or Prototyping:** Expo CLI is generally better suited for beginners or those who need to validate an MVP quickly. The ease of starting and lack of complex native configurations lower the entry barrier.
- **For Large-Scale Apps / Advanced Native Features:** When an app requires features not directly supported by Expo (such as proprietary native modules or specific build configurations), **React Native CLI** offers full control over native code.
- **Gradual Migration:** It is possible to start with Expo for its fast setup and, if limitations arise, migrate to the bare workflow or React Native CLI. Most JavaScript code remains reusable, ensuring a smooth transition.

Chosen for this Book

Expo CLI is the fastest and simplest way to create React Native apps without worrying about native configurations; while **React Native CLI** is ideal for developers who need deep platform control.

Both options are officially supported, and the choice depends on whether the team wants to simplify the experience or requires advanced customization capabilities. However, in this book, we will be using **Expo CLI** because it is easier to understand and offers a quicker learning curve. For more details, you can consult https://expo.dev/.

JavaScript XML

Before diving into your first project, it is essential to understand that JavaScript XML (JSX) is a syntax extension that allows you to write UI components in a way that resembles HTML while still leveraging the full power of JavaScript. Let us see about it in the next section.

Another important point before creating our first project is understanding that JavaScript XML (JSX) is a syntax extension adopted by React (and consequently by React Native) that resembles HTML but internally converts each element into JavaScript function calls. Despite its friendly appearance, JSX is not pure HTML—it acts as a declarative layer that simplifies the creation of complex interfaces, allowing the use of variables, conditional expressions, loops, and other JavaScript features directly within the "layout" of components.

Basic Concept

- Instead of `<div>` and `<span>` (as in the web), React Native uses `<View>` and `<Text>` to represent containers and text. JSX recognizes these elements and converts them into actual native components when executed.
- Unlike HTML, where attributes follow specific rules, JSX of React Native uses camelCase for properties and callback functions (`onPress`, `onLayout`, and so on), reflecting JavaScript conventions.

Mixing Logic and Layout

JSX allows JavaScript logic to be inserted directly into the interface structure. This means you can use conditional structures, loops, functions, and other constructs without needing to concatenate HTML strings, as was common in older front-end approaches. For example:

```
import React from 'react';
import { Text } from 'react-native';
```

```
export default function Hello() {
const name = 'Alice';

  return (
<Text>Hello, {name}!</Text>
  );
}
```

In this example, JSX inserts the value of the local variable **`name`** directly into the **`<Text>`** component, displaying the message **"Hello, Alice!"** without relying on any props or external variables. Thus, the interpolation syntax **`{name}`** allows React Native to render **Alice** declaratively, keeping the code simple and easy to understand.

Transformation into Function Calls

- When JSX code is processed, each snippet such as **`<View>`** or **`<Text>`** is transformed into an equivalent function call, such as **`React.createElement(View, {...props}, ...)`**. In the case of React Native, these calls do not generate HTML nodes but rather structures that the framework interprets to build and update native components.
- This automatic conversion is typically handled by **Babel** (in the default configuration of React Native), eliminating the need to manually create HTML or use DOM manipulation functions, as was common in other libraries.

Advantages of the Declarative Style

- **Simplified Reading:** Combining layout and logic in a single file makes it easier to understand how the interface is built and updated.
- **Composition Flexibility:** With JSX, creating smaller and reusable components becomes natural, as each component can be imported as **`<MyComponent />`** and embedded within another.
- **Reduced Maintenance:** The complexity of handling HTML/markup strings and manually updating each element is replaced by a **declarative model**—simply change the state or props, and JSX reflects the updates in the interface.

Direct Use of Conditions and Loops

One of the significant advantages of JSX is that it allows the use of JavaScript features to control what is displayed, when, and how many elements are rendered. For example:

```
import { View, Text } from 'react-native';

export default function ListNames() {
constnomes = ['Alice', 'Bob', 'Charlie'];

  return (
<View>
      {nomes.map((nome, index) => (
<Text key={index}>Olá, {nome}!</Text>
      ))}
</View>
  );
}
```

In this example, we have a component that displays a fixed list of names, where each name is transformed into a `<Text>` element with a unique identifier `(key={index})` to prevent React warnings and optimize rendering.

Best Practices

- **Componentization:** It divides the layout into smaller, more specific components (for instance, separate a list into `<ListaNomes>` and an individual item `<ItemNome>`).
- **Rendering Optimizations:** For large lists or performance-intensive components, using hooks such as `React.memo`, `useCallback`, or `useMemo` helps prevent unnecessary re-renders, ensuring optimal performance.
- **Consistent Styling:** Maintains a standardized naming convention (such as `container`, `title`, and so on) and use `StyleSheet.create(...)` to organize and reuse styles, keeping JSX cleaner.

JSX is fundamental in providing a development experience similar to the web ecosystem while focusing on creating native interfaces. It eliminates the need to manipulate HTML nodes directly and simplifies the integration of logic (conditionals, loops, variables) with the layout structure. Combined with the declarative model of React, JSX enables developers to build React Native applications in a more readable, scalable, and efficient way, aligning mobile interface development with modern web application practices.

We will read about **components** in this section. Components are the building blocks of any React Native application. They are self-contained, reusable pieces of code that define how a particular section of your user interface should appear and behave. Think of them as individual "widgets" or "modules" that, when combined, create a complete, dynamic application.

At this point, you do not need to worry about mastering every detail of components. Throughout the book, we will progressively explore how to create, compose, and optimize components. Our goal is to gradually introduce you to these concepts so that you become comfortable with the idea of breaking down your interface into manageable, reusable parts.

For now, just remember that components help organize your code and make it more maintainable by isolating functionality and appearance. As we move forward, you will gain hands-on experience with components and learn best practices for structuring and integrating them, ensuring that your applications are both robust and scalable. Let us create our first project in React Native now!

Setting up the Development Environment

Properly configuring the development environment is the first step to ensuring that your React Native project runs smoothly throughout the coding, testing, and debugging phases.

- **Hardware Requirements**: To emulate Android or iOS, it is recommended to have a computer with at least **8GB of RAM** (ideally **16GB**) and a modern processor. Simulating mobile devices is resource-intensive, requiring significant CPU and memory usage.
- **Operating System**: You can develop on **Windows, macOS, or Linux**, but each system has specific requirements:
    - To compile **iOS**, you need a **Mac** with **Xcode** installed.
    - On **Windows and Linux**, iOS development is not officially supported.
- **Node.js**: Node.js is essential for running JavaScript outside the browser. Install the **LTS version** from https://nodejs.org and verify the installation with the commands on the terminal:`node -v` and `npm -v`.

- **Expo CLI**: Responsible for simplifying the creation of React Native projects, eliminating the need for manual Gradle (Android) and pods (iOS) configurations.
- **Code Editor**: **Visual Studio Code (VS Code)** is widely used due to its helpful extensions (ESLint, Prettier, Git) and native **TypeScript support**.
- **Emulators and Simulators**:
    - **Android**: Requires **Android Studio**, where you configure the SDK and create an **Android Virtual Device (AVD)**.
    - **iOS**: For **macOS users**, **Xcode** provides a built-in iOS simulator ready to use.

Now that you have familiarized yourself with the simulators required for testing on both Android and iOS, it is time to put your environment into action. In the next section, we will guide you through creating your first React Native project, laying the groundwork for your journey into mobile app development.

Creating Your First React Native Project

For beginners, the simplest way to get hands-on experience with React Native is by using **Expo**, as this platform abstracts various environment configurations. The following is a basic guide:

1. **Install Node.js**
    a. Visit nodejs.org and download the Long-Term Support (LTS) version.
    b. After installation, verify in the terminal with **`node -v`** and **`npm -v`** to ensure everything is set up.
2. **Expo CLI**
    a. Currently, instead of installing **`expo-cli`** globally, the recommended approach is to use **`create-expo-app`**, which comes with Expo updates.
3. **Create the project**
    a. In the terminal, run:
    ```
    npx create-expo-app MyProject --template blank
    ```
    b. It may ask about installing the latest version of the **`create-expo-app`** package. Confirm by pressing **y**.
    c. This will create a new project using the default **blank** template in JavaScript. If you want to use a different template, run:
    ```
    npx create-expo-app --template
    ```
    and replace **`--template`** with the desired one.
    d. This command generates the basic app structure, including folders like **assets** (for images and fonts) and files such as **App.js**.
4. **Navigate to the folder**
    a. Use **`cd MyProject`** to access the newly created project directory.
5. **Run the project**
    a. Use **`npm start`** or **`npx expo start`** to launch **Metro Bundler**, a web interface that manages your compilation of the app.
    b. Metro provides instructions to open emulators or scan a QR code with **Expo Go**.

6. **Test on Physical Devices or Emulators**
    a. **Physical Device:** Install the **Expo Go** app from the Play Store (Android) or App Store (iOS). Ensure your device is on the same Wi-Fi network as your computer, then point the camera at the QR code displayed in Metro.
    b. **Emulator:** If you prefer running on an **Android emulator** or **iOS simulator**, set them up (**Android Studio / Xcode**) and click **"`Run on Android device/emulator`"** or **"`Run on iOS simulator`"** in the Metro interface.

Once you have successfully run your application on an emulator or simulator, it is time to take a closer look at the underlying project structure. In the next section, we will walk through the typical folder organization created by Expo (as shown in *Figure 1.1*), which will help you understand where each piece of your project resides and how to navigate and customize it for your development needs.

Project Structure

After creating your project with Expo, a typical folder organization includes the following folders, we can see that in *Figure 1.1*.

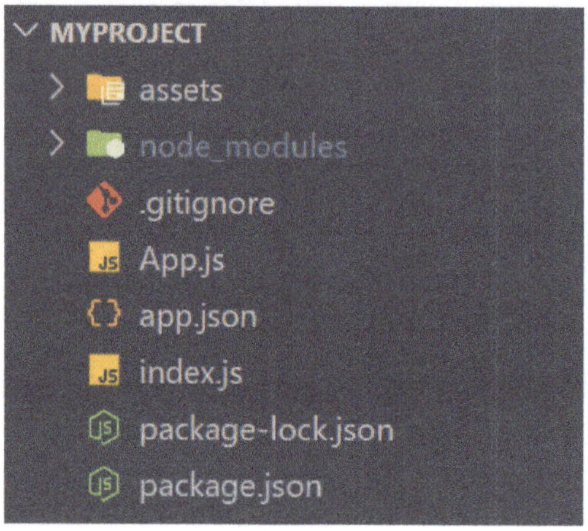

***Figure 1.1**: Basic Structure of a New Project on React Native*

- **`.git/`:** It is a hidden folder that stores the entire Git versioning history and metadata. It is created when initializing a repository **`git init`** or cloning a project.
- **`assets/`:** It is a folder dedicated to static resources such as images, icons, fonts, and other files used in the application. Expo/React Native projects usually contain images (logos, illustrations) and custom fonts.
- **`node_modules/`:** It is the directory where dependencies installed via **`npm`** (or **`yarn`**) are stored. It contains all the libraries and packages required for the project, along with their subdependencies.
- **`.gitignore`:** This is a text file specifying which files or folders Git should ignore (not version). It typically includes **`node_modules/`**, log files, build artifacts and other sensitive or transient information.
- **App (JavaScript file):** It is the main application file (**`App.js`** or **`App.jsx`**). It usually serves as the entry point, defining the root component of the project while importing React Native libraries and other modules.
- **app (file or folder):** This may be another JavaScript file (say **`app.js`**) or a folder containing subcomponents. The name suggests it stores core logic or additional components. Its exact function varies depending on the conventions of the development team.

- `index` **(JavaScript file) :** Generally, it is an initial file that registers the main `App` component. In some cases, it registers it with `AppRegistry` (in pure React Native) or initializes specific services. It may act as a bridge between native configuration and the main component.
- `package` **(JSON file):** Typically named `package.json`, this file describes the name, version, execution scripts, dependencies, and project metadata of the app. If only named **"package"**, the `.json` extension might be hidden or renamed. Ensure it is actually `package.json`.
- `package-lock` **(JSON file):** Usually named `package-lock.json`. It records the exact versions of installed dependencies and subdependencies in `npm`, ensuring reproducible installations across different machines.

In summary, this structure reflects the basic components of a JavaScript project: version control (Git), resource folders (assets), dependencies (node_modules), main application files (App, index), and configuration files (.gitignore, package.json/package-lock.json). As your app grows, it becomes natural to add directories to keep the code modular. Let us talk about the best practices, now that we have already created our first project.

Best Practices

To achieve high-quality results with React Native, it is crucial to adopt best practices that cover everything from project organization to monitoring the application in production. Before diving into each aspect, rest assured that we will cover all of these best practices in detail throughout the book. There is no need to memorize or fully grasp them immediately; we will gradually explore how to implement and integrate these principles into your React Native workflow. In the following subsection, there are some recommendations.

Framework

- **Componentization:** Screens, cards, buttons, and lists can be divided into smaller, reusable components.
- **Separation of Responsibilities:** Business logic and access to external services should be placed in service modules, not inside interface components.
- **Document Routes:** If using React Navigation, keep screen definitions organized to facilitate future maintenance.
- **Consistent Styling:** Use `StyleSheet` or libraries such as Styled Components to standardize layout and styling.
- **Version Control:** Always use Git for project versioning.

Code Organization

- **Folder Structure:** Separating components, services, screens, and modules coherently (like `components`, `screens`, and `services`) improves scalability.
- **TypeScript:** Using static typing prevents errors and speeds up development.
- **Hooks and Functional Components:** Prefer functional components and hooks over class components to better leverage the features of React and keep the code concise.
- **State Management:** For complex apps, adopting solutions such as Redux, MobX, or Context API helps keep state logic organized.

Performance

- **Optimized Lists:** Use `FlatList` and `SectionList` for large collections instead of `ScrollView` with extensive data.
- **Conditional Rendering:** Minimize unnecessary re-renders using `React.memo`, `PureComponent`, or `shouldComponentUpdate` in critical areas.
- **Native Animations:** Use `Animated` with `useNativeDriver: true` or libraries such as React Native Reanimated for smooth transitions and gestures.
- **Image Caching:** Implement image caching (for example, with `react-native-fast-image`) and optimized formats (WebP) to reduce download size and memory usage.

Accessibility

- **Screen Readers:** Add properties such as `accessible={true}`, `accessibilityLabel`, and `accessibilityRole` to interactive or informational components.
- **Inclusive Layout:** Ensure proper contrast, font resizing, and clear icon descriptions.
- **Verification Tools:** Use Accessibility Inspector (iOS) or Accessibility Scanner (Android) to identify and fix navigation flow issues.

Testing

- **Multiple Levels:** Cover business logic with unit tests using Jest and the UI with libraries such as React Native Testing Library.
- **End-to-End (E2E):** Automate end-to-end flows with tools such as Detox or Appium, simulating real interactions on devices or emulators.
- **Continuous Integration:** Integrate tests into the CI pipeline to detect regressions before release.

By applying these practices, you can build robust, high-performance, and sustainable React Native applications, maximizing the benefits of the technology while minimizing the risks associated with cross-platform development. With a strong foundation in place, let us now look ahead. React Native continues to evolve, meeting the ever-changing demands of the mobile market and unlocking new possibilities for developers. In the next section, we will explore the key trends and future perspectives that are shaping the ongoing development of the framework.

Trends and Future

React Native continues to evolve steadily, meeting the demands of the mobile market and offering new possibilities for developers. The main trends and future perspectives for the framework are explained in the following subsection.

Adoption of the New Architecture

React Native is transitioning to a redesigned architecture, which includes **JSI, TurboModules, and Fabric**, aiming to improve performance and interoperability. By reducing dependency on the asynchronous bridge between JavaScript and native code, the framework is expected to achieve even lower latency in UI operations, enabling smoother and more synchronized animations, even in demanding scenarios.

The new **Fabric renderer** also supports modern React features such as **Concurrent Rendering** and **Suspense**, facilitating the development of even more responsive applications. Although full adoption is gradual—since it depends on adjustments to existing libraries and native code—it is expected that, in the coming years, most apps will run in **"`bridgeless`" mode**.

Meta (formerly Facebook) continues to invest in improvements for this transition, adopting **Hermes** as the default JavaScript engine and optimizing modules to become **TurboModules**. It is important to note that the classic architecture remains supported, ensuring backward compatibility for those who prefer a more gradual migration.

Growth of the Expo Ecosystem

Expo has gained traction as a key platform within the React Native ecosystem, simplifying development at various levels. It provides an **SDK** packed with ready-to-use modules like camera, sensors, authentication, cloud-based build services, and **over-the-air (OTA) updates**.

With the release of features such as **Development Builds** and **Config Plugins**, Expo has become useful not only for rapid prototyping but also for large-scale enterprise applications. Recent studies indicate that over 70% of React Native developers use Expo at some stage of their workflow, whether for quickly starting projects or managing CI/CD pipelines with **Expo Application Services (EAS)**.

The distinction between **"bare RN"** and **"Expo-based"** is becoming increasingly blurred, positioning Expo as the preferred solution for starting—and often evolving—React Native applications.

Cross-Platform Expansion beyond Mobile

The "learn once, use anywhere" concept is materializing as React Native extends beyond **Android** and **iOS**. Official support for Windows and macOS has been introduced, thanks to the initiative of Microsoft. This allows developers to share business logic between desktop and mobile versions of the same app, as seen in **Microsoft Teams**.

At the same time, projects such as **React Native Web** enable RN components to run in **browsers**, while **Apple TV** and **Android TV** benefit from community-driven adaptations. There are even cases of React Native being used in **VR glasses** and **IoT devices**.

The idea of centralizing development in React/JavaScript while selectively adapting for different platforms is appealing to companies seeking consistency across multiple platforms.

Competition and Market Evolution

The cross-platform mobile development segment is highly competitive, with solutions such as **Flutter (Google), Jetpack Compose Multiplatform (Kotlin), and .NET MAUI (Microsoft)**. Each brings a different approach, but this competition drives React Native to innovate continuously, closing performance gaps and improving the developer experience.

For example, the growth of Flutter has pushed React Native to accelerate initiatives such as the **Fabric renderer** and startup optimizations. Meanwhile, the huge installed base of RN and its reliance on **JavaScript** (the most popular language of the world) ensures that many companies have no incentive to migrate to another platform.

Interestingly, there is a convergence of ideas:

- Features pioneered by React Native (such as **hot reload**) are now seen in competitors.
- React Native, in turn, incorporates innovations from other frameworks.

With a strong community and backing from tech giants such as **Meta and Microsoft**, React Native is expected to remain a leading cross-platform framework.

Impact on Mobile Development

React Native has permanently changed mobile app development by integrating web development practices (like fast updates, high iteration levels) into the native ecosystem. This approach has enabled more teams to adopt cross-platform solutions, reducing costs and delivery time.

App stores have adapted their update policies, facilitating fast bug fixes (such as via **CodePush**). Looking ahead, as React Native becomes more robust—whether through its new architecture or tools such as Expo—its market presence is expected to grow.

The ability to unify web and mobile development in JavaScript is extremely attractive from an organizational perspective, driving adoption even in large-scale products.

React Native maintains a strong position thanks to continuous technical improvements and a thriving ecosystem. **Meta** continuously enhances the foundation of the framework, while the community expands its functionalities and best practices.

For developers and companies investing in React Native today, the future looks promising. Far from stagnating, RN is expanding its capabilities in performance and platform reach, solidifying itself as a reliable choice for building cross-platform mobile experiences.

Conclusion

In this chapter, we followed React Native from its origins, when Facebook faced the challenge of unifying code for iOS and Android, to its widespread adoption by companies of various sizes and industries. The idea of combining JavaScript with native components not only increased team productivity—previously hindered by duplicated efforts—but also preserved the performance and smoothness expected in a top-tier app.

Throughout the reading, we have seen that React Native has made significant progress, achieving better integration with platforms (Android and iOS), along with tools such as **Hermes, JSI, Fabric, and TurboModules**, which make mobile development even faster and more responsive. Features such as **Hot Reload** and **Fast Refresh** have optimized the testing and interface refinement cycle, while the large community ensures a rich supply of libraries, guides, and support.

We also explored real-world use cases, support for modern technologies (**TypeScript, GraphQL, Firebase, and so on**), and the benefits and limitations of the framework. We found that in scenarios requiring extreme graphical performance or extensive use of highly specific hardware resources, native development may still be preferable. However, for most applications, React Native strikes a balance between high performance, cost reduction, and faster feature deployment.

Finally, we analyzed best practices for code organization, testing, accessibility, and CI/CD, as well as the dual approach of **Expo CLI versus React Native CLI**—on one hand, the convenience of starting projects without dealing with native configurations; on the other, the flexibility to customize every aspect of the build. Each decision depends on the context and goals of the project.

With this foundation, it is clear that React Native is a robust and continuously evolving tool. It is a highly viable alternative for developing cross-platform applications, combining the JavaScript/React ecosystem with native components to ensure a smooth user experience. This versatility, coupled with a strong community and continuous improvements from Meta and contributors, reinforces React Native as one of the top choices for building modern and scalable mobile applications.

Before diving into React Native, it is essential to have a solid foundation in JavaScript and TypeScript. The next chapter reviews key ES6+ concepts such as arrow functions, async/await, destructuring, and modules. We will introduce TypeScript, and demonstrate the advantages of typing your code in medium to large projects. The second part of the chapter will cover React fundamentals, including functional components, props, state, and the component lifecycle. This knowledge will be critical for building robust, maintainable applications in React Native.

Self-Assessment Questions

Before consolidating what has been studied throughout this chapter, it is useful to reflect on how React Native handles mobile app development, its differences from other approaches, and the tools that optimize the development workflow. The following questions serve as a guide to review the fundamental concepts presented, identify any doubts, and reinforce the understanding of the structure and best practices within the React Native ecosystem:

1. In what ways does React Native differ from hybrid applications based on WebView?
2. What is the importance of Hot Reload in the development cycle?
3. What factors make the React Native CLI more suitable than the Expo CLI in certain cases?
4. What are the main elements that make up the structure of a React Native project?
5. What are the main advantages of working with React Native compared to other hybrid or native solutions?

Answering these questions helps review and consolidate the material, allowing you to assess whether you have satisfactorily understood the concepts covered or if you need to explore any specific aspect further.

Key Terms

- **JavaScript XML (JSX):** A syntax extension that allows writing UI components using a structure similar to HTML, which is later converted into JavaScript function calls.
- **Hot Reload/Fast Refresh:** Features that enable instant code updates without losing the application state, improving development speed and debugging efficiency.
- **Hermes:** A lightweight and optimized JavaScript engine designed specifically for React Native to improve startup time and execution performance.
- **JavaScript Interface (JSI):** A new abstraction layer that enhances communication between JavaScript and native code, replacing the old bridge architecture.
- **Fabric:** A redesigned rendering engine in React Native that enables smoother animations, lower latency, and better integration with modern React features such as Concurrent Rendering and Suspense.
- **TurboModules:** A new way of handling native modules, improving performance by making JavaScript-native interactions more efficient.
- **Expo CLI:** A tool that simplifies React Native development by handling native configurations, allowing quick project setup without requiring direct interaction with native code.
- **React Native CLI:** The standard command-line interface for React Native, offering greater flexibility and control over native configurations.
- **Flexbox:** A layout system used in React Native (similar to CSS Flexbox) that helps create responsive and adaptable UI structures.
- **React Navigation:** A popular library for managing navigation in React Native apps, offering support for stacks, tabs, and drawer navigation.

- **State Management (Redux, Context API, MobX):** Approaches used to manage application state efficiently, improving data flow and UI consistency.
- **Expo Application Services (EAS):** A cloud-based service that simplifies building, updating, and deploying React Native apps without requiring direct access to native build tools.
- **CodePush:** A technology that enables over-the-air (OTA) updates for React Native apps, allowing bug fixes and minor changes to be deployed without requiring a full app store update.
- **End-to-End Testing (E2E):** Testing methodology using tools such as Detox or Appium to simulate real user interactions in mobile applications.
- **React Native Web:** A project that allows React Native components to be used in web applications, promoting code reuse across mobile and browser platforms.
- **Platform-Specific Code:** The ability to write code that runs only on specific platforms (Android/iOS) using platform checks or file extensions such as **`.ios.js`** and **`.android.js`**.
- **Over-the-Air (OTA) Updates:** A method of updating apps dynamically without requiring users to download a new version from the app store.

These key terms summarize some of the essential concepts covered in this chapter, helping reinforce the understanding of the ecosystem and development practices of React Native.

CHAPTER 2

JavaScript/TypeScript and React Fundamentals

Introduction

Before you start coding with React Native, it is essential to have a solid foundation in JavaScript and TypeScript. After all, behind every beautiful mobile app interface lies the logic built with these languages.

React Native is a powerful tool for creating cross-platform mobile applications, but it requires a strong understanding of key concepts from modern JavaScript—especially features introduced in ES6, such as arrow functions, async/await, modules, and destructuring. These features help make your code cleaner, more efficient, and easier to maintain.

Additionally, TypeScript has become almost indispensable in medium to large-scale projects. It adds static typing to JavaScript, which helps catch errors early in development, improves code readability, and makes long-term maintenance much easier.

In this chapter, we will review the essential concepts of these languages that every React Native developer should master. We will also dive into the core principles of the React library, including functional components, props, state, hooks, and the component lifecycle. With this knowledge, you will be ready to build robust, well-structured, and scalable mobile applications.

Structure

In this chapter, we will cover the following topics:

- JavaScript Fundamentals (ES6+)
  - Variables and Scope (Let, Const, Var)
  - Arrow Functions and Their Uses
  - Template Literals
  - Destructuring (Arrays and Objects)
  - Spread and Rest Operators
  - Modules (Import/Export)
  - Async/Await and Promises

- Introduction to TypeScript
  - What is TypeScript
  - Key Features and Benefits
  - Basic Types (String, Number, Boolean, Array, Tuple, Enum)
  - Interfaces and Type Aliases
  - Functions and Typing
  - Classes and Objects with TypeScript
- React Fundamentals
  - Introduction to React and its Core Concepts
  - Functional Components versus Class Components
  - JSX Syntax and Expressions
  - Props: Passing Data between Components
  - State: Managing Internal Component Data
- Hooks and Component Lifecycle
  - Introduction to Hooks
  - useState Hook: Managing State in Functional Components
  - useEffect Hook: Side Effects and Lifecycle Management
  - Custom Hooks and Their Uses
  - Comparison to Class Component Lifecycle Methods

JavaScript Fundamentals (ES6+)

JavaScript was created by Brendan Eich in 1995, originally under the name Mocha, later renamed to LiveScript, and finally to **JavaScript**. In 1997, aiming to standardize the language and ensure interoperability across different browsers, Netscape submitted JavaScript to **Ecma International**, resulting in the first edition of **ECMAScript**, known as **ES1**.

The following versions, **ES2** (1998) and **ES3** (1999), brought incremental improvements, such as more robust regular expressions and better string handling. However, the attempt to launch **ES4** faced significant challenges due to disagreements about the direction of the language, leading to the abandonment of that version.

The Road to ES6

After the release of **ES3**, developers encountered limitations when building more complex web applications. The need for more advanced features and a more expressive syntax became increasingly clear. Although **ES5**, released in 2009, introduced improvements like strict mode and native **JSON** support, the language still lacked many features found in other modern programming languages.

In this context, the development of **ES6** officially began in 2009, with the goal of equipping JavaScript with more robust tools to meet the growing demands of web development. After years of discussions and refinements, **ES6** was officially published in June 2015.

Key Features Introduced by ES6

ECMAScript 6 (ES6), also known as **ECMAScript 2015**, marks a significant milestone in the history of JavaScript, introducing features that enhanced the language and made it more efficient and powerful. With ECMAScript 6 (ES6), JavaScript gained several new features that significantly enhanced the language. Among these improvements are arrow functions, which offer a more concise syntax for defining functions; template literals, which simplify the creation of multiline strings and variable interpolation; and modules (import/export), which allow developers to organize code into separate files, promoting modularity and reusability. These features made JavaScript more robust and better suited to modern web development needs. ES6 introduced a wide range of features that transformed the way developers write JavaScript:

- **Classes and Modules:** New syntax for class and module declarations, making it easier to organize and reuse code.
- **Arrow Functions:** A more concise syntax for writing functions, which also inherit the lexical context of this.
- **Block-Scoped Variables:** Introduction of let and const for block-scoped variable declarations, replacing the function-scoped behavior of var.
- **Iterators and Generators:** New ways to iterate over collections and generate sequences of values on demand.
- **Promises:** A standard for handling asynchronous operations, simplifying processes like network requests.
- **Template Literals:** Enable expression interpolation and the creation of multi-line strings in a more intuitive way.

These additions made JavaScript a more modern language, better aligned with the needs of contemporary development.

Variables and Scope (Let, Const, Var)

Before ES6, JavaScript used only the **var** keyword for declaring variables. However, var has function scope, which can lead to unexpected behavior due to hoisting, where variable declarations are moved to the top of their scope. For example:

```
function example() {
    if (true) {
var message = "Hello from inside the block!";
    }
    console.log(message); // "Hello from inside the block!"
}
example();
```

In this case, message is accessible outside the if block because var does not respect block scope. To address these limitations, ES6 introduced **let and const**, which have block scope. Variables declared with let can be reassigned, while const defines constants whose values cannot be changed after initialization. Let us see this example:

```
function example() {
    if (true) {
        let count = 1;
const name = "JavaScript";
        console.log(count); // 1
        console.log(name);  // "JavaScript"
    }

console.log(typeof count); // "undefined"
console.log(typeof name);  // "undefined"
}
example();
```

Here, count and name are only accessible within the if block, demonstrating the block scoping behavior of let and const. The example clearly demonstrates why `let` and `const` are preferred in modern development: they respect block scope, preventing accidental leakage of variables outside their intended context. This makes the code more predictable, secure, and easier to maintain—especially in structures like `if`, `for`, or nested functions.

Arrow Functions and Their Use Cases

Arrow functions provide a more concise syntax for writing functions and have the important characteristic of not binding their own context, instead inheriting it from the surrounding lexical scope. This is especially useful in callbacks and anonymous functions. For example:

```
const greetings = ["Hi", "Hello", "Hey"];
const excited = greetings.map(word => `${word}!`);
console.log(excited); // ["Hi!", "Hello!", "Hey!"]
```

In this example, the arrow function word => `\${word}!` returns each string with an exclamation mark added, using a compact syntax. Their concise syntax not only makes the code cleaner and easier to read but also encourages developers to write smaller, more focused functions. As shown in the example with map, arrow functions are especially effective for transforming arrays, handling promises, and working with functional patterns.

So, arrow functions are a powerful addition to JavaScript that combine syntactic simplicity with more intuitive behavior regarding this keyword. By not binding their own context, they avoid common pitfalls associated with traditional function expressions—particularly in asynchronous code, event handlers, and callbacks. While they are not suitable for every situation—such as when a function needs its own arguments, or is used as a constructor—they are an essential tool in modern JavaScript, and understanding when and how to use them is key to writing elegant, efficient code.

Template Literals

Template literals allow for more flexible and readable string creation. They support expression interpolation and multi-line strings using backticks (`) and **${}** for embedded expressions. For example:

```
const user = 'Emily';
const day = 'Monday';
const message = `Good morning, ${user}!
Today is ${day}. Ready to start the week?`;
console.log(message);
```

This eliminates the need for manual concatenation and improves the readability of the code. By using backticks and ${} for interpolation, template literals simplify dynamic content generation—whether you are building messages, generating HTML, or formatting output for logs and reports. As seen in the example, a few lines of code can now do what previously required much more verbose syntax.

Template literals are a modern and elegant solution for working with strings in JavaScript. They make code more readable and expressive by allowing developers to embed variables directly into strings and create multi-line outputs without the need for cumbersome concatenation or escape characters. Overall, template literals contribute to cleaner code and a smoother developer experience, making them a fundamental feature in any modern JavaScript project.

Destructuring (Arrays and Objects)

Destructuring is a powerful feature in modern JavaScript that lets you extract values from arrays or properties from objects into individual variables. This simplifies code and enhances clarity.

Example of an Array Destructuring:

```
const colors = ["red", "green", "blue"];
const [primary, secondary] = colors;
console.log(primary);   // "red"
console.log(secondary); // "green"
```

Example of an Object Destructuring:

```
const book = { title: "1984", author: "George Orwell" };
const{ title, author } = book;
console.log(title);  // "1984"
console.log(author); // "George Orwell"
```

This approach is especially helpful when dealing with function parameters or API responses. Whether you're handling function parameters, working with API responses, or accessing nested data, destructuring provides a straightforward way to extract only what you need. As shown in the examples, you can assign meaningful variable names and avoid repetitive access to array indices or object keys.

Destructuring is a modern JavaScript feature that promotes cleaner and more intuitive code by allowing you to unpack values from arrays or objects directly into variables. This not only reduces repetition but also enhances readability, especially when working with structured data. By embracing destructuring, developers can write code that is more concise, expressive, and aligned with the declarative nature of modern JavaScript.

Spread and Rest Operators

The spread and rest operators share the same syntax but serve opposite purposes. The Spread operator expands elements of an iterable, while the Rest operator gathers multiple elements into a single variable.

Spread Operator: The Spread operator is useful for copying arrays, merging arrays, or passing variable arguments to functions.

Example of merging arrays:

```
const frontend = ["HTML", "CSS"];
const backend = ["Node.js", "Express"];
constfullstack = [...frontend, ...backend];
console.log(fullstack); // ["HTML", "CSS", "Node.js", "Express"]
```

Example of passing arguments to a function:

```
const numbers = [3, 7, 2];
const max = Math.max(...numbers);
console.log(max); // 7
```

Rest Operator: The Rest operator allows functions to accept an indefinite number of arguments or to collect the remaining elements during destructuring.

Example of a function with variable arguments:

```
function multiply(multiplier, ...values) {
    return values.map(value => value * multiplier);
}
console.log(multiply(2, 1, 3, 5)); // [2, 6, 10]
```

Example of an array destructuring with Rest:

```
const fruits = ["apple", "banana", "cherry", "date"];
const [first, ...others] = fruits;
console.log(first);   // "apple"
console.log(others);  // ["banana", "cherry", "date"]
```

In this example, the first gets the first element, and others collects the rest of the array elements into a new array.

The Spread and Rest operators are versatile tools in modern JavaScript that significantly simplify how we work with arrays, objects, and function parameters. Despite sharing the same syntax, they serve opposite, yet complementary purposes.

The Spread operator allows you to expand elements—whether to merge arrays, clone objects, or pass values into functions with ease. It enables a more readable and declarative style of coding, removing the need for manual loops or verbose operations. On the other hand, the Rest operator provides a convenient way to gather multiple values into a single structure. Whether collecting extra arguments in a function or unpacking parts of an array while grouping the rest, it brings flexibility and clarity to common coding patterns. Together, these operators promote cleaner, more expressive code and reduce boilerplate, making them essential in everyday JavaScript development.

Modules (Import/Export)

Before ES6, JavaScript lacked a native module system, which led developers to rely on external libraries and patterns (like IIFE or CommonJS) to structure and reuse code. With the introduction of modules in ES6, it became possible to break down code into smaller, reusable parts, greatly improving code organization, maintainability, and scalability in modern applications.

Exporting Modules

To make functions, constants, or objects accessible to other files, we use the export keyword. There are two main types of exports: named and default.

Named Export: It allows you to export multiple items from a single module.

```
// file: utils.js
export function multiply(x, y) {
    return x * y;
}
export const E = 2.718;
```

Default Export: It is used when a module exports a single primary function or value.

```
// file: greet.js
export default function greet(name) {
    return `Welcome, ${name}!`;
}
```

Importing Modules

To use values exported from another module, we use the import keyword.

Importing Named Exports: You must use the same names as those defined in the original module.

```
import { multiply, E } from './utils';

console.log(multiply(4, 5)); // 20
console.log(E);              // 2.718
```

Importing a Default Export:

You can name the imported value however you like.

```
import welcome from './greet';

console.log(welcome('Alex')); // Welcome, Alex!
```

ES6 modules significantly improved code organization, allowing developers to build more maintainable, testable, and reusable applications by dividing projects into manageable components.

Async/Await and Promises

In modern JavaScript development, handling asynchronous operations efficiently and clearly is essential. ES6 introduced Promises as a cleaner alternative to callbacks, which often led to deeply nested logic, known as "callback hell", that was hard to read and maintain.

A **Promise** represents a value that may be available now, later, or never. It can be in one of three states: pending, fulfilled, or rejected. Promises use **`.then()`** for handling success and **`.catch()`** for handling errors. Example with Promises:

```
function fetchUserData() {
    return new Promise((resolve, reject) => {
setTimeout(() => {
const success = true;

            if (success) {
resolve("User data loaded");
            } else {
reject("Failed to load data");
            }
        }, 1500);
    });
}

fetchUserData()
.then(data => console.log(data))
.catch(error =>console.error(error));
```

To make asynchronous code even more readable and resemble synchronous flow, ECMAScript 2017 (ES8) introduced the async and await keywords. An **`async function`** returns a Promise automatically, and await pauses the function execution until the Promise resolves or rejects. Example with async/await is as follows:

```
async function showUserData() {
    try {
const data = await fetchUserData();
        console.log(data);
    } catch (error) {
console.error("An error occurred:", error);
    }
}

showUserData();
```

This cleaner and more intuitive approach has become the standard in modern JavaScript development, especially for apps that interact heavily with APIs, files, or timers. Managing asynchronous behavior is a critical aspect of modern JavaScript development—especially when working with APIs, file systems, user interactions, or timed operations. Promises brought a major improvement over the traditional callback-based approach, helping to eliminate deeply nested, hard-to-read code structures commonly known as "callback hell."

With Promises, asynchronous operations become more manageable, using `.then()` and `.catch()` to handle success and failure in a linear and predictable flow. This model alone improves code readability and error handling. However, the real game-changer came with the introduction of async/await in ES2017. By allowing developers to write asynchronous code that looks and behaves like synchronous code, async/await simplifies control flow and enhances clarity. It also makes debugging and reasoning about asynchronous logic far easier.

As shown in the examples, wrapping Promises in async functions and using await leads to cleaner, more maintainable code. Today, this pattern is considered the standard for working with asynchronous tasks in JavaScript and is widely adopted in frameworks, libraries, and applications across the ecosystem.

JavaScript and TypeScript

Mastering the fundamentals of modern JavaScript, especially the features introduced with ES6 and beyond is essential for any developer aiming to build efficient, maintainable, and scalable applications. From arrow functions and template literals to modules, destructuring, and asynchronous programming with promises and **`async/await`**, these tools have transformed the way we write JavaScript and have paved the way for more readable, modular, and powerful codebases.

As JavaScript has evolved, so have the demands of large-scale applications. While ES6+ has addressed many limitations of the past, developers often still face challenges related to code reliability, type safety, and scalability, especially as applications grow in complexity.

This is where TypeScript comes into play. TypeScript builds on top of JavaScript by adding static typing, better tooling, and more robust code validation—all without sacrificing the flexibility of JavaScript. In the next section, we will explore the fundamentals of TypeScript, understand how it enhances the development process, and learn how to integrate it into your modern JavaScript projects. Let us dive in and discover how TypeScript can elevate your code quality and development experience.

Introduction to TypeScript

TypeScript is a superset of JavaScript that adds static typing to the language. Created by Microsoft, TypeScript was designed to address many of the challenges developers face when working with large-scale JavaScript applications, such as code reliability, scalability, and maintainability. While JavaScript is dynamic and flexible, this same flexibility can lead to hard-to-detect bugs and unpredictable behavior, especially as applications grow in size.

By introducing type annotations and other structural features, TypeScript allows developers to catch errors at compile time rather than at runtime. It also provides a more robust development experience through features like autocompletion, refactoring tools, and inline documentation—making the language more productive and safer to use in professional software development.

Despite these enhancements, TypeScript compiles down to plain JavaScript, which means it can run anywhere JavaScript runs. This compatibility ensures that adopting TypeScript does not mean abandoning the existing JavaScript ecosystem; rather, it enhances it.

Key Features and Benefits

TypeScript brings several advantages to modern development. Among the most notable are:

- **Optional Static Typing:** Developers can explicitly declare types for variables, function parameters, and return values. This improves code clarity and allows many errors to be caught during development.

- **Type Inference:** TypeScript is smart enough to infer types even when you don't explicitly declare them, offering a good balance between flexibility and safety.
- **Better Tooling:** With TypeScript, IDEs provide richer experiences—like smarter autocompletion, inline error checking, and advanced navigation features.
- **Modern JavaScript Features:** TypeScript supports all the latest JavaScript (ES6+) syntax, and even enables the use of upcoming features through configuration.
- **Improved Refactoring:** The presence of types makes refactoring code safer and more reliable, reducing the chances of breaking unrelated parts of your application.

These benefits make TypeScript especially valuable in collaborative environments or long-term projects where code quality, readability, and maintenance are top priorities.

Basic Types

TypeScript introduces a rich system of types to describe your variables and data structures. Let us look at some of the most commonly used types.

String, Number, and Boolean

These are the fundamental data types used in most programming languages.

```
let message: string = "Hello";
let age: number = 30;
let isActive: boolean = true;
```

Here, we declare three variables with explicit types. If you try to assign a value of the wrong type (like assign a number to a message), TypeScript will throw an error at compile time. Understanding the basic types – string, number, and boolean – is essential for working effectively with TypeScript. These types form the foundation of most applications and are used to represent common forms of data: text, numerical values, and true/false logic.

By explicitly declaring these types, developers gain the advantage of compile-time type checking, which helps catch mistakes early in the development process. This reduces bugs and increases the reliability of the code. For example, if a variable is expected to store a string but receives a number instead, TypeScript will raise an error before the code even runs.

This type safety not only improves the developer experience but also makes codebase easier to read, maintain, and scale. Embracing these simple yet powerful types is the first step toward writing robust and predictable TypeScript applications.

Array

Arrays in TypeScript can be typed in two ways: using square brackets or using the generic **`Array<T>`** syntax.

```
let colors: string[] = ["red", "green", "blue"];
let numbers: Array<number> = [1, 2, 3];
```

Both notations are equivalent and define arrays that should only contain elements of the specified type. Arrays are essential for managing collections of data, and TypeScript enhances their use by allowing you to explicitly define the type of elements they contain. This type enforcement helps prevent unexpected behavior at runtime, since TypeScript will immediately warn you if, for example, you try to insert a string into a number array.

In larger applications, this becomes especially useful for maintaining consistency and avoiding logic errors. By leveraging typed arrays, your code becomes more predictable, easier to debug, and safer to refactor—benefits that align perfectly with the goal of the TypeScript of improving code quality and developer confidence.

Tuple

Tuples allow you to define an array with a fixed number of elements, each with a known type.

```
let user: [string, number] = ["Alice", 25];
```

In this case, the user must always have a string as the first element and a number as the second. Tuples provide a powerful way to represent structured data where the position and type of each element are strictly defined. Unlike regular arrays, which can grow dynamically and contain multiple values of the same type, tuples enforce a fixed length and precise typing for each position.

This is especially useful when working with data that has a clear format—such as a pair of values representing a name and age, or coordinates with fixed dimensions. For example, **`[string, number]`** ensures that only a string followed by a number is valid, offering both clarity and type safety. By using tuples, you make your intent explicit in the code, reduce ambiguity, and gain stronger compiler checks. They are a great fit for scenarios where the structure of the data is just as important as the data itself.

Enum

Enums are a feature that does not exist in JavaScript natively. They are useful for defining a set of named constants.

```
enum Direction {
  Up,
  Down,
  Left,
  Right,
}

let move: Direction = Direction.Up;
```

By default, enum members are assigned numeric values starting from 0, but you can also assign custom values. Enums bring structure and readability to your code by allowing you to define a set of named constants—something that JavaScript does not support natively. Instead of using arbitrary values like strings or numbers scattered throughout your code, enums let you group related options in a clear, centralized way. For React Native with **`TypeScriptenums`** emit runtime JavaScript (extra bundle code). Many RN/TS codebases prefer string-literal unions (say **`type Direction = 'Up' | 'Down' | 'Left' | 'Right'`**) unless you specifically need a runtime enum object (for iteration, mapping, or interop).

They are especially helpful when dealing with fixed sets of values, such as directions, user roles, or statuses. By default, TypeScript assigns numeric values starting from 0, but you can customize these values or use string enums for more meaningful representation. Using enums improves code clarity, prevents magic numbers or strings, and makes it easier to manage and validate values across your application—all while leveraging the benefits of strong typing and autocomplete support.

Interfaces and Type Aliases

TypeScript allows you to define the shape of data using interfaces and type aliases.

Interface

Interfaces are primarily used to describe the structure of objects.

```
interface User {
  name: string;
  age: number;
isAdmin?:boolean; // optional property
}

const user1: User = {
  name: "Bob",
  age: 28,
};
```

Interfaces support optional properties (with ?), readonly properties, and can even extend other interfaces, making them extremely versatile. Interfaces are a cornerstone of the type system of TypeScript, offering a clean and a scalable way to define the shape of objects. They allow you to specify what properties an object should have, along with their types, while still offering flexibility through optional (?) and read only properties.

By using interfaces, you make your code more self-documenting and easier to maintain, especially in collaborative or large-scale projects. They help catch structural mismatches at compile time, reducing runtime errors and improving overall reliability. Interfaces can also extend other interfaces, enabling reuse and composition of complex types in a modular way. Whether you're defining the structure of data models, API responses, or component props, interfaces provide a powerful and elegant solution for keeping your code organized and type-safe.

Type Alias

Type aliases allow you to give a name to any type, including union and intersection types.

```
type ID = string | number;

let userId: ID = 123;
```

Type aliases are often used when working with more complex types or when describing function signatures. Type aliases are a flexible tool in TypeScript that let you assign a custom name to any type, making your code more readable and maintainable. They are particularly useful when dealing with complex or repetitive type structures, such as unions, intersections, or detailed object shapes.

By using a type alias like type **`ID = string | number`**, you can simplify function parameters, variables, or return types without repeating long or complicated definitions. This not only improves clarity but also makes future changes easier—since updating the alias automatically updates every place it is used. While similar to interfaces, type aliases shine when describing non-object types, function signatures, or combining multiple types in creative ways. They are a powerful addition to your TypeScript toolkit, helping you write expressive and scalable type-safe code.

Classes and Objects with TypeScript

TypeScript enhances object-oriented programming in JavaScript by supporting classes with strict type definitions, access modifiers, constructors, and inheritance.

```
class Person {
  protected name: string;
  protected age: number;

constructor(name: string, age: number) {
```

```
    this.name = name;
this.age = age;
  }

  public greet(): void {
console.log(`Hello, my name is ${this.name}.`);
  }
}
```

In this example, we use private, protected, and public to control access to class members. These access modifiers help enforce encapsulation and better class design.

We can extend the class using extends:

```
class Employee extends Person {
  private role: string;

constructor(name: string, age: number, role: string) {
super(name, age);
this.role = role;
  }

  public describe(): void {
    console.log(`${this.name} is a ${this.role}.`);
  }
}
```

We can also use interfaces to define contracts for classes:

```
interface Shape {
area(): number;
}

class Rectangle implements Shape {
constructor(private width: number, private height: number) {}

area(): number {
    return this.width * this.height;
  }
}
```

Using interfaces in this way makes your classes more flexible and testable. TypeScript brings a robust, statically typed layer to the object-oriented capabilities of JavaScript, enabling developers to write structured, maintainable, and scalable code using familiar OOP principles such as classes, inheritance, encapsulation, and interfaces.

A best practice (React / React Native): While TypeScript supports OOP features (classes, inheritance, access modifiers), most React and React Native codebases favor composition and functional components with Hooks for UI logic. Class components are still supported, but React recommends function components for new code, and newer React patterns are primarily designed around Hooks.

With features like access modifiers (private, protected, public), you can clearly define what should or should not be accessible from outside a class, encouraging better encapsulation and reducing potential bugs from unintended usage. The constructor allows for type-checked initialization of class instances, and extends make inheritance straightforward and type-safe.

In addition, TypeScript allows you to implement interfaces in classes, enforcing contracts that ensure consistent structure and behavior across different implementations. This pattern is especially helpful for large applications, where decoupling logic from concrete implementations can improve testing and code reuse.

By combining strong typing with classic OOP patterns, TypeScript empowers developers to write cleaner, more reliable object-oriented code—making it an excellent choice for both small utilities and complex application architectures.

Thoughts about TypeScript

TypeScript provides a strong, expressive type system on top of JavaScript that helps developers write cleaner, safer, and more maintainable code. Whether you are building a small project or a large enterprise application, TypeScript offers features that enhance every stage of development—from catching bugs early to improving code documentation and team collaboration.

Now that you have mastered the basics of TypeScript, it is time to explore some of its more advanced features. In the next section, we will cover union and intersection types, generics, utility types, and more—tools that will allow you to write even more expressive and reusable code while maintaining strong type safety.

Advanced TypeScript Features

As your applications grow in complexity, writing code that is both expressive and type-safe becomes increasingly important. TypeScript offers a powerful type system that can be extended through advanced features designed to model complex data structures, enforce strict typing, and support reusable components.

Union Types

A union type allows a variable or parameter to hold more than one possible type. This is useful in cases where a value may be of different forms—for example, an ID that can be either a string or a number.

```
function printId(id: number | string) {
console.log(`ID: ${id}`);
}
printId(123);       // valid
printId("abc123");  // valid
```

In the example above, the function printId accepts either a number or a string. Union types are particularly helpful when dealing with APIs or user input, where the format of data may vary.

You can use type narrowing to handle each type appropriately within the function:

```
function process(value: number | string) {
  if (typeof value === "string") {
    console.log(value.toUpperCase());
  } else {
    console.log(value.toFixed(2));
  }
}
```

TypeScript automatically narrows down the type based on the condition, allowing safe access to type-specific methods. Union types provide the flexibility to accept multiple possible types for a single value, making your code more adaptable to real-world scenarios—such as when working with APIs, form inputs, or configuration options that can come in different formats.

By using the | symbol, you can declare that a value can be one type or another, like string | number. This allows your functions and variables to remain flexible while still benefiting from the static type checking of TypeScript. What makes union types even more powerful is type narrowing. TypeScript uses conditions like type of checks to automatically determine the actual type at runtime, giving you safe and precise access to methods and properties appropriate for each type. This balance between flexibility and safety makes union types an essential feature for building robust, real-world applications where input and data types can vary without compromising code quality.

Intersection Types

An intersection type combines multiple types into one. The resulting type must satisfy all included types, meaning it will have all their properties.

```
interface Person {
  name: string;
}

interface Employee {
employeeId: number;
}

type Staff = Person & Employee;

conststaffMember: Staff = {
  name: "Alice",
employeeId: 101,
};
```

This is ideal when you want to compose multiple behaviors or roles into a single type. Intersection types are frequently used in component props, configuration objects, or models that extend shared characteristics. Intersection types allow you to merge multiple type definitions into one, creating a new type that must include all properties and requirements from each source. This makes them especially valuable when a value needs to fulfill multiple roles or behaviors at once.

For example, combining a Person and an Employee into a single Staff type ensures that any object of this type has both a name and an employeeId. This pattern is useful for modeling real-world data structures where entities often share and combine different characteristics. Intersection types are commonly used when designing component props, configuration objects, or data models that build upon multiple layers of functionality. They promote code reuse, enhance type precision, and make your models more expressive and composable, all while maintaining the strong type safety that TypeScript provides.

Generics

Generics allow you to write reusable and flexible code that maintains type safety. Instead of hardcoding types, generics let you define types dynamically when the function, class, or interface is used.

Generic Function

```
function identity<T>(value: T): T {
  return value;
}

const a = identity<string>("hello");
const b = identity<number>(42);
```

The type, T is a placeholder that gets replaced at usage time. This makes the function reusable for any type while preserving strict type checking. In most cases, TypeScript infers generic type parameters from the arguments you pass. For example, **`identity("hello")`** infers `T` as **`string`** automatically. You typically only specify explicit type parameters (say **`identity<string>("hello")`**) for edge cases—

such as when inference is ambiguous, when you need to widen/narrow a type intentionally, or when the generic is not directly inferable from the inputs.

Generic Interface

```
interface Box<T> {
  content: T;
}

conststringBox: Box<string> = { content: "TypeScript" };
constnumberBox: Box<number> = { content: 123 };
```

Generics with Constraints

You can restrict generic types using the extends keyword to ensure that they meet certain requirements:

```
function logLength<T extends { length: number }>(item: T): void {
  console.log(item.length);
}

logLength("Hello");      // valid
logLength([1, 2, 3]);     // valid
// logLength(42);         // error: number does not have 'length'
```

Generics are one of the most powerful features of TypeScript, enabling you to write reusable, flexible, and type-safe code. Instead of locking your functions, classes, or interfaces to specific types, generics let you define type placeholders—like T—that are filled in when the code is used. This approach allows you to create utilities and components that adapt to different data types without sacrificing the benefits of strong typing. Whether you're building a `Box<T>` to hold any kind of content or an `identity<T>` function that works with any value, generics ensure type consistency while maximizing flexibility.

You can also apply constraints with extends to ensure the provided types meet certain conditions, giving you even more control over how generics behave. This is especially useful when working with values that must have specific properties (like `.length`). Generics are essential for designing robust, scalable codebases—particularly in libraries, frameworks, or applications where type precision and reusability are key to maintaining clean architecture and reducing bugs.

Utility Types

TypeScript includes several utility types that simplify type transformations and make your code more expressive and DRY (Don't Repeat Yourself). Let us explore some of the most useful ones.

Partial<T>

It converts all properties of a type to optional.

```
interface User {
  name: string;
  age: number;
}

constupdateUser = (data: Partial<User>) => {
  console.log(data);
};

updateUser({ name: "Bob" });
```

Readonly<T>

It marks all properties as read-only, preventing reassignment.

```
const user: Readonly<User> = {
  name: "Alice",
  age: 30,
};

// user.age = 31; // Error: Cannot assign to 'age'
```

Readonly<T> is shallow, it makes only the top-level properties read-only, but nested objects/arrays remain mutable. If you need deep immutability, use a custom **DeepReadonly** utility type (recursive) or adopt dedicated patterns/libraries for immutable state management.

Pick<T, K>

It creates a new type by selecting a subset of properties from an existing type.

```
type UserName = Pick<User, "name">;

const u: UserName = { name: "Alice" };
```

Omit<T, K>

It creates a new type by excluding certain properties from an existing type.

```
type UserWithoutAge = Omit<User, "age">;

const u2: UserWithoutAge = { name: "Bob" };
```

These utility types reduce repetition, improve maintainability, and allow you to work with derived types in a clean and declarative way. They are built-in helpers in TypeScript that allow you to manipulate and transform types in a concise, expressive, and type-safe way. They reduce duplication, promote consistency, and make your codebase easier to maintain—especially when working with complex data structures.

For instance, **Partial<T>** is useful when you want to make all properties optional, which is perfect for update functions or form inputs. On the other hand, **Readonly<T>** allows you to enforce immutability, helping prevent unintended changes to data.

Types like **Pick<T, K>** and **Omit<T, K>** enable you to extract or exclude specific fields from existing types, giving you the flexibility to reuse and reshape data models without redefining them from scratch. By leveraging utility types, you can build types dynamically and declaratively, leading to more scalable and maintainable code. These tools are especially valuable in larger applications or libraries, where type precision and reusability are essential. Embracing them is a smart way to write clean, DRY, and powerful TypeScript.

Type Guards

Type guards allow you to narrow down the type of a variable using runtime checks, ensuring that the value is of the expected type before performing operations on it.

```
function isString(value: unknown): value is string {
  return typeof value === "string";
}
```

This custom type guard function can now be used to safely treat values as strings:

```
function handle(value: unknown) {
  if (isString(value)) {
    console.log(value.toUpperCase());
  }
}
```

Type guards are an essential feature in TypeScript that allow you to safely work with dynamic or unknown values by narrowing them to specific types at runtime. This ensures that you're not calling methods or accessing properties that don't exist on a given type—helping you avoid runtime errors. Using simple checks like typeof, instanceof, or custom guard functions, you can tell TypeScript how to refine the type of a variable based on logic inside your code. This gives you access to type-specific behavior only when it is safe to do so.

For example, a custom type guard like **`isString`** allows you to confidently call string methods only when the value is truly a string. This pattern is especially useful when working with unknown, union types, or external data like API responses.

Here is a practical React Native focused example, in which we can add right after your **`isString`** guard. It demonstrates validating an **API response** with a discriminated union and narrowing via a **`'status' in obj`** check plus **`typeof`** checks.

```
// Example: validating an API response in a React Native app

type ApiSuccess = {
  status: 'ok';
  data: {
userId: string;
    name: string;
  };
};

type ApiError = {
  status: 'error';
  message: string;
};

type ApiResponse = ApiSuccess | ApiError;

function isRecord(value: unknown): value is Record<string, unknown>
{
  return typeof value === 'object' &&value !== null;
}

function isApiResponse(value: unknown): value is ApiResponse {
  if (!isRecord(value)) return false;
  if (!('status' in value)) return false;

const status = value.status;
  if (status !== 'ok' && status !== 'error') return false;

  if (status === 'ok') {
    if (!('data' in value) || !isRecord(value.data)) return false;
    return (
typeofvalue.data.userId === 'string' &&
typeof value.data.name === 'string'
    );
  }
```

```
  // status === 'error'
  return typeofvalue.message === 'string';
}

// Usage in an RN fetch flow
async function fetchUser(): Promise<void> {
const res = await fetch('https://example.com/api/user');
constjson: unknown = await res.json();

  if (!isApiResponse(json)) {
    throw new Error('Unexpected API response shape');
  }

  // Narrowing via discriminant `status`
  if (json.status === 'ok') {
    // json is ApiSuccess here
    console.log(json.data.name);
  } else {
    // json is ApiError here
console.warn(json.message);
  }
}
```

Ultimately, type guards bring the dynamic flexibility of JavaScript together with the static safety of TypeScript, allowing you to write code that is both powerful and reliable.

Literal Types

Literal types restrict a variable to a specific set of values. This is useful for defining finite options, such as directions or states.

```
type Direction = "up" | "down" | "left" | "right";

function move(dir: Direction) {
console.log(`Moving ${dir}`);
}
```

Literal types allow you to strictly define the exact values a variable can take, offering a powerful way to represent limited options with complete type safety. By specifying literal values—like specific strings or numbers—you ensure that only those exact values are allowed. This is especially useful when working with fixed choices, such as directions, statuses, modes, or predefined actions. For example, the Direction type ensures that only "**up**", "**down**", "**left**", or "**right**" are valid inputs for the move function—reducing the chance of bugs caused by typos or unexpected values.

Literal types help make your code self-documenting, predictable, and easier to validate at compile time. They're often used in combination with union types and discriminated unions to model well-defined and controlled data flows, especially in configuration options or component props. In short, literal types add precision and clarity to your TypeScript code while improving safety and developer experience.

What to Expect about TypeScript

By mastering advanced TypeScript features such as union types, intersection types, generics, utility types, type guards, and more, you equip yourself with a powerful set of tools to write code that is not only reusable and flexible, but also robust and scalable.

TypeScript goes far beyond simple type annotations—it gives you the ability to model complex data structures, enforce strict contracts, and express intent clearly in your code. With these features, you can describe the shape of your data and logic with precision, leading to fewer runtime errors and more predictable behavior.

This level of type safety becomes increasingly important in larger codebases or team environments, where maintaining consistency and preventing bugs are critical to long-term success. Features like generics and utility types help you write DRY (Don't Repeat Yourself) code, while tools like type guards and literal types allow you to handle dynamic scenarios safely.

Moreover, TypeScript enhances the overall developer experience—providing better IDE support, intelligent code completion, refactoring tools, and early error detection, which significantly boosts productivity and confidence during development. In short, learning about the advanced capabilities of TypeScript prepares you not just to write better code, but to design better systems. You will be ready to tackle more sophisticated challenges, build cleaner APIs, and contribute effectively to modern, professional JavaScript projects.

With a solid foundation in JavaScript and TypeScript, we are now ready to dive into the world of React — a powerful library for building web and mobile interfaces. Next, we will explore how React naturally integrates with JS and TS, enabling the development of modern, reusable, and scalable applications.

React Fundamentals

React is a widely-used JavaScript library created by Jordan Walke at Facebook in 2011 and publicly released in 2013. Initially designed to tackle complex UI challenges on the own platform of Facebook, React quickly became renowned for simplifying the creation of interactive, stateful user interfaces. Its adoption rapidly grew, and today, React is among the most prominent tools used to build scalable, maintainable web and mobile applications.

Historical Background of React

In the early 2010s, Facebook was facing difficulties managing increasingly complex user interfaces. Traditional methods—like manipulating the DOM directly—proved inefficient and error-prone at scale. React emerged as a response to these challenges, introducing a component-driven architecture and the concept of a virtual DOM, radically changing how developers approached UI design.

On mobile, we do not manipulate DOM; the same React mental model applies, but the renderer targets native views. In React Native, we describe this as "React reconciliation / a virtual tree" rather than "virtual DOM," since there is no browser DOM. Consider a short clarification: React builds a virtual representation and the RN renderer commits updates to native views.

By open-sourcing React in 2013, Facebook allowed the broader development community to contribute improvements and build a vibrant ecosystem. React quickly gained popularity due to its simplicity, performance, and strong developer experience, leading to widespread industry adoption.

In 2015, Facebook introduced React Native, extending the philosophy of React to mobile app development, enabling the creation of native apps for iOS and Android using JavaScript and React. React continues to evolve through ongoing development and extensive community contributions, shaping the way modern web and mobile interfaces are built.

Core Concepts of React

React applications are fundamentally built on several key pillars that serve as the foundation for how interfaces are structured, updated, and maintained. Understanding these core concepts is essential for developing efficient, scalable, and maintainable React applications.

- **Components**: React follows a component-based architecture, where the user interface is broken down into small, reusable pieces. Each component is an independent and isolated part of the UI that can manage its own logic and presentation. Components can be nested, combined, and reused across different parts of the application, making development more modular and organized.
- **JSX (JavaScript XML)**: JSX is a syntax extension for JavaScript that allows you to write HTML-like code within your JavaScript files. It makes the structure of your UI components more readable and expressive. JSX is not required to use React, but it has become the de facto standard due to its clarity and developer-friendly syntax. This concept was thoroughly introduced and explained in Chapter 1, where we explored how JSX compiles into regular JavaScript using **`React.createElement`** under the hood.
- **Props (Properties)**: Props are a mechanism for passing data from parent to child components. They are read-only and allow components to be dynamic and reusable. With props, components become more flexible, as they can render different outputs based on the data they receive. Props also help enforce a unidirectional data flow, which is a core principle of the architecture of React.
- **State**: While props are used to receive data, state is used to manage data internal to a component. State is mutable and allows components to react to user input, API responses, and other dynamic changes over time. React provides the **`useState`** hook for managing state in functional components, enabling reactivity and UI updates when data changes.
- **Component Lifecycle**: Every React component goes through a lifecycle that includes mounting, updating, and unmounting. Understanding these phases is crucial for executing side effects, cleaning up resources, or initializing data at the appropriate time. While class components use methods like **`componentDidMount`**, **`componentDidUpdate`**, and **`componentWillUnmount`**, functional components achieve similar behavior using the **`useEffect`** hook.

These core concepts work together to empower developers to create rich, interactive web applications with confidence. Mastering them is the first step toward building robust React applications – and a solid preparation for transitioning into React Native development.

Functional Components versus Class Components

React provides two primary ways of creating components: functional components and class components. Historically, class components were more prevalent because they offered features such as internal state management and lifecycle methods like **`componentDidMount`** and **`componentDidUpdate`**. However, since the release of React Hooks in version 16.8, functional components have become the standard due to their simplicity, readability, and ease of maintenance.

Let us examine both types of components in more depth, comparing their syntax, capabilities, and ideal use cases, to understand why modern React development strongly favors functional components.

Functional Components

Functional components are plain JavaScript functions that return JSX. They are easy to read and write, and were originally used only for presentational purposes – components that received props and rendered UI based on them. However, with the introduction of **Hooks** (such as **`useState`** and **`useEffect`**), functional components gained the ability to manage state and perform side effects, effectively replacing most use cases for class components.

Example with Function:

```
function Welcome(props) {
  return <h1>Hello, {props.name}!</h1>;
}
```

Example with Hooks:

```
import React, { useState } from 'react';
import { View, Text, Button } from 'react-native';

export function Counter() {
const [count, setCount] = useState(0);

  return (
<View>
<Text>You clicked {count} times</Text>
<Button title="Click me" onPress={() =>setCount(count + 1)} />
</View>
  );
}
```

In summary, functional components represent the modern and preferred approach to building React applications. They offer a simpler, more readable syntax and, with the power of Hooks, are capable of handling complex behaviors such as managing state and side effects. What once required verbose class syntax can now be expressed cleanly within a function, leading to more maintainable and testable code. Whether you are creating a simple UI or a fully interactive application, functional components provide the flexibility and power needed to build scalable and elegant interfaces in the contemporary React development landscape.

Class Components

Class components extend **`React.Component`** and must include a **`render()`** method that returns JSX. They were the primary way to handle state and lifecycle events before Hooks were introduced. Although still valid and supported, they are now considered more verbose and harder to test and maintain compared to their functional counterparts.

Example:

```
class Welcome extends React.Component {
render() {
    return <h1>Hello, {this.props.name}!</h1>;
  }
}
```

With state:

```
class Counter extends React.Component {
  constructor(props) {
    super(props);
this.state = { count: 0 };
  }

handleClick = () => {
this.setState((prev) => ({ count: prev.count + 1 }));
  };

render() {
    return (
<div>
<p>You clicked {this.state.count} times</p>
<button onClick={this.handleClick}>Click me</button>
</div>
```

```
        );
    }
}
```

While class components were once the foundation of stateful and dynamic behavior in React, they have gradually taken a back seat to functional components with Hooks. They remain fully supported and are still useful in some legacy codebases, but their verbose syntax and more complex structure make them less ideal for modern development.

Class components require constructors, manual binding of methods in some cases, and a deeper understanding of the component lifecycle, which can increase the learning curve and reduce code readability. As React continues to evolve, class components serve as an important historical step in the development of the library, but the simplicity and elegance of functional components have made them the go-to choice for most developers today.

Why Functional Components are Preferred

Today, **functional components** are the recommended standard for building React applications—and for good reason. They offer a modern, streamlined approach to building components that makes development faster, more consistent, and easier to maintain. Here is why functional components have become the preferred choice:

- **Less Boilerplate, More Readability**: Functional components are concise and focus directly on what matters—rendering UI. There is no need to write constructors, bind methods, or extend classes, which makes the code cleaner and easier to follow.
- **Hooks Unlock Powerful Capabilities**: With the introduction of Hooks like `useState`, `useEffect`, `useContext`, and custom hooks, functional components are no longer limited to being stateless. They can now handle complex logic, stateful behavior, and side effects while maintaining clear separation of concerns.
- **Improved Testing and Reusability**: Functional components promote a more functional programming style, where logic can be broken into reusable pieces through hooks. This modularity makes testing and refactoring easier, as business logic can be isolated from presentation.
- **Performance in Practice:** Functional components align with modern React patterns and are often simpler to compose and reuse. However, performance primarily depends on **how often components re-render** and whether you apply the right patterns (say memoization and stable references) to avoid unnecessary work—not on the component being a class versus a function.
- **Modern Best Practices**: The React team and broader ecosystem now encourage the use of functional components in all new code. Most official documentation, third-party libraries, and community patterns are centered around hooks and functional paradigms, ensuring better support and future-proof practices.
- **Consistency across the App**: Using functional components throughout a codebase helps maintain consistency in code style, which improves readability and reduces onboarding time for new developers.

While **class components** are still fully supported and useful in existing applications, embracing **functional components** is key to staying aligned with modern React. They represent the future of the framework, enabling developers to build more scalable, maintainable, and expressive interfaces with less complexity and greater clarity.

Props: Passing Data between Components

In React, **props** (short form of **properties**) are the primary way to pass data from parent to child components. They enable components to be dynamic and reusable by allowing you to customize their behavior or output based on the values received.

Props are **read-only**, meaning that child components cannot modify the props they receive. Instead, they consume the props to render content or perform logic based on the input provided. This one-way data flow—from parent to child—ensures predictable component behavior and supports the declarative nature of React.

Example:

```
function Greeting(props) {
  return <p>Hello, {props.user}!</p>;
}

function App() {
  return <Greeting user="Carlos" />;
}
```

In the example above:

- The **`App`** component passes the value **`"Carlos"`** as the **`user`** prop to **`Greeting`**.
- The **`Greeting`** component uses this prop to display a personalized message.

This simple pattern is at the heart of how React builds complex UIs: components can be composed and nested, each receiving specific props that define their content, logic, or behavior.

Why Props Matter

- **Reusability**: Instead of hardcoding values, you can reuse the same component with different props across your app.
- **Clarity and Maintainability**: The one-way flow of data makes it easier to reason about what a component is rendering and why.
- **Separation of Concerns**: Components become more focused and easier to test because their output depends solely on the props they receive.

Common Use Cases

- Displaying dynamic values (like user names, titles, numbers)
- Passing event handlers (such as **`onClick`**)
- Configuring component behavior (say **`disabled`**, **`size`**, **`theme`**)
- Passing children elements to be rendered inside other components

Props are foundational to the design philosophy of React. They make it possible to **compose flexible, declarative interfaces** and enable components to behave like configurable building blocks. Mastering the use of props is essential for creating clean, maintainable, and scalable React applications.

State: Managing Internal Component Data

In React, the concept of **state** refers to the internal data of a component that can change over time. Unlike **props**, which are passed from a parent component to a child and are immutable, state is managed and maintained locally within each component.

One of the most important characteristics of state in React is that any change to its value automatically triggers a re-render of the component. This ensures that the user interface is always synchronized with the internal data and behavior of the component.

State Management in Class Components

Before the introduction of Hooks, class components were the primary way to handle state and lifecycle in React. State is defined within the class constructor using **`this.state`**, and it can be updated with the **`this.setState()`** method.

The **`setState`** method merges the new state with the previous one and notifies React that the component needs to be re-rendered. This process is essential to ensure that the UI stays in sync with the most up-to-date data.

Example:

```
class Counter extends React.Component {
  constructor(props) {
    super(props);
this.state = { count: 0 };
  }

  increment = () => {
this.setState((prev) => ({ count: prev.count + 1 }));
  };

render() {
    return (
<div>
<p>Counter: {this.state.count}</p>
<button onClick={this.increment}>Increment</button>
</div>
    );
  }
}
```

In the example above, the **`Counter`** component starts with the **`count`** state set to zero. Each button click triggers the **`increment`** method, which updates the state using **`setState`**. React then re-renders the component with the new value, keeping the user interface in sync.

State in Functional Components

With the release of React 16.8, the introduction of Hooks brought a new way to handle state in functional components through the **`useState`** Hook. This allowed functional components—previously used mainly for simple rendering tasks—to become fully capable of managing state and handling side effects.

The Hooks approach is more concise and easier to understand, which led to widespread adoption across the React community and is now the recommended way to develop new stateful components.

The Importance of State

State is fundamental to building interactive and dynamic applications with React. It allows the UI to respond to events, user actions, and data changes. Common situations where state is essential include:

- Storing user input data in forms
- Controlling the visibility of UI elements (such as menus, modals, and tabs)

- Tracking clicks, item selections, scroll position, or navigation
- Storing API responses and dynamically loaded content

When state changes, React runs reconciliation to compare the previous and next element trees, then the platform renderer commits the minimal set of updates to the native UI (via the renderer of React Native), helping avoid unnecessary work and keeping updates efficient.

State is one of the core pieces of the component architecture of React. It represents the "internal knowledge" of the component—everything that can change while the component is rendered on screen. Proper state management enables developers to build interfaces that are not only reactive but also consistent and scalable.

In class components, state is managed using **`this.state`** and **`this.setState`**, whereas in modern functional components, the **`useState`** Hook is used—an approach that will be explored in greater depth in the next section. The adoption of this functional paradigm represents a significant evolution in how we build modern interfaces with React.

Hooks and Component Lifecycle

Hooks are special functions introduced in React starting from version 16.8 with the goal of bringing features like state management and lifecycle control to functional components, which until then were mainly used to display content based on props. With the arrival of Hooks, functional components became just as powerful as class components – but with the advantage of a cleaner, more readable, and reusable syntax.

Hooks allow developers to better organize component logic by separating responsibilities into reusable functions. They encourage code composition, eliminate the need for classes, and promote a more modern and functional development model with React.

Some of the most commonly used Hooks include:

- **`useState`**: Manages the internal state of a component.
- **`useEffect`**: Handles side effects and lifecycle-like behavior (such as fetching data, subscriptions).
- **`useContext`**, **`useRef`**, **`useMemo`**, **`useCallback`**: Used to manage context, references, performance optimizations, and memoization. **`useMemo`** and **`useCallback`** are **optimization tools**, not defaults. Overusing them can reduce readability and does not always improve performance; prefer clear code first, and add memoization only when profiling shows unnecessary re-renders or expensive computations.
- **Custom Hooks**: Developer-defined functions that encapsulate and reuse logic across multiple components.

Hooks have become a cornerstone of modern React development, empowering developers to write cleaner, more modular, and maintainable code.

Managing State with useState

The **`useState`** Hook allows you to add state to functional components in React. It returns an array with two elements: the current state value and a function to update that value.

Example:

```
import React, { useState } from "react";
import { View, Text, Button } from "react-native";

export function Counter() {
const [count, setCount] = useState(0);
```

```
  return (
<View>
<Text>Counter: {count}</Text>
<Button title="Add" onPress={() =>setCount((prev) =>prev + 1)} />
</View>
  );
}
```

In the example above:

- **`useState(0)`** initializes the state with a value of **`0`**.
- **`setCount`** is the function used to update that value.
- Every time **`setCount`** is called, the component re-renders with the updated state.

This behavior is essential for creating reactive interfaces, where the UI automatically updates in response to user interactions.

Controlling Side Effects with useEffect

The **`useEffect`** Hook is used to handle side effects—work that runs outside the render phase—such as data fetching (API calls), setting up timers/intervals, subscribing to events (including **`AppState`**, **`Dimensions`**, NetInfo), and registering/unregistering listeners (for example, navigation focus/blur handlers).

For example:

```
import React, { useState, useEffect } from "react";

function Timer() {
const [seconds, setSeconds] = useState(0);

useEffect(() => {
const interval = setInterval(() => {
setSeconds(prev =>prev + 1);
    }, 1000);

    return () =>clearInterval(interval); // cleanup on unmount
  }, []);

  return <p>Time: {seconds}s</p>;
}
```

In this example:

- **`useEffect`** runs after the component is mounted.
- The empty dependency array (`[]`) ensures the effect runs once **per mount** (similar to **`componentDidMount`**), but in development with **StrictMode** (React 18+/19) React may intentionally re-run effects to detect unsafe side effects; in production it runs once as expected.
- The return function inside **`useEffect`** is executed when the component unmounts, helping to clean up the interval and avoid memory leaks.

The **`useEffect`** Hook is incredibly powerful because it can replicate the behavior of all lifecycle methods from class components. For example:

- **`componentDidMount`** → **`useEffect(() => {...}, [])`**

- **`componentDidUpdate`** → **`useEffect(() => {...}, [dependencies])`**
- **`componentWillUnmount`** → cleanup function inside **`useEffect`**

Creating Custom Hooks

Custom Hooks allow developers to reuse component logic without duplicating code. These are functions that start with the word **`use`** and may internally use other Hooks. This approach helps separate logic from UI, keeping components smaller, clearer, and easier to test.

Example of a Custom Hook:

```
import { useEffect, useState } from "react";
import { Dimensions } from "react-native";

export function useWindowWidth(): number {
const [width, setWidth] = useState(Dimensions.get("window").width);

useEffect(() => {
const subscription = Dimensions.addEventListener("change", ({ window }) => {
setWidth(window.width);
    });

    return () =>subscription.remove();
  }, []);

  return width;
}
```

Using the Hook:

```
function ScreenInfo() {
const width = useWindowWidth();
  return <p>Screen width: {width}px</p>;
}
```

This pattern is especially useful for handling things like validations, browser data, event listeners, and shared logic across multiple components.

Hooks versus Class Lifecycle Methods

Before Hooks, component behavior over time was managed using class lifecycle methods. With Hooks, we now have a clearer, more functional alternative. Here is how common class lifecycle methods translate to Hooks:

- **`componentDidMount`** → **`useEffect(() => {...}, [])`**
- **`componentDidUpdate`** → **`useEffect(() => {...}, [dependencies])`**
- **`componentWillUnmount`** → **`useEffect`** with a return cleanup function

This functional approach simplifies logic and gives developers fine-grained control over when and how effects are executed, all while reducing code complexity.

Thoughts on Hooks and Lifecycle

The introduction of Hooks brought a major shift in how React components were written; fundamentally redefining the way developers' structure and organize their applications. Prior to Hooks, functional components were limited to simple rendering logic, while class components carried the burden of managing state and lifecycle events—often resulting in verbose, harder-to-maintain code. Hooks changed that by empowering functional components with the same capabilities as classes, but in a more concise and expressive form.

With **useState**, developers can manage internal component state in a straightforward way, and with **useEffect**, they can handle side effects like data fetching, subscriptions, and DOM manipulation—all within functional components. These core Hooks reduce boilerplate and simplify how components behave over time.

Beyond the built-in Hooks, Custom Hooks allow developers to encapsulate reusable logic into self-contained functions that can be shared across components. This not only promotes modularity but also leads to cleaner and more testable code, especially in large-scale applications.

Hooks represent the evolution of the component model of React—providing a more declarative, composable, and scalable approach to building user interfaces. They encourage best practices, improve developer experience, and enhance the performance and maintainability of applications.

Mastering Hooks is not just about writing cleaner code—it is about embracing the full potential of modern React. For any developer aiming to build robust, responsive, and future-proof applications, a deep understanding of Hooks is absolutely essential.

Conclusion

In this chapter, we laid a strong foundation by exploring the core features of modern JavaScript (ES6+), TypeScript, and the essential principles of React. We began with key JavaScript concepts such as `let`, `const`, arrow functions, destructuring, spread/rest operators, and modular code organization. We then introduced TypeScript, emphasizing how its static typing, interfaces, and generics help improve code quality, scalability, and developer confidence. Together, these languages establish the groundwork for more robust and maintainable code. We also examined component-based architecture of React, JSX syntax, data flow with props and state, and the power of Hooks like `useState` and `useEffect`. This modern approach to UI development fosters modularity, reusability, and cleaner logic through custom Hooks.

With a solid understanding of these tools, developers are well-prepared to transition into React Native development, where these concepts are directly applicable to creating high-performance, scalable, and intuitive mobile applications. With these key skills in place, you are now ready to move into the next stage: applying them within real-world React Native projects, where the same principles will be essential to building intuitive, efficient, and cross-platform mobile experiences.

Self-Assessment Questions

Before moving forward, it is important to reflect on the foundational concepts explored in this chapter—ranging from modern JavaScript features and the static typing of TypeScript to the architecture of React components and their behavior. These self-assessment questions are designed to help reinforce your understanding, identify areas that may require deeper review, and ensure you are well-prepared to apply these concepts in practical development, including React Native projects.

1. What are the differences between **var**, **let**, and **const** in JavaScript, and how do they impact variable scope?
2. What are arrow functions, and in what ways do they improve code readability and behavior?
3. How do Spread and Rest operators work, and what are the common use cases for each?
4. What are Promises in JavaScript, and how do they improve asynchronous code handling compared to callbacks?
5. How does the **useState** Hook enable state management in functional React components?

6. When and why should you use the `useEffect` Hook in a React component?
7. What are the main advantages of using TypeScript in JavaScript-based projects like React or React Native?
8. How does destructuring simplify working with arrays and objects in modern JavaScript?
9. What are props in React, and how do they differ from component state?
10. Why are functional components with Hooks generally preferred over class components in modern React development?

Reviewing and answering these questions will help consolidate your knowledge of the content of the chapter and ensure you are building a strong foundation for more advanced topics ahead. If any of the answers are unclear, it is a great opportunity to revisit the relevant sections before progressing further.

Key Terms

This chapter introduced several important terms and concepts that form the foundation of modern JavaScript development, TypeScript usage, and React architecture. Understanding these terms will help reinforce the material covered and prepare you for more advanced topics, especially in the context of building React Native applications.

- **ES6+**: Refers to the versions of ECMAScript starting from ES6 (ECMAScript 2015) and beyond. These versions introduced significant improvements such as arrow functions, classes, modules, destructuring, and more.
- **let / const / var**: Keywords used to declare variables in JavaScript. `let` and `const` respect block scope and are preferred in modern code, while `var` is function-scoped and often leads to unintended behavior due to hoisting.
- **Arrow Function**: A concise way to write functions using `=>`. They do not bind their own `this`, making them ideal for callbacks and inline logic.
- **Destructuring**: A syntax that allows you to extract values from arrays or properties from objects and assign them to variables, improving code readability and reducing repetition.
- **Spread / Rest Operators**: The spread operator (`...`) expands elements from arrays or objects, while the rest operator gathers multiple elements into a single array or object. They simplify operations such as merging, copying, and parameter handling.
- **Modules (import/export)**: ES6 modules provide a native mechanism for splitting code into reusable files. The `import` and `export` statements enable clean, modular application design.
- **Promise**: An object representing the eventual result (or failure) of an asynchronous operation. Promises are used to manage asynchronous code in a more readable and structured way.
- **async / await**: Syntactic sugar built on top of Promises, allowing asynchronous code to be written in a synchronous-like style. Improves readability and simplifies error handling.
- **React**: A JavaScript library developed by Facebook for building declarative, component-based user interfaces, especially useful for single-page applications and dynamic web/mobile UIs.
- **Functional Component**: A React component defined as a plain JavaScript function that returns JSX. It is the modern standard in React development, especially with the use of Hooks.
- **Props**: Short for properties, these are read-only values passed from parent to child components to render dynamic and reusable UI elements.

- **State**: Represents internal data managed by a component that can change over time, triggering UI updates when modified.
- **Hook**: Special functions introduced in React 16.8 that let you use state and other React features in functional components without writing a class.
- **useState / useEffect**: The most commonly used Hooks. `useState` allows you to manage state in a functional component, while `useEffect` is used for handling side effects such as data fetching or setting up subscriptions.
- **TypeScript**: A statically typed superset of JavaScript that adds type annotations and tooling benefits, improving code quality, refactorability, and maintainability—especially in large-scale applications.

These key terms serve as a vocabulary reference for the core technologies and concepts introduced in this chapter and are essential for building well-structured, scalable, and maintainable React (and React Native) applications.

CHAPTER 3
Core React Native Concepts and Project Structure

Introduction

In this chapter, you will gain a detailed understanding of how React Native works "under the hood" and explore key differences between native and web rendering. We will dive into the internal architecture of React Native, including how JavaScript interoperates with iOS and Android. Historically, this interaction was mediated by the classic, batched asynchronous "Bridge" (legacy architecture). In modern React Native, the platform is moving toward the New Architecture—built on JSI, TurboModules, and Fabric—often described as "bridgeless," which changes how JS-native communication is modeled and optimized. Additionally, you will learn about the standard project structure of a React Native application, understanding the role and purpose of each file and folder on both Android and iOS platforms.

To begin with, we will present an overview of the architecture of React Native, which enables JavaScript to drive a native UI. At a high level, React Native work is split across the **JavaScript thread** (application logic and React reconciliation), the **UI (main) thread** (native view updates and user interactions), and additional **native/background threads** used by the platform (for example, networking, image decoding, and other native work).

How layout and rendering are coordinated depends on the architecture in use. **In the classic (legacy) architecture**, layout calculations (Yoga) and view updates were coordinated through an asynchronous, batched Bridge model. **In the New Architecture**, the renderer is **Fabric** and JS-native interoperability is built on **JSI** (with TurboModules), which changes how rendering and updates are scheduled and reduces reliance on the legacy "Bridge" mental model.

A crucial part of this discussion is the difference between native rendering and WebView rendering. Unlike hybrid frameworks such as Cordova or Ionic—which rely on WebView to render HTML and JavaScript inside a mobile app—React Native uses native components for UI rendering. This means buttons, lists, and other interface elements are rendered directly using the native APIs of the platform, leading to better performance and a more consistent user experience. Understanding this distinction helps developers appreciate the balance React Native strikes between flexibility and performance.

We shall also discuss **Expo**, a toolchain built around React Native that simplifies the development process, especially for beginners or those looking to prototype quickly. You will gradually learn that when Expo is the right choice, then transitioning to the React Native CLI provides more control and flexibility, particularly for integrating custom native modules or optimizing performance.

By the end of this chapter, you will not only understand how the architecture of React Native supports cross-platform development but also recognize its strengths and trade-offs compared to web-based rendering approaches. With this foundational knowledge, you will be better equipped to design efficient, scalable, and maintainable mobile applications that fully leverage the power of native components—without sacrificing the productivity of a unified JavaScript codebase.

Structure

In this chapter, we will cover the following topics:

- Introduction
  - Overview of React Native architecture
  - Differences between Native Rendering and WebView Rendering
  - Chapter Objective and Its Relevance to Cross-Platform Development
- How React Native Works Internally
  - Native Modules and the Bridge Architecture
  - What is New in React Native 0.74
- Best Practices for Code Organization in React Native Projects
  - Componentization, Reusability, and Separation by Responsibility
  - Naming Conventions and Best Practices
- Project Folder Structure
  - Overview of Folder Structure in a React Native Project
  - Shared Code Structure (`src/`)
- Expo versus React Native CLI
  - Differences between the Two Approaches
  - Advantages and Limitations of Expo
  - Ideal Scenarios for Using Expo
  - When to Opt for the Pure CLI
  - Migrating from Expo to React Native CLI
- Debugging Tools and Build Lifecycle
  - Debugging Methods: Current Default Tools
  - Build Lifecycle: Development, Testing, Build, Publication
  - Distribution Strategies: Internal Beta, CI/CD, Progressive Rollout
  - Post-Launch Monitoring with Sentry, Bugsnag, and Metrics
- Code Conventions and Project Standardization
  - Naming Conventions (**`camelCase`**, **`PascalCase`**, **`UPPER_SNAKE_CASE`**)
  - ESLint and Prettier for Automatic Standardization
  - Maintaining Consistency in Large Teams
  - Code Review, Documentation, Onboarding, and CI Automations

How React Native Works Internally

Before diving into the technical details of how React Native handles multiple threads, it is essential to understand the foundation of its architecture. React Native was designed to combine the power of native rendering with the productivity of JavaScript development. Unlike traditional hybrid solutions that render components inside a WebView, React Native directly translates your JavaScript components into native views, ensuring a smooth and high-performance user experience.

This architecture is composed of multiple layers and communication channels that operate in parallel. The core of the application is written in JavaScript — leveraging modern frameworks like React — while the execution of graphical interface actions is delegated to native APIs on both Android and iOS. The secret lies in how these two "realms" communicate asynchronously.

React Native operates through multiple specialized threads, each with a well-defined responsibility:

- **JS Thread (JavaScript Thread):** This is the environment where all the JavaScript code of the application runs. It handles business logic, state management, component lifecycle, and navigation logic. Everything you write in `.js` or `.ts` files runs here.
- **UI Thread (or Main Thread):** This is the native thread of the operating system, responsible for everything displayed to the user — layouts, animations, touches, and interactions. It is the same thread used by fully native apps to render their interfaces.
- **Shadow Thread:** Used to calculate the layout of components using the Flexbox-based layout engine. These calculations are done in parallel to optimize performance and are then applied to the UI Thread.

Take a look at *Figure 3.1*, which illustrates in a simplified way how React Native manages different threads to ensure a smooth user experience, even when complex logic is being processed in the background.

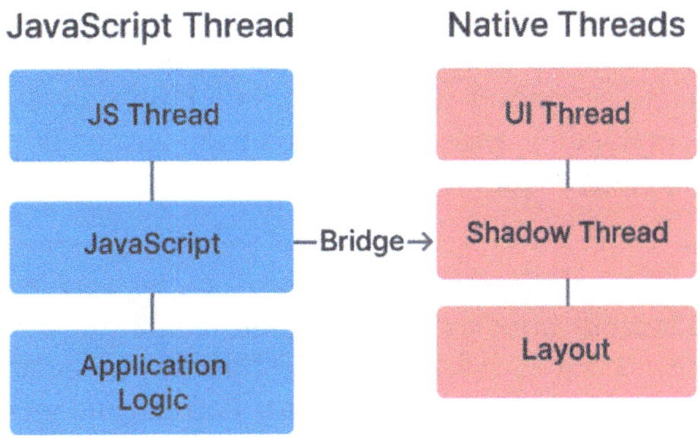

***Figure 3.1**: Basic Differences between JavaScript Thread Threads Nativas*

On the left side, we have highlighted the JavaScript Thread (in blue), where all the app logic resides — from state management to the execution of components and React interactions. In the center of the image is the **Bridge**, which serves as the communication link between the JavaScript world and the native elements of the platforms.

On the right side (in pink), we can see the **Native Threads**, composed of the UI Thread, responsible for rendering visual elements and animations, and the Layout Thread (sometimes called the Shadow Thread), which handles layout calculations via Flexbox.

This architectural separation ensures that even when complex operations are processed in the JavaScript Thread, the interface remains responsive — as long as each part respects its execution boundaries. The image reinforces how React Native provides an efficient bridge between JS code and the native elements of Android and iOS.

This separation ensures that, even with complex tasks running on the JS Thread, the interface stays smooth and responsive – provided the code is well-optimized. However, if the developer overloads the JS Thread (say with heavy loops or poor state management) performance can suffer.

Native Modules and the Bridge Architecture

The communication between the JS Thread and the native threads happens through a fundamental structure known as the **Bridge**. This bridge is responsible for translating JavaScript instructions into native commands specific to Android and iOS. When you use a React Native component, such as a button or list, React Native sends commands through the Bridge to render these components using the corresponding native elements, ensuring both performance and appearance similar to fully native apps.

Native modules are fundamental parts of this architecture. They allow developers to implement specific functionalities that require direct access to the APIs of the operating system, such as the camera, geolocation, sensors, or advanced platform-specific features. In this way, React Native offers powerful and flexible integration with the native capabilities of each device.

Having a deep understanding of how this architecture works enables developers to optimize performance, debug more effectively, and create smoother and more natural experiences for the end users.

Hermes is an open-source JavaScript engine developed by Meta, specifically optimized for running React Native applications on Android devices. When enabled, Hermes compiles JavaScript into an efficient bytecode format ahead of time (AOT), resulting in faster app startup, reduced memory consumption, and improved overall performance.

One of the key advantages of Hermes is its ability to minimize the time required to parse and execute JavaScript code – which directly impacts how quickly the app becomes interactive. This is particularly important for low-end or resource-constrained Android devices, where performance bottlenecks are more noticeable.

Activating Hermes can lead to significant gains in runtime efficiency and is highly recommended for production builds. Understanding and choosing to use Hermes is part of making thoughtful architectural decisions that prioritize performance, scalability, and a better user experience.

Metro Bundler is the bundler and transform pipeline of React Native used during development and builds. It resolves modules and platform-specific entry points, applies transformations (such as `Babel/TypeScripttranspilation`), bundles JavaScript into an output that the JavaScript engine of an app can execute, and also, handles asset resolution (images, fonts, and other static resources). During development, Metro also powers features like **Fast Refresh** and incremental rebuilds for rapid iteration.

Metro is not responsible for runtime `JavaScript↔native` communication inside the running app; that interaction is handled by the runtime architecture of React Native—historically via the legacy Bridge, and in modern React Native via the JSI-based interop of the New Architecture (with systems like TurboModules and Fabric).

Metro plays a crucial role in the internal architecture by handling module resolution, dependency graph creation, code transformation (via Babel), and hot reloading support. It ensures that the application code is structured in a format that allows for seamless communication through the Bridge between the JavaScript Thread and the native platform.

By optimizing bundle size, enabling fast refresh, and supporting efficient updates during development, Metro contributes significantly to both performance and developer productivity. Understanding how Metro works helps developers troubleshoot build issues and make informed decisions when customizing the build process or improving performance.

What is New in React Native 0.83.1

React Native **0.83** is the current stable release line, and **0.83.1** is a patch release that mainly delivers targeted fixes on top of the feature set of 0.83. In this generation, the headline improvements are less about introducing a brand-new architectural model and more about upgrading the React foundation, strengthening modern debugging workflows, and improving performance instrumentation.

React Native 0.83 ships with **React 19.2**, and the release highlights React 19.2 features such as **`<Activity>`** and **`useEffectEvent`** now being available in React Native projects. A major day-to-day developer experience upgrade is the expansion of **React Native DevTools**: since 0.83, DevTools includes first-class **Network inspection** and **Performance tracing**, making it easier to trace where requests originate (via an "**`Initiator`**" view), inspect request/response details, and correlate network activity with runtime performance in a unified timeline. React Native 0.83 also promotes a subset of **Web Performance APIs** to **stable**, enabling more consistent measurement and user-timing instrumentation that can feed into the DevTools Performance view.

From an upgrade-risk perspective, the 0.83 release is explicitly positioned as the first React Native release with **no user-facing breaking changes**, which helps teams treat upgrades more like routine maintenance while still gaining meaningful tooling improvements. Finally, React Native **0.83.1** (as a patch) focuses on correctness: it includes an **Android-specific fix** for a network error that could occur during **`FormData` uploads with binary data** (a common file-upload scenario).

Best Practices for Code Organization in React Native Projects

Building high-quality mobile applications with React Native goes far beyond just making the code work. To ensure that a project is scalable, maintainable, and understandable for the entire team – including new members who may join in the future – it is essential to adopt good code organization practices from the start. A well-planned structure facilitates continuous development, reduces errors, improves productivity, and contributes to the longevity of the application.

In the following subsection, we will highlight key guidelines that can be applied to React Native projects to ensure higher code quality, clarity, and organization.

Component-Centered Architecture for Reusability

One of the main strengths of React Native is its component-based architecture, which promotes the modular, decoupled, and highly reusable construction of user interfaces. Components function as independent blocks that encapsulate both visual elements and their logic, making development more cohesive and standardized.

To maximize the benefits of this approach, the following principles are recommended:

- **Code Reusability:** Whenever possible, create generic and parameterizable components. This avoids duplication and promotes visual and functional consistency throughout the app. A custom button, for example, can be used across multiple screens with small style and behavior variations.

- **Independence and Clear Purpose:** A well-designed component should be self-contained and have a single, clear responsibility. This improves readability, simplifies maintenance, and enhances testability.

- **Component Composition:** Instead of building large, complex components, break the interface into smaller, reusable parts. Use composition to build screens from these smaller blocks. This makes the code cleaner and more flexible.

A component-based architecture also fosters collaboration among developers, as each person can work on different parts of the application without interfering with others. Moreover, this responsibility-based division allows for natural project scalability, making it easier to maintain large codebases and add new features without compromising the existing structure. When applied well, this approach promotes not only development efficiency but also quality, organization, and robustness in the final product.

Separation of Concerns and Modular Organization

Another important pillar for maintaining clean code is the clear **separation of responsibilities**. Each part of the system should handle a specific, well-defined function. This favors modularity and allows developers to work more efficiently, with fewer conflicts and greater predictability.

Here are some practical recommendations for structuring the project:

- **Layered Architecture:** Structure your app in separate layers, such as:
    - **Presentation (UI):** Responsible for the interface and visual components.
    - **Business Logic:** Manages state, validation rules, and user interactions.
    - **Services and APIs:** Handles server communication, authentication, local storage, and the like.
    - **Data Persistence:** Deals with offline storage using tools like SQLite, Realm, or `AsyncStorage`.
- **Functionality Isolation:** Avoid having a component or module handle multiple tasks. The single responsibility principle is crucial for enabling unit testing, refactoring, and long-term evolution of the application.
- **Standardization:** Define coding and naming standards for the entire team. This includes file naming conventions, use of semicolons, indentation, variable types, and so on. Tools like `ESLint` and `Prettier` are great allies in automating standardization.

Regarding **folder organization**, use a well-defined directory structure. *Figure* 3.2 below presents a clear visual representation of a typical `src/` structure in a modern React Native project. This modular organization improves scalability and maintainability as the project grows:

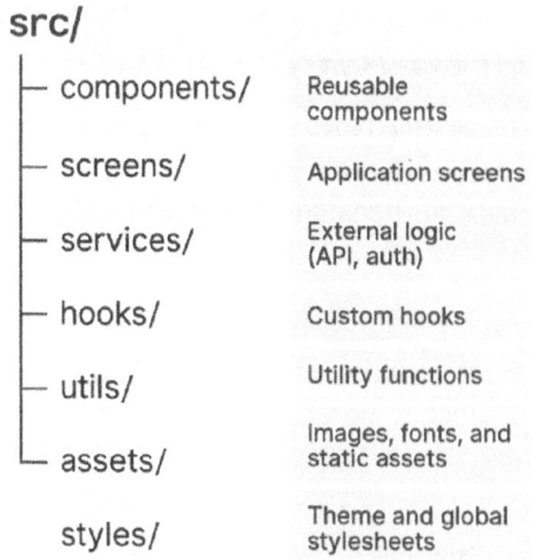

***Figure 3.2**: Structure of a Project with Good Practices*

The image in *Figure* 3.2 shows how the `src/` folder can be structured to accommodate different parts of the application. Each subfolder serves a specific function:

- `components/` stores reusable components.

- **`screens/`** gathers the main screens of the app.
- **`services/`** contains external logic such as APIs and authentication.
- **`hooks/`** holds custom hooks.
- **`utils/`** centralizes utility functions.
- **`assets/`** organizes static resources like images and fonts.
- **`styles/`** consolidates theme and global style files.

This organization promotes a clean, intuitive, and scalable codebase, especially in collaborative teams. Adopting this modular organization strengthens maintainability and scalability, allowing new features to be added safely and clearly, while also making it easier for developers to integrate into the project.

Animations and Performance with Reanimated

Animations are a critical part of delivering a smooth and engaging user experience in mobile applications. While React Native provides basic animation capabilities out of the box, libraries like **`react-native-reanimated`** offer advanced control and performance optimization by allowing animations to run directly on the UI Thread.

Unlike traditional JavaScript-driven animations — which can suffer from dropped frames or lag due to JS Thread congestion — Reanimated enables declarative animations that execute natively, providing fluid transitions and interactions that closely resemble those found in fully native apps.

Integrating Reanimated into your component-based architecture allows you to build interactive, reusable, and highly performant components. It is especially valuable in complex UIs where responsiveness and visual feedback are essential. Using this library strategically enhances not only the aesthetic appeal but also the overall performance and user satisfaction of your app.

Internationalization (i18n)

Adding internationalization support early in your project is essential for building scalable apps that can reach a global audience. Libraries like **`i18next`** or **`react-intl`** simplify the process of managing translations, date and number formats, and locale-specific behaviors. Hence, by planning for multilingual support from the start, you avoid costly refactoring later and create a more inclusive, accessible application experience.

Security

Security is a fundamental aspect of scalable and trustworthy mobile applications. As apps often handle sensitive user data, it is important to implement secure storage solutions such as **`react-native-keychain`** or **`Expo SecureStore`** to protect authentication tokens and other confidential information. Additionally, practices like code obfuscation, secure communication (HTTPS), and reverse engineering prevention help safeguard your application against common vulnerabilities. Prioritizing security from the beginning builds user trust and ensures compliance with data protection standards.

Other Key Points for Scalability

Beyond project structure itself, other considerations directly contribute to the scalability and maintainability of the application:

- **State Management:** Choose a clear strategy for managing application state. Libraries such as **Redux**, **Zustand**, **Recoil**, or **Context API** can be used, depending on the complexity of the app. The important thing is to have a centralized, easily accessible, and manageable state.

- **Documentation:** Whenever possible, document component behaviors, functions, and modules. This helps onboard new developers and reduces confusion during maintenance.
- **Testing:** Implement automated tests, especially for critical components and business logic. Unit, integration, and UI tests help prevent regressions and provide confidence when making changes.
- **Internationalization (i18n):** To ensure global scalability and facilitate the expansion of your application into multiple languages, it is essential to implement internationalization strategies from the beginning. Using libraries like `i18next` or react-`intl` allows you to easily manage texts and formats in different languages, making the application adaptable to various cultures and regions.
- **Sensitive Data Security:** Professional applications often handle sensitive information that needs to be adequately protected. Utilize tools like react-native-keychain or Expo `SecureStore` to securely store confidential data. Additionally, practices such as code obfuscation and reverse engineering prevention significantly enhance the security of your app.
- **Optimization with Hermes and Metro Bundler:** Hermes is a JavaScript engine specifically optimized for React Native, offering substantial improvements in performance, reduced memory usage, and faster startup times. Complementarily, Metro Bundler performs the bundling and optimization of JavaScript code, ensuring efficient application execution. Using both effectively can greatly improve the end-user experience.
- **Native Animations with Reanimated:** Well-implemented animations provide fluidity and an experience closer to native applications. The react-native-reanimated library enables animations to run directly on the UI Thread, resulting in smooth movements and high performance. Investing in animation quality positively impacts the overall perception of the app of the user.

It is important to emphasize that the combination of a well-defined project structure, consistent coding standards, and good practices in organization and testing not only improves the technical quality of the application but also strengthens team collaboration.

Reflections

Scalable and sustainable projects are a direct result of conscious decisions made from the very first commits. Investing time in architecture, standardization, and documentation from the beginning is essential to ensure the healthy evolution of the codebase, facilitate team growth, and support continuous delivery of value to the user.

Keeping an application organized goes far beyond aesthetics or personal preference. It is an essential practice to ensure that the project grows with quality, remains stable, and is sustainable in the long term. By adopting a component-based architecture, clearly separating responsibilities, using a modular structure, and enforcing well-defined standards, development becomes more efficient, collaborative, and free of unnecessary rework.

Regardless of team size or project complexity, investing in code organization is a **strategic decision** that brings countless technical and managerial benefits.

Project Folder Structure

A clear and organized structure is essential for the success of React Native projects – especially considering that this framework integrates JavaScript code with native elements specific to Android and iOS. In the following paragraphs, we break down each essential part of a typical React Native project structure.

Android-Specific Directories and Files

The **`android/`** folder contain all the native files and configurations related to the Android operating system. Even though most of the development is done in JavaScript, this folder is indispensable for the final Android app build. It allows you to configure permissions, define icons, splash screens, minimum versions, and app compatibility, as well as add native code (Java/Kotlin) when necessary.

- **`android/app`**: This is the core of the Android app within the project. It contains files like **`build.gradle`** (module level), where you configure specific dependencies, permissions, environment variables, app identifiers, and versioning settings.
- **`android/app/src/main`**: Inside this folder are the main elements of the Android application, including native code and visual resources. It includes the **`java/`** structure, where custom native modules in Java or Kotlin can be added, as well as the **`res/`** folder (for visual assets) and **`AndroidManifest.xml`**.
- **`android/app/src/main/AndroidManifest.xml`**: A fundamental file that defines app permissions (such as camera or location access), declares activities (screens) and native services, and centralizes initialization settings and required metadata for proper app behavior.
- **`android/gradle`**: Stores Gradle configuration files, the automation system used to compile and package the Android app. The global project configuration, such as the Gradle wrapper and **`gradle.properties`**, is also managed here.

These directories and files form the backbone of the integration between JavaScript code and the Android native environment within a React Native project. Although much of the app logic is developed using web technologies, this structure is where critical configurations take place to ensure the app runs correctly on Android devices. Understanding the role of each component is essential for making specific adjustments, resolving build issues, integrating native features, or customizing the user experience more deeply.

iOS-Specific Directories and Files

The **`ios/`** folder follows the same logic as **`android/`**, but for the platform of Apple, it contains the native files, configurations, and resources specific to iOS, all structured for integration with **Xcode** — the official development environment of Apple.

- **`ios/[project_name].xcodeproj`**: It is the Xcode project file. Opening this in Xcode lets you configure app identity, distribution certificates, icons, splash screens, integrate native libraries, and perform builds.
- **`ios/[project_name]/AppDelegate.m` (or `AppDelegate.swift`)**: It is the file responsible for launching the iOS application. It defines the entry point of the app, sets up the bridge between JavaScript and native code, and can be customized to include native integrations.
- **`ios/Podfile`**: It is used by **CocoaPods**, a dependency manager for iOS projects. This is where external libraries (such as Firebase, camera, and the like) to be installed natively are defined.
- **`ios/[project_name]/Info.plist`**: It is one of the most sensitive files in an iOS project. It defines mandatory settings such as the app name, requested permissions (like microphone or location access), status bar style, privacy settings, and other properties that directly affect the behavior and appearance of the app.

As with the Android structure, the **`ios/`** folder is critical to ensuring the app runs properly on Apple devices. Even if the main development happens in JavaScript, this is where essential configurations, native library integrations, and Apple-required definitions are handled — especially for publishing on the App Store. Mastering these files is vital for customizing the app, setting permissions, fixing build issues, and ensuring compliance with the guidelines of Apple.

Shared Code Structure

The core and most actively developed part of a React Native project is the **`src/`** directory, where all the JavaScript or TypeScript code shared between Android and iOS lives. A well-organized structure in this folder facilitates maintenance, speeds up development, and helps the team stay oriented.

- **`src/components`:** It stores reusable UI components like buttons, modals, inputs, cards, headers, and so on. Each component should be self-contained and flexible, so it can be used across different screens with minimal variation.
- **`src/screens`:** It contains the main screens of the app, usually organized by sections or flows (for example, **`LoginScreen`**, **`ProfileScreen`**, **`SettingsScreen`**). This separation helps with navigation and screen-specific logic.
- **`src/services`:** It holds logic for communicating with external services, such as REST or GraphQL API calls, Firebase or Auth0 authentication, and database integrations. It is the ideal place to centralize business logic that is decoupled from the UI.
- **`src/hooks`:** This stores custom hooks that encapsulate reusable logic – like network status detection, form management, or animations with **`useAnimated`**. Hooks help reduce code duplication and improve readability.
- **`src/utils`:** It contains generic utility functions such as date and currency formatters, CPF validators, text masks, percentage calculations, and more. Anything commonly used but not directly tied to the UI can go here.
- **`src/assets`:** This is a repository for static files such as images (PNG, SVG), icons, videos, custom fonts, configuration JSON files, and so on. Keeping this directory well-organized prevents path issues and makes managing visual assets easier.
- **`src/styles`:** Consolidates global themes of the application – including colors, font sizes, standard styles for buttons, paddings, borders, and other reusable visual elements. This helps maintain visual consistency throughout the app.

This modular and segmented structure directly supports productivity, code reuse, ongoing maintenance, and long-term project growth. In larger teams, it also improves collaboration, as developers can work on different parts of the project without conflicts. By applying the best structuring practices from the beginning, you prepare your app to grow in a solid, organized, and sustainable way.

Expo versus React Native CLI

When starting a React Native project, one of the most important decisions you will need to make is whether to use **Expo** or the **pure React Native CLI**. This choice will directly impact your development workflow, customization possibilities, and the level of control you will have over the project. Both approaches offer specific advantages but also impose certain limitations that should be considered based on the requirements and goals of your app. A deep understanding of the differences between these two options is essential for making a decision aligned with the project scope, team experience, and available development resources.

Pros and Cons of Expo

Expo is a tool that abstracts much of the complexity of native development, offering a smoother and more accessible experience – especially for beginners. It provides a convenience layer on top of pure React Native, bundling a set of tools, services, and pre-integrated APIs that make it easy to build functional apps without touching native code. However, this convenience comes at the cost of technical limitations and reduced freedom compared to the traditional CLI.

Advantages:

- The main advantage of Expo is the **ease of initial setup**, allowing anyone with basic JavaScript knowledge to quickly start building an app.
- It includes **many pre-configured features** out of the box, such as push notifications, authentication, geolocation, camera access, and more, thereby eliminating the need for manual setup.
- You can **test your app directly on your phone** using the Expo Go app, without needing to set up Android Studio or Xcode at the beginning.
- The **OTA (over-the-air) update system** and active community make Expo a reliable solution, always aligned with best practices in the ecosystem.

Disadvantages:

- Expo **Go** does not allow direct addition of custom native modules, which can limit certain libraries or deeper native integrations; however, Expo projects **can** use custom native code when using an **Expo Development Build** (custom dev client) or the **prebuild/bare workflow** (often via config plugins).
- The **final app size tends to be larger**, as it includes several libraries you might not use, but which are needed for the infrastructure of Expo.
- There is some reliance on the tooling and services of Expo in typical workflows of the same (for example, EAS Build and EAS Update), but this is not strictly required in every case. Teams can choose alternatives—such as self-hosted CI/build pipelines, different push notification providers, or custom native integrations—depending on their requirements.

In summary, Expo is an excellent choice for those seeking convenience, speed, and a smoother learning curve when developing mobile apps with React Native. Its integrated tools and quick testing capabilities make the process much more efficient, especially for short-term projects or less experienced teams.

However, as the project grows and requires more control over native behavior, its limitations can become a barrier. That is why it is crucial to evaluate your technical requirements before fully committing to Expo, understanding that while it is ideal in many cases, it may eventually require migration to the pure CLI in more advanced scenarios.

Ideal Scenarios for Using Expo

Expo is highly recommended for projects that need to be launched quickly, without the need for manual native environment setup. Its ecosystem is especially beneficial for small teams, beginners in mobile development, or for those building fast and functional prototypes.

Expo is ideal when:

- The focus is on **development speed and simplicity**, especially during the initial phases of the project.
- There is **no need for custom native modules**, such as specific SDKs or hardware integrations not supported by Expo.
- The project involves **simple to medium-sized applications**, like informational apps, content generators, registration and lookup systems — where ease of use and maintainability are more important than full technical flexibility.
- **Fast distribution and constant testing** are priorities — something made simple with Expo Go and the OTA update system.

These scenarios show how Expo can be a powerful ally in mobile development when the project requirements are aligned with its proposal. By removing initial technical barriers and offering a streamlined, optimized experience, Expo allows ideas to quickly come to life – making concept validation and rapid delivery much easier.

However, it is important to remember that this approach prioritizes convenience over flexibility. So when choosing Expo, it is essential to ensure the goals of your app fall within the capabilities of the platform, which will guarantee a more productive development process with fewer roadblocks in the future.

Steps to Migrate from Expo to Pure React Native CLI

At certain points, your project may grow in complexity beyond what Expo can offer. This is common when there is a need to integrate specific native libraries, access low-level APIs, or perform customizations that Expo does not support. In such cases, migrating to the pure React Native CLI becomes not only recommended but essential to ensure scalability and full control over the behavior of your app. The following are the key steps to perform this transition safely and efficiently:

1. Run the **prebuild** step instead of "eject" by executing `npx expo prebuild`. This generates the native `android/` and `ios/` directories for your project, enabling full native configuration and integration with native SDKs while still keeping the configuration-first workflow of Expo (including config plugins). You typically use **prebuild** when you need custom native modules, native project changes, or you want to create an **Expo Development Build** (custom dev client). For production builds, many teams then use **EAS Build** to compile App Store/Play Store binaries (or build locally/CI if preferred).

2. **Set up native development environments** by installing and configuring Android Studio (for Android) and Xcode (for iOS). This includes installing SDKs, setting up emulators, and configuring environment variables on your system. This step is crucial because from this point on, you will need to build and test your app directly in these environments.

3. **Remove Expo-specific dependencies** that will no longer work after ejecting, such as `expo-camera`, `expo-notifications`, and others. Replace these libraries with compatible CLI alternatives, many of which require manual installation of native dependencies and adjustments to files like `AndroidManifest.xml` and `Info.plist`.

4. **Reconfigure services** that were previously managed automatically by Expo, such as push notifications, over-the-air (OTA) updates, analytics, permissions, and deep linking. These services will now need to be integrated and configured manually, following the documentation of the libraries you choose to use.

5. **Thoroughly test the app** on real devices and emulators to ensure everything is working correctly after the migration. Check that all permissions are properly set, UI elements render as expected, and there are no build errors on either Android or iOS platforms.

Performing this migration requires more technical knowledge and attention to detail but rewards you with much greater control over the project. By carefully following these steps, you will be able to take full advantage of native platform features, deliver more robust solutions, and prepare your app for more advanced challenges in the mobile development landscape.

Debugging Tools and Build Lifecycle

In React Native app development, one of the most important aspects to ensure the quality of the final product is the application of proper **debugging practices** and a deep understanding of the **build and deployment lifecycle**. More than just writing functional code, it is essential to monitor each stage of development using the right tools to quickly and accurately identify, isolate, and fix issues. At the same time, understanding how an app is prepared, tested, packaged, and delivered to the user is critical to avoid major errors, optimize performance, and ensure safe, continuous updates. A well-structured approach to these two aspects directly impacts the stability, performance, and scalability of the app.

Introduction to Debugging Methods

Debugging is an essential part of any app development process, and React Native is no exception. Several tools and techniques are available to help identify bugs, unexpected behaviors, slowness, and inconsistencies — allowing developers to make faster, more informed decisions throughout the development cycle.

- **React Native Debugger:** One of the most complete debugging tools for React Native. It combines the features of Chrome DevTools with advanced capabilities such as inspecting props, state, and Redux store, allowing real-time monitoring of the data flow of your app. It supports features like time-travel debugging, action tracking, and grouped log viewing. This tool is especially valuable in Redux-based projects, offering a full visualization of actions and global state mutations.
- **Flipper:** Developed by Facebook, Flipper is a modern graphical interface that connects to your app in real time, offering a rich visual debugging experience. It supports a wide range of plugins — including layout inspection, log analysis, performance tracking, network request debugging, animations, and database monitoring (like Realm, SQLite). You can also create custom plugins, making it highly customizable to suit the specific needs of your project.
- **Console Logs:** Although it is the simplest approach, using `console.log()` remains a valuable day-to-day tool. It is ideal for understanding app behavior during execution, identifying unexpected variable values, tracking function flow, and confirming that specific code blocks are being executed. When used moderately and organized well, this technique can be extremely effective — especially in early development phases or when fixing specific bugs quickly.
- **Breakpoints and IDE Debugging:** Some IDEs like Visual Studio Code allow you to set breakpoints and debug JavaScript code step-by-step. This is particularly useful for exploring the logic of app in real time, viewing the call stack, and inspecting variable values at different stages of execution.

Using these tools together creates a powerful debugging strategy. They support a **proactive approach** to problem-solving, streamline development time, and significantly contribute to building more stable, high-performance, and professional-grade applications.

Fast Refresh

Fast Refresh is a native feature of React Native that significantly accelerates the local development cycle. It allows code changes to be instantly reflected in the running application without requiring a full recompilation — and most importantly, it preserves the current state of the component whenever possible.

This functionality is especially useful during visual adjustments, layout testing, or minor logic tweaks, enabling developers to see the impact of their changes almost in real time. By streamlining the process, Fast Refresh reduces frustration and the wasted time caused by full rebuilds, which are common in traditional native environments.

Activating and understanding how Fast Refresh works is essential for a fast, iterative, and productive development cycle. When used alongside tools like console logs and React Native Debugger, it becomes a key element in building interfaces with greater efficiency and speed.

Overview of the Build Lifecycle and Deployment Strategies

The **build and deployment lifecycle** of a React Native application involves a series of steps, from writing the first lines of code to delivering the final product to users via app stores. Fully understanding this flow is essential to ensure successful deliveries, identify potential bottlenecks, and efficiently automate processes. Each step requires attention to both technical and strategic details and is crucial for the quality and longevity of the project.

Local Development

This is the initial phase, where developers work on the code in their local environments. The focus here is on building core features, visually testing the UI, and ensuring that the flows align with the business logic. The use of simulators, emulators, and real devices helps validate the behavior of the app across different scenarios and operating systems.

Testing and Validation

Once features are developed, it is critical to validate the app behavior through testing. This includes:

- **Unit tests** for verifying individual functions,
- **Integration tests** to ensure components work together properly,
- **UI tests** to validate user experience and visual interactions.

Tools like **Jest**, **Detox**, and **React Native Testing Library** are widely used in this phase.

Building the Application

With code validated, the next step is compiling the app to generate the final executable files: APK or AAB for Android, and IPA for iOS. At this stage, tools like **Gradle** (Android) and **Xcode** (iOS) handle transpilation, packaging, and digital signing. This is also when app versioning, naming, icons, permissions, and certificates are configured.

Distribution and Release

After generating the builds, the app is prepared for distribution to stores (Google Play and App Store). Before that, many projects go through internal or public **beta testing phases** using tools like **Firebase App Distribution**, **TestFlight** (iOS), or CI/CD services for automation. A common practice is to use **progressive rollouts**, releasing the app gradually to a subset of users, which helps mitigate large-scale issues.

Post-Launch Monitoring

Deployment is not the end — it is the start of real user interaction. After release, it is essential to monitor app performance using error tracking tools like **Sentry** and **Bugsnag**, and to collect usage metrics such as average session time, retention, crashes, and resource consumption. Based on this data, the team can confidently plan updates, fix bugs, and introduce new features.

Mastering the build and deployment lifecycle is an essential skill for teams aiming to deliver reliable, high-quality products. The more **structured and predictable** the process, the more efficient the team becomes — and the better the final user experience.

Code Conventions and Project Standardization

Building a robust, scalable, and maintainable application goes far beyond implementing features. One of the core pillars for the success of any project — especially within large or collaborative teams — is adopting clear **code conventions** and solid **project structure standardization**. These practices not only reduce onboarding time for new developers but also significantly minimize errors, improve code readability and review processes, and result in a more organized and sustainable project in the long run. Additionally, a standardized foundation makes refactoring, testing, and future integrations much easier.

Recommended Naming Conventions

The way we name files, variables, functions, and components has a direct impact on the clarity and navigability of codebase. Well-defined names communicate intent and purpose clearly, making it easier for the team — or even your future self — to read and understand the code. Following a common naming convention avoids ambiguity and ensures cohesion across the repository.

Naming Recommendations

- **Files and Folders:** Always use short, descriptive names in English and avoid unclear abbreviations. Use **PascalCase** for component files (say **`UserProfile.js`**), and **camelCase** for utility files, functions, and services (like **`fetchUserData.js`**). Folder names can follow **kebab-case** (such as **`user-profile/`**) or **camelCase**, as long as consistency is maintained.
- **React Components:** Should be named using **`PascalCase`**, such as **`LoginScreen`**, **`PrimaryButton`**, or **`UserCard`**. Avoid generic names like **`Component1`** or **`Page2`**, which do not express the purpose of the component.
- **Variables and Functions:** Use **`camelCase`**, say **`userEmail`**, **`handleLogin`**, **`fetchProfileData`**. Names should be clear and descriptive, representing what they are or what they do.
- **Global Constants:** Use **`UPPER_SNAKE_CASE`** (like **`API_BASE_URL`**, **`MAX_RETRIES`**) to clearly indicate fixed values and prevent accidental changes.

Establishing and following these conventions creates a smoother workflow where all team members can quickly understand the structure and purpose of code written by others.

Global ESLint and Prettier Configuration

To ensure these conventions are applied automatically and consistently, using linting and formatting tools like **ESLint** and **Prettier** is essential. These tools help enforce coding rules, prevent bad practices, and maintain a uniform code style across the entire project.

ESLint:

- Configure ESLint with rules tailored to JavaScript and TypeScript.
- Recommended rules include:
  - **`no-unused-vars`**: Prevents unused variable declarations.
  - **`no-undef`**: Avoids using undeclared variables.
  - **`consistent-return`**: Enforces consistent return behavior in functions.
  - React-specific rules, like **`react-hooks/rules-of-hooks`**, to prevent incorrect use of Hooks.

  - Required typing for functions and props, especially with TypeScript (**`explicit-function-return-type`**).

Prettier:

- Prettier should be integrated into the project to ensure consistent formatting.
- Recommended settings:
  - **`printWidth: 80`** or **`100`**: Sets the maximum line width.
  - **`singleQuote: true`**: Enforces the use of single quotes in strings.
  - **`trailingComma: 'es5'`**: Adds trailing commas in objects and arrays where valid.
  - **`tabWidth: 2`**: Uses two spaces for indentation.
  - **`semi: true`**: Ensures all statements end with a semicolon.

These tools can be integrated into development environments (like VS Code) and configured to run automatically on pre-commit hooks or in CI/CD pipelines, ensuring all committed code complies with the defined standards – with no exceptions.

Maintaining Consistency in Large Teams and Projects

As the project grows and new developers join, maintaining consistency in codebase becomes increasingly challenging. To prevent different styles, logic patterns, and structures from mixing within the same repository, it is essential to adopt strategies that reinforce standardization practically and continuously.

Best practices for consistency:

- **Technical Documentation:** Maintain clear and accessible documentation (say a **`CONTRIBUTING.md`** file or internal wiki) that explains code conventions, ESLint rules, Prettier usage, folder structure, commit standards, and architectural decisions.

- **Code Reviews:** Establish a mandatory code review process before every merge. The goal is not just to catch bugs, but also to ensure adherence to style and standards, while fostering knowledge sharing within the team.

- **Internal Workshops and Onboarding:** Host periodic training sessions to reinforce established conventions. New team members should go through an onboarding process that covers these standards to ensure alignment from the start.

- **CI/CD with Linters and Formatters:** Automate checks with ESLint and Prettier in the CI pipeline. This ensures that any code violating the rules is detected before it is merged into the main codebase.

- **Use of Templates and Generators:** Standardize the creation of components, services, and screens through templates or tools like **Plop**, ensuring that all new files follow the predefined structure by default.

Adopting and maintaining code conventions and project structure standardization is not just about aesthetics or organization – it is an **investment in quality, agility, and collaboration**. Well-structured projects with clear rules are easier to scale, less prone to bugs, and offer a smoother development experience for everyone involved.

Beyond memorizing processes, commands, and tools, it is essential for the developer to understand the why behind things. Why is the architecture structured this way? Why do we separate responsibilities? Why should we care about threads, performance, and file organization?

The answer lies in **technical maturity**.

Working with React Native — and mobile development in general — is a journey that increasingly demands architectural awareness. It is not enough for the code to simply work. It needs to work well — predictably, scalably, and collaboratively. And that is not achieved through shortcuts, but through conscious decisions. Every architectural choice we make — from how we name files to how we manage state — carries consequences that accumulate over time. Maturity means anticipating those consequences and shaping the project with a long-term vision.

When Technical Mastery is not Enough: The Value of Organization

Early in career, the focus is often on "getting something on the screen" — creating a button, a form, a working navigation. Undeniably, this is certainly an achievement. But as projects grow, the ability to **maintain** code becomes more valuable than simply writing it.

Directory organization, meaningful naming, structure standardization, automated tests, and good debugging practices are the pillars that sustain a living application, especially in team environments. React Native projects tend to grow quickly, and without a solid, cohesive foundation from the start, what began as a simple login screen can become a constant source of frustration.

This is when many developers realize they need to relearn what they thought they already knew: writing **less** can be better; separating responsibilities may seem time-consuming, but it prevents chaos; and standardization, far from being bureaucratic, is an act of collective respect in teamwork.

React Native as a Bridge: Between the Web and the Native World

React Native plays a fascinating role in the modern development ecosystem. It is a bridge between the **declarative, productive, and familiar world of JavaScript** and the **power of native code**. To get the best of both worlds, developers must understand how this bridge works. Knowing how threads, the Bridge, native modules, and JavaScript execution limits relate to native rendering enables better decisions, avoids bottlenecks, and allows you to fully harness the potential of the tool.

More than that, this understanding helps us avoid the "black box" trap — that moment when something breaks in the app and we are unsure whether the issue lies in logic, the Bridge, native code, or a thread conflict. Architectural knowledge brings autonomy and confidence. It shifts the role of the developer from operator to **solution architect**.

Scalability is a Matter of Intention

Finally, it is worth reflecting on the concept of scalability. Scaling a project is not just about making it bigger — it is about enabling it to grow without losing integrity. This applies to the codebase, the team, the delivery cycle, and the user experience.

Scalability starts with a well-thought-out structure. With the humility to understand that even in small projects, it is worth investing in the foundation. The time spent creating a reusable component, separating files, configuring ESLint and Prettier, writing tests, or documenting architectural decisions will be rewarded when the project grows — and it will grow, if you do a good job.

In the end, what we build with React Native goes beyond beautiful interfaces and functional apps. We are building a **way of thinking** — a technical mindset that combines clarity, intentionality, consistency, efficiency, and empathy for the next developer who will inherit that code.

This is the kind of engineering that turns ordinary projects into **memorable products**.

Conclusion

Throughout this chapter, we have delved into the internal workings of React Native, examining its architecture, threading model, project structure, and the role of tools like the Bridge and Expo. We have also highlighted how understanding the "why" behind technical decisions—such as separating responsibilities, naming conventions, and file organization—is essential for building scalable and maintainable applications. Technical maturity comes not just from making things work, but from building with intention and anticipating the long-term impact of our architectural choices.

As we move forward, we shall build upon this architectural foundation to explore practical implementation techniques in React Native. In the next chapter, we will focus on Basic Components, Styling, and Responsive Layout, thinking about best practices for structuring multi-screen apps. These topics will equip you to create seamless user experiences while applying the performance-conscious and organized mindset established in this chapter.

Questions

The following questions are designed to help you reflect on these concepts, identify any gaps in your understanding, and strengthen your technical foundation for the challenges ahead.

1. How does React Native differ from traditional hybrid solutions, such as those using WebView, in terms of component rendering?
2. What is the role of the JavaScript Thread in React Native, and why can overloading it negatively impact app performance?
3. What is the Bridge in React Native, and how does it enable communication between JavaScript code and native elements on Android/iOS?
4. What are the main responsibilities of the UI Thread and Shadow Thread within the React Native rendering cycle?
5. In what situation is the use of native modules necessary, and how do they integrate into the architecture of React Native?
6. What are the main directories inside the **`android/`** folder in a React Native project, and what is the purpose of each one?
7. How is the **`ios/`** folder structured, and why is it essential even when most development is done in JavaScript?
8. Why is modular organization of the **`src/`** directory important, and how does it contribute to the scalability and maintainability of the project?
9. Why is it recommended to separate components, services, hooks, utilities, and styles in a React Native project?
10. What are the key criteria for choosing between Expo and the React Native CLI when starting a new project?
11. In what context is it more appropriate to use Expo, and when does migrating to the pure CLI become necessary?
12. Which tools can be used for debugging in React Native, and how do they support the development and bug-fixing process?
13. How does the build and deployment lifecycle of a React Native app work – from local development to publishing in app stores?

14. Why is adopting code standards (with tools like ESLint and Prettier) essential in projects with multiple developers?
15. How do clear documentation and regular code reviews contribute to the consistency and quality of a project?

Key Terms

- **JavaScript Thread:** Responsible for executing all JavaScript code in the app, including business logic, state management, and navigation. It is the core of the React Native app on the JS side and should be used carefully to avoid compromising UI performance.
- **UI Thread (Main Thread):** The native thread responsible for visually rendering the app interface. It handles animations, user inputs, and all visual elements, ensuring a smooth experience when well managed.
- **Shadow Thread:** An intermediate thread responsible for calculating layouts using the Flexbox algorithm. It processes the visual structure and passes the results to the UI Thread, optimizing performance.
- **Bridge:** The asynchronous communication bridge between the JavaScript world and native Android/iOS components. It enables native rendering via JS commands and integration with native modules.
- **Native Module:** Platform-specific code implemented in Java (Android) or Swift/Objective-C (iOS) to access OS-level APIs. It allows React Native to integrate with features like the camera, sensors, and GPS in a native manner.
- **Modular Structure (`src/`):** The central directory where the JavaScript/TypeScript code of the app is organized. It contains subfolders like **`components`**, **`screens`**, **`services`**, **`hooks`**, **`utils`**, **`assets`**, and **`styles`**, each with a clear responsibility in the project.
- **Expo:** A framework that simplifies React Native development by providing ready-to-use APIs and an automated build environment. Ideal for simple, fast projects or small teams, but with limitations in native customizations.
- **React Native CLI:** The pure React Native approach, offering full control over the **`android/`** and **`ios/`** folders. It allows the use of native libraries and advanced integrations, making it suitable for complex and highly customized projects.
- **Eject:** The process of migrating an Expo project to pure React Native CLI. It generates native structures and requires manual configuration of dependencies, offering more freedom for customization.
- **AndroidManifest.xml:** A key file in Android projects that defines permissions, activities (screens), and metadata used by the app. Any integration with system features must be declared here.
- **Info.plist:** The iOS equivalent of **`AndroidManifest.xml`**. It defines app name, requested permissions, privacy settings, and status bar behavior.
- **React Native Debugger:** A powerful debugging tool that allows inspection of state, props, and Redux data flow, with integration into DevTools.
- **Flipper:** A graphical debugging tool developed by Facebook for React Native apps. It supports log inspection, performance tracking, network analysis, animations, and more – with plugin support.

- **useState / useEffect:** Fundamental hooks in functional components. `useState` manages local state, while `useEffect` handles side effects such as requests, timers, or lifecycle events.
- **ESLint / Prettier:** Linting and code formatting tools that help maintain consistent standards in projects with multiple developers, avoiding common errors and style mismatches.
- **Code Review:** The practice of peer reviewing code to ensure standardization, catch bugs, and promote collective learning within the team.
- **CI/CD:** Continuous Integration and Continuous Deployment. An automated process for testing, building, and deploying apps, used to ensure that the delivered code is stable and follows the defined standards.

CHAPTER 4

Basic Components, Styling, and Responsive Layout

Introduction

In this chapter, we will delve deeply into the core React Native components—**View**, **Text**, **Image**, and **TextInput**—which are essential for building intuitive, functional interfaces. Each component will be illustrated with practical examples that highlight its use cases and nuances, ensuring you gain a solid understanding of when and how to apply them effectively.

Mastering these fundamental components is vital for any React Native developer, as they form the very foundation of every visual interface in the framework. Knowing how to work with them correctly lets you create robust apps with an outstanding user experience, regardless of device or platform.

We will also cover advanced styling techniques using **CSS-in-JS** and **Flexbox** concepts. These approaches make your apps truly responsive—dynamically adapting to varying screen sizes and resolutions. Crafting responsive layouts is key to delivering a consistent, enjoyable experience on both smartphones and tablets.

Additionally, we will highlight the best practices for responsive design to ensure visual consistency and intuitive functionality across **iOS** and **Android**. Embracing these practices not only improves the user experience but also streamlines development by enabling style and component reuse across platforms.

Finally, we will emphasize the importance of accessibility and performance optimization in React Native. A well-structured, responsive design not only boosts user satisfaction but also enhances app performance, making your applications efficient and a pleasure to use.

Structure

In this chapter, we will cover the following topics:

- React Native Basic Components
- View Component: Structuring the Interface in React Native
    - The Role of View in Visual Organization
    - Creating Layouts with Flexbox

    - Common Issues and Bad Practices
    - Building a Complete Layout
    - Reflections on the View Component
- Text Component: Displaying and Styling Text in React Native
    - Displaying Text Elements
    - Styling and Formatting Text
    - Specific Text Behaviors
    - Nesting and Advanced Formatting
    - Accessibility Considerations
    - Reflections on the Text Component
- Image Component: Working with Images in React Native
    - Loading Local and Remote Images
    - Handling Image Assets Efficiently
    - Resizing with resizeMode
    - Reflections on the Image Component
- TextInput Component: Capturing and Managing User Input
    - Customizing Inputs for Various Use Cases
    - Accessibility Considerations
    - Reflections about TextInput
- ScrollView Component: Managing Scrollable Content in React Native
    - Handling Content Overflow with ScrollView
    - Nested Scrolling
    - Reflections about ScrollView
- Styling in React Native
    - Using StyleSheet
    - Creating and Managing Styles
    - Dynamic and Responsive Styling in React Native
    - Adapting to Different Screen Sizes
    - Using the Dimensions API
    - Advanced Responsiveness Techniques

React Native Basic Components

The basic components in React Native are the fundamental elements used to build graphical interfaces in mobile applications. They function as modular building blocks, capable of composing complete screens in an organized and scalable way. A deep understanding of these components not only increases development efficiency but also facilitates code maintenance, reduces the likelihood of bugs, and significantly improves the end-user experience.

These components represent powerful abstractions that hide the native complexity of each platform (iOS and Android), thereby providing a unified interface for UI construction. This means that when working with components such as `View`, `Text`, `Image`, or `TextInput`, developers do not need to interact directly with native elements like **UIView** on iOS or **ViewGroup** on Android. React Native coordinates JavaScript and native code for you (historically via the legacy Bridge, and in modern versions via the JSI-based interop of the New Architecture), aiming for consistent cross-platform behavior and efficient UI updates—though actual performance depends on rendering patterns and workload.

Each basic component has a specific role in the React Native UI ecosystem:

- **View**: It acts as a generic container, allowing grouping of other components and layout control via Flexbox.
- **Text**: It renders textual content and supports rich styling, including custom fonts, spacing, and transformations (uppercase/lowercase).
- **Image**: It simplifies display of local and remote images, with options for caching, automatic resizing, and quality control.
- **TextInput**: It manages user data entry, offering support for custom keyboards, input masks, real-time validation, and focus events.

In addition to these, there are other essential components for common use cases:

- **ScrollView** and **FlatList**: Both of these enable content scrolling, supporting both static and large dynamic lists with on-demand rendering optimizations.
- **SectionList**: It is ideal for grouped or sectioned lists, displaying fixed headers and categorized items.
- **SafeAreaView**: It ensures content respects safe areas on devices with notches or system bars.
- **TouchableOpacity**, **TouchableHighlight**, and **Pressable**: These are touchable components that capture user interactions, provide visual feedback, and handle simple gestures.

One of the key differentiators of React Native is its ability to style these components using the Flexbox layout system, offering flexibility to create responsive interfaces that adapt to different screen sizes and resolutions—without writing separate native code for each platform. Combining **StyleSheet** and inline styles allows clear CSS-in-JS organization, style reuse, and visual consistency across the app.

Another crucial aspect is the focus on performance and accessibility. Many basic components include built-in accessibility properties (such as **accessibilityLabel**, **accessible**, and **importantForAccessibility**), making it easier to build inclusive apps for screen readers and users with special needs. Moreover, by avoiding unnecessary re-renders; for example, using **shouldComponentUpdate** in class components or React.memo in functional components—you can ensure a smoother and more responsive user experience.

Finally, these basic components also serve as the foundation for advanced UI libraries and custom component development. By combining animations (via the **Animated** API), complex gestures (with **react-native-gesture-handler**), and integration with native modules (through **Native Modules** and **TurboModules**), developers can extend the potential and deliver robust of React Native, sophisticated applications—while retaining the simplicity and control provided by the basic components.

View Component: Structuring the Interface in React Native

In React Native application development, the View component is one of the most fundamental and frequently used elements. It acts as a generic container that visually groups and organizes other interface components, playing a role similar to the **<div>** tag in HTML. Although it has no visual appearance of its own, View serves as an invisible structure that defines the layout, positioning, and visual behavior of the elements within it.

The true strength of View lies in its versatility. It is used on virtually every screen of an application—whether to create distinct areas such as headers, footers, columns, and sections, or to align and organize content like buttons, text, forms, and images. In many cases, it serves as the starting point for building complete and well-structured layouts.

The Role of View in Visual Organization

By using View, developers can apply styles such as margins, paddings, background colors, borders, and shadows. Moreover, it supports flexible layout systems, especially Flexbox, which makes it possible to build interfaces that automatically adapt to different screen sizes and device orientations. This is crucial in mobile environments, where a wide variety of screen dimensions and aspect ratios exist.

For instance, with the proper combination of **`flexDirection`**, **`justifyContent`**, and **`alignItems`**, developers can create anything from simple horizontal alignments to complex content grids. This capability makes View an essential tool for organizing the visual logic of an application.

A simple example of how View can be used to center text in the middle of the screen is as follows:

```
import React from 'react';
import { View, Text, StyleSheet } from 'react-native';

export default function App() {
  return (
<View style={styles.container}>
<Text style={styles.title}>Hello World!</Text>
</View>
  );
}

const styles = StyleSheet.create({
  container: {
    flex: 1,
backgroundColor: '#F5F5F5',
justifyContent: 'center',
alignItems: 'center',
  },
  title: {
fontSize: 24,
fontWeight: 'bold',
  },
});
```

In this example, the View takes up the entire screen space (**`flex: 1`**) and centers its content both vertically and horizontally.

Creating Layouts with Flexbox
The power of the View becomes even more evident when combined with Flexbox—the default layout system in React Native. With Flexbox, it is easy to control how elements align and are distributed within a given space.

Here is an example where three colored squares are positioned side by side with spacing between them:

```
<View style={styles.row}>
<View style={styles.boxRed} />
<View style={styles.boxGreen} />
<View style={styles.boxBlue} />
```

```
</View>

const styles = StyleSheet.create({
  row: {
flexDirection: 'row',
justifyContent: 'space-around',
    padding: 10,
  },
boxRed: {
    width: 60,
    height: 60,
backgroundColor: 'red',
  },
boxGreen: {
    width: 60,
    height: 60,
backgroundColor: 'green',
  },
boxBlue: {
    width: 60,
    height: 60,
backgroundColor: 'blue',
  },
});
```

Now compare this with the *Figure 4.1*, that represents this code:

***Figure 4.1**: Example with Flexbox*

This type of structure is essential for creating dynamic, well-distributed interfaces, ensuring a smooth and visually balanced user experience.

Common Issues and Bad Practices

Despite its importance, incorrect usage of the View component can lead to serious performance and maintenance problems. One of the most frequent mistakes is excessive nesting of View components—placing multiple Views inside one another without a real need. This can result in slower rendering times and make the code harder to read and maintain.

Another common issue is improper use of Flexbox, especially failing to correctly configure properties like **`flex`**, **`flexDirection`**, **`justifyContent`**, and **`alignItems`**. These oversights often lead to misaligned components or inconsistent behavior across different devices.

Therefore, it is crucial to follow best practices when using the View component, such as:

- Limiting the number of nested levels.
- Properly naming and organizing styles using StyleSheet.create.
- Using reusable components instead of duplicating similar structures.
- Testing the layout on different screen sizes and orientations.

Building a Complete Layout

The following is an example of a complete screen structure with a header, content area, and footer—all organized using View:

```
<View style={styles.wrapper}>
<View style={styles.header}>
<Text style={styles.headerText}>My App</Text>
</View>

<View style={styles.content}>
<Text style={styles.paragraph}>Main screen content.</Text>
</View>

<View style={styles.footer}>
<Text style={styles.footerText}>Footer</Text>
</View>
</View>

const styles = StyleSheet.create({
  wrapper: {
    flex: 1,
backgroundColor: '#fff',
  },
  header: {
    padding: 20,
backgroundColor: '#0066cc',
  },
headerText: {
    color: '#fff',
fontSize: 20,
fontWeight: 'bold',
  },
  content: {
    flex: 1,
    padding: 20,
  },
  paragraph: {
fontSize: 16,
  },
  footer: {
    padding: 10,
backgroundColor: '#f1f1f1',
alignItems: 'center',
  },
footerText: {
fontSize: 14,
    color: '#333',
  },
});
```

This example demonstrates how the View component can be used to create a complete and organized screen layout, with each section clearly defined and logically separated.

Reflections on the View Component

Mastering the **View** component is essential for any developer aiming to create clean, responsive, and functional interfaces with React Native. More than just stacking components on the screen, using **View** with intention and understanding enables the development of scalable applications with a solid visual foundation.

Learning to use **View** correctly involves a deep understanding of how Flexbox works, how styles are applied, and how to avoid common pitfalls. By following the best practices and striving for clarity and simplicity in layout design, developers ensure not only a great user experience but also a cleaner and more maintainable code in the long run.

Text Component: Displaying and Styling Text in React Native

The **Text** component is one of the most fundamental elements in any mobile application built with React Native. It is responsible for displaying any textual content on the screen: titles, paragraphs, captions, button labels, error messages, notifications, and much more. Functionally, **Text** is comparable to HTML elements such as **<p>**, **<h1>**, or **<span>**, but fully adapted to the mobile ecosystem.

As a highly versatile component, Text can be customized in various ways, allowing for style adjustments, alignment, line breaks, spacing, responsiveness, and accessibility. Mastering the use of Text is essential to ensure clear and pleasant communication with the end user.

Displaying Text Elements

Using the Text component is very straightforward. Simply wrap a string within **<Text>** tags, and the content will be rendered on the screen. Here is a simple example:

```
import React from 'react';
import { Text, View } from 'react-native';

export default function App() {
  return (
<View>
<Text>Hello World!</Text>
</View>
  );
}
```

In the aforesaid example, the phrase "*Hello, world!*" will be displayed on the screen. However, despite its simplicity, the **Text** component offers a wide range of features that go far beyond merely rendering plain text.

Styling and Formatting Text

React Native provides a wide variety of style properties that can be applied to the **Text** component. These include colors, font sizes, spacing, alignment, font weight, letter and word spacing, text decoration (underline, strikethrough), and much more.

```
<Text style={styles.title}>Welcome to the app!</Text>
<Text style={styles.subtitle}>Explore the features below!</Text>

const styles = StyleSheet.create({
  title: {
```

```
fontSize: 24,
fontWeight: 'bold',
    color: '#333',
marginBottom: 10,
  },
  subtitle: {
fontSize: 16,
    color: '#666',
  },
});
```

Additionally, you can apply styles conditionally based on the state of the application, making the text interactive and dynamic.

Specific Text Behaviors

Beyond styling, the Text component has specific behaviors worth noting:

- **Automatic Line Wrapping**: By default, text adjusts to the size of its container and wraps to the next line automatically.
- **Number of Lines**: You can limit the number of visible lines using the numberOfLines property.

```
<Text numberOfLines={2}>
  This is an example of very long text that will be cut off after two lines.
</Text>
```

- **Selectable Text**: By default, the text is not selectable. To change this behavior:

```
<Text selectable={true}>
  You can select this text and copy it.
</Text>
```

- **Text with Links**: By combining the Text component with events like **`onPress`**, it is possible to simulate hyperlinks:

```
<Text onPress={() =>Linking.openURL('https://reactnative.dev')}>
  Access official documentation.
</Text>
```

Nesting and Advanced Formatting

`Text` component allows nesting other **`Text`** components within it, which is useful for applying different styles to specific parts of a sentence:

```
<Text>
  This is a <Text style={{ fontWeight: 'bold' }}>bold text</Text> inside another.
</Text>
```

This is especially useful in messages that combine static text and variables with distinct styles, such as error or status messages.

Accessibility Considerations

Accessibility is a critical aspect of modern interface development—especially on mobile devices, where many users rely on assistive technologies like screen readers. The **`Text`** component supports various properties that help make content more accessible. Here are some accessibility practices best with Text:

- Use **`accessible={true}`** on elements with interaction or semantic meaning.
- Set **`accessibilityLabel`** to provide more precise descriptions for screen readers.
- **Do not rely on color alone** to communicate meaning (such as, error states). Use icons, labels, or additional text cues as well.
- **Ensure sufficient color contrast** between text and background to meet WCAG guidance, especially for smaller font sizes.
- Avoid using text within images. Whenever possible, use real text instead of images with embedded text.
- One should prioritize readability. Choose appropriate font sizes, ensure sufficient color contrast, and avoid very small text.

```
<Text>
  accessible={true}
accessibilityLabel="Welcome message for the user"
  style={{ fontSize: 18 }}>
  Welcome to our app!
</Text>
```

Using accessibility features with the Text component helps promote inclusion and compliance with standards such as the WCAG (Web Content Accessibility Guidelines). Below is an example of a screen that brings together several of the best practices discussed so far:

```
import React from 'react';
import { View, Text, StyleSheet, Linking } from 'react-native';

export default function WelcomeScreen() {
  return (
<View style={styles.container}>
<Text style={styles.title}>Hello!</Text>
<Text style={styles.subtitle}>Welcome to our app.</Text>
<Text style={styles.paragraph}>
           Access the <Text style={styles.link} onPress={() =>Linking.
openURL('https://reactnative.dev')}>official documentation</Text> to learn
more.
</Text>
</View>
  );
}

const styles = StyleSheet.create({
  container: {
    padding: 20,
  },
  title: {
fontSize: 28,
fontWeight: 'bold',
    color: '#222',
marginBottom: 8,
  },
  subtitle: {
fontSize: 18,
    color: '#555',
marginBottom: 16,
```

```
  },
  paragraph: {
fontSize: 16,
lineHeight: 24,
    color: '#333',
  },
  link: {
    color: '#0066cc',
textDecorationLine: 'underline',
  },
});
```

Reflections on the Text Component

The Text component is much more than just a way to display words on the screen. It represents the primary means of communication with the user, playing a key role in guiding, informing, alerting, and instructing within an application.

With proper styling, attention to best practices, and a focus on accessibility, Text becomes a powerful tool for creating interfaces that are not only visually appealing but also functional and inclusive.

Understanding and mastering the properties of the **Text** component allows developers to create rich, expressive, and accessible content, directly enhancing the overall user experience. Together with other components like **View**, **TouchableOpacity**, and **Image**, **Text** brings life to interfaces that engage and deliver real value.

Image Component: Working with Images in React Native

Images are an essential part of visual communication in any mobile application. They help convey information, reinforce brand identity, illustrate features, and enhance the user experience. In React Native, the **Image** component is responsible for displaying images in a versatile way, supporting both local files and remotely hosted images.

While basic usage is straightforward, working with images in mobile apps requires attention to several factors, such as performance, memory usage, resizing, caching, and adaptation to different screen sizes. This chapter will cover how to use the **Image** component efficiently and effectively in React Native.

Loading Local and Remote Images

The Image component can be used to display images stored locally in the project or images hosted externally on remote servers.

To load local images (stored in the project directory), you need to use the **require()** function:

```
import React from 'react';
import { Image, View, StyleSheet } from 'react-native';

export default function LocalImageExample() {
  return (
<View style={styles.container}>
<Image
        source={require('./assets/logo.png')}
        style={styles.image}
```

```
      />
</View>
  );
}

const styles = StyleSheet.create({
  container: {
    padding: 20,
alignItems: 'center',
  },
  image: {
    width: 200,
    height: 200,
  },
});
```

Important: *The path provided to* ***require()*** *must be static. It is not possible to dynamically load local images using* ***require****.*

To load remote images, use the **uri** property inside an object passed to the **source** prop.

```
<Image
  source={{ uri: 'https://reactnative.dev/img/tiny_logo.png' }}
  style={{ width: 100, height: 100 }}
/>
```

React Native will download the image as soon as it is rendered in the interface, respecting the size specified in the **style** prop. It is essential to always define both **width** and **height** when loading remote images. React Native begins fetching a remote image as soon as the **<Image>** is rendered, and then lays it out using the dimensions you provide in **style**. Since, the framework cannot know the intrinsic size of a network image at layout time (until it is fetched/decoded), you have to explicitly set both **width** and **height** (or otherwise compute them) to avoid layout ambiguity and rendering issues.

Handling Image Assets Efficiently

Managing images in mobile projects goes beyond simply displaying them. You need to think about strategies to reduce memory usage, avoid unnecessary reloads, and adapt images to different screen densities (DPI).

Devices with different screen densities require images in various resolutions to maintain sharpness. React Native handles this well through a naming convention:

```
/assets
 ├── icon.png       → standard density (1x)
 ├── icon@2x.png    → medium density (2x)
 └── icon@3x.png    → high density (3x)
```

When using **require('./assets/icon.png')**, React Native automatically selects the appropriate version based on the screen density of the device.

Resizing with `resizeMode`

The **resizeMode** property defines how the image should be scaled within the available space:

- **cover**: It fills the container completely, potentially cropping parts of the image.
- **contain**: It ensures the entire image is visible, scaling it to fit within the space.
- **stretch**: It stretches the image to fill the space (may cause distortion).

- **center**: It centers the image without resizing it.
- **repeat**: It tiles the image to fill the space (limited support on iOS/Android).

```
<Image
  source={{ uri: 'https://reactnative.dev/img/tiny_logo.png' }}
  style={{ width: 300, height: 150 }}
resizeMode="contain"
/>
```

Even with app-level optimizations, poorly prepared images can negatively impact performance. Best practices include:

- Using images optimized for web/mobile (like **.webp**, progressive **.jpeg**).
- Reducing resolution to the minimum required.
- Compressing images before adding them to the project.
- Avoiding large images as backgrounds, especially when loaded remotely.

Image Optimization Checklist (React Native)

Here are a few main principles:

- **Prefer modern formats when appropriate:** Use WebP (or AVIF where supported in your pipeline) for photos to reduce size; be cautious if you rely on platform-specific support, transparency requirements, or if compression introduces artifacts—validate on both iOS and Android.
- **Right-size assets:** Export images close to the maximum on-screen size you actually render to avoid wasted memory and decode time.
- **Use the correct format:** Prefer SVG/vector (where your setup supports it) for icons/illustrations; use raster for photos.
- **Set remote image dimensions:** Provide width and height (or compute them) for network images to avoid layout issues.
- **Cache and prioritize:** Use caching strategies and avoid re-downloading the same assets unnecessarily.
- **Accessibility:** Do Provide meaningful accessibility, and label text for non-decorative images. Also, mark purely decorative images as not accessible when appropriate.

```
<Image
  source={require('./assets/logo.png')}
  style={{ width: 120, height: 120 }}
accessibilityLabel="Logo of the company"
/>
```

For decorative images (without semantic importance), you can omit the label or set accessible={false} to avoid distractions for visually impaired users.

Reflections on the Image Component

The Image component in React Native is a powerful tool for incorporating visual elements into mobile interfaces. However, using it efficiently requires more than simply rendering images on the screen. Developers must consider resolution, performance, resizing, caching, compression, and accessibility.

By following the best practices, it is possible to ensure that images not only serve their aesthetic purpose but also contribute to a smooth, inclusive, and optimized experience for all users. Whether using local or remote images—or leveraging helper libraries—developers should always balance visual quality with performance.

TextInput Component: Capturing and Managing User Input

The **`TextInput`** component is the main interface between the user and manually entered data in a React Native application. Whether in login forms, search fields, comment boxes, or any other scenario involving text input, TextInput provides the necessary tools to make the interaction efficient, customizable, and accessible.

Although it may seem like a simple component, TextInput includes a wide range of features and properties that must be well understood to ensure good usability, accurate validation, and proper integration with other elements of the application.

The basic use of TextInput is straightforward. It allows users to type text and can be either controlled or uncontrolled through state management.

```
import React, { useState } from 'react';
import { TextInput, View, StyleSheet } from 'react-native';

export default function App() {
const [name, setName] = useState('');

  return (
<View style={styles.container}>
<TextInput
        placeholder="Enter your name"
        value={name}
onChangeText={setName}
        style={styles.input}
      />
</View>
  );
}

const styles = StyleSheet.create({
  container: {
    padding: 20,
  },
  input: {
    height: 40,
borderColor: '#ccc',
borderWidth: 1,
paddingHorizontal: 10,
borderRadius: 5,
  },
});
```

In this example, the input field is controlled using the useState hook, meaning the typed value is maintained in the state of the application.

Customizing Inputs for Various Use Cases

The **TextInput** component can be highly customized to suit different purposes: password fields, numbers, emails, multiline text, search fields, and more. The following are some useful properties:

```
<View>
<TextInput
    placeholder="E-mail"
keyboardType="email-address"
autoCapitalize="none"
    style={styles.input}
  />
<TextInput
    placeholder="Senha"
secureTextEntry={true}
    style={styles.input}
  />
</View>
```

This example demonstrates how you can tailor the TextInput component for different input types. The first field is configured for email input by setting keyboardType="email-address" and disabling automatic capitalization using autoCapitalize="none", which is ideal for fields like email or usernames where capitalization could lead to errors.

The second field uses secureTextEntry={true} to hide the entered characters, making it suitable for password inputs and other sensitive information. Beyond these options, TextInput supports a wide range of props for additional customization:

- **multiline={true}**: It allows users to enter multiple lines of text.
- **maxLength={number}:** It limits the number of characters.
- **onChangeText={function}:** It handles text changes in real-time.
- **returnKeyType="done":** It customizes the return key on the keyboard.
- **editable={false}:** It disables editing for read-only fields.

These capabilities make TextInput a powerful and flexible component for capturing user input across a variety of form scenarios. Always consider accessibility and user experience when designing inputs—ensure labels are clear, inputs are appropriately sized, and keyboard types match the expected data format.

Accessibility Considerations

Inputs are critical elements for accessibility. Ensuring that they are understandable to assistive technologies is part of the responsibility of the developer.

- **accessible={true}**: It makes the input readable by screen readers.
- **accessibilityLabel**: It provides a clear description of the purpose of the input field.
- **importantForAccessibility="yes"**: It ensures the field gets priority focus from the screen reader.
- Avoid visual-only instructions (for example, "**click the blue button**") and prefer descriptive text.

```
<TextInput
  placeholder="Full name"
accessibilityLabel="Full name field"
```

```
                accessible={true}
                style={styles.input}
            />
```

In addition, for multilingual applications, accessible text should take into account the language settings of the device or use i18n (internationalization) tools.

Reflections about TextInput

The TextInput component is one of the pillars of interactivity in React Native. When used correctly, it allows developers to capture and validate user input efficiently, securely, and accessible. Although it may appear simple, it plays a crucial role in building functional and inclusive interfaces.

By customizing inputs for different contexts, managing state and interaction with focus control, and applying solid validation and accessibility practices, developers can ensure their applications are intuitive, smooth, and responsive to user needs.

Mastering TextInput, alongside Text, Button, and View, is essential for any modern application aiming to deliver an excellent experience on mobile devices.

`ScrollView` Component: Managing Scrollable Content in React Native

Mobile applications often need to handle content that exceeds the screen size, such as long lists, lengthy forms, or interfaces with multiple sections. For these cases, React Native provides the ScrollView component, which enables vertical (or horizontal) scrolling for any group of elements.

While easy to implement, **`ScrollView`** should be used mindfully, as improper usage can directly impact performance—especially when rendering large amounts of data. In this chapter, we will explore how to use **`ScrollView`** correctly and avoid common pitfalls. For large or "infinite" lists, the recommended default is **`FlatList`** (or **`SectionList`**), using features like **`onEndReached`** to load more items efficiently, since these components virtualize rows instead of rendering everything at once.

Handling Content Overflow with ScrollView

The main purpose of **`ScrollView`** is to ensure that content larger than the screen can be accessed by the user through scrolling. Any component or group of components can be placed inside a **`ScrollView`**.

```
import React from "react";
import { ScrollView, Text, StyleSheet, View } from "react-native";

const items = Array.from({ length: 30 }, (_, i) => ({
  id: `item-${i + 1}`, // stable key for this list
  label: `Item ${i + 1}`,
}));

export default function SimpleScroll() {
  return (
<ScrollView style={styles.scrollContainer}>
<Text style={styles.title}>Scrollable Items</Text>

      {items.map((item) => (
<View key={item.id} style={styles.item}>
<Text>{item.label}</Text>
</View>
```

```
        ))}
    </ScrollView>
      );
    }

    const styles = StyleSheet.create({
    scrollContainer: {
        padding: 16,
    backgroundColor: "#f2f2f2",
      },
      title: {
    fontSize: 20,
    marginBottom: 10,
      },
      item: {
    backgroundColor: "#fff",
        padding: 20,
    marginBottom: 10,
    borderRadius: 8,
        elevation: 1,
      },
    });
```

Avoid using the array index as **key** for dynamic lists (items added/removed/reordered). Prefer a stable, unique **id** from your data to prevent incorrect UI reuse and state bugs. Without ScrollView, content that exceeds the screen height would be cut off. With it, scrolling is automatically enabled.

Nested Scrolling

While possible, nested scroll views (**ScrollView** inside another **ScrollView**) should be avoided whenever possible, as they can cause gesture conflicts and performance issues. When absolutely necessary, use **nestedScrollEnabled={true}** on Android to enable support:

```
<ScrollViewnestedScrollEnabled={true}>
<ScrollView style={{ height: 200 }}>
    {/* Inner scrollable content */}
</ScrollView>
</ScrollView>
```

The main drawback of **ScrollView** is that it renders all of its child elements at once—even those that are off-screen. This means that lists with hundreds or thousands of items may cause lag or high memory usage. Here is some best practices to improve performance:

- Use **ScrollView** only for content with a limited number of elements.
- For large lists, prefer **FlatList** or **SectionList**, which render items on demand.
- Avoid deep nesting of **ScrollViews**.
- Use **removeClippedSubviews={true}** where applicable.
- Use **keyboardShouldPersistTaps="handled"** to prevent conflicts with the virtual keyboard.

Reflections about ScrollView

The ScrollView component is essential for handling content that exceeds screen size in React Native applications. It allows users to navigate through long forms, lengthy text, and complex layouts with ease. However, developers must be cautious when dealing with large datasets and should prefer optimized components like FlatList whenever performance is a concern.

Hence, by mastering **ScrollView**, developers gain full control over scroll behavior, related events, and the visual flow of content. With good performance practices, smooth scrolling, and smart interactions—like infinite scroll—the user experience can be significantly enhanced.

Styling in React Native

The appearance of an application is equally important as its functionality. In React Native, component styling follows a declarative approach inspired by CSS, but with some important differences. The styling system is flexible and powerful, offering several ways to control the appearance of elements: **StyleSheet**, inline styles, CSS-in-JS libraries, and theming strategies.

In this chapter, you will learn how to efficiently create, apply, and organize styles in React Native—mastering key concepts such as Flexbox, reusability, customization, and visual consistency.

Using StyleSheet

StyleSheet is a common, recommended way to define **static** styles in React Native and can help keep style code organized. Inline or dynamic styles are also fine when needed—just try to keep style objects **stable** (for instance, reuse **StyleSheet.create**, avoid recreating large style objects every render) to minimize unnecessary re-renders. It allows you to organize style rules in JavaScript objects, similar to traditional CSS, but with differences in naming conventions and value types.

```
import { StyleSheet, Text, View } from 'react-native';

export default function App() {
  return (
<View style={styles.container}>
<Text style={styles.text}>Hello, world!</Text>
</View>
  );
}

const styles = StyleSheet.create({
  container: {
    flex: 1,
justifyContent: 'center',
alignItems: 'center',
backgroundColor: '#f5f5f5',
  },
  text: {
fontSize: 20,
    color: '#333',
  },
});
```

Advantages of **StyleSheet.create()**:

- Static validation of styles.
- Potential for internal performance optimization.
- Cleaner and a more organized code structure.

Creating and Managing Styles

A well-structured React Native project requires organized styling to ensure visual consistency, easier maintenance, and style reuse. Styles can be:

- **Local** (within the same file as the component).
- **Shared** (in separate files like `styles.js`).
- **Dynamically generated** (using conditional logic).
- **Themed or global** (via context or styling libraries).

Best Practices for Organized Styles

- **Avoid duplication**: Reuse styles whenever possible.
- **Use descriptive names**: Improves code readability and structure.
- **Separate style from logic**: Do not mix UI code with business rules.
- **Centralize color palette and spacing**: Makes future maintenance easier.

Styling in React Native is a vast and essential topic for building functional, accessible, and visually pleasing interfaces. By mastering `StyleSheet`, understanding the differences between inline and reusable styles, applying Flexbox effectively, and adopting strategies like theming and CSS-in-JS when appropriate, developers can build scalable, well-organized, and maintainable UIs.

There is no one-size-fits-all approach to styling—but rather best practices suited to different contexts and project scales. The key lies in consistency, clarity, and a strong focus on the user experience.

Dynamic and Responsive Styling in React Native

With the wide variety of screen sizes, pixel densities, and platform-specific features across Android and iOS devices, responsive design is no longer optional—it is a fundamental requirement in mobile app development.

This chapter introduces techniques and best practices for making your React Native application adaptable, functional, and visually consistent across any device. We shall explore essential APIs, helpful components, and modern patterns for creating truly responsive and accessible interfaces.

Adapting to Different Screen Sizes

The first step toward responsiveness is to understand how React Native measures and renders layout. Style values like `width`, `height`, `margin`, and `fontSize` use **unitless numbers** that represent **density-independent pixels (dp)**, so that the same numeric value maps appropriately across different screen densities. For text, scaling is influenced by the accessibility settings of the user (say the device **font scale**), so responsive typography should account for user-configured font scaling rather than assuming fixed "pixel" sizing.

In React Native, measurements are made using density-independent pixels (dp), meaning a single unit can represent a different number of physical pixels depending on the device.

- **dp/sp:** Abstract units that scale based on screen density.
- **Physical pixel:** Varies according to DPI (Dots per Inch).
- **Density:** Higher DPI means more pixels per inch.

This abstraction improves visual consistency but requires attention when designing layouts or selecting font/image sizes.

Using the Dimensions API

The Dimensions API allows you to dynamically access the screen size of the device.

```
import { Dimensions } from 'react-native';

const{ width, height } = Dimensions.get('window');
```

These values can be used to adjust styles based on actual screen size:

```
const styles = StyleSheet.create({
  container: {
    width: width * 0.9,
    padding: 16,
  },
});
```

Note: Window represents the usable screen area (excluding status bar). Use screen to get full screen dimensions.

Advanced Responsiveness Techniques

In mobile development, especially on devices with modern screen designs such as the iPhone X and beyond, it is essential to ensure that user interface elements do not clash with or get hidden behind hardware-specific screen features. These include notches, status bars, curved screen edges, and home indicators. This is where the SafeAreaView component becomes a critical tool in React Native development.

The **`SafeAreaView`** is designed to wrap content and automatically apply padding so that nothing is obscured by these system UI areas. It acts as a safety zone, making the content of your app remains fully visible and accessible to users regardless of the physical screen layout of the device.

```
import { SafeAreaView } from 'react-native-safe-area-context';

<SafeAreaView style={{ flex: 1 }}>
  {/* Safe visible content */}
</SafeAreaView>
```

Without using **`SafeAreaView`**, important UI elements such as buttons, titles, or forms might end up under the notch or be covered by the iOS home bar, leading to a poor user experience or even unusable screens. This is especially problematic in full-screen layouts where the content spans the entire device screen. By wrapping your main views or screens with **`SafeAreaView`**, you prevent such issues automatically and ensure your app adheres to platform UI standards.

The **core `SafeAreaView`** (from **`react-native`**) of React Native is now **deprecated** in the official documentation. For modern apps, the recommended approach is to use **`react-native-safe-area-context`**, which provides a **`SafeAreaProvider`**, **`SafeAreaView`**, and hooks (say **`useSafeAreaInsets`**) for consistent safe-area handling across platforms and navigation setups.

The enhanced version allows better management of insets and even offers hooks and context for more advanced use cases, like dynamically adjusting padding based on orientation, device type, or nesting multiple safe zones. It is also better maintained and aligned with current design trends in mobile device manufacturing.

On Android devices, although notches and system bars are less varied compared to iOS, similar issues can occur—especially with devices using gesture-based navigation or immersive modes. SafeAreaView helps to standardize these edge cases across platforms so developers do not need to write custom logic for each device type or OS version.

Best Practices and Use Cases:

- **Apply safe area insets selectively:** Rather than wrapping an entire screen (or navigator) in **`SafeAreaView`**, React Navigation recommends using **`useSafeAreaInsets()`** and applying only the padding you actually need (like **`paddingTop`** for a custom header, **`paddingBottom`** for a footer). This avoids common "jumpy" or flickery behavior during animations and keeps layouts predictable.
- **Combine with navigation:** When working with navigation libraries like **`React Navigation`**, **`SafeAreaView`** should be considered around screen content, not around the entire navigation container unless necessary.
- **Avoid UI clipping:** Essential for header bars, bottom menus, or any fixed-positioned UI elements that live near screen edges.
- **Consistency:** Using SafeAreaView ensures your app feels native and polished on every device, improving user trust and overall UX.

The use of SafeAreaView is not just a best practice; it is a necessity in the contemporary landscape of mobile development. Devices continue to evolve, with increasingly unique screen shapes and interaction zones. By using SafeAreaView from react-native-safe-area-context, you are future-proofing your interface and ensuring that it works seamlessly across all devices, orientations, and UI constraints. It is one of those small components that, when used properly, can make a big difference in the polish and professionalism of your app.

`KeyboardAvoidingView` prevents text inputs from being obscured by the keyboard. When building mobile interfaces that include forms, chat inputs, or any type of text field, a common challenge arises: the virtual keyboard can cover critical parts of the UI. This often leads to a frustrating experience where users cannot see the field they are typing into, or worse, cannot reach the submit button without closing the keyboard manually.

React Native addresses this issue with the KeyboardAvoidingView component, which helps automatically adjust your layout when the keyboard appears, ensuring that input fields and interactive elements remain visible and accessible.

```
import { KeyboardAvoidingView, Platform } from 'react-native';

<KeyboardAvoidingView
  behavior={Platform.OS === 'ios' ? 'padding' : 'height'}
  style={{ flex: 1 }}
>
  {/* Form or input fields */}
</KeyboardAvoidingView>
```

Unlike desktops, mobile screens are small and have to make room for the software keyboard, which can take up nearly half the screen. Without properly handling this behavior, your carefully designed forms can become unusable. Users may have to guess what they are typing, or will not be able to tap "Send" or "Next" unless they dismiss the keyboard manually.

The KeyboardAvoidingView component solves this by shifting, resizing, or padding the view when the keyboard is triggered. This ensures a smooth and seamless interaction between text input fields and the keyboard, improving the usability of your app dramatically.

KeyboardAvoidingView works by measuring the space taken by the keyboard and then automatically adjusting the layout based on the behavior you define. The behavior prop dictates how the component reacts:

- **`"padding"`:** Adds padding to the bottom of the view equal to the height of the keyboard. Ideal for iOS, where layout shifts need to be gentle and predictable.

- `"height"`: Adjusts the height of the container to make space for the keyboard, typically used on Android for more native-feeling behavior.
- `"position"`: Moves the entire view up. Less commonly used but useful in specific scenarios.

The behavior can and should be adapted based on the platform to maintain consistency. The Platform API of React Native makes this easy and allows your layout to respond intelligently to the device environment.

Best Practices and Scenarios:

- **Forms:** Always wrap forms inside a KeyboardAvoidingView to prevent the keyboard from covering fields or buttons.
- **Chats or Comments:** In chat-style interfaces where there is an input fixed at the bottom of the screen, this component becomes essential.
- **Modals or Scrollable Views:** Combine with ScrollView if your inputs need scrolling as well. For deeply nested content, consider using KeyboardAvoidingView along with KeyboardAwareScrollView from community packages.

Keep in mind that certain layouts may still require fine-tuning. KeyboardAvoidingView does a great job in most cases, but testing across different devices, platforms, and screen sizes is key to getting a polished result.

KeyboardAvoidingView is one of several tools that React Native offers to adapt layouts dynamically. Alongside it, components like SafeAreaView, and APIs like Dimensions, PixelRatio, and Platform enable developers to build interfaces that respond to screen size, orientation, device type, and input method.

Together, these tools help achieve true responsiveness, not just visually, but behaviorally—ensuring that UI components not only look good but act correctly in context.

Final Thoughts

Styling interfaces to adapt across various devices is a central challenge in mobile development. In React Native, responsiveness is achieved through a combination of dynamic measurements, smart use of APIs like Dimensions, PixelRatio, and Platform, and helpful components such as **`SafeAreaView`** and **`KeyboardAvoidingView`**.

By applying these techniques, you ensure your application is pleasant, functional, and consistent—regardless of screen size, pixel density, or platform. The key lies in testing, modularizing, and always designing with the end-user experience in mind.

Conclusion

Throughout this chapter, we explored the fundamental components of React Native—such as **`View`**, **`Text`**, **`Image`**, **`TextInput`**, and **`ScrollView`**—understanding their purposes, practical uses, and common pitfalls. These building blocks are essential for any mobile application, and mastering them allows you to structure, display, and capture information with clarity, fluidity, and accessibility. Through concrete examples, we learned how to align content, display visual and textual data, capture user input, and manage extensive content with smooth, responsive scrolling.

We advanced further by learning how to apply styles efficiently using **`StyleSheet`**, balancing organization, performance, and reusability. We also explored modern styling approaches such as CSS-in-JS, theming, and global styling, along with mastering the layout system using Flexbox. Additionally, we deeply examined responsive styling techniques. We concluded with an in-depth dive into UI/UX practices that ensure visual clarity, accessibility, and performance—essential pillars of any quality application. Creating intuitive, inclusive, and efficient interfaces requires attention to detail, conscious use of available tools, and a strong commitment to user experience. By mastering these foundations, developers do more than write functional code—they deliver real value, creating apps that adapt, delight, and remain relevant across any device. Next, we will explore navigation in React Native—understanding how to move between screens, pass parameters, and structure the user journey effectively.

Self-Assessment Questions

Before moving on, it is important to pause and reflect on the key concepts covered in this chapter. The following self-assessment questions are designed to help you review your understanding of the core components of React Native, styling techniques, and best practices for responsive and accessible UI design. Take your time to answer each one thoughtfully—this reflection will reinforce your knowledge and highlight any topics you may want to revisit before advancing:

1. What is the role of the View component in structuring a React Native interface, and how does it differ from <div> of HTML?
2. How can the Text component be styled, nested, and made accessible for screen readers?
3. What are the performance considerations when using ScrollView, and when should FlatList or SectionList be preferred?
4. Why is it necessary to explicitly set width and height when using the Image component to load remote images?
5. What are some key properties of TextInput, and how can it be customized and validated for accessibility?
6. How does Flexbox enhance responsive layout in React Native, and what are the essential properties to master?
7. What are the advantages of using StyleSheet.create() over inline styles in terms of performance and organization?
8. How do tools like Dimensions, PixelRatio, and Platform API contribute to responsive and platform-specific design?
9. What are the strategies and components—like SafeAreaView, KeyboardAvoidingView, and ThemeProvider— that help build adaptive and accessible layouts?
10. How do UI/UX best practices, such as feedback on interaction and proper focus management, improve usability in mobile apps?

Answering these questions helps review and consolidate the material, allowing you to assess whether you have satisfactorily understood the concepts covered or if you need to explore any specific aspect further.

Key Terms

- **`View`:** A fundamental container component used to group and organize interface elements. It is equivalent to the **`<div>`** in HTML and is widely used to structure layout using Flexbox.
- **`Text`:** A component responsible for displaying textual content on the screen. It supports rich styling, accessibility properties, and allows nesting of other Text components.
- **`Image`:** A component for rendering local or remote images. It allows resizing, cache control, and supports accessibility features.

- **`TextInput`:** A text input field used to capture user-provided data. It supports focus events, real-time validation, and keyboard customization.
- **`ScrollView`:** A component that enables vertical or horizontal scrolling for content that exceeds the screen size. Should be used sparingly for large lists, as it renders all elements at once.
- **`FlatList` / `SectionList`:** Optimized components for rendering large lists. They render items on demand and offer better performance than ScrollView in data-heavy scenarios.
- **`StyleSheet.create()`:** A method used to create static and optimized style objects. It ensures better performance and type validation.
- **`Flexbox`:** A layout system natively used in React Native to align, distribute, and dynamically resize components.
- **`PixelRatio`:** An API that provides information about the pixel density of the screen, useful for scaling fonts, borders, and icons proportionally.
- **`Dimensions`:** An API that allows retrieving the screen dimensions of the device (width and height), often used for responsive layouts.
- **`Platform API`:** Enables detection of the current platform (iOS or Android) and applying platform-specific styles or behaviors.
- **`SafeAreaView`:** A component that ensures content respects safe areas of the interface, such as the notch or status bar.
- **`KeyboardAvoidingView`:** A component that automatically adjusts the layout to prevent the virtual keyboard from overlapping input fields.
- **styled-components:** A popular CSS-in-JS library used in React and React Native projects for component-based styling, with support for themes and conditional styles.
- **Responsive Design:** A design technique that ensures the interface adapts to different screen sizes and pixel densities, providing a consistent visual experience.
- **Accessibility (a11y):** A set of practices for making apps usable by people with disabilities. In React Native, you can apply properties like **`accessible`**, **`accessibilityLabel`**, and **`importantForAccessibility`**.
- **Responsive Font Scaling:** A technique for scaling fonts based on screen density or user settings, ensuring readability on any device.
- **Global Theming:** A strategy for defining and reusing colors, sizes, and spacing in a centralized manner. Can be implemented using Context API or styled-components.
- **Performance Optimization:** Practices such as using **`React.memo`**, organizing styles with **`StyleSheet`**, and on-demand rendering with optimized lists to improve UI fluidity and performance.
- **Inline Styles versus StyleSheet:** Inline styles are applied directly in JSX and are useful for quick adjustments. Using **`StyleSheet`** offers better performance, readability, and code organization.

These key terms summarize some of the essential concepts covered in this chapter, helping reinforce the understanding of the ecosystem and development practices of React Native.

CHAPTER 5
Navigation with React Navigation

Introduction

Navigation lies at the heart of any mobile application that spans multiple screens, shaping the way users explore content, access features, and accomplish tasks. A thoughtfully designed navigation structure does more than simply moving people from one view to another; it establishes a clear path through the functionality of the app, reduces friction, and ultimately keeps users engaged. In React Native, where there is no built-in routing mechanism, selecting the right navigation library is crucial to delivering a native-like experience. React Navigation has emerged as the de facto standard, combining a modular architecture with first-class support for both iOS and Android gestures, seamless animations, and out-of-the-box TypeScript integrations—most notably, typed route params and strongly typed navigator APIs that catch navigation mistakes at compile time.

Since its introduction, React Navigation has evolved to handle everything from the simplest stack of screens to intricate, nested navigators that include bottom tabs, side drawers, and even combinations of both. Version 7.x brought a redesigned static API that streamlines common patterns, significant performance enhancements through the use of native components under the hood, and refined tooling for deep linking—making it easier than ever to configure your application to respond to external URLs or incoming notifications.

In practice, "static" means your navigator structure and screen definitions are declared up front as a stable configuration, rather than being assembled dynamically at runtime based on conditional logic. This makes navigation easier to reason about, improves TypeScript inference, and enables tooling to validate routes and linking configuration earlier—reducing runtime surprises. By using a single, unified approach, you can avoid the cognitive overhead of multiple libraries and focus instead on crafting the flows and interactions that matter most to your users.

In this chapter, you will be guided step by step through the process of integrating React Navigation into a new or existing React Native project. You will learn how to install the core packages and auxiliary dependencies, and how to adjust your Babel and native configurations so that key features such as **`react-native-reanimated`** and gesture handling work correctly in both Expo and React Native CLI environments. You will then explore each navigator type—stack, tabs, and drawer—seeing how to configure screens, customize headers, and apply transition animations that feel natural on each platform. Along the way, you will uncover techniques for passing parameters between screens, using hooks like **`useNavigation`** and **`useRoute`**, and nesting navigators to build scalable, maintainable flows.

Beyond the mechanics of setup and configuration, you will also discover best practices for organizing your navigation logic into discrete modules, preventing common pitfalls such as duplicate navigations or unmounting issues, and optimizing performance for complex apps. By the end of this chapter, you will not only have a fully functional navigation system but also a deep understanding of how React Navigation works beneath the surface—empowering you to deliver robust, efficient, and delightful user experiences in your React Native applications.

Structure

In this chapter, we will cover the following topics:

- Introduction to Navigation in React Native
    - Overview of React Navigation and Its Advantages
- Initial Setup of React Navigation
    - Installing Core Packages
    - Additional Required Dependencies
    - Specific Configurations for Expo and React Native CLI
    - Wrapping the Application with NavigationContainer
- Stack Navigation
    - Using createNativeStackNavigator
    - Comparison between `@react-navigation/native-stack` and `@react-navigation/stack`
    - Customizing Screen Transitions and Animations
    - Advanced Customizations with `@react-navigation/stack`
    - Choosing the Right Stack Navigator
    - Stack Navigation Summary
- Tab Navigation
    - Basic Implementation of `createBottomTabNavigator`
    - Customizing Tab Icons
    - Advanced Customization of Tab Styles
    - Combining Navigators (Nested Navigation)
    - Tab Navigation Summary
- Drawer Navigation
    - Setting Up `createDrawerNavigator` for Side Navigation
    - Customizing Drawer Content with `drawerContent`
    - Styling and Positioning the Drawer
    - Combining Drawer Navigation with Stack Navigation
    - Drawer Navigation Summary
- Passing Parameters between Screens
    - How to Send Parameters with `navigation.navigate`
    - How to Access Parameters with route.params
    - Using Hooks: `useNavigation` and `useRoute`

Introduction to Navigation in React Native

In mobile applications, navigation plays a crucial and decisive role in the user experience. It directly influences how users move between different screens, how they access specific features, and how they interact with the content provided within the app. The efficiency of navigation is not merely a technical concern; it is a feature that deeply affects user satisfaction and retention. Well-structured navigation significantly reduces friction, providing a smooth, intuitive, and pleasant experience, which increases the likelihood that users will continue engaging with the app regularly.

Effective navigation is also vital to ensure that users can quickly find what they are looking for, translating into greater efficiency in completing desired tasks. Whether for apps that contain a large amount of content, like news platforms or social networks, or apps focused on specific functionalities, such as productivity tools and games, clear and predictable navigation is fundamental. Users often abandon apps when they encounter difficulties or feel frustrated due to confusing or complicated navigation.

In React Native development, the need for a robust navigation solution is even more evident. By default, React Native does not come with a built-in navigation system. This means developers must rely on external solutions—specialized libraries that efficiently handle navigation between different screens and data flows. Among the various available options, React Navigation stands out as the preferred solution for most developers. Its widespread adoption is a direct result of its core characteristics: flexibility, ease of integration, and optimized performance.

Overview of React Navigation and Its Advantages

React Navigation is a routing and navigation management library specifically created for React Native applications, although it can also be used in certain web application contexts. One of the main reasons this library has gained broad acceptance is its ability to offer several navigator models, such as Stack Navigator, Tab Navigator, and Drawer Navigator. This diversity of navigators allows developers to quickly implement everything from simple navigation flows to complex architectures involving multiple layers and different types of interactions.

The key Advantages of React Navigation are as follows:

- **Easy to Use**: One of the most notable features of React Navigation is its simplicity. With intuitive interfaces and pre-integrated navigators, even beginner developers can quickly set up basic navigation flows. This significantly speeds up development, especially for projects requiring rapid delivery or immediate functional prototypes.

- **Optimized Components for iOS and Android**: React Navigation offers specific support for both iOS and Android platforms. Navigators are developed with close attention to interface guidelines of each platform, ensuring that transitions, animations, and gestures feel natural and intuitive for end users. This means that React Native apps built with React Navigation provide a native app feel, with a familiar experience for users on each platform.
- **Fully Customizable**: Another major advantage is the complete customization React Navigation offers. If you are familiar with JavaScript and React Native, you can customize virtually any aspect of the navigation system—from screen visuals to specific transition behaviors and event handling. This flexibility allows developers to tailor navigation exactly to the needs of the project, without arbitrary limitations imposed by the library.
- **Extensible Platform**: Extensibility is another strong point. React Navigation allows for the creation of custom navigators and even the replacement or expansion of its internal APIs. This extensibility ensures that as your project evolves and gains complexity, you will not be limited by the chosen library and can adapt and expand it as needed.

In addition to its technical advantages, React Navigation enjoys strong community support and backing from major players in the React Native ecosystem, such as Expo, Software Mansion, and Callstack. This ongoing support ensures the library stays up to date with the latest best practices and mobile development trends, constantly benefiting from active community contributions.

Throughout this chapter, we will cover all these aspects in depth—from installation and basic configuration to advanced topics like nested navigation, dynamic parameter passing, deep linking, and advanced UI and animation customizations. By the end of this chapter, you will be well prepared to implement a complete and robust navigation system, delivering an exceptional experience to the users of your React Native applications.

Initial Setup of React Navigation

To start working with navigation in React Native applications, the first essential step is to properly configure React Navigation. This library is highly modular and requires the installation of several core packages and additional dependencies to function fully. Correct setup is crucial to ensure stability, performance, and a smooth experience when navigating between screens.

Installing Core Packages

React Navigation offers several specific navigators for different types of user interfaces and experiences (stack, tabs, and drawers). To install the main required packages, use the following commands in the terminal of your React Native application.

With npm:

```
npm install @react-navigation/native &&npm install @react-navigation/native-stack #
ou @react-navigation/bottom-tabs ou @react-navigation/drawer
```

Or, if you are using Yarn:

```
yarn add @react-navigation/native @react-navigation/native-stack @react-navigation/
bottom-tabs @react-navigation/drawer
```

Once the installation is complete, here is a brief overview of what each package is responsible for:

- **`@react-navigation/native`**: The core of the React Navigation library, it provides context and basic functionalities for all types of navigators.

- **`@react-navigation/native-stack`**: It provides high-performance, native stack-based navigation, ideal for fast and optimized transitions.
- **`@react-navigation/bottom-tabs`**: It enables the creation of bottom tab-based interfaces, very common in mobile applications.
- **`@react-navigation/drawer`**: It allows lateral navigation via drawers that slide from the side of the screen, offering easy access to various features and screens.

These packages work together to give you a flexible, modular, and scalable navigation system, capable of adapting to simple and complex app structures alike.

Additional Required Dependencies

Besides the main packages, React Navigation depends on some auxiliary libraries that improve the overall experience and provide native support for gestures, animations, and optimized performance. These additional dependencies must also be installed:

With npm:

```
npm install react-native-gesture-handler react-native-reanimated react-native-screens
react-native-safe-area-context
```

With Yarn:

```
yarn add react-native-gesture-handler react-native-reanimated react-native-screens
react-native-safe-area-context
```

After installing the libraries, it is important to understand their roles in enhancing gesture handling, animation performance, screen optimization, and safe area management across different devices:

- **`react-native-gesture-handler`**: It enables advanced gesture support in React Native, which is essential for smooth interaction with interfaces like drawers and navigation gestures. **Common gotcha:** Gesture Handler setup may require specific root/entry configuration depending on your project (for example, wrapping the app with the appropriate root view and ensuring the entry file imports are in the right place); if it is misconfigured, you can see runtime crashes when gestures or drawers initialize.
- **`react-native-reanimated`**: It offers a robust and performant API for complex native animations, essential for transitions and custom animations.
- **`react-native-screens`**: It improves navigation performance by using native screens directly from the operating system, reducing memory usage and optimizing performance.
- **`react-native-safe-area-context`**: It properly manages safe areas on mobile devices, such as notches and system navigation bars.

After installing these additional dependencies, some specific configurations are necessary to ensure the project correctly recognizes the native libraries.

Specific Configurations for Expo and React Native CLI

In Expo, the setup is simplified because Expo automatically integrates these native dependencies. However, you must ensure the project is properly configured with the following additional command:

```
npx expo install react-native-screens react-native-safe-area-context react-native-
gesture-handler react-native-reanimated
```

Additionally, to enable react-native-reanimated, you must add the following plugin to your babel.config.js file. Reanimated setup is version-sensitive—follow the official installation steps for *your*

Reanimated version, since Babel plugin requirements and configuration details can change between releases.

```
module.exports = function(api) {
api.cache(true);
  return {
    presets: ['babel-preset-expo'],
    plugins: ['react-native-reanimated/plugin'],
  };
};
```

After making this change, restart the development server with:

```
npx expo start --clear
```

For React Native CLI users, execute the following additional command to finalize the setup of native dependencies:

```
npx pod-install ios
```

Then, add the required plugin to the **babel.config.js** file to ensure **react-native-reanimated** works properly:

```
module.exports = {
  presets: ['module:metro-react-native-babel-preset'],
  plugins: ['react-native-reanimated/plugin'],
};
```

Restart the Metro server after these changes to correctly apply the configuration:

With npm:

```
npm run start -- --reset-cache
```

Or with Yarn:

```
yarn start --reset-cache
```

Following these steps carefully ensures that gesture handling, animations, and screen optimizations are fully functional, providing a stable foundation for building seamless and performant navigation experiences in your React Native application.

Wrapping the Application with NavigationContainer

After installing the dependencies and completing the configurations, you need to wrap your React Native application inside a special component called **NavigationContainer**. This component is responsible for managing the navigation state of the application and providing the necessary context for navigators to function correctly.

Simple example of basic setup:

```
// App.tsx or index.tsx
import React from 'react';
import { NavigationContainer } from '@react-navigation/native';
import { createNativeStackNavigator } from '@react-navigation/native-stack';
import HomeScreen from './screens/HomeScreen';
import DetailScreen from './screens/DetailScreen';

const Stack = createNativeStackNavigator();

export default function App() {
```

```
  return (
<NavigationContainer>
<Stack.NavigatorinitialRouteName="Home">
<Stack.Screen name="Home" component={HomeScreen} />
<Stack.Screen name="Details" component={DetailScreen} />
</Stack.Navigator>
</NavigationContainer>
  );
}
```

The **NavigationContainer** is the central configuration point that wraps the navigators of all apps, allowing different types of navigators—stack, tabs, and drawers—to be configured later, as well as supporting advanced features like deep linking and navigation analytics integration.

Initial Setup Summary

- Installation of the core packages (**@react-navigation/***).
- Installation and setup of additional dependencies (gestures, animations, native screens, safe areas).
- Specific configurations based on whether you are using Expo or React Native CLI.
- Wrapping the main component of the application with **NavigationContainer**.

Following these steps ensures a solid foundation to start implementing various types of navigation in your React Native application, offering a smooth and pleasant experience for the end user.

Stack Navigation

Stack navigation is one of the most common and fundamental types used in mobile application development. It organizes screens into a sequential structure, similar to a stack, where you can navigate by pushing a new screen onto the stack or popping it off to return to the previous screen. React Navigation provides two main navigators to implement this pattern: **@react-navigation/native-stack** and **@react-navigation/stack**.

Using createNativeStackNavigator

To implement stack-based navigation with React Navigation, it is recommended to start with **createNativeStackNavigator**, as it offers better performance and direct integration with native APIs, resulting in a faster and smoother experience.

Basic example using **createNativeStackNavigator**:

```
import React from 'react';
import { NavigationContainer } from '@react-navigation/native';
import { createNativeStackNavigator } from '@react-navigation/native-stack';

import HomeScreen from './screens/HomeScreen';
import DetailsScreen from './screens/DetailsScreen';

const Stack = createNativeStackNavigator();

export default function App() {
  return (
<NavigationContainer>
<Stack.NavigatorinitialRouteName="Home">
```

```
<Stack.Screen
          name="Home"
          component={HomeScreen}
          options={{ title: 'Home Screen' }}
        />
<Stack.Screen
          name="Details"
          component={DetailsScreen}
          options={{ title: 'Details' }}
        />
</Stack.Navigator>
</NavigationContainer>
  );
}
```

In this example:

- **`Stack.Navigator`** defines the basic structure of navigation.
- **`Stack.Screen`** specifies each accessible screen.
- The **`initialRouteName`** parameter determines which screen is loaded first.

Comparison between @react-navigation/native-stack and @react-navigation/stack

Both navigators support stack navigation, but they have important differences in terms of performance and customization:

Feature	Native-stack	Stack
Performance	High performance (native component)	Intermediate performance (pure JavaScript)
Animation customization	Limited to native animations	Fully customizable (JavaScript animations)
Default transitions	Smooth and consistent (native platform)	Flexible, but dependent on JavaScript performance
Web support	Limited	Full (works well with React Native Web)
Recommended use	Apps prioritizing native performance and standard transitions	Apps requiring highly customized animations

Table 5.1: *Comparison of Native-stack and Stack Navigation in React Navigation*

While both navigators are powerful tools, choosing between them depends on the specific needs of your project. If you value maximum performance and a native feel, especially on mobile devices, native-stack is usually the best option. Some important points:

- **Transition customization: `@react-navigation/stack`** offers deeper control over transition animations (custom interpolators/gestures) and is generally easier to fine-tune for bespoke motion. **`native-stack`** supports common transitions well, but can be more constrained when you need highly custom interpolators.

- **Header behavior and styling: `native-stack`** uses the platform-native header, which can behave differently from the JS header in **`@react-navigation/stack`**—especially around dynamic title updates, large titles (iOS), and certain styling/layout edge cases. If you need pixel-perfect, fully custom headers, **`@react-navigation/stack`** may be simpler.

- **Presentation modes and edge cases: `native-stack`** excels at native presentation styles (say iOS-style modals) but there can be behavioral differences across platforms and OS versions (including modal gestures, transparent backgrounds, and stacking modals). **`@react-navigation/stack`** can be more predictable when you want consistent cross-platform behavior, at the cost of less "native" feel.

However, if your application demands highly customized transitions, advanced animations, or needs full compatibility with web environments, stack provides the flexibility required to deliver a richer and more tailored user experience. Understanding these trade-offs helps ensure that your navigation architecture remains efficient, scalable, and perfectly aligned with the design of your app and performance goals.

Customizing Screen Transitions and Animations

Even with some limitations compared to the JavaScript-based **`stack`** navigator, **`native-stack`** allows basic transition customizations using predefined options like system default animations, modal animations, or even disabling animations entirely.

Simple example using **`native-stack`**:

```
<Stack.NavigatorinitialRouteName="Home" screenOptions={{
  animation: 'slide_from_right', // other options: 'fade', 'none', 'slide_from_
bottom'
}}>
<Stack.Screen
    name="Home"
    component={HomeScreen}
    options={{ title: 'Home Screen' }}
  />
<Stack.Screen
    name="Details"
    component={DetailsScreen}
    options={{ title: 'Details', animation: 'fade' }} // Custom animation for this
screen
  />
</Stack.Navigator>
```

Common **`native-stack`** animation options include:

- **`'default'`** (system default)
- **`'fade'`** (fade-in effect)
- **`'slide_from_right'`** (horizontal slide, iOS-style)
- **`'slide_from_bottom'`** (vertical modal-style slide)
- **`'none'`** (no animation)

These animation options, while simpler than fully customized transitions, offer enough flexibility for most apps aiming for native-like performance and behavior.

They help maintain a consistent user experience across platforms while ensuring fast and smooth navigation transitions, especially important in high-performance mobile applications.

Advanced Customizations with `@react-navigation/stack`

If your project requires more control over custom transitions, it is recommended to use the **`stack`** navigator. Here is an advanced example:

```
import { createStackNavigator, TransitionPresets } from '@react-navigation/stack';

const Stack = createStackNavigator();

export default function App() {
  return (
<NavigationContainer>
<Stack.NavigatorinitialRouteName="Home" screenOptions={{
gestureEnabled: true,
        ...TransitionPresets.SlideFromRightIOS,
      }}>
<Stack.Screen
          name="Home"
          component={HomeScreen}
          options={{ headerShown: false }}
        />
<Stack.Screen
          name="Details"
          component={DetailsScreen}
          options={{
            ...TransitionPresets.ModalSlideFromBottomIOS,
headerShown: true,
          }}
        />
</Stack.Navigator>
</NavigationContainer>
  );
}
```

In this example:

- **`gestureEnabled`** allows swipe gestures to return to the previous screen.
- **`TransitionPresets`** provides predefined animation sets.
- You can also create fully custom animations using the **`cardStyleInterpolator`** property.

Example of a custom animation with **`stack`**:

```
screenOptions={{
cardStyleInterpolator: ({ current, layouts }) => ({
cardStyle: {
      transform: [
        {
translateX: current.progress.interpolate({
inputRange: [0, 1],
outputRange: [layouts.screen.width, 0],
          }),
        },
      ],
    },
  }),
}}
```

By using `cardStyleInterpolator`, you gain complete control over how screens transition — from simple slides to more complex movements like scaling, rotating, or fading effects.

This level of customization enables you to create unique and highly polished navigation experiences, making your application stand out with smooth, immersive transitions that feel tailor-made for your brand and user interaction design.

Choosing the Right Stack Navigator

When building your navigation architecture, it is important to understand when to use each type of stack navigator, as the decision directly impacts performance, user experience, and the flexibility of your app.

Choose **`native-stack`** when native performance and standard transitions are top priorities. It is highly optimized because it uses native components under the hood, providing smoother transitions, better memory management, and a more "native feel" across iOS and Android. This makes it ideal for most applications where default system behaviors are sufficient and fast responsiveness is critical.

Choose **`stack`** when highly customized animations or transition behaviors are essential, especially for applications that require visually rich experiences or that are intended to run cross-platform, including React Native Web.

Since it is based on JavaScript, **`stack`** offers maximum flexibility to design unique, complex animations and fully control screen transitions, even at the cost of slightly lower performance compared to **`native-stack`**.

Stack Navigation Summary

`createNativeStackNavigator` is recommended for projects that prioritize performance, simplicity, and adherence to platform-native behaviors. It is lightweight, faster, and easier to maintain for most standard navigation flows.

`createStackNavigator` is better suited for projects that demand complex, visually distinctive animations and customized transition effects, especially when creating premium, brand-specific experiences across different platforms.

By understanding the strengths of each navigator, you can make smarter architectural choices for your app — balancing performance, flexibility, and user experience based on the specific goals of your project.

With this knowledge, you will be able to confidently implement the best stack navigation strategy, ensuring that your React Native applications offer seamless, intuitive, and engaging user journeys that scale alongside the growth of your product.

Tab Navigation

Tab navigation is widely used in modern mobile applications, especially those that have multiple main sections or categories that users need quick access to. React Navigation offers full support for tabbed navigation through the **`createBottomTabNavigator`**, allowing the creation of intuitive and practical interfaces where users can easily switch between main screens.

Basic Implementation of `createBottomTabNavigator`

To implement bottom tab navigation with React Navigation, we use the **`createBottomTabNavigator`**. This navigator makes it easy to create user-friendly interfaces and supports features like smooth animations, custom icons, and full visual control over the tabs.

Basic example:

```
import React from 'react';
import { NavigationContainer } from '@react-navigation/native';
import { createBottomTabNavigator } from '@react-navigation/bottom-tabs';

import HomeScreen from './screens/HomeScreen';
import ProfileScreen from './screens/ProfileScreen';
import SettingsScreen from './screens/SettingsScreen';

const Tab = createBottomTabNavigator();

export default function App() {
  return (
<NavigationContainer>
<Tab.NavigatorinitialRouteName="Home">
<Tab.Screen name="Home" component={HomeScreen} />
<Tab.Screen name="Profile" component={ProfileScreen} />
<Tab.Screen name="Settings" component={SettingsScreen} />
</Tab.Navigator>
</NavigationContainer>
  );
}
```

In this example:

- Each **`Tab.Screen`** represents a distinct tab.
- The **`initialRouteName`** defines the screen displayed initially.

Using **`createBottomTabNavigator`** not only simplifies the user journey across major sections of your app but also enhances usability by providing intuitive, quick-access navigation. By combining it with custom icons, personalized labels, and responsive styles, you can further tailor the tab bar experience to align perfectly with the branding of your applications and user expectations.

Mastering this setup will enable you to create professional, modern, and highly interactive bottom tab navigations, elevating both the visual appeal and functionality of your mobile application.

Customizing Tab Icons

A very common and expected feature by users is intuitive icons on the bottom tabs. To customize icons in React Navigation, you often use popular libraries like **`react-native-vector-icons`** or **`expo/vector-icons`**.

Example using **`react-native-vector-icons`**:

First, install the library:

```
npm install react-native-vector-icons
# or with Yarn
yarn add react-native-vector-icons
```

Now, customize tab icons:

```
import Icon from 'react-native-vector-icons/Ionicons';

<Tab.Navigator
initialRouteName="Home"
screenOptions={({ route }) => ({
```

```
tabBarIcon: ({ focused, color, size }) => {
      let iconName;

      if (route.name === 'Home') {
iconName = focused ? 'home' : 'home-outline';
      } else if (route.name === 'Profile') {
iconName = focused ? 'person' : 'person-outline';
      } else if (route.name === 'Settings') {
iconName = focused ? 'settings' : 'settings-outline';
      }

      return <Icon name={iconName} size={size} color={color} />;
    },
tabBarActiveTintColor: '#6200EE',   // Active icon color
tabBarInactiveTintColor: 'gray',    // Inactive icon color
  })}
>
<Tab.Screen name="Home" component={HomeScreen} />
<Tab.Screen name="Profile" component={ProfileScreen} />
<Tab.Screen name="Settings" component={SettingsScreen} />
</Tab.Navigator>
```

In this example:

- The **tabBarIcon** property defines which icon is shown, depending on whether the tab is focused or not.
- Popular icon sets such as Ionicons, Material Icons, and FontAwesome are frequently used.

Adding meaningful and visually consistent icons significantly improves user navigation by providing immediate visual cues about the purpose of each tab. Icons not only enhance the aesthetic of your application but also contribute to usability, helping users to find and recognize important sections of the app more quickly and intuitively.

By thoughtfully designing and implementing your tab icons, you create a more polished and engaging user experience that reflects the professionalism and attention to detail of your overall application.

Advanced Customization of Tab Styles

React Navigation offers multiple options to fully customize the visual style of bottom tabs, enabling you to match the design of your app precisely.

Advanced example:

```
<Tab.Navigator
initialRouteName="Home"
screenOptions={{
tabBarActiveTintColor: '#ffffff',
tabBarInactiveTintColor: '#cccccc',
tabBarActiveBackgroundColor: '#6200EE',
tabBarInactiveBackgroundColor: '#3700B3',
tabBarLabelStyle: {
fontSize: 12,
fontWeight: '600',
marginBottom: 4,
    },
```

```
tabBarStyle: {
      height: 60,
paddingVertical: 5,
backgroundColor: '#121212',
borderTopWidth: 0,
    },
  }}
>
<Tab.Screen name="Home" component={HomeScreen} options={{ title: 'Home' }} />
<Tab.Screen name="Profile" component={ProfileScreen} options={{ title: 'Profile' }} />
<Tab.Screen name="Settings" component={SettingsScreen} options={{ title: 'Settings'
}} />
</Tab.Navigator>
```

Important customization options:

- **`tabBarActiveTintColor`** and **`tabBarInactiveTintColor`**: Icon and text colors for active/ inactive tabs.
- **`tabBarActiveBackgroundColor`** and **`tabBarInactiveBackgroundColor`**: Background colors for tabs.
- **`tabBarLabelStyle`**: Label text style for tabs.
- **`tabBarStyle`**: Overall styling of the bottom tab bar.

By taking advantage of these advanced styling options, you can create a navigation experience that feels fully integrated with the branding of your application and overall design language. Well-designed tab bars not only improve visual consistency but also enhance the usability of the app, giving users a more intuitive and visually engaging interface at every interaction.

When customizing tab appearance—icons, labels, active/inactive states, and backgrounds—treat accessibility as a first-class requirement. Verify color contrast for text and icons (especially for inactive states), and test both light and dark mode to ensure labels and glyphs remain readable across themes and device settings.

Thoughtful customization transforms basic navigation into a polished, professional user experience — making your app not just functional, but truly memorable.

Combining Navigators (Nested Navigation)

It is common to combine tab navigation with other types of navigators, like stack or drawer, creating complex yet intuitive interfaces.

Simplified example combining tabs and stack navigation:

```
constHomeStack = createNativeStackNavigator();

function HomeStackScreen() {
  return (
<HomeStack.Navigator>
<HomeStack.Screen name="HomeMain" component={HomeScreen} />
<HomeStack.Screen name="Details" component={DetailsScreen} />
</HomeStack.Navigator>
  );
}

<Tab.NavigatorinitialRouteName="Home">
<Tab.Screen name="Home" component={HomeStackScreen} />
```

```
<Tab.Screen name="Profile" component={ProfileScreen} />
<Tab.Screen name="Settings" component={SettingsScreen} />
</Tab.Navigator>
```

In this example:

- Each tab can have its own stack navigator, allowing independent navigation within each tab.

Nested navigation is a powerful pattern that enables you to organize the screens of your application logically and modularly. By isolating navigation flows inside individual tabs or drawers, you improve maintainability and create a more predictable user experience.

```
NavigationContainer
└ RootStack
   ├ AuthStack
│  ├ SignIn
│  └ SignUp
   └ AppTabs
      ├ HomeStack
│  ├ Home
│  └ Details
      ├ SearchStack
│  ├ Search
│  └ Filters
      └ SettingsDrawer
         ├ SettingsStack
│  ├ Settings
│  └ Account
         └ Help
```

This diagram highlights the key mental model: **a single root navigator** decides the high-level flow (say Auth versus App), while each tab/drawer can encapsulate its own stack for localized navigation without polluting the route structure of the rest of the app.

It also allows different sections of the app to manage their own history independently, ensuring that users can navigate deeply within a section without affecting the global navigation structure. Mastering nested navigators is crucial for scaling your app as new features and sections are added, keeping the architecture clean, flexible, and easy to evolve over time.

Tab Navigation Summary

When building mobile applications, organizing the main sections clearly and intuitively is fundamental to delivering a great user experience. Tab navigation plays a central role in this, providing users with immediate access to key areas of the app through an interface that feels familiar, fast, and user-friendly.

Here are the main reasons why tab navigation is so important:

- **Tab navigation is ideal for organizing multiple main sections**: It allows users to move effortlessly between core areas of the app, such as Home, Profile, Settings, or Search, without needing to dive deep into nested menus.
- **Clear and intuitive icons significantly enhance usability**: Well-designed icons help users recognize sections at a glance, speeding up interactions and improving the overall flow through the application.

- **Custom styles allow seamless integration with the design of your app**: With full control over colors, fonts, backgrounds, and iconography, you can create a tab bar that perfectly matches the identity of your brand, contributing to a more cohesive visual experience.
- **Easily combinable with other navigation types like Stack and Drawer**: By nesting Stack Navigators inside each Tab or combining Tabs within a Drawer, you can build powerful, modular, and flexible navigation structures suitable for apps of any size and complexity.

Mastering this technique will offer users an intuitive, clear, and organized experience, contributing positively to the success of your React Native application. It not only improves navigation efficiency but also reinforces a sense of stability, professionalism, and care for detail – essential qualities that differentiate truly exceptional mobile apps in the current competitive landscape.

Thus, by strategically implementing and customizing tab navigation, you build the foundation for scalable, elegant, and user-centered applications that will continue to grow and adapt to the evolving needs of your user.

Drawer Navigation

Drawer navigation is a widely used design pattern in mobile applications, where a side menu slides out from the edge of the screen, providing quick access to different sections of the app. This pattern is especially useful in applications with multiple categories, settings, or grouped information.

React Navigation makes implementing drawer navigation easy through the **`createDrawerNavigator`**, providing flexibility to customize the content, style, and behavior of the drawer.

Setting up `createDrawerNavigator` for Side Navigation

To set up drawer navigation, first import and use **`createDrawerNavigator`** in your project.

Basic example:

```
import React from 'react';
import { NavigationContainer } from '@react-navigation/native';
import { createDrawerNavigator } from '@react-navigation/drawer';

import HomeScreen from './screens/HomeScreen';
import ProfileScreen from './screens/ProfileScreen';
import SettingsScreen from './screens/SettingsScreen';

const Drawer = createDrawerNavigator();

export default function App() {
  return (
<NavigationContainer>
<Drawer.NavigatorinitialRouteName="Home">
<Drawer.Screen name="Home" component={HomeScreen} />
<Drawer.Screen name="Profile" component={ProfileScreen} />
<Drawer.Screen name="Settings" component={SettingsScreen} />
</Drawer.Navigator>
</NavigationContainer>
  );
}
```

In this example:

- Each **`Drawer.Screen`** defines a menu option in the side panel.
- The **`initialRouteName`** sets the first screen displayed when the app opens.

Drawer navigation is particularly effective for applications that have multiple sections, settings, or tools that users may need to access from anywhere within the app. By presenting a persistent side menu, you provide an organized and space-efficient way to structure navigation – especially useful for apps with a larger number of features or deeper navigation hierarchies.

With careful implementation and customization, drawer navigation can enhance user accessibility, improve content discoverability, and maintain a clean, uncluttered main interface – resulting in a smoother and more professional user experience.

Customizing Drawer Content with `drawerContent`

React Navigation allows full customization of the content of the drawer through the **`drawerContent`** prop, which receives a React component. This makes it possible to create fully customized menus, including user avatars, custom buttons, external links, and more.

Customization example:

```
function CustomDrawerContent(props) {
  return (
<DrawerContentScrollView {...props}>
<DrawerItemList {...props} />
<DrawerItem
        label="Help"
onPress={() => alert('Help link')}
      />
</DrawerContentScrollView>
  );
}

export default function App() {
  return (
<NavigationContainer>
<Drawer.Navigator
initialRouteName="Home"
drawerContent={(props) =><CustomDrawerContent {...props} />}
>
<Drawer.Screen name="Home" component={HomeScreen} />
<Drawer.Screen name="Profile" component={ProfileScreen} />
<Drawer.Screen name="Settings" component={SettingsScreen} />
</Drawer.Navigator>
</NavigationContainer>
  );
}
```

In this example:

- **`DrawerContentScrollView`** creates a scrollable area for the drawer content.
- **`DrawerItemList`** automatically renders the list of registered screens in **`Drawer.Navigator`**.
- **`DrawerItem`** adds custom items at the end of the menu, such as help links or logout buttons.

Thus, you can combine main navigation with extra elements to enrich the user experience.

Styling and Positioning the Drawer

`createDrawerNavigator` offers several options to configure the appearance of the drawer and behavior, such as:

- Drawer position (**`left`** or **`right`**)
- Drawer width
- Background styles, borders, and typography for menu items

Example of Styling and Repositioning:

```
<Drawer.Navigator
initialRouteName="Home"
screenOptions={{
drawerPosition: 'left', // or 'right'
drawerStyle: {
backgroundColor: '#f0f0f0',
      width: 250,
    },
drawerLabelStyle: {
fontSize: 16,
fontWeight: 'bold',
    },
drawerActiveTintColor: '#6200EE',
drawerInactiveTintColor: 'gray',
  }}
>
<Drawer.Screen name="Home" component={HomeScreen} />
<Drawer.Screen name="Profile" component={ProfileScreen} />
<Drawer.Screen name="Settings" component={SettingsScreen} />
</Drawer.Navigator>
```

Important options:

- **`drawerPosition`**: It defines which side of the screen the drawer appears (**`left`** or **`right`**).
- **`drawerStyle`**: It allows styling the drawer container (background color, width, and so on).
- **`drawerLabelStyle`**: It controls the style of the menu item labels.
- **`drawerActiveTintColor`** and **`drawerInactiveTintColor`**: Both of these define colors for selected and unselected items.

These settings help create a drawer navigation that naturally integrates with the overall design of your app.

Combining Drawer Navigation with Stack Navigation

In larger and more dynamic applications, it is very common – and highly recommended – to combine **drawer navigation** with **stack navigation**. This hybrid approach offers the best of both worlds: a side menu for quick section switching and independent, and linear flows of screens inside each section.

For example, each drawer option can open its own stack navigator containing multiple related screens, maintaining a clear and organized navigation hierarchy while keeping the user experience simple and intuitive.

Simplified example:

```
import { createNativeStackNavigator } from '@react-navigation/native-stack';

constHomeStack = createNativeStackNavigator();

function HomeStackScreen() {
  return (
<HomeStack.Navigator>
<HomeStack.Screen name="HomeMain" component={HomeScreen} />
<HomeStack.Screen name="Details" component={DetailsScreen} />
</HomeStack.Navigator>
  );
}

export default function App() {
  return (
<NavigationContainer>
<Drawer.Navigator>
<Drawer.Screen name="Home" component={HomeStackScreen} />
<Drawer.Screen name="Profile" component={ProfileScreen} />
<Drawer.Screen name="Settings" component={SettingsScreen} />
</Drawer.Navigator>
</NavigationContainer>
  );
}
```

In this example:

- Each **Drawer.Screen** links to a different flow.
- The **Home** drawer item opens a stack where users can navigate between **HomeMain** and **Details**, maintaining independent navigation history inside the Home section.
- Other drawer items like **Profile** and **Settings** could also have their own nested stacks if needed.

Why Combine Drawer and Stack

- **Logical grouping**: Related screens stay together in dedicated flows, improving user orientation inside the app.
- **Independent navigation**: Users can explore different screens within a section without affecting the navigation of other sections.
- **Better scalability**: New features and screens can be easily added to the right section without changing the global navigation structure.
- **Clear back behavior**: Stack navigation preserves the natural "back" action within sections, while the drawer remains available for switching top-level areas.

Best Practices When Combining Navigators

- Clearly define which of the sections deserves their own stacks.
- Keep the drawer menu clean and organized, limiting it to top-level categories.
- Maintain consistent header styles and gestures between the stack and drawer navigators to ensure a smooth, cohesive experience.

Thus, by combining drawer and stack navigators properly, you can offer users a navigation system that feels intuitive, professional, and effortlessly scalable – essential for delivering polished React Native applications that grow along with user demands and app complexity.

Drawer Navigation Summary

When designing mobile applications that have multiple independent areas – such as user profiles, settings, dashboards, or resource libraries – **drawer navigation** becomes an excellent tool to organize and present these sections in an accessible and efficient way. Drawer menus allow users to quickly jump between key parts of the app without cluttering the main interface, keeping the user experience clean, intuitive, and scalable.

Here is a summary of why drawer navigation is so powerful:

- **`createDrawerNavigator` easily implements sliding side menus**: It offers a straightforward way to add a side navigation drawer to your app, significantly enhancing usability for apps with multiple top-level sections.
- **Drawer content can be fully customized with the `drawerContent` prop**: You can completely redesign the drawer, inserting personalized menus, user avatars, external links, logout buttons, and more, creating a truly tailored navigation experience.
- **Various styling options are available to integrate the drawer into the layout of the app**: Background colors, label fonts, icon colors, drawer width, and even gesture behavior can be customized, ensuring that the drawer feels like a natural extension of the design of your application.
- **Drawer navigation can be combined with stack navigation to create robust and organized experiences**: By nesting stack navigators inside drawer items, you can maintain complex, independent navigation flows for each section without sacrificing clarity or performance.

With proper use of drawer navigation, your React Native application can offer accessible, efficient, and elegant navigation, especially for projects that require access to many sections or features at any point in the app.

Moreover, a well-designed drawer enhances not only the structural organization of your application but also its perceived quality and user engagement. When implemented thoughtfully – with clean grouping, custom visuals, and a fluid user experience – drawer navigation transforms from a simple menu into a powerful and strategic tool for navigating complex applications with ease and sophistication.

Hence, mastering drawer navigation ensures that your app remains scalable, intuitive, and ready to handle growing functionality without overwhelming the user.

Passing Parameters between Screens

In mobile app development, it is very common to need to send information from one screen to another. In React Navigation, passing parameters between screens is simple, efficient, and naturally integrates with the navigation flow.

This process is mainly done through the **`navigation.navigate`** method to send parameters and the **`route.params`** object to receive them. Additionally, useful hooks like **`useNavigation`** and **`useRoute`** make it more flexible to access navigation information within components.

How to Send Parameters with navigation.navigate

When navigating to a new screen, you can attach data by passing it as the second argument to the **navigate** method.

Example of sending parameters:

```
function HomeScreen({ navigation }) {
  return (
<Button
      title="Go to Details"
onPress={() =>navigation.navigate('Details', {
itemId: 42,
otherParam: 'Some information',
      })}
    />
  );
}
```

In this example:

- We are navigating to the **Details** screen.
- We are sending two parameters: **itemId** and **otherParam**.

Passing parameters during navigation is a fundamental technique to make screens more dynamic and contextual. It allows screens to adapt their content based on user actions, specific selections, or real-time data, creating more personalized and meaningful experiences.

Properly structuring parameter passing also ensures greater flexibility when scaling your application, as screens can be reused for multiple contexts simply by varying the parameters they receive — improving both code maintainability and user satisfaction.

How to Access Parameters with route.params

Once parameters are sent during navigation, you need a way to retrieve and use them on the destination screen. React Navigation provides a straightforward method for this: you can access the Passed parameters through the **route.params** object, which is automatically injected into the props of your screen.

This allows screens to become truly dynamic, adjusting their behavior or content based on what was passed when navigating.

Here is a basic example of how to access the received parameters:

```
function DetailsScreen({ route, navigation }) {
const{ itemId, otherParam } = route.params;

  return (
<View>
<Text>Item ID: {itemId}</Text>
<Text>Other Parameter: {otherParam}</Text>
<Button title="Go Back" onPress={() =>navigation.goBack()} />
</View>
  );
}
```

In this example:

- **route.params** contains all the parameters sent during navigation.
- The values **itemId** and **otherParam** are destructured from **route.params** and displayed on the screen.
- We also provide a "Go Back" button that uses **navigation.goBack()** to return to the previous screen.

This simple pattern enables a wide range of possibilities, such as:

- Displaying specific details for a selected item (such as a product, user profile, or an article).
- Loading content based on an identifier or type passed from another screen.
- Personalizing messages, titles, or layouts dynamically without hardcoding.

Always make sure to handle parameters safely, especially if there is a possibility that a screen might be accessed without all expected parameters. Using default values or optional chaining helps prevent runtime errors and ensures a more robust navigation flow.

By effectively leveraging **route.params**, you enable your React Native application to offer personalized, context-aware experiences that feel fluid, intelligent, and responsive to user actions, which is a key ingredient for building professional-grade mobile applications.

Using Hooks: useNavigation and useRoute

In modern React Native development, it is increasingly common to build applications with **functional components** rather than class-based ones. Because functional components often do not automatically receive **navigation** and **route** as props – especially when they are deeply nested components or UI elements like buttons, cards, or list items – React Navigation provides **dedicated hooks** to solve this in a clean, flexible, and powerful way.

useNavigation

The **useNavigation** hook allows you to programmatically access the **navigation object** from any component, not just screens. This enables components like buttons, icons, or custom cards to trigger navigation actions without needing to manually pass navigation props down the component tree.

Example:

```
import { useNavigation } from '@react-navigation/native';

function GoToDetailsButton() {
const navigation = useNavigation();

  return (
<Button
      title="Go to Details"
onPress={() =>navigation.navigate('Details', { itemId: 101 })}
    />
  );
}
```

In this example:

- We call **useNavigation()** inside a simple button component.
- When the button is pressed, it triggers navigation to the **Details** screen and passes a parameter (**itemId: 101**).

The key benefits of **useNavigation** are as follows:

- It decouples navigation logic from screen components.
- It increases reusability. Buttons, cards, or list items can independently handle navigation.
- It simplifies props management. There is no need to propagate **navigation** through intermediate components manually.

This approach makes the codebase cleaner, easier to maintain, and more scalable as your app grows.

useRoute

The **useRoute** hook allows you to access the **route object** from anywhere inside a component, providing easy access to parameters passed during navigation.

Example:

```
import { useRoute } from '@react-navigation/native';

function DetailsScreen() {
const route = useRoute();
const{ itemId } = route.params;

  return (
<View>
<Text>Item ID: {itemId}</Text>
</View>
  );
}
```

In this example:

- We call **useRoute()** to access the current route information inside the **DetailsScreen**.
- We destructure**itemId** from **route.params** to display it on the screen.

The key benefits of **useRoute** are as follows:

- Direct access to route parameters without relying on screen props.
- It has cleaner and more modular components. Components can dynamically adapt based on the navigation context.
- Essential for deeper nested components that still need access to route data.

Best Practices When Using useNavigation and useRoute

Always **check for the existence of parameters** before using them to avoid runtime errors.

- Use **typed navigation and route hooks** with TypeScript for even safer and more predictable navigation (say **useNavigation<MyStackNavigationProp>()**).
- Keep navigation actions centralized when possible, but do not hesitate to use these hooks for localized navigation needs in specific components.
- Avoid overusing navigation inside very small components if it complicates their responsibility. Maintain clean separation of concerns when possible.

Why Hooks are Essential for Scalable Navigation Architectures

Hooks like **`useNavigation`** and **`useRoute`** transform how navigation logic is written in modern React Native applications.

They allow you to:

1. Create more modular and flexible UI components.
2. Reduce dependency on props drilling.
3. Enhance code readability by keeping navigation logic close to the component that triggers it.
4. Build dynamic, responsive components that adapt based on both navigation flow and passed parameters.

By mastering these hooks, you unlock a new level of architecture quality and scalability in your React Native projects, preparing your app to grow in complexity without sacrificing maintainability.

Important Tip: Optional Parameters

Sometimes, a screen might be accessed with or without parameters. To avoid errors when accessing non-existent properties, it is important to safely handle optional parameters:

Example:

```
function DetailsScreen({ route }) {
const{ itemId = 0, otherParam = 'Parameter not provided' } = route.params || {};

  return (
<View>
<Text>Item ID: {itemId}</Text>
<Text>Other Parameter: {otherParam}</Text>
</View>
  );
}
```

Using default values ensures that the app continues to function correctly even if parameters are not passed.

Nested Navigation and Deep Linking

More robust mobile applications often require **nested navigation**, where different types of navigators (Stack, Tab, Drawer) are combined to create complex navigation flows. Additionally, integrating **deep linking** allows users to directly access specific screens via URLs, whether by clicking external links or notifications.

React Navigation offers full support for both scenarios, providing flexibility and power to build advanced navigation experiences.

Setting up Nested Navigators

Nested navigation occurs when one navigator is placed inside another. For example, you might have:

- A Tab containing different Stacks for each tab.
- A Drawer grouping different Stacks or Tabs.

This setup helps organize navigation logic cleanly while maintaining scalability.

Example: Stack inside a Tab

Imagine a flow where each tab has its own stack of screens:

```
import { createBottomTabNavigator } from '@react-navigation/bottom-tabs';
import { createNativeStackNavigator } from '@react-navigation/native-stack';

const Tab = createBottomTabNavigator();
constHomeStack = createNativeStackNavigator();
constSettingsStack = createNativeStackNavigator();

function HomeStackScreen() {
  return (
<HomeStack.Navigator>
<HomeStack.Screen name="HomeMain" component={HomeScreen} />
<HomeStack.Screen name="Details" component={DetailsScreen} />
</HomeStack.Navigator>
  );
}

function SettingsStackScreen() {
  return (
<SettingsStack.Navigator>
<SettingsStack.Screen name="SettingsMain" component={SettingsScreen} />
<SettingsStack.Screen name="Profile" component={ProfileScreen} />
</SettingsStack.Navigator>
  );
}

export default function App() {
  return (
<NavigationContainer>
<Tab.Navigator>
<Tab.Screen name="HomeTab" component={HomeStackScreen} options={{ title: 'Home' }} />
<Tab.Screen name="SettingsTab" component={SettingsStackScreen} options={{ title:
'Settings' }} />
</Tab.Navigator>
</NavigationContainer>
  );
}
```

In the aforesaid example:

- Each tab (`HomeTab` and `SettingsTab`) has its own stack navigator.
- This isolates navigation history between tabs, allowing independent navigation within each.

Example: Tab inside a Drawer

You can also create a Drawer where each item opens a Tab navigator:

```
import { createDrawerNavigator } from '@react-navigation/drawer';

const Dr

export default function App() {
  return (
```

```
<NavigationContainer>
<Drawer.Navigator>
<Drawer.Screen name="Tabs" component={TabsScreen} />
<Drawer.Screen name="Profile" component={ProfileScreen} />
</Drawer.Navigator>
</NavigationContainer>
  );
}
```

Where **TabsScreen** would be the Tab navigator configured previously.

Handling Deep Links (Deep Linking)

Deep linking allows your app to open directly on a specific screen via a link, such as: **myapp://details/42**

This is especially useful for notifications, marketing campaigns, content sharing, and app integrations.

Basic Deep Linking Configuration

Deep Linking allows your React Native app to be opened directly to specific screens when a user clicks on a URL — whether from a website, an email, a notification, or another application. Configuring Deep Linking ensures seamless navigation experiences and is essential for improving user engagement, content sharing, and app interoperability.

The first step to enable deep linking is to define a URL scheme inside the **NavigationContainer**. React Navigation makes this process straightforward by using a **linking** configuration object.

Here is a basic example:

```
import { NavigationContainer } from '@react-navigation/native';

const linking = {
  prefixes: ['myapp://', 'https://myapp.com'],
config: {
    screens: {
HomeTab: {
        screens: {
HomeMain: 'home',
          Details: 'details/:id',
        },
      },
SettingsTab: {
        screens: {
SettingsMain: 'settings',
          Profile: 'profile',
        },
      },
    },
  },
};

export default function App() {
  return (
<NavigationContainer linking={linking}>
```

```
      {/* your navigators here */}
</NavigationContainer>
  );
}
```

Breaking Down the Configuration:

- **prefixes**: It defines which URL patterns the app should recognize and respond to.
  - **myapp://** is a custom app-specific scheme (works like a deep link for installed apps).
  - **https://myapp.com** allows web links to be handled as well.
- **config**: It maps the internal navigation routes to URL paths. You can organize screens inside navigators (such as Tabs, Stacks, or Drawers) and associate each route with a specific path.

For Example:

- A link like **myapp://details/42** would open the **Details** screen and automatically pass **id=42** as a parameter.
- A link like **myapp://settings** would directly open the **Settings** screen inside the Settings tab.

Why Deep Linking Matters

- **Improves user experience**: Users can jump straight to specific content instead of navigating manually from the home screen.
- **Enhances app engagement**: Campaigns, notifications, and external sites can drive users directly into relevant parts of your app.
- **Facilitates content sharing**: Users can share links that lead directly to particular screens, posts, profiles, or features inside your app.
- **Supports universal apps**: Deep linking unifies the presence of your app across web, mobile, and notifications.

Setting up Deep Linking is a crucial step in making your React Native application **more integrated, discoverable, and user-friendly**. Once properly configured, you ensure that your app can handle navigation both internally and externally, responding intelligently to incoming URLs – a must-have feature for modern mobile experiences.

Customizing Headers and Transition Animations

In professional-grade applications, the navigation experience goes beyond simple screen switches. How headers appear and how transitions happen between screens greatly impacts the perceived quality, fluidity, and visual identity of the app.

React Navigation provides robust options for header customization and a range of transition behaviors (depending on whether you use **native-stack** or the JS stack). However, it is important to clarify that **sharedTransitionTag** is typically associated with the shared element/shared transition capabilities of the Reanimated (like Reanimated shared transitions), not a core React Navigation API. Availability and behavior can be **version- and setup-dependent** (Reanimated version, Babel plugin configuration, and the navigator implementation), so that readers should verify compatibility against the official Reanimated documentation for their installed versions before adopting this pattern.

Customizing Headers Using the header Property

Each screen registered in a navigator (like Stack) can have its own customized header using the **options** prop, or you can define global styles using **screenOptions**. Customizing headers is fundamental for creating a visually cohesive application that aligns with your brand and improves the overall user experience.

Basic example:

```
<Stack.Navigator
screenOptions={{
headerStyle: { backgroundColor: '#6200EE' },
headerTintColor: '#fff',
headerTitleStyle: { fontWeight: 'bold' },
  }}
>
<Stack.Screen
    name="Home"
    component={HomeScreen}
    options={{ title: 'Home' }}
  />
<Stack.Screen
    name="Details"
    component={DetailsScreen}
    options={{
      title: 'Details',
headerBackTitle: 'Back',
    }}
  />
</Stack.Navigator>
```

After configuring headers this way, all your screens will either inherit the global settings from **`screenOptions`**, or they can individually override these settings using their own **`options`**.

In this example, we can see that:

- **`headerStyle`** changes the header container style (like background color).
- **`headerTintColor`** changes the header icons and text color.
- **`headerTitleStyle`** customizes the text style of the title (say bold, font size).
- **`headerBackTitle`** sets the text shown on the back button in iOS (useful for improving navigation clarity).

These properties allow you to establish consistent branding across your application while also enabling screen-specific customizations where necessary.

Dynamic Headers

In many real-world applications, a static title or fixed header style is not always enough. Sometimes you need the header to **adapt dynamically** based on the data associated with the current screen – for example, displaying the name of a product, the title of an article, or even the name of a user when viewing their profile.

React Navigation makes it easy to achieve this by allowing the **`options`** prop of a **`Stack.Screen`** to be a **function** instead of a static object. This function receives the **`route`** and **`navigation`** props, letting you access parameters and dynamically configure header behavior.

```
<Stack.Screen
  name="Details"
  component={DetailsScreen}
```

```
  options={({ route }) => ({
    title: `Item ${route.params.itemId}`,
  })}
/>
```

In this example:

- We use the **route** parameter received by the **options** function.
- The title of the header is dynamically constructed using the **itemId** sent during navigation.
- Each time the **DetailsScreen** is opened with a different **itemId**, the header title updates accordingly (like "Item 42", "Item 101" and so on).

Best Practices and Final Considerations

When building navigation in a React Native application, it is not enough to simply connect screens – it is essential to structure navigation efficiently, scalably, and robustly. As a project grows, poorly planned navigation can lead to confusion, subtle bugs, and performance degradation. This chapter gathers key best practices to ensure your application has solid navigation, ready to evolve alongside the project.

Structuring Navigation Efficiently for Scalability

- **Organize navigators into separate modules**: For larger projects, separate Stack Navigators, Tab Navigators, and Drawer Navigators into distinct files. For example, you might create files like **HomeStack.tsx**, **AuthStack.tsx**, **MainTabs.tsx**, and **AppDrawer.tsx** to maintain a clean project structure.
- **Adopt a clear navigation tree**: Think of your app as a "navigation map. "Define the main flow – such as authentication → home → profile → settings – before you start coding, only to ensure a logical and scalable navigation hierarchy.
- **Use consistent naming for screens and navigators**: Name your routes and navigators clearly and consistently, like **HomeScreen**, **ProfileScreen**, and **SettingsScreen**. Consistent naming helps avoid ambiguities, simplifies deep linking setups, and improves maintainability.
- **Centralize common configurations**: Define default **screenOptions** in each navigator to maintain consistent visual styles, such as header designs, default animations, and transitions. Centralization reduces repetition and ensures uniformity across the app.

Managing Navigation State and Preventing Undesired Behavior

- **Use the useNavigationState hook when needed**: This hook allows you to access the current navigation state and make dynamic decisions based on it – for example, preventing users from navigating multiple times rapidly to the same screen.
- **Prevent double-click and duplicate navigations**: Implement protections to avoid users opening multiple instances of the same screen by repeatedly tapping buttons. This can be done by checking navigation availability or by managing internal component states to block navigation during transitions.
- **Properly handle route parameters**: Always validate the existence of **route.params** to avoid crashes due to missing values. Use default values or safe checks like optional chaining to make your navigation flow more resilient.

- **Manage protected navigations carefully**: If access to certain screens depends on authentication or user permissions, apply conditional logic before navigating. Redirect unauthenticated users appropriately, ensuring a secure and logical app experience.

Performance Optimization Tips for Complex Navigation

- **Use lazy loading in navigators**: Especially in Tab Navigators, configure screens to load only when accessed. This reduces the initial load time of the app and improves perceived performance.
- **Avoid rendering heavy components off-screen**: Use the **`useIsFocused`** hook to ensure that components fetch data or render expensive content only when the screen is actually visible to the user. This avoids unnecessary memory usage and improves responsiveness.
- **Properly configure `detachInactiveScreens`**: In Stack and Tab Navigators, enabling this option can help reduce memory usage by **detaching** inactive screens from the native view hierarchy (and, depending on the navigator and platform, limiting what stays rendered). **This is not the same as unmounting** the React component tree: screen state and lifecycle behavior may be preserved even when views are detached. Because the exact detach behavior can vary by navigator implementation (such as native-stack versus JS stack) and by platform, readers should validate the effect in their specific setup—especially if they rely on background rendering, animations, or side effects in inactive screens.
- **Prefer `createNativeStackNavigator` whenever possible**: Native Stack navigators are lighter and faster because they rely on native platform components rather than pure JavaScript rendering.
- **Minimize unnecessary complex animations**: Although custom animations can enhance UX, overly complex transitions can harm performance, especially on older or less powerful devices. Prefer native transitions or lightweight animations to maintain a smooth, high-performance user experience.

Best Practices Summary

- Modularize and plan your navigation carefully for better scalability and maintainability.
- Prevent undesired behaviors such as multiple simultaneous navigations or crashes from missing parameters.
- Use hooks like **`useIsFocused`** and **`useNavigationState`** to gain fine-grained control over navigation behavior.
- Implement optimization strategies to ensure smooth, efficient navigation even as your app grows in size and complexity.

Thus, by following these practices, you will build solid, scalable, and high-quality navigation experiences, preparing your React Native application for structured growth and long-term success — with minimal maintenance headaches and maximum user satisfaction.

Conclusion

In this chapter, we have explored navigation in React Native in depth, understanding how React Navigation has become the leading solution for structuring screen flows in modern mobile applications. We saw that beyond simply switching between screens, well-planned navigation is essential to ensure a smooth, intuitive, and scalable user experience.

We learned how to set up basic navigators such as Stack, Tab, and Drawer, implementing nested navigation and combining different types of flows in a modular and organized way. We also covered how to safely pass parameters between screens, how to handle navigation events using hooks like **`useNavigation`** and **`useRoute`**, and how to structure the project to maintain clarity and scalability as the app grows.

When addressing header customization, implementing smooth transitions between screens, and using animations with **`sharedTransitionTag`**, we realized that attention to the visual behavior and aesthetics of navigation makes a significant difference in the perceived quality of an application.

Additionally, we have discussed fundamental best practices for managing navigation state, preventing common mistakes like duplicate navigations, and implementing performance optimization strategies in complex apps, ensuring that navigation remains fast, efficient, and free of inconsistencies.

With these tools and practices, it becomes clear that mastering React Navigation is essential for developing high-quality React Native applications. It enables the creation of robust navigation experiences, aligned with the expectations of users on modern mobile platforms.

Just as React Native has evolved to meet a wide range of needs in cross-platform development, React Navigation keeps pace with this growth, offering flexibility, performance, and a broad set of features to address any navigation challenge a project may require.

With a solid foundation in navigation, you will be prepared to build applications that not only function but truly delight users — delivering fluidity, organization, and excellence with every interaction. Next, we will unlock the power of centralized state management by integrating Redux and the Context API in React Native. This chapter will show you how to keep data cohesive, predictable, and effortlessly debuggable—even as your app scales in complexity.

Self-Assessment Questions

Before consolidating what has been studied throughout this chapter, it is useful to reflect on how navigation is structured within React Native applications, the differences between the available navigators, and the best practices for managing complex navigation flows. The questions below serve as a guide to review the fundamental concepts presented, identify any doubts, and reinforce the understanding of scalable and efficient navigation architectures:

- What is the main difference between **`createNativeStackNavigator`** and **`createStackNavigator`** in React Navigation?
- How does nesting navigators (such as Stack inside Tab or Tab inside Drawer) contribute to building complex navigation flows?
- What are the benefits of using **`useNavigation`** and **`useRoute`** hooks in React Navigation?
- How can deep linking improve user experience in mobile applications?
- What strategies can be applied to optimize the performance of navigation in large and complex apps?
- How can customizing headers and implementing shared transitions enhance the visual quality of navigation?
- What are the potential issues caused by multiple rapid navigations, and how can they be prevented?
- Why is it important to modularize navigators in large applications?

Answering these questions helps review and consolidate the material, allowing you to assess whether you have satisfactorily understood the concepts covered or if you need to explore any specific aspect further. Mastering these navigation concepts ensures that your applications will deliver intuitive, responsive, and highly scalable user experiences.

Key Terms

- **Stack Navigator:** A navigation pattern that organizes screens in a stack, where new screens are pushed onto the top and the back action pops them off, mimicking the standard mobile navigation behavior.
- **Tab Navigator:** A navigation system that displays tabs at the bottom (or sometimes at the top) of the screen, allowing users to quickly switch between different main sections of the app.
- **Drawer Navigator:** A side navigation panel (drawer) that slides from the left or right side of the screen, typically containing navigation links and actions for accessing different parts of the application.
- **`NavigationContainer`:** A core component that wraps the entire navigation structure of the app, providing the navigation context and state management.
- **`navigation.navigate`:** A function used to move from one screen to another, optionally passing parameters between them.
- **`route.params`:** An object containing the parameters passed to a screen during navigation, allowing screens to dynamically adapt based on the data received.
- **`useNavigation`:** A hook that provides access to the navigation object inside any component, making it possible to programmatically navigate without relying on props.
- **`useRoute`:** A hook that provides access to the current route object, including any parameters passed during navigation.
- **Deep Linking:** A feature that allows external URLs to directly open specific screens within the mobile app, improving integration with web content, marketing campaigns, and notifications.
- **Shared Element Transitions:** Animations where a visual element is seamlessly shared between two screens, creating a smooth and visually appealing transition effect.
- **Screen Options:** A configuration object that defines styling and behavior for screens within a navigator, such as header appearance, animation style, or gestures.
- **Lazy Loading:** A technique where screens are only loaded when needed, optimizing memory usage and reducing the initial load time of the app.
- **`useIsFocused`:** A hook that allows detection of whether the current screen is focused, useful for triggering actions like data refreshes only when necessary.
- **`detachInactiveScreens`:** An optimization setting that unmounts screens not currently visible, freeing up memory and improving navigation performance.
- **`headerStyle / headerTitleStyle`:** Style properties that allow customization of the appearance of the header (navigation bar) on each screen.
- **`cardStyleInterpolator`:** A function used in Stack Navigators to define custom animations for transitions between screens.

These key terms summarize the essential concepts covered in this chapter, helping reinforce the understanding of navigation patterns, best practices, and optimization strategies within the React Navigation ecosystem.

CHAPTER 6
State Management with Redux and Context API

Introduction

In this chapter, we will explore the key strategies for managing state in React Native applications in an organized and scalable way. We shall begin by covering the fundamentals of Redux—including the creation of stores, actions, and reducers—and examine how its unidirectional data flow ensures predictability and simplifies debugging through tools like Redux DevTools. Next, we will set up Redux in a real project, integrate middleware (Redux Thunk or Redux Saga) to handle side effects and asynchronous calls, and structure our state into modular slices that follow the best practices.

In the second part, we will introduce the Context API as a lighter, native alternative—ideal for localized scenarios such as themes, user preferences, or small pieces of shared logic. You will also learn how to create providers and custom hooks to consume contexts, and how to combine useReducer to replicate Redux-like reducer behavior. Finally, we will be discussing the criteria that will help you choose between Redux and Context in different situations, ensuring a robust global state architecture that is easy to maintain and minimizes unnecessary re-renders.

Structure

In this chapter, we will cover the following topics:

- Introduction to State Management
  - Why We Need State Management in Complex Apps
  - The Problems of "Prop Drilling" and Data Inconsistencies
  - Overview: Redux versus Context API
- Redux Fundamentals
  - The Unidirectional Data Architecture
  - Store: Concept and Responsibilities
  - Actions: Definition, Payloads, and Type Constants
  - Reducers: Pure Functions, Immutable State, and Composition

- Setting Up Redux in React Native
    - Installing Libraries (`redux`, `react-redux`, `@reduxjs/toolkit`)
    - Creating the Store with `configureStore`
    - Store Provider (`<Provider>`) and Entry-Point Configuration
    - Core Hooks: `useSelector` and `useDispatch`
- Managing Asynchronous Flows
    - Issues with HTTP Calls and Side Effects
    - Redux Thunk: Definition, Setup, and Examples
    - Redux Saga: Generator Functions, Watchers, and Workers
    - Quick Comparison: Thunk versus Saga
- Testing Practices in Redux
    - Testing Pure Reducers and Actions
    - Mocking the Store for Component Tests
    - Testing Thunks and Sagas
- Context API as a Simple Alternative
    - When Context Makes More Sense than Redux
    - Creating Contexts (`StateContext` and `DispatchContext`)
    - Custom Hook with `useContext`
    - Using `useReducer` Within Context for Reducer-Like Logic
- Integration of Context and Redux
    - Hybrid Use Cases (for example, Context for Theming, Redux for Data)
    - Best Practices for Isolating Responsibilities
- Best Practices for Global State Architecture
    - Selectors and Memoization (Reselect)
    - Avoiding Unnecessary Re-renders (`React.memo`, `useCallback`)
    - Separation of UI Logic and Data Logic
    - File Naming and Organization
- Final Considerations and Next Steps
    - Criteria for Deciding Between Redux and Context in New Projects
    - Advanced Tools (Redux Toolkit, RTK Query)

Introduction to State Management

In modern React Native applications, components often need to share and consume data at various levels of the component tree. As an app grows in complexity—adding screens, features, and asynchronous operations—relying solely on local component state (**`useState`**) becomes cumbersome and error-prone. Centralized state management provides a single source of truth for the data of your application, ensuring that all parts of the app read and update state in a predictable and organized way.

There are two principal approaches within the React ecosystem for handling global state:

- **Redux**: A standalone library that implements a strict unidirectional data flow. Redux maintains the state of your entire application in a single store, with changes described by plain action objects and processed by pure reducer functions. Its strong conventions and rich middleware ecosystem (Thunk, Saga, and so on) make it ideal for large-scale or highly interactive applications where predictable state transitions and debugging tools (like Redux DevTools) are essential.
- **Context API**: A built-in React feature that allows you to pass data through the component tree without manually threading props at every level. By creating a Context provider, you can expose values (state, dispatch functions, and the like) to any descendant component via the `useContext` hook. When paired with `useReducer`, Context can serve as a lightweight alternative to Redux for simpler or medium-sized apps.

Before diving into implementation details, let us explore why state management matters, the pitfalls of "prop drilling," and how Redux and Context API compare.

Why We Need State Management in Complex Apps

In a simple app, you might store a few pieces of information—such as the text of an input, the on/off status of a toggle, or the result of a single API call—in local component state. However, enterprise-grade applications with multiple interdependent screens introduce several challenges:

- **Data Sharing**: Information like authenticated user details, theme preferences, shopping cart contents, or fetched lists often needs to be accessed by different parts of the UI.
- **Data Synchronization**: Updates made in one component must be immediately reflected everywhere else that depends on the same data, without discrepancies.
- **History and Traceability**: Centralizing state changes enables powerful debugging tools (Redux DevTools) that log every action, making it easier to trace and reproduce bugs.
- **Predictability**: A strictly unidirectional data flow prevents unintended side effects when one part of the app directly mutates the state of another component.

Without a clear strategy for global state management, an app is prone to subtle bugs, unpredictable behavior, and high coupling between components.

The Pitfalls of "Prop Drilling" and Data Inconsistencies

Prop drilling occurs when you pass props through multiple levels of components simply to reach the one that actually consumes the data. For example, consider a five-level tree: to provide the `user` object to a `NetworkIndicator` component, every intermediate component must declare and forward the same prop:

```
<Root>
<ScreenA user={user}>
<ScreenB user={user}>
<ScreenC user={user}>
<NetworkIndicator user={user} />
</ScreenC>
</ScreenB>
</ScreenA>
</Root>
```

This pattern leads to:

- **Verbose, repetitive code**: This makes refactoring tedious.
- **Risk of inconsistency**: In case, any level forgets or renames the prop, the consumer will receive undefined or incorrect data.
- **Poor maintainability**: Adding new shared state requirements multiplies the number of props to manage throughout the app.

Moreover, without centralization, components may each hold their own copy of the same data. When one component updates that data locally, the others remain out of sync, leading to state divergence and hard-to-reproduce bugs.

Overview: Redux versus Context API

Before we dive into specific differences, let us briefly define each approach:

Redux is a standalone state management library based on the principles of a single, immutable store and a strict unidirectional data flow. All state changes are described by plain action objects and handled by pure reducer functions, making side effects explicit and traceable via middleware (say, Thunk or Saga). The conventions of Redux and ecosystem of DevTools, middleware, and abstractions (Redux Toolkit, RTK Query) make it a powerful choice for large-scale applications with complex business logic and asynchronous workflows.

Context API is a built-in feature of React that enables you to pass data through the component tree without manually threading props at each level. By creating one or more Context providers, you expose values—such as theme settings, user info, or dispatch functions—to any descendant via the `useContext` hook. When paired with `useReducer`, Context can emulate Redux-style reducers in a lightweight, dependency-free way, making it ideal for simpler or medium-sized apps that do not require the full rigor of Redux.

A high-level comparison of Redux and the Context API for managing global state is explained in the following table:

Aspect	Redux	Context API
Complexity	Medium to high: requires defining actions, reducers, middleware, and additional setup (say Redux Thunk, Saga).	Low to medium: uses `createContext`, `useContext`, and optionally `useReducer`.
Scope	Best for large applications with multiple domains of state and complex business logic.	Suited for less dynamic state such as theming, localization, or simple auth.
Tooling	Rich ecosystem: DevTools, middleware, Redux Toolkit, RTK Query.	Native to React, no external dependencies.
Data Flow	Strictly unidirectional: store → reducers → view.	Similar conceptually, but less formal: any provider can supply and consume values.
Performance	Memoized selectors (reselect) and slice-based splitting mitigate excessive re-renders.	Can trigger re-renders of all consumers when context value changes unless carefully segmented.
Learning Curve	Steeper, due to architectural patterns and middleware knowledge.	Gentler, leveraging familiar React hooks API.

Table 6.1: *High-level Comparison of Redux and the Context API for Managing Global State*

While Redux and the Context API are common baselines, the React Native ecosystem also uses lighter-weight state libraries such as **Zustand** (minimal store pattern), **Jotai** (atomic state), and **Recoil** (graph-based/atom-selector model). These can be good fits when you want simpler ergonomics than Redux or more structure than Context alone, depending on the complexity and performance needs of your app.

In the coming sections, we will dive deeper into configuring and using each approach, helping you decide which fits the size of your project, complexity, and team expertise.

Redux Fundamentals

Redux is built on a set of guiding principles designed to make application state predictable, centralized, and easy to debug. At its core lies the concept of a single immutable state tree: rather than having multiple, potentially conflicting sources of truth, Redux keeps all state in one place, ensuring consistency across your app. Every change is triggered by dispatching a plain action object, which describes *what* happened but not *how* the state should change—this separation of intent from implementation fosters clearer reasoning about state transitions.

Reducers, which are pure functions, then process these actions to produce a new state without mutating the previous one, enabling features like time-travel debugging and state replay. Middleware sits between dispatching an action and reaching the reducers, allowing you to handle asynchronous logic, logging, error reporting, or other side effects in a clean, composable fashion. Together, these building blocks; unidirectional data flow, a single store, explicit actions, pure reducers, and a rich middleware ecosystem, provide a robust framework for maintaining complex application state in a predictable and maintainable manner.

Unidirectional Data Flow

At the heart of Redux is a strictly unidirectional flow of data, which contrasts with more ad hoc or bidirectional patterns. The flow proceeds as follows:

1. **Dispatch an Action:** A component or middleware dispatches a plain JavaScript object called an *action*, describing "what happened."
2. **Reducers Process the Action:** The action is sent to reducer functions, each of which examines the **`type`** of the action and returns a new state slice based on the payload of the action.
3. **Store Updates State:** The Redux store collects the results from all reducers, merges them into a new global state object, and replaces the old state.
4. **View Re-renders:** Components subscribed to the store (via **`connect`** or **`useSelector`**) receive the updated state and re-render as needed.

This loop ensures that data always travels the same path—action → reducer → new state → view—making side effects easier to track, debugging more straightforward (with time-travel debugging), and reasoning about state changes much clearer.

Store: Concept and Responsibilities

The **store** is a plain object that holds your entire application state tree. There is only one store in a Redux app. Its responsibilities include:

- **Holding State:** The store contains the current state tree, which can be accessed via **`store.getState()`**.
- **Dispatching Actions:** The store exposes a **`dispatch(action)`** method for sending actions into the system.
- **Registering Listeners:** Components or custom code can subscribe to state changes with **`store.subscribe(listener)`**, which returns an unsubscribe function.

- **Integrating Middleware:** Middleware wraps the dispatch method of the store to intercept or modify actions before they reach the reducers (for instance, to handle async logic or logging).

Example of creating a store with Redux Toolkit:

```
import { configureStore } from '@reduxjs/toolkit';
import rootReducer from './reducers';

const store = configureStore({
  reducer: rootReducer,
  // middleware: (getDefaultMiddleware) => [...getDefaultMiddleware(),
logger],
});

export default store;
```

Actions: Definition, Payloads, and Type Constants

Actions are plain objects that describe changes in the application. Every action must have a **type** property (usually a string constant) and may include an optional **payload** carrying additional data.

```
// actionTypes.ts
export const ADD_TODO = 'todos/add';
export const REMOVE_TODO = 'todos/remove';

// actions.ts
import { ADD_TODO, REMOVE_TODO } from './actionTypes';

export interface AddTodoAction {
  type: typeof ADD_TODO;
  payload: { id: string; text: string };
}

export interface RemoveTodoAction {
  type: typeof REMOVE_TODO;
  payload: { id: string };
}

export type TodoActions = AddTodoAction | RemoveTodoAction;

export const addTodo = (id: string, text: string): AddTodoAction => ({
  type: ADD_TODO,
  payload: { id, text },
});

export const removeTodo = (id: string): RemoveTodoAction => ({
  type: REMOVE_TODO,
  payload: { id },
});
```

The key points that we should remember are:

- **Type Constants** avoid typos and help tools like TypeScript infer correct action shapes.
- **Payload** carries the minimal data needed to update the state.
- **Action Creators** are helper functions that return action objects, centralizing creation logic and ensuring consistency.

Reducers: Pure Functions, Immutable State, and Composition

Reducers are pure functions that take the previous state and an action, then return the next state. They must follow two rules:

1. **Pure Functions:** Given the same inputs (state and action), a reducer must always return the same output, with no side effects (no API calls, random numbers, or mutations).
2. **Immutable Updates:** Instead of mutating the existing state object, reducers return a new object reflecting the updates. This enables change detection via shallow equality checks.

Example of a simple todo reducer:

```
import { ADD_TODO, REMOVE_TODO } from './actionTypes';
import { TodoActions } from './actions';

export interface Todo {
  id: string;
  text: string;
}

export type TodosState = Todo[];

const initialState: TodosState = [];

export function todosReducer(
  state = initialState,
  action: TodoActions
): TodosState {
  switch (action.type) {
    case ADD_TODO:
      return [...state, { id: action.payload.id, text: action.payload.text }];

    case REMOVE_TODO:
      return state.filter((todo) => todo.id !== action.payload.id);

    default:
      return state;
  }
}
```

Composition of Reducers

For large apps, you split your state into slices, each managed by its own reducer, and combine them:

```
import { combineReducers } from 'redux';
import { todosReducer } from './todosReducer';
import { userReducer } from './userReducer';

const rootReducer = combineReducers({
  todos: todosReducer,
  user: userReducer,
});

export default rootReducer;
```

This modular approach keeps each reducer focused on its own slice of state, improving maintainability and testability. With these fundamentals in place—the unidirectional data flow, a single store, clear action definitions, and pure, immutable reducers—you are ready to integrate Redux into your React Native projects. In the next section, we will walk through step-by-step setup and best practices.

Configuring Redux in React Native

Once you understand the core principles of Redux, the next step is integrating it into your React Native project. This involves installing the required packages, creating and configuring a store, wrapping your app with the Redux provider, and using the primary hooks (**useSelector** and **useDispatch**) to interact with state.

Installing Dependencies

Begin by installing the core Redux libraries and the React bindings. We recommend using Redux Toolkit (**@reduxjs/toolkit**), which bundles **redux** and common utilities into a single, batteries-included package:

```
npm install @reduxjs/toolkit react-redux
# or
yarn add @reduxjs/toolkit react-redux
```

- **@reduxjs/toolkit** includes **redux**, **redux-thunk** by default, plus helper functions like **createSlice** and **configureStore**.
- **react-redux** provides React-specific bindings, including the **<Provider>** component and custom hooks.

Creating the Store with configureStore

The **configureStore** of Redux Toolkit simplifies store setup by automatically combining reducers, adding sensible middleware (including **redux-thunk**), and enabling Redux DevTools integration:

```
// src/store/index.ts
import { configureStore } from '@reduxjs/toolkit';
import todosReducer from '../features/todos/todosSlice';
import userReducer from '../features/user/userSlice';

export const store = configureStore({
  reducer: {
    todos: todosReducer,
    user: userReducer,
  },
  // Optional: customize middleware or devTools settings here
});

// Infer the `RootState` and `AppDispatch` types from the store itself
export type RootState = ReturnType<typeof store.getState>;
export type AppDispatch = typeof store.dispatch;
```

- **reducer**: Accepts an object mapping slice names to slice reducers.
- **DevTools**: Enabled by default in development.
- **Middleware**: Includes **redux-thunk** out of the box; you can add additional middleware via the **middleware** option.

Wrapping Your App with <Provider>

To make the store available throughout your component tree, wrap your root component (usually in **App.tsx** or **index.js**) with React Redux's **<Provider>**:

```
// App.tsx
import React from 'react';
import { Provider } from 'react-redux';
import { store } from './src/store';
import MainNavigator from './src/navigation/MainNavigator';

export default function App() {
  return (
<Provider store={store}>
<MainNavigator />
</Provider>
  );
}
```

- The **<Provider>** component takes a single **store** prop and injects it into the context of React.
- Now any nested component can access the Redux state or dispatch actions.

Using the Primary Hooks: useSelector and useDispatch

With the store in place, you can read state and dispatch actions via the hooks of React Redux:

```
// src/features/todos/TodoList.tsx
import React, { useEffect } from 'react';
import { useSelector, useDispatch } from 'react-redux';
import { fetchTodos, selectAllTodos } from './todosSlice';

export function TodoList() {
  const dispatch = useDispatch();
  const todos = useSelector(selectAllTodos);
  const status = useSelector((state: RootState) => state.todos.status);

useEffect(() => {
    if (status === 'idle') {
      dispatch(fetchTodos());
    }
  }, [status, dispatch]);

  return (
    // render your todo items
  );
}
```

- **useDispatch** returns the **dispatch** function of the store, typed as **AppDispatch**.
- **useSelector** accepts a selector function **(state: RootState) => T** and returns the selected slice of state; it subscribes to the store and re-renders the component when the selected state changes.
- Create reusable selectors in your slice files (such as **selectAllTodos**) for better encapsulation and potential memoization with **reselect**.

When you implement "derived" selectors (for example, filtering only completed todos) as plain functions, that computation runs again whenever any part of the Redux state changes. In addition, operations like **filter()** create a **new array** on every call, which can trigger **unnecessary re-renders** in components that consume the selector—even if the todos themselves did not change.

```
// todosSlice.ts
import { createSelector } from "@reduxjs/toolkit";
import type { RootState } from "../store";

export const selectAllTodos = (state: RootState) =>state.todos.items;

// Memoized selector: recomputes only when selectAllTodos output changes
export const selectCompletedTodos = createSelector(
  [selectAllTodos],
  (todos) =>todos.filter((t) => t.completed)
);
```

By using **`createSelector`**, the selector output becomes **memoized**. If the input selector (**`selectAllTodos`**) returns the same reference (that is the todos list has not changed), **`createSelector`** returns the **previously computed result** instead of allocating a new array, thereby reducing wasted work and helping prevent re-renders when unrelated slices of state update. Note that **Redux Toolkit re-exports `createSelector`** (from **`reselect`**), so that you can typically import it from **`@reduxjs/toolkit`** without installing **`reselect`** separately.

With these steps completed, your React Native application is now wired up to Redux. In the next section, we will be exploring how to handle asynchronous logic and side effects using middleware such as Redux Thunk and Redux Saga.

Asynchronous Flow Management

In real-world applications, many state changes depend on asynchronous operations—fetching data from APIs, interacting with device storage, or performing complex computations off the main thread. Out of the box, Redux only handles synchronous updates: dispatching an action immediately invokes reducers. To handle side effects (asynchronous calls, logging, and so on) you introduce **middleware**, which can intercept dispatched actions and perform additional work before (or instead of) passing them on to reducers.

HTTP Calls and Side Effects

When you trigger an HTTP request from a component (for example, **`fetch('/api/items')`**), you must:

1. **Dispatch a "request started" action** so that the UI can show loading state.
2. **Perform the asynchronous operation** (HTTP, database, file I/O).
3. **Dispatch a "success" action** (with retrieved data) or a **"failure" action** (with error info).

Without middleware, you would usually perform the fetch inside the component and manually dispatch "started" and "success/failure" actions. That approach scatters async logic across UI layers, makes testing harder, and mixes side effects with presentation. Middleware centralizes side-effect logic in one place, keeps components focused on rendering, and makes async flows easier to test and reuse.

Error Handling Strategies (Real-World Baseline)

In production apps, error handling is part of the primary flow—not an afterthought. A common pattern is to store both **`loading`** and **`error`** in state, so that the UI can reliably communicate what happened:

- **On request start:** Set **`loading = true`**, clear **`error`**.
- **On success:** Set **`loading = false`**, store **`data`**.
- **On failure:** Set **`loading = false`**, store a user-safe **`error`** message (and optionally an error code/status for debugging).

This enables consistent UI behavior such as showing a spinner during the request, rendering an error banner/toast on failure, and providing a "Try again" action.

Request Cancellation (`AbortController`)

Network requests often outlive the UI that initiated them (navigation away, unmounts, rapid repeated searches). In those cases, cancellation prevents wasted work and avoids updating state for a screen that is no longer active. With **`fetch`**, the standard approach is **`AbortController`**:

- Create an **`AbortController`** when starting a request.
- Pass **`signal`** to **`fetch`**.
- Abort in cleanup (or when a new request supersedes the old one).
- Treat **`AbortError`** as a non-failure path (does not show an error UI for an intentional cancel).

In middleware, you can apply the same idea by keeping a controller per request (or per resource key) and aborting when appropriate, rather than leaving cancellation logic inside components.

Retry Logic for Transient Failures

Mobile networks are unreliable, so many apps implement retries for **transient** failures (timeouts, temporary connectivity drops, or 5xx server errors). A safe default retry strategy includes:

- **A small attempt limit** (for example, 2-3 retries).
- **Backoff** between attempts (wait longer after each failure).
- **Rules for when *not* to retry** (for example, 4xx validation/auth errors usually require user action, not retries).

Retries are best implemented in middleware, and hence, they are consistent across screens and easy to test. The UI can still participate by presenting a clear error message and offering a manual "Retry" button when automatic retries fail.

Why Middleware Remains the Recommended Structure

Middleware is the right place to manage the full lifecycle of side effects—**loading state, success/failure actions, cancellation, and retry policies**—because it provides a single, testable layer for async behavior. Components can then remain declarative: they dispatch intent ("load items"), render based on state (**`loading/data/error`**), and avoid embedding networking concerns directly in the UI layer.

Redux Thunk: Definition, Configuration, and Examples

Redux Thunk is the simplest and most common middleware for handling async logic. It allows action creators to return **functions** (thunks) instead of action objects. These functions receive **`dispatch`** and **`getState`** as arguments and can perform side effects before dispatching real actions.

Setup

Redux Toolkit includes Thunk middleware by default, so you rarely need to add it manually. In modern Redux codebases, the recommended approach for async logic is often **`createAsyncThunk`**, which generates a standard async action lifecycle—**`pending`** / **`fulfilled`** / **`rejected`**—and integrates cleanly with slices and TypeScript. This reduces boilerplate versus manually writing "request started / success / failure" actions while keeping async flows testable and consistent.

```
import { createAsyncThunk, createSlice } from "@reduxjs/toolkit";

type Item = { id: string; name: string };
```

```
export const fetchItems = createAsyncThunk<Item[]>(
  "items/fetchItems",
  async (_, { rejectWithValue, signal }) => {
    try {
      const res = await fetch("/api/items", { signal });
      if (!res.ok) return rejectWithValue(`HTTP ${res.status}`);
      return (await res.json()) as Item[];
    } catch (err: any) {
      // Abort is not a "real" error for UI purposes
     if (err?.name === "AbortError") return rejectWithValue("Request cancelled");
      return rejectWithValue(err?.message ?? "Unknown error");
    }
  }
);

type ItemsState = { data: Item[]; loading: boolean; error: string | null };

const initialState: ItemsState = { data: [], loading: false, error: null };

const itemsSlice = createSlice({
  name: "items",
  initialState,
  reducers: {},
  extraReducers: (builder) => {
    builder
.addCase(fetchItems.pending, (state) => {
state.loading = true;
state.error = null;
      })
.addCase(fetchItems.fulfilled, (state, action) => {
state.loading = false;
        state.data = action.payload;
      })
.addCase(fetchItems.rejected, (state, action) => {
state.loading = false;
state.error =
          (action.payload as string) ??
action.error.message ??
          "Request failed";
      });
  },
});

export const itemsReducer = itemsSlice.reducer;
```

`createAsyncThunk` uses **`AbortController`** via the provided **`signal`**, so you can cancel requests (like on unmount) by aborting the underlying request of Thunk in your calling code or middleware flow.

This configuration ensures that any action creator returning a function (a "thunk") is properly handled before reaching your reducers.

```
import { configureStore } from '@reduxjs/toolkit';
import thunk from 'redux-thunk';
import rootReducer from './reducers';
```

```
export const store = configureStore({
  reducer: rootReducer,
  middleware: (getDefault) => getDefault().concat(thunk),
});
```

What just happened?

- We imported **thunk** from **redux-thunk** and concatenated it onto the default middleware array.
- Now, when you dispatch a function instead of an object, Thunk middleware will call that function with **dispatch** and **getState**.

Creating a Thunk Action

Next, we will define a slice that manages our posts state, then write a **thunk** that performs an HTTP request and dispatches the appropriate actions based on the result:

```
// features/posts/postsSlice.ts
import { createSlice, PayloadAction } from '@reduxjs/toolkit';
import { AppDispatch, RootState } from '../../store';

interface Post { id: number; title: string; body: string; }
interface PostsState { items: Post[]; status: 'idle' | 'loading' | 'failed'; }

const initialState: PostsState = { items: [], status: 'idle' };

const postsSlice = createSlice({
  name: 'posts',
  initialState,
  reducers: {
    fetchStart(state) { state.status = 'loading'; },
fetchSuccess(state, action: PayloadAction<Post[]>) {
state.status = 'idle';
state.items = action.payload;
    },
    fetchFailure(state) { state.status = 'failed'; }
  }
});

export const { fetchStart, fetchSuccess, fetchFailure } = postsSlice.actions;
export default postsSlice.reducer;

// Thunk function
export const fetchPosts = () => async (dispatch: AppDispatch, getState: () => RootState)
=> {
  dispatch(fetchStart());
  try {
    const response = await fetch('https://jsonplaceholder.typicode.com/posts');
    const data: Post[] = await response.json();
    dispatch(fetchSuccess(data));
  } catch (error) {
    dispatch(fetchFailure());
  }
};
```

Why "mutating" state works here: In reducers created with Redux Toolkit (**`createSlice`**), you can write code that looks like it mutates state (like **`state.status = 'loading'`**). Redux Toolkit uses **`Immer`** under the hood to track these changes and produce a new immutable state object safely. This is different from traditional Redux reducers, where direct mutation would cause bugs and break update detection.

Key takeaways:

- The slice defines three reducers for loading status and saving fetched data.
- The **`fetchPosts thunk`** dispatches **`fetchStart()`** before the request, then either **`fetchSuccess(data)`** or **`fetchFailure()`** based on the outcome.
- By moving **`async`** logic into **`thunks`**, components remain clean and focus solely on UI.

Usage in Component

Finally, we trigger our **`thunk`** from a React component and render UI based on the state of the slice:

```
import React, { useEffect } from 'react';
import { useDispatch, useSelector } from 'react-redux';
import { fetchPosts } from './postsSlice';
import { RootState } from '../../store';

export function PostList() {
  const dispatch = useDispatch();
  const { items, status } = useSelector((state: RootState) => state.posts);

useEffect(() => {
    if (status === 'idle') dispatch(fetchPosts());
  }, [status, dispatch]);

  if (status === 'loading') return <LoadingIndicator />;
  if (status === 'failed')  return<ErrorMessage />;

  return (
<FlatList
      data={items}
      renderItem={({ item }) =><PostItem post={item} />}
      keyExtractor={(item) =>item.id.toString()}
    />
  );
}
```

How it works:

- On mount, the component checks if the posts slice is idle and dispatches **`fetchPosts()`**.
- While the request is in progress, we show a loading indicator; on failure, an error message; on success, we render the list.
- Separating data fetching into thunks keeps the component focused on rendering logic.

Redux Saga: Generators, Watchers, and Workers

Redux Saga uses ES6 generator functions to express side effects sequentially in a more declarative style. Sagas watch for specific actions and spawn "worker" sagas that perform the asynchronous work, and then dispatch new actions.

Setup

```
import createSagaMiddleware from 'redux-saga';
import { configureStore } from '@reduxjs/toolkit';
import rootReducer from './reducers';
import rootSaga from './sagas';

const sagaMiddleware = createSagaMiddleware();

export const store = configureStore({
  reducer: rootReducer,
  middleware: (getDefault) => getDefault().concat(sagaMiddleware),
});

sagaMiddleware.run(rootSaga);
```

Writing a Saga

```
// sagas/postsSaga.ts
import { call, put, takeLatest } from 'redux-saga/effects';
import { fetchStart, fetchSuccess, fetchFailure } from '../features/posts/
postsSlice';

function* fetchPostsWorker() {
  try {
    yield put(fetchStart());
    const response = yield call(fetch, 'https://jsonplaceholder.typicode.com/
posts');
    const data = yield response.json();
    yield put(fetchSuccess(data));
  } catch (error) {
    yield put(fetchFailure());
  }
}

export function* watchFetchPosts() {
  yield takeLatest('posts/fetchPostsRequest', fetchPostsWorker);
}

// sagas/index.ts
import { all } from 'redux-saga/effects';
import { watchFetchPosts } from './postsSaga';

export default function* rootSaga() {
  yield all([
watchFetchPosts(),
    // other watchers...
  ]);
}
```

Explanation:

- **`takeLatest`** watches for actions of type '**`posts/fetchPostsRequest`**' and runs **`fetchPostsWorker`**, cancelling any previous unfinished worker if a new action arrives.
- In the worker, call performs the HTTP request, and put dispatches actions—making the sequence of side effects explicit.
- All in **`rootSaga`** starts multiple watcher sagas in parallel.

Dispatching and Listening

- Components dispatch a simple action, like `{ type: 'posts/fetchPostsRequest' }`.
- The watcher saga (`takeLatest`) intercepts that action and runs the worker.
- The worker performs side effects (`call`, `put`) in sequence.

Quick Comparison: Thunk versus Saga

Feature	Redux Thunk	Redux Saga
Style	Function-based, inline async code	Generator-based, declarative effects (`yield` statements)
Readability	Familiar async/await syntax, but can get messy for complex flows	Clear separation of watchers/ workers; sequential flow control
Testability	Easy to test action creators by mocking dispatch	Easy to test generator functions step by step
Concurrency Control	Manual (e.g., track in-flight requests, cancel tokens)	Built-in via effects (`race`, `cancel`, `debounce`)
Learning Curve	Gentle—just JavaScript functions	Steeper—requires understanding generators and saga effects
Bundle Size	Small	Larger, adds saga runtime

Table 6.2: *Comparison between Thunk versus Saga*

Both middleware patterns are battle-tested and widely used. `Thunk` is great for straightforward `async` needs, and teams comfortable with plain JS. **Saga** excels when you need advanced flow control, cancellation, or coordination between multiple async tasks. Choose according to the complexity of your app and the familiarity of your team.

When to Use Redux Saga (And When Not To)

Redux Saga is a middleware for managing side effects using **generator functions**. It has a steeper learning curve (generators, effects, and orchestration patterns), so it is not the default choice for most React Native apps. In many cases, `createAsyncThunk` (or **RTK Query** for data fetching/caching) is simpler and more maintainable.

Use Redux Saga when you need fine-grained control over complex async orchestration, such as:

- **Complex async flows and race conditions:** Coordinating competing requests, "take latest" versus "take every," and canceling outdated work reliably.
- **Debouncing and throttling:** Search-as-you-type, rate-limiting actions, and smoothing bursts of events without pushing timing logic into components.
- **Background sync tasks:** Periodic refresh, offline/online synchronization strategies, and long-lived workflows that should outlast individual screens.
- **Coordinating multiple API calls:** Sequencing or parallelizing requests, handling dependencies between them, and implementing rollback/compensation logic when part of a workflow fails.

Prefer Thunk / RTK Query when:

- You mainly need straightforward request lifecycles (**loading/success/error**) and simple branching.

- Your async logic is mostly CRUD-style API calls with caching and invalidation needs (RTK Query is often the most ergonomic fit).
- You want to minimize conceptual overhead and keep the middleware surface area small.

Redux Testing Practices

Automated testing is a cornerstone of maintainable, production-ready Redux applications. By verifying that each piece of your state management logic works in isolation—and that they integrate correctly—you reduce the risk of subtle bugs slipping into complex user flows. In this section, we will establish a comprehensive strategy for testing Redux code, organized around three key pillars:

- **Unit-testing pure functions:** Reducers and action creators are inherently deterministic: given the same inputs, they always produce the same outputs. Unit tests for these building blocks are fast to run, easy to write, and provide immediate feedback on the correctness of your state transitions.
- **Component-level integration tests with a mocked store:** While unit tests cover individual functions, your UI components integrate Redux state and dispatch actions. By wrapping components in a `<Provider>` with a lightweight, mock store, you can verify that they render correctly based on given state and that user interactions dispatch the expected actions—without depending on network requests or a full store configuration.
- **Testing asynchronous flows:** Real-world apps often include complex side-effects—fetching data, debouncing input, or orchestrating multi-step processes. You need confidence that your Thunks and Sagas handle success, failure, and edge cases correctly. By mocking network calls and driving these middleware functions in isolation, you can assert the precise sequence of dispatched actions and ensure proper error handling and cancellation behavior.

Together, these testing layers form a safety net: unit tests catch logic errors early, integration tests validate your UI-store contract, and async tests guarantee that your side-effect orchestration behaves predictably under all conditions. In the following subsections, we shall dive into each pillar, providing patterns, code examples, and best practices to help you build a robust test suite for your Redux-powered React Native applications.

Testing Pure Reducers and Action Creators

Because reducers are pure functions—given the same inputs, they always return the same output—they are straightforward to test with unit tests. Likewise, action creators simply produce objects and can be validated with simple assertions.

```
// features/todos/todosSlice.ts (excerpt)
import { createSlice, PayloadAction } from '@reduxjs/toolkit';

export interface Todo { id: string; text: string; completed: boolean; }
export type TodosState = Todo[];

const initialState: TodosState = [];

const todosSlice = createSlice({
  name: 'todos',
  initialState,
  reducers: {
addTodo(state, action: PayloadAction<Todo>) {
state.push(action.payload);
    },
```

```
toggleTodo(state, action: PayloadAction<string>) {
      const todo = state.find((t) => t.id === action.payload);
      if (todo) todo.completed = !todo.completed;
    }
  }
});

export const { addTodo, toggleTodo } = todosSlice.actions;
export default todosSlice.reducer;

// __tests__/todosSlice.test.ts
import todosReducer, { addTodo, toggleTodo, Todo } from '../features/todos/
todosSlice';

describe('todos reducer', () => {
  const initialState: Todo[] = [];

it('should handle addTodo', () => {
    const newTodo: Todo = { id: '1', text: 'Write tests', completed: false };
    const nextState = todosReducer(initialState, addTodo(newTodo));
    expect(nextState).toEqual([newTodo]);
  });

it('should handle toggleTodo', () => {
    const state: Todo[] = [{ id: '1', text: 'Write tests', completed: false
}];
    const nextState = todosReducer(state, toggleTodo('1'));
    expect(nextState[0].completed).toBe(true);
  });
});
```

Tips:

- *Use descriptive test names matching your reducer and action names.*
- *Test both the happy path (expected use) and edge cases (unknown action types, missing payload).*

Expanding Reducer Tests: Edge Cases, Parameterized Tests, and Snapshots

Solid reducer tests should cover both the "happy path" and common edge cases. In real apps, reducers regularly receive empty collections, optional/null fields, and boundary inputs (including `0`, negative values, max limits). Testing these cases helps prevent regressions that only appear with real production data.

Edge Cases and Boundary Conditions

Include tests for scenarios such as:

- **Empty arrays** (such as "remove item" on an empty list should be a no-op).
- **Null/undefined values** for optional fields (ensure that reducers handle missing data predictably).
- **Boundary values** (like counters should not go below 0; pagination should stop at the end; duplicates should not be inserted).

```
import reducer, { addTodo, removeTodo } from "./todosSlice";

describe("todos reducer - edge cases", () => {
it("removeTodo is a no-op on an empty list", () => {
```

```
    const state = { items: [] as any[] };
    const next = reducer(state as any, removeTodo("missing-id"));
    expect(next.items).toHaveLength(0);
  });
});
```

Parameterized Tests with `test.each()`

When you want to validate the same behavior across multiple inputs, parameterized tests keep your suite concise and readable:

```
import reducer, { setFilter } from "./todosSlice";

describe("setFilter parameterized", () => {
test.each([
    ["all"],
    ["active"],
    ["completed"],
  ] as const)("sets filter to %s", (filter) => {
    const initial = { filter: "all", items: [] };
    const next = reducer(initial as any, setFilter(filter));
    expect(next.filter).toBe(filter);
  });
});
```

This pattern is especially useful for boundary and validation checks (for example, different error payloads, empty versus populated arrays, multiple status values).

Snapshot Testing for Complex State Shapes

For reducers that produce larger, nested state (especially when you add new fields over time), snapshots can catch unintended changes. Use them selectively—snapshots are most valuable when the state shape is complex and the test should alert you to unexpected structural changes.

```
import reducer, { fetchItems } from "./itemsSlice";

describe("items reducer snapshots", () => {
it("fulfilled state shape stays consistent", () => {
    const initial = { data: [], loading: false, error: null };
    const action = fetchItems.fulfilled([{ id: "1", name: "A" }], "req-1");
    const next = reducer(initial as any, action);

    expect(next).toMatchSnapshot();
  });
});
```

The **`createSlice`** of Redux Toolkit generates **action creators** and **action types** for you, so tests can import and dispatch the real actions (say **`addTodo()`**, **`removeTodo()`**) instead of hand-crafting action objects. This reduces duplication, keeps tests aligned with production code, and makes refactors safer since action payload types are enforced by TypeScript.

Mocking the Store for Component Tests

When testing React components that connect to Redux, you often do not want to spin up the real store or deal with network calls. Instead, mock a minimal store and wrap your component with **`<Provider>`**, passing in a custom store created with known state.

```
// __tests__/TodoList.test.tsx
import React from 'react';
import { render, screen, fireEvent } from '@testing-library/react-native';
import { Provider } from 'react-redux';
import configureStore from 'redux-mock-store';
import thunk from 'redux-thunk';
import TodoList from '../features/todos/TodoList';

const middlewares = [thunk];
const mockStore = configureStore(middlewares);

describe('<TodoList />', () => {
it('renders todos from store and dispatches toggle action', () => {
    const initialState = {
      todos: [{ id: '1', text: 'Test Redux', completed: false }]
    };
    const store = mockStore(initialState);

render(
<Provider store={store}>
<TodoList />
</Provider>
    );

expect(screen.getByText('Test Redux')).toBeTruthy();
    fireEvent.press(screen.getByText('Toggle')); // assuming button label
    const actions = store.getActions();
    expect(actions[0]).toEqual({ type: 'todos/toggleTodo', payload: '1' });
  });
});
```

Notes:

- **redux-mock-store** records dispatched actions without running reducers.
- You can assert that components render based on initial state and dispatch the correct actions on interactions.

Testing Thunks and Sagas

Testing thunks and sagas involves validating asynchronous state-management logic to ensure actions are dispatched correctly, side effects are handled as expected, and error or loading states are properly managed throughout the flow.

Testing Thunks

For **thunks**, you can create a fake dispatch and state, then call the **thunk** directly and assert on the sequence of dispatched actions. Use Jest mocks for any network calls.

```
// __tests__/fetchPostsThunk.test.ts
import { fetchPosts } from '../features/posts/postsSlice';
import * as slice from '../features/posts/postsSlice';

describe('fetchPosts thunk', () => {
it('dispatches start and success actions on successful fetch', async () => {
    const fakePosts = [{ id: 1, title: 'Hello', body: 'World' }];
```

```
global.fetch = jest.fn().mockResolvedValue({
      json: () => Promise.resolve(fakePosts)
    });

    const dispatch = jest.fn();
    const getState = jest.fn();

    await fetchPosts()(dispatch, getState, undefined);

    expect(dispatch).toHaveBeenNthCalledWith(1, slice.fetchStart());
    expect(dispatch).toHaveBeenNthCalledWith(2, slice.
fetchSuccess(fakePosts));
  });

it('dispatches failure action on fetch error', async () => {
global.fetch = jest.fn().mockRejectedValue(new Error('Network error'));

    const dispatch = jest.fn();
    const getState = jest.fn();

    await fetchPosts()(dispatch, getState, undefined);

    expect(dispatch).toHaveBeenLastCalledWith(slice.fetchFailure());
  });
});
```

Testing Sagas

Saga effects can be tested step-by-step by invoking the generator and checking yielded effects:

```
// __tests__/postsSaga.test.ts
import { runSaga } from 'redux-saga';
import * as api from '../api/posts';
import { fetchPostsWorker } from '../sagas/postsSaga';
import { fetchStart, fetchSuccess, fetchFailure } from '../features/posts/
postsSlice';

describe('fetchPostsWorker saga', () => {
it('dispatches success action if API call succeeds', async () => {
    const fakePosts = [{ id: 1, title: 'Saga', body: 'Test' }];
api.fetchPosts = jest.fn().mockResolvedValue(fakePosts);

    const dispatched: any[] = [];
    await runSaga(
      {
        dispatch: (action) =>dispatched.push(action)
      },
      fetchPostsWorker
).toPromise();

    expect(dispatched).toContainEqual(fetchStart());
    expect(dispatched).toContainEqual(fetchSuccess(fakePosts));
  });

it('dispatches failure action if API call fails', async () => {
api.fetchPosts = jest.fn().mockRejectedValue(new Error('Fail'));
```

```
    const dispatched: any[] = [];
    await runSaga(
      {
        dispatch: (action) =>dispatched.push(action)
      },
      fetchPostsWorker
).toPromise();

    expect(dispatched).toContainEqual(fetchStart());
    expect(dispatched).toContainEqual(fetchFailure());
  });
});
```

Best practices:

- Isolate side effects by mocking network or I/O functions.
- For sagas, use **runSaga** or step through the generator manually.
- Keep tests fast and deterministic by avoiding real network calls.

Hence, by covering these three areas—pure functions, component integration, and async flows—you will have a comprehensive suite of tests that safeguard your Redux logic and ensure confidence as your application evolves.

Context API as a Lightweight Alternative

For smaller applications or slices of state that do not warrant the full weight of Redux, the built-in Context API of React —especially when combined with **useReducer**—can provide a clean, dependency-free way to share global data. In this section, we shall explore when Context is the right choice, how to set it up, and patterns for maintaining reducer-style logic without external libraries.

When Context Makes More Sense than Redux

Although Redux excels in large, complex apps with extensive asynchronous flows and strict conventions, Context is often preferable when:

- **State domains are small and cohesive** (like theme, locale, authentication flag).
- **Logic is relatively simple**; you do not need elaborate middleware or advanced debugging tools.
- **You wish to avoid extra dependencies**, keeping your bundle size minimal.
- **You are fine with fewer constraints** on where and how you update state, trading off some predictability for simplicity.

Using Context in these scenarios leads to less boilerplate and faster setup, making it ideal for prototypes, medium-sized apps, or isolated features within a larger codebase.

Performance Caveat (Context)

When a Context **value changes**, React will re-render **all consumers** of that Context (and any components that read it), even if a given consumer only uses a small part of the value. In React Native, this can become a bottleneck for **frequently updating state** (such as form keystrokes, live search, and gesture/animation-driven updates).

Recommendations:

1. **Split contexts by update frequency and responsibility** (including **AuthContext**, **ThemeContext**, **FormStateContext**) so high-churn values do not force unrelated re-renders.
2. **Memoize consumer components** with **React.memo()** (and keep props stable) to reduce downstream re-render work.
3. **Stabilize the context value.** Wrap object values in **useMemo()** (and functions in **useCallback()**) so you do not create a new **{...}** object every render when nothing meaningful changes.

Creating Contexts (StateContext and DispatchContext)

A common pattern is to split your context into two: one for state values, and another for the dispatch function produced by **useReducer**. This separation prevents unnecessary re-renders when only dispatch changes.

```
// src/context/CounterContext.tsx
import React, { createContext, useReducer, ReactNode } from 'react';

interface CounterState {
  count: number;
}

type CounterAction = { type: 'increment' } | { type: 'decrement' };

const initialState: CounterState = { count: 0 };

function counterReducer(state: CounterState, action: CounterAction):
CounterState {
  switch (action.type) {
    case 'increment':
      return { count: state.count + 1 };
    case 'decrement':
      return { count: state.count - 1 };
    default:
      return state;
  }
}

// Create two contexts: one for state, one for dispatch
export const CounterStateContext = createContext<CounterState |
undefined>(undefined);
export const CounterDispatchContext = createContext<React.
Dispatch<CounterAction> | undefined>(undefined);

export function CounterProvider({ children }: { children: ReactNode }) {
  const [state, dispatch] = useReducer(counterReducer, initialState);

  return (
<CounterStateContext.Provider value={state}>
<CounterDispatchContext.Provider value={dispatch}>
        {children}
</CounterDispatchContext.Provider>
</CounterStateContext.Provider>
  );
}
```

Key points:

- **CounterStateContext** carries the current state.
- **CounterDispatchContext** carries the **dispatch** function.
- The provider wraps your app (or a subtree), initializing the reducer once.

Custom Hook with useContext

To simplify consumption, define a custom hook that abstracts away the two contexts and throws clear errors if used outside the provider:

```
// src/hooks/useCounter.ts
import { useContext } from 'react';
import { CounterStateContext, CounterDispatchContext } from '../context/
CounterContext';

export function useCounter() {
  const state = useContext(CounterStateContext);
  const dispatch = useContext(CounterDispatchContext);

  if (state === undefined || dispatch === undefined) {
    throw new Error('useCounter must be used within a CounterProvider');
  }

  return { state, dispatch };
}
```

Benefits:

- Consumers access **{ state, dispatch }** in a single call.
- You guard against misuse by throwing an error if the hook is invoked outside the provider.

Using useReducer Inside Context for Reducer-Style Logic

Because **useReducer** shares the same signature as Redux reducers, you can maintain a familiar pattern—pure reducer functions, action objects, and predictable updates—without adding any third-party libraries:

```
// src/components/CounterDisplay.tsx
import React from 'react';
import { useCounter } from '../hooks/useCounter';

export function CounterDisplay() {
  const { state, dispatch } = useCounter();

  return (
<View style={{ alignItems: 'center' }}>
<Text>Current Count: {state.count}</Text>
<Button title="+" onPress={() => dispatch({ type: 'increment' })} />
<Button title="-" onPress={() => dispatch({ type: 'decrement' })} />
</View>
  );
}
```

How it works:

- `dispatch({ type: 'increment' })` invokes your `counterReducer`, updating state immutably.
- Components re-render only when the slice of context they consume changes.
- You enjoy clear separation between state changes (reducers) and UI, just like Redux, but without external dependencies.

By following this pattern—splitting state and dispatch contexts, creating a custom hook, and using `useReducer`, you gain many Redux-like benefits with minimal setup, making Context API a compelling choice for smaller-scale state management.

Integration of Context and Redux

In larger applications, it is often advantageous to combine the strengths of both, Redux and the Context API rather than choosing one exclusively. By using Context for concerns that benefit from minimal boilerplate and Redux for domains requiring rigorous state logic and middleware support, you can keep your codebase lean, performant, and well organized.

Hybrid Uses (Context for Theming, Redux for Data)

Theming and Localization: Use Context to expose UI configuration such as color schemes, font sizes, or language strings. These values change infrequently and are consumed by deeply nested components; Context avoids prop drilling while introducing very little overhead.

```
// ThemeContext provides a palette and a toggleTheme() function
                              <ThemeProvider>
                              <Provider store={store}>
                              <App />
                              </Provider>
                              </ThemeProvider>
```

Authentication Status: You can store the raw auth token or permissions in Redux (for easy inspection, middleware, and persistence) while using Context to expose a simple `isAuthenticated` boolean, login/logout callbacks, or user profile info to UI components.

Feature Flags and A/B Testing: Context is ideal for passing down feature-flag configurations loaded once at startup, without coupling flag lookups to Redux actions and reducers.

By clearly delineating:

- **Context = light, UI-centric state**
- **Redux = complex, business-logic state;** you avoid overloading Redux with trivial concerns and keep Context from growing into unwieldy global stores.

Best Practices for Isolating Responsibilities

- **Keep Contexts Focused:**
  - Define one small context per concern (including `ThemeContext`, `LocaleContext`).
  - Avoid creating a "mega-context" that holds unrelated state—this reduces unnecessary re-renders when one value changes.
- **Segregate Providers:**
  - Nest your providers in a logical order: UI contexts (theme, i18n) at the top, then `<Provider>` of Redux, then feature-specific contexts.

   - This layering ensures that UI settings are available within Redux-connected components and that Redux state is isolated from UI-only concerns.
- **Encapsulate Mutation Logic:**
   - Context should expose only setter functions or dispatch-like callbacks, not the entire reducer internals.
   - Redux slices should encapsulate their actions and selectors; components call well-defined APIs instead of reaching into the store directly.
- **Minimize Cross-Dependencies:**
   - Avoid having Context providers dispatch Redux actions or vice versa in arbitrary places. Instead, compose them at the application root or within dedicated integration modules.
   - If a context action needs to trigger a Redux update, define a single coordination layer (say a custom hook) that imports both **`useContext`** and **`useDispatch`** and orchestrates the interaction.
- **Performance Considerations:**
   - Memoize context values (like via **`useMemo`**) so that consumers only re-render when truly relevant data changes.
   - In Redux, leverage selectors and **`React.memo`** to prevent unnecessary renders when unrelated slices update.

By following these guidelines, you will leverage Context and Redux where they shine, maintain a clear separation of concerns, and build an application architecture that scales gracefully as new features and complexity are added.

Best Practices for Global State Architecture

A well-designed global state architecture not only simplifies development but also enhances application performance and maintainability. The following are four key practices to follow when organizing and accessing your Redux or Context state.

Selectors and Memoization (`reselect`)

Use Selectors: Encapsulate state queries in reusable selector functions, rather than accessing state slices directly in your components. This centralizes the logic for deriving data and makes refactoring easier.

```
// features/todos/selectors.ts
import { createSelector } from 'reselect';
import { RootState } from '../../store';

const selectTodosState = (state: RootState) =>state.todos;

export const selectAllTodos = createSelector(
  selectTodosState,
  (todosState) => todosState.items
);

export const selectCompletedTodos = createSelector(
  selectTodosState,
  (todosState) =>todosState.items.filter((t) => t.completed)
);
```

- **Memoize Expensive Computations:** When deriving data—for example, filtering, sorting, or aggregating large lists; memoization prevents re-running the computation unless its inputs have changed. **reselect**'s **createSelector** provides this out of the box.

Avoiding Unnecessary Re-renders (React.memo, useCallback)

- **React.memo for Pure Components:** Wrap function components in **React.memo** so they only re-render when their props actually change.

```
const TodoItem = React.memo<{ todo: Todo }>(({ todo }) => {
  return <Text style={todo.completed ? styles.completed :
undefined}>{todo.text}</Text>;
});
```

- **useCallback for Handler Functions:** When passing callbacks down to memoized children, wrap them in **useCallback** to preserve referential identity across renders, preventing needless updates.

```
function TodoList() {
  const dispatch = useDispatch();
  const onToggle = useCallback(
    (id: string) => dispatch(toggleTodo(id)),
    [dispatch]
  );
  // …
  return items.map((todo) => (
<TodoItem key={todo.id} todo={todo} onToggle={onToggle} />
  ));
}
```

Separation of UI Logic and Data Logic

- **Keep Components Focused on Presentation:** UI components should consume data via props or hooks and dispatch intent through callbacks, but not contain data-fetching logic or business rules.
- **Extract Data Logic into Slices or Hooks:** All state mutations, side effects, and derived state should reside in Redux slices (or custom Context hooks). This separation aids testability and reusability.

```
// features/posts/postsSlice.ts – handles fetching and caching
// components/PostList.tsx – purely renders posts via selectors and dispatches thunks
```

File Naming and Organization

Feature Folders: Organize code by feature, grouping related slices, selectors, types, and tests together. For example:

```
src/
  features/
    todos/
      todosSlice.ts
      selectors.ts
      types.ts
      __tests__/
```

```
        todosSlice.test.ts
    posts/
      postsSlice.ts
      selectors.ts
      sagas.ts
      __tests__/
        postsSaga.test.ts
  store/
    index.ts
```

Consistent Naming Conventions

- Slice files: **`<feature>Slice.ts`**
- Selector files: **`selectors.ts`**
- Hook files: **`use<Feature>.ts`**
- Test files mirror the module name: **`todosSlice.test.ts`**

Thus, by applying these best practices—memoized selectors, render-optimizing patterns, clear separation of concerns, and logical file structure—you will create a scalable, performant, and maintainable global state architecture that stands the test of growing application complexity.

Final Considerations and Next Steps

As you wrap up your exploration of global state management in React Native, it is important to synthesize what you have learned and establish guidelines for future decision-making and continuous improvement. This section offers criteria to help you choose the right tool for your next project, highlights advanced libraries that extend the capabilities of Redux, and points you to resources for deepening your expertise.

Criteria for Deciding between Redux and Context in New Projects

- **Complexity of State Logic**
  - **Redux**: Opt for Redux when your app requires multiple independent domains of state (such as user data, caching layers, multi-step forms), complex asynchronous flows, or middleware for logging, analytics, or error handling.
  - **Context**: Choose Context when state domains are small, independent, and change infrequently (like theme selection, locale strings, simple authentication flags).
- **Team Familiarity and Onboarding**
  - **Redux**: Has a steeper learning curve—actions, reducers, middleware, and the Redux devtools ecosystem—but offers strong conventions that new team members can quickly adopt once trained.
  - **Context**: Leverages the native API of React and hooks, reducing onboarding friction for teams already comfortable with hooks.
- **Performance Requirements**
  - **Redux**: With memoized selectors and fine-grained slicing, you can minimize unnecessary re-renders even under heavy update loads.
  - **Context**: Simpler to set up, but large or frequently changing context values can trigger wide re-renders unless contexts are carefully partitioned.

- **Tooling and Debugging Needs**
  - **Redux**: Access to time-travel debugging, action replay, and middleware introspection makes it ideal for mission-critical applications.
  - **Context**: Lacks built-in devtools, but is lightweight and free of external dependencies.

Use these criteria as a quick decision matrix: if your project checks off more Redux boxes—complex logic, heavy async, rigorous debugging—Redux is the safer bet. Otherwise, Context delivers faster setup with less boilerplate.

Advanced Tools: Redux Toolkit and RTK Query

Even if you choose Redux, you do not have to write all boilerplate by hand. Two modern libraries streamline development:

- **Redux Toolkit:** Provides `configureStore`, `createSlice`, and `createAsyncThunk` to reduce boilerplate for store setup, action creators, and reducers. Built-in support for TypeScript, Immer-powered immutable updates, and DevTools integration makes it the de facto standard for new Redux projects.
- **RTK Query:** An opinionated data-fetching and caching solution built on top of Redux Toolkit. It automatically generates hooks for REST or GraphQL endpoints, handles caching, cache invalidation, polling, and error states, all with minimal code. RTK Query often eliminates the need to write manual thunks for standard API interactions.

Adopting these tools accelerates development, enforces best practices, and lets you focus on business logic, rather than boilerplate. By following these guidelines and leveraging the tools and resources above, you will be well equipped to design scalable, maintainable, and performant state management solutions for any React Native project.

Conclusion

In this chapter, we have journeyed from understanding the fundamental challenges of state management in React Native—prop drilling, scattered local state, and unpredictable side effects—to mastering two powerful solutions: Redux and the Context API. We started by exploring the unidirectional data flow of Redux, the single immutable store, and the clear contract between actions and pure reducers, then saw how middleware like Thunk and Saga cleanly handle asynchronous operations. We learned how to configure a robust store with Redux Toolkit, wire up our React Native app with `<Provider>`, and leverage `useSelector` and `useDispatch` to connect UI to state.

We then delved into testing, establishing strategies for unit-testing reducers and actions, mocking stores for component tests, and validating our async flows with thunks and sagas—ensuring every layer of our state logic is reliable and maintainable. Next, we introduced the Context API as a lightweight alternative: splitting state and dispatch into separate contexts, creating custom hooks with `useContext`, and using `useReducer` to emulate Redux-style logic without extra dependencies. Real-world applications often benefit from a hybrid approach—using Context for UI-centric concerns like theming or localization, while reserving Redux for complex data domains and middleware-driven workflows. We covered best practices for isolating responsibilities, organizing files by feature, writing memoized selectors with Reselect, and preventing unnecessary re-renders through `React.memo` and `useCallback`.

Finally, we provided criteria to guide your choice between Redux and Context: assess the complexity of your state logic, team familiarity, performance needs, and debugging requirements. We also highlighted advanced tools—Redux Toolkit and RTK Query—that further reduce boilerplate and streamline data fetching. With these patterns, tools, and best practices in hand, you are equipped to architect global state in any React Native project—balancing predictability, performance, and simplicity according to the unique needs of your app. As your application grows, revisit these techniques to ensure that your state layer remains organized, testable, and easy to evolve.

Coming up, we will shift our focus to connecting your app with the outside world. The next chapter dives into API integration, persistent data storage, and robust offline first patterns—so that your React Native experience remains seamless even when the network does not.

Questions

Before wrapping up your study of centralized state management with Redux and the Context API, it is valuable to pause and test your grasp of the key concepts, patterns, and best practices presented in this chapter. Reflecting on these questions will help you identify any gaps and reinforce your understanding of both approaches:

1. What are the core reasons for adopting centralized state management in complex React Native applications?
2. In broad terms, how do Redux and the Context API differ in their approach to solving these problems?
3. Describe the unidirectional data architecture of Redux—how does it enforce predictability?
4. What responsibilities does the Redux store have, and how does middleware augment its behavior?
5. Why do we use action type constants and action creators rather than dispatching plain objects inline?
6. What makes a reducer a pure function, and why is immutability crucial when writing reducers?
7. What challenges arise when handling HTTP calls and side effects in Redux without middleware?
8. How does Redux Thunk allow you to write asynchronous logic, and what does a basic thunk look like?
9. How do you unit-test pure reducers and action creators to guarantee correct state transitions?
10. What advantage does mocking the Redux store provide when testing React components?
11. Under which circumstances is the Context API (with **`useReducer`**) more appropriate than Redux?
12. What pattern splits state and dispatch into separate contexts, and why does it improve performance?
13. In what scenarios should you apply **`React.memo`** or **`useCallback`** to prevent unnecessary re-renders?
14. Why is it important to separate UI logic from data logic, and how can the file/folder structure reinforce this separation?
15. What criteria will you use to choose between Redux and Context in your next project?

Answering these questions will help you review the material of the entire chapter—from architectural principles to practical implementation and testing—ensuring that you are ready to apply Redux and Context API effectively in your React Native projects.

Key Terms

- **Centralized State Management:** A pattern where application state is held in a single, global store rather than scattered across individual components, ensuring a single source of truth and predictable data flow.
- **Store:** The object that holds the entire state tree in Redux. It provides methods to read the state (**`getState()`**), dispatch actions (**`dispatch()`**), and subscribe to changes (**`subscribe()`**).

- **Action:** A plain JavaScript object describing *what happened* in the app. Every action has a `type` property (usually a constant) and may include a `payload` carrying additional data.
- **Reducer:** A pure function that takes the previous state and an action, then returns a new state. Reducers must not mutate the existing state and should handle actions via immutable updates.
- **Unidirectional Data Flow:** The architectural principle in Redux where data follows a single cycle: dispatch an action → reducer processes it → store updates state → views re-render, making state changes predictable and traceable.
- **Middleware:** A layer that sits between dispatching an action and reaching the reducers, allowing you to intercept or augment actions—for example, to handle asynchronous logic (Redux Thunk) or orchestrate side effects (Redux Saga).
- **Redux Thunk:** A middleware that allows action creators to return functions (thunks) instead of plain objects. Thunks receive `dispatch` and `getState` and can perform asynchronous operations before dispatching real actions.
- **Redux Saga:** A middleware leveraging ES6 generator functions to handle side effects in a declarative style. Sagas watch for specific actions (watchers) and run worker functions to perform async tasks and dispatch results.
- **configureStore:** A helper from Redux Toolkit that simplifies store creation by combining reducers, adding default middleware (including Thunk), and enabling Redux DevTools out of the box.
- **Provider (`<Provider>`):** A React Redux component that makes the Redux store available to nested components via context mechanism of React.
- **useSelector:** A React Redux hook that extracts and subscribes to a specific slice of state from the Redux store, causing the component to re-render when that slice changes.
- **useDispatch:** A React Redux hook that returns the `dispatch` function of the store, allowing components to dispatch actions.
- **Context API:** The built-in feature of React for passing data through the component tree without prop drilling. By creating a context provider, you can share state or functions across deeply nested components.
- **createContext:** A React function to create a Context object, containing `Provider` and `Consumer` components for distributing values.
- **useContext:** A React hook to consume the nearest context value, avoiding the need to wrap components with `<Context.Consumer>`.
- **useReducer:** A React hook that manages state transitions via a reducer function, mirroring the reducer pattern of Redux but scoped to a specific component subtree when used within a Context provider.
- **Selector:** A function that extracts or derives a specific piece of state from the store. When memoized (say with Reselect), selectors prevent expensive recalculations unless their inputs change.
- **Memoization (Reselect):** A technique to cache the results of expensive selector computations, recomputing only when input state slices differ, thereby optimizing performance.
- **React.memo:** A higher-order component that prevents re-rendering of a functional component if its props remain unchanged, reducing unnecessary UI updates.
- **useCallback:** A React hook that memoizes callback functions, preserving their identity across renders and preventing child components from re-rendering when passed as props.

CHAPTER 7

API Integration, Data Storage, and Offline Synchronization

Introduction

The vast majority of mobile applications depend on external data to deliver value to users. In this chapter, you will learn how to integrate your app with REST and GraphQL APIs, mastering tools like Axios and Apollo Client to perform reliable and efficient requests. We will also cover how to handle errors and consistently indicate loading states. Next, we will further explore local storage options – from simple **`AsyncStorage`** to more complete solutions like SQLite and Realm – ensuring your app continues to function even without a connection. Finally, we shall introduce "offline-first" strategies and automatic synchronization mechanisms so that changes made while offline are reconciled as soon as the device reconnects, providing users with a smoother and more resilient experience.

Structure

In this chapter, we will cover the following topics:

- Introduction to API Integration
  - Difference between REST and GraphQL APIs
  - Data flow in Mobile Applications
  - Most Used Libraries: Axios and Apollo Client
- Consuming REST APIs with Axios
  - Organizing Endpoints and Services (Service/Repository pattern)
  - Interceptors for Authentication and Response Handling
  - Pagination, Filters, and Query Parameters
- Consuming GraphQL APIs with Apollo
  - Core Concepts: Queries, Mutations, and Subscriptions
  - Configuring Apollo Client in React Native
  - Apollo Hooks (`useQuery`, `useMutation`)
  - Cache Updates and Fetch Policies (`fetchPolicy`)

- Error Handling and Loading States
  - Patterns for Loading Spinners and Progress Indicators
  - Displaying Error Messages to the User
  - Automatic Retry and Exponential Backoff
  - Failure Logging for Diagnostics
- Local Data Storage
  - `AsyncStorage`: When to Use and Limitations
  - More Robust Databases: SQLite and Realm
  - Schema Modeling
  - Basic CRUD Operations
  - Organizing a Persistence Layer (Data Access Layer)
- "Offline First" Strategies
  - Principles of "Offline First"
  - In-memory Cache versus Persistent Cache
  - Responsive UI without Connectivity: Placeholders and Stale Data
  - Network State Detection (`NetInfo`)
- Data Synchronization on Reconnection
  - Pending Operations Queue (Write Queue)
  - Synchronization Conflicts and Resolution Strategies (Last-Write-Wins, Manual Merge)
  - Reconnection Events and Triggers for Automatic Sync
  - User Feedback on Synchronization Progress
- Testing and Best Practices
  - Unit Tests for API services (Mocking Axios/Apollo)
  - Integration Tests in Offline Scenarios
  - Monitoring: Performance and Availability Metrics
  - Pre-Deploy Review Checklist

Introduction to API Integration

When building mobile applications, one of the most critical capabilities is the ability to both retrieve and submit data to remote servers. API integration empowers your app to leverage existing services—whether that means fetching a product catalog, authenticating users, or synchronizing usage metrics. In this expanded introduction, we will dive into the core principles you need to design a network layer that is modular, reliable, and easy to maintain. You will learn how to structure your codebase for clear separation of concerns, handle versioning and authentication, and adopt patterns that scale as your application grows.

Difference between REST and GraphQL APIs

REST (Representational State Transfer)

- **Resource-Oriented**: Every endpoint corresponds to a resource (say `/users`, `/orders`).
- **HTTP Verbs**: CRUD operations map directly to **`GET`**, **`POST`**, **`PUT/PATCH`**, and **`DELETE`**.

- **Over-fetching and Under-fetching**: Clients may receive more or less data than they need, leading to extra network overhead or additional requests.
- **Statelessness**: Each request contains all the information the server needs to process it—servers do not store client context between calls.

```
// Example: REST request using Axios
import axios from 'axios';

constapi = axios.create({ baseURL: 'https://api.example.com/v1' });

// Fetch all users
async function fetchUsers() {
  try {
const response = await api.get('/users');
    return response.data;
  } catch (error) {
console.error('Failed to fetch users:', error);
    throw error;
  }
}
```

GraphQL

- **Single Endpoint**: All operations—queries, mutations, and subscriptions—are sent to one **/graphql** endpoint.
- **Client-Specified Queries**: Clients request exactly the fields they need, eliminating over-fetching and under-fetching.
- **Strong Typing and Schema**: The server exposes a self-documenting schema, enabling powerful developer tooling.
- **Real-time Support**: Built-in support for subscriptions allows for live updates.

```
// Example: GraphQL query with Apollo Client
import { ApolloClient, InMemoryCache, gql } from '@apollo/client';

const client = new ApolloClient({
uri: 'https://api.example.com/graphql',
  cache: new InMemoryCache(),
});

async function fetchUsersGraphQL() {
const{ data } = await client.query({
    query: gql`
      query GetUsers {
        users {
          id
          name
          email
profilePicture
        }
      }
    `,
  });
  return data.users;
}
```

Figure 7.1 summarizes the typical asynchronous data flow in a React Native app. A user interaction triggers an intent (an action) that is handled by an async layer (Thunk, RTK Query, or Saga). The app enters a loading state, performs the API call, and then routes the result through either response handling (normalize/validate/transform) on success or error handling (store an error message and optionally retry) on failure. Finally, state updates drive the UI re-render, and—when applicable—the flow also updates a cache (for example, cache of RTK Query or local persistence) to keep subsequent reads fast and consistent.

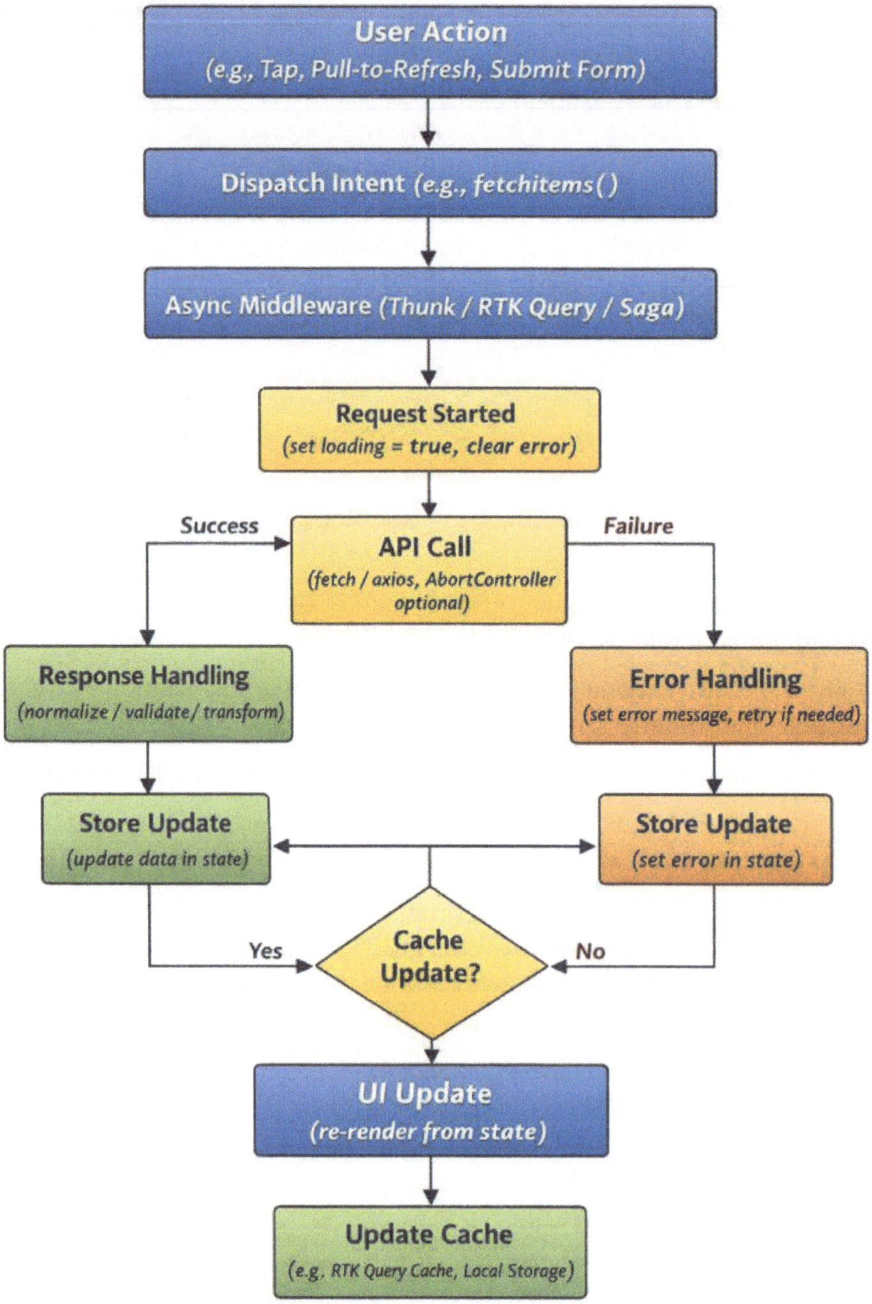

Figure 7.1: *End-to-End Async Request Cycle in React Native: User Action →Async Middleware → API Call → Success/Error Handling → Store/UI Update, with An Optional Cache Update Step*

Typical Data Flow in Mobile Applications

This section outlines how data typically moves through a mobile application, from user input and API interactions to local state updates, storage, and UI rendering.

1. **User Action Triggers:**
    - A screen mounts, or the user taps a button.
    - Your view model or controller dispatches an action.
2. **API Call Execution:**
    - A network service sends the request (REST or GraphQL).
    - Authentication headers, query parameters, and request bodies are assembled.
3. **Response Handling:**
    - **Success:** Data is parsed, normalized if needed, and stored in local state or cache.
    - **Error:** Errors are caught, translated into user-friendly messages, and optionally retried or escalated.
4. **UI Update:**
    - Loading indicators are shown while awaiting the network.
    - **On success:** UI components re-render with new data.
    - **On failure:** Error banners or dialogs inform the user.

By isolating this logic inside a dedicated **network layer**—often called "services" or "repositories"—you keep your UI components focused purely on rendering and user interaction.

Popular Libraries: Axios and Apollo Client

This section introduces two widely used libraries for handling data communication in mobile applications, with Axios commonly used for REST APIs and Apollo Client for GraphQL-based data management.

Axios

- **Lightweight and Flexible**: Easily configure base URLs, timeouts, and headers.
- **Interceptors**: Inject authentication tokens, handle global errors, and transform requests/responses in one place.

```
// axiosAuth.ts
import axios, { AxiosError, AxiosInstance, AxiosRequestConfig } from "axios";

/**
 * Assumptions:
 * - AuthService.getAccessToken(): string | null
 * - AuthService.getRefreshToken(): string | null
 * - AuthService.refreshTokens(refreshToken: string): Promise<{ accessToken:
string; refreshToken?: string }>
 * - AuthService.setTokens(tokens): void
 * - AuthService.logout(): void  (clears tokens + navigates to login)
 */

type RefreshResult = { accessToken: string; refreshToken?: string };

declare constAuthService: {
getAccessToken: () => string | null;
getRefreshToken: () => string | null;
refreshTokens: (refreshToken: string) => Promise<RefreshResult>;
setTokens: (tokens: RefreshResult) => void;
```

```
  logout: () => void;
};

// Create instance as usual
export constapi: AxiosInstance = axios.create({
baseURL: "https://example.com",
  timeout: 15000,
});

// ---- Token refresh queue state ----
let isRefreshing = false;
let refreshPromise: Promise<RefreshResult> | null = null;

type QueueItem = {
  resolve: (token: string) => void;
  reject: (err: unknown) => void;
};

let failedQueue: QueueItem[] = [];

function processQueue(err: unknown, token: string | null) {
failedQueue.forEach(({ resolve, reject }) => {
    if (err) reject(err);
    else if (token) resolve(token);
    else reject(new Error("No token after refresh"));
  });
failedQueue = [];
}

function shouldAttemptRefresh(error: AxiosError): boolean {
const status = error.response?.status;
  return status === 401;
}

// Optional: avoid refreshing for auth endpoints themselves
function isAuthEndpoint(config?: AxiosRequestConfig): boolean {
consturl = config?.url ?? "";
  return url.includes("/auth/login") || url.includes("/auth/refresh");
}

// ---- Request interceptor: attach access token ----
api.interceptors.request.use(
  (config) => {
const token = AuthService.getAccessToken();
    if (token) {
config.headers = config.headers ?? {};
config.headers.Authorization = `Bearer ${token}`;
    }
    return config;
  },
  (error) =>Promise.reject(error)
);

// ---- Response interceptor: refresh + retry on 401 ----
api.interceptors.response.use(
  (response) => response,
```

```
async (error: AxiosError) => {
constoriginalRequest = error.config as (AxiosRequestConfig&{ _retry?: boolean })
| undefined;

    // If we don't have a request config, we can't retry
    if (!originalRequest) return Promise.reject(error);

    // Only handle 401s, and avoid infinite loops
    if (!shouldAttemptRefresh(error) || originalRequest._retry) {
      return Promise.reject(error);
    }

    // Don't try to refresh if the 401 came from the refresh endpoint itself
    if (isAuthEndpoint(originalRequest)) {
AuthService.logout();
      return Promise.reject(error);
    }

constrefreshToken = AuthService.getRefreshToken();
    if (!refreshToken) {
      // No refresh token => cannot recover, go to login
AuthService.logout();
      return Promise.reject(error);
    }

originalRequest._retry = true;

    // If a refresh is already in progress, queue this request until refresh
completes
    if (isRefreshing) {
      return new Promise((resolve, reject) => {
failedQueue.push({
          resolve: (newAccessToken) => {
originalRequest.headers = originalRequest.headers ?? {};
originalRequest.headers.Authorization = `Bearer ${newAccessToken}`;
            resolve(api(originalRequest));
          },
          reject,
        });
      });
    }

    // Start a single refresh request
isRefreshing = true;
refreshPromise = AuthService.refreshTokens(refreshToken);

    try {
const tokens = await refreshPromise;
AuthService.setTokens(tokens);

      // Replay queued requests with the new access token
processQueue(null, tokens.accessToken);

      // Retry the original request
originalRequest.headers = originalRequest.headers ?? {};
originalRequest.headers.Authorization = `Bearer ${tokens.accessToken}`;
```

```
      return api(originalRequest);
    } catch (refreshErr) {
      // Refresh failed (e.g., refresh token expired/revoked) => logout only
now
processQueue(refreshErr, null);
AuthService.logout();
      return Promise.reject(refreshErr);
    } finally {
isRefreshing = false;
refreshPromise = null;
    }
  }
);
```

Apollo Client

- **Advanced Caching**: Normalizes and caches data by object identifiers, reducing redundant network calls.
- **React Integration**: Hooks like **`useQuery`** and **`useMutation`** make it simple to bind data fetching to component lifecycles.
- **Fetch Policies**: Choose between **`cache-first`**, **`network-only`**, **`cache-and-network`**, and others to balance freshness and performance.

```
import { useQuery, gql } from '@apollo/client';

const GET_POSTS = gql`
  query GetPosts {
    posts {
      id
      title
      author { id name }
    }
  }
`;

function PostsList() {
const{ data, loading, error, refetch } = useQuery(GET_POSTS, {
fetchPolicy: 'cache-and-network',
  });

  if (loading) return <Text>Loading posts...</Text>;
  if (error)   return <Text>Error loading posts.</Text>;

  return (
<FlatList
      data={data.posts}
keyExtractor={item => item.id}
renderItem={({ item }) => (
<Text>{item.title} by {item.author.name}</Text>
      )}
    />
  );
}
```

Expanding API Versioning (and Rate Limiting) for Mobile Clients

API versioning is not only a backend concern—mobile apps ship to app stores, update slowly and often run for months on older builds. A good versioning strategy therefore needs (1) a clear contract boundary, (2) a migration path, and (3) an explicit end-of-life policy.

Header-based Versioning (Media Type / Accept Header)

In addition to URL-based versioning (like /v1/items), many teams use header-based or media-type versioning so URLs remain stable while the contract evolves. A common pattern is embedding the version in the Accept header:

```
GET /items HTTP/1.1
Accept: application/vnd.api+json;version=1
Authorization: Bearer <token>
```

It is considered quite useful because of the following reasons:

- Keeps endpoints stable (no **`/v1/...`** proliferation).
- Allows gradual rollout and A/B testing by switching headers per client build.
- Encourages clients to be explicit about the contract they expect.

Its trade-offs are as follows:

- Harder to debug manually (version is not visible in the URL).
- Requires consistent tooling/documentation so clients send the correct header.

Mobile guidance: Centralize your API client so *every* request includes the correct **`Accept`** header, and log in the negotiated version in debug builds to reduce support time.

GraphQL "Versioning" (Schema Evolution Instead of Versioned Endpoints)

GraphQL typically avoids explicit version numbers in the API surface. Instead, it evolves the **schema** in a backwards-compatible way:

- **Add fields** instead of changing existing fields.
- **Avoid breaking changes** to types/field signatures whenever possible.
- Use the built-in **`@deprecated` directive** to steer clients away from old fields while keeping them available during migration.

Example:

```
type User {
  id: ID!
fullName: String! @deprecated(reason: "Use `name` instead.")
  name: String!
}
```

Mobile guidance:

- Deprecate first, remove later (with a sunset policy).

- Use analytics (or server logs) to measure usage of deprecated fields by app version.
- Coordinate removal with mobile release cycles (App Store lag).

When you truly need breaking changes: Some teams introduce a new root field (like `userV2`) or a parallel type (`UserV2`) and migrate queries incrementally—still avoiding "v2 endpoints."

Version Sunset Policies and Client Migration Guidance

Versioning without a **sunset policy** eventually creates an unmaintainable matrix of behaviors. A practical mobile-friendly policy includes:

- **Support window:** It is, for instance, "We support the last N versions or last X months."
- **Deprecation timeline:** It announces a deprecation date, then a hard sunset date.
- **Runtime signaling:** It communicates deprecation/sunset to clients via headers and structured errors.

Example headers:

```
Deprecation: true
Sunset: Wed, 30 Sep 2026 00:00:00 GMT
Link: <https://api.example.com/docs/migrations/v1-to-v2>;
rel="deprecation"
```

Client Migration Guidance (What to Document):

- What changed (fields, semantics, validation).
- How to migrate (code examples, mapping tables).
- Recommended minimum app version(s) to support the new API.
- A "known issues" section for older builds.

Mobile best practice: Implement a lightweight "server notice" capability (say, a response header or a config endpoint) to warn users on very old builds and encourage upgrades before hard cutoffs.

Handling API Rate Limiting in Mobile Apps

Mobile clients are especially prone to rate-limit issues (poor connectivity, retries, background resume bursts, multiple screens requesting the same data). Treat rate limiting as a first-class concern.

Common Signals

Servers often indicate rate limits via:

- **HTTP 429 Too Many Requests**
- A **Retry-After** header (seconds or a date)
- Rate limit metadata headers (varies by provider), such as:
  - **`X-RateLimit-Limit`**, **`X-RateLimit-Remaining`**, **`X-RateLimit-Reset`**

Recommended Client Behavior

1. **Respect `Retry-After`**
   - If you receive **`429`**, wait the suggested time before retrying.
2. **Use exponential backoff + jitter for transient failures**
   - Avoid synchronized retry storms by adding randomness ("jitter").

3. **Deduplicate requests**
    - Avoid triggering the same call from multiple screens simultaneously (cache or share in-flight requests).
4. **Prefer caching for read-heavy endpoints**
    - RTK Query (or similar) can reduce duplicate fetching and centralize caching/invalidation.
5. **Provide user-visible feedback when appropriate**
    - For actions (submit/payment), show "Try again in a moment."
    - For background refresh, silently delay rather than surfacing errors.

Simple Retry Policy (Conceptual)

- Retry `429` only after `Retry-After`.
- Retry network timeouts/5xx with backoff (2–3 attempts).
- Do not automatically retry 4xx validation/auth errors (requires user action).

Operational note: Rate limiting becomes much easier if your backend provides consistent headers and the API layer of your app centralizes retries/cancellation/deduplication.

Best Practices and Advanced Considerations

This section highlights key best practices and advanced considerations that help improve application scalability, maintainability, performance, and long-term development efficiency.

- **API Versioning**: Prefix your endpoints (like, `/v1/users`) to allow non-breaking changes and smooth migrations.
- **Authentication and Security**:
    - Use OAuth2 or JWT tokens with short lifespan and secure storage (Keychain or Keystore).
    - Refresh tokens automatically when expired.
- **Error Handling Strategies**:
    - Distinguish between network errors, client errors (4xx), and server errors (5xx).
    - Provide user feedback (toasts, dialogs) and retry logic for transient failures.
- **Offline-First and Synchronization**:
    - Queue writes operations locally and replays them when connectivity returns.
    - Resolve conflicts using timestamps, server-assigned IDs, or merging strategies.
- **Testing Your Network Layer**:
    - Mock HTTP clients (Axios mocks or `MockedProvider of Apollo`) to write deterministic unit tests.
    - Simulate network latency and failures to ensure graceful degradation.

With this comprehensive overview, you are equipped to choose the integration approach that best fits the needs of your project, design a clean and maintainable network layer, and implement robust error-handling and offline synchronization strategies. By adhering to these patterns and best practices, your mobile app will deliver a seamless, performant user experience—regardless of network conditions.

Consuming REST APIs with Axios

To begin consuming REST APIs in React Native—or any JavaScript application—it is best practice to create a custom **Axios** instance. This centralizes settings such as the **baseURL**, timeouts, common headers, and credentials:

```
// src/services/api.js
import axios from 'axios';

constapi = axios.create({
baseURL: 'https://api.example.com/v1',
  timeout: 10000,                    // 10 seconds timeout
  headers: { 'Content-Type': 'application/json' },
});

export default api;
```

With this instance, all of your service modules can import **api** and make requests without repeating the base URL or other configuration.

Organizing Endpoints into Services

It is a good idea to group related endpoints into "service" or "repository" modules. For example, a **userService** might look like this:

```
// src/services/userService.js
import api from './api';

export constUserService = {
asyncgetAll({ page = 1, limit = 20, filters = {} } = {}) {
constparams = { page, limit, ...filters };
const response = await api.get('/users', { params });
    return response.data;
  },

asyncgetById(id) {
const response = await api.get(`/users/${id}`);
    return response.data;
  },

async create(payload) {
const response = await api.post('/users', payload);
    return response.data;
  },

  // other methods: update, delete...
};
```

In this approach, your UI layer simply calls **UserService.getAll({ page, filters })** and does not need to know anything about URL paths or query-string serialization.

Handling Authentication, Errors, and Logging with Interceptors

To inject authentication tokens, handle global errors, or add logging for every request, use Axios interceptors. For example, a **request interceptor** can attach the access token, while a **response interceptor** can handle 401 errors:

```
// src/services/api.js (with interceptors)
import axios from 'axios';
import { getToken, handleLogout } from '../auth';

constapi = axios.create({
baseURL: 'https://api.example.com/v1',
  timeout: 10000,
  headers: { 'Content-Type': 'application/json' },
});

api.interceptors.request.use(config => {
const token = getToken();
  if (token) {
config.headers.Authorization = `Bearer ${token}`;
  }
  return config;
});

api.interceptors.response.use(
  response => response,
  error => {
    if (error.response?.status === 401) {
handleLogout(); // redirect to login, clear token, etc.
    }
    // You can throw a custom error or notify the user here
    return Promise.reject(error);
  }
);

export default api;
```

Pagination, Filters, and Query Parameters

When you need pagination, filtering, or other query parameters, Axios makes it simple: just pass a **params** object, and it will be serialized automatically:

```
// Example: pagination and filters
const{ data } = await api.get('/products', {
params: {
    page: 2,
    limit: 50,
    category: 'electronics',
    sort: 'price_desc',
  },
});
```

Axios also supports arrays and nested objects in query strings. For more complex serialization you can integrate libraries like **qs**. By organizing your code into a dedicated instance, clear service modules, and well-placed interceptors, your integration layer remains clean, reusable, and easy to evolve as new requirements emerge.

Consuming GraphQL APIs with Apollo

When your application requires more flexibility than a traditional REST API can offer, GraphQL emerges as an excellent alternative. With it, you can request exactly the fields you need, reduce multiple requests, and define mutations clearly. To streamline this flow in React Native, the reference library is Apollo Client, which provides everything from network configuration to an intelligent cache and support for real-time subscriptions.

Core Concepts

Core concepts in Apollo Client provide the foundation for working efficiently with GraphQL in React Native, including queries, mutations, caching, and subscriptions for managing application data in a structured and scalable way.

Queries

These are read operations in GraphQL. Unlike REST, where each endpoint returns a fixed resource, here you specify exactly which fields you want to receive:

```
query GetUser($id: ID!) {
user(id: $id) {
    id
    name
    email
profilePicture
  }
}
```

In this example, the client sends a single request and gets only **`id`**, **`name`**, **`email`**, and **`profilePicture`**, avoiding unnecessary data and speeding up loading.

Mutations

These are the equivalent of write operations (POST/PUT/DELETE in REST). You define the input structure and the server returns only the requested fields:

```
mutation CreatePost($input: CreatePostInput!) {
createPost(input: $input) {
    id
    title
createdAt
  }
}
```

This ensures consistency in the response payload and simplifies API versioning, since the response format is always specified by the client.

Subscriptions

Subscriptions allow you to receive notifications from the server as soon as specific events occur, using WebSockets under the hood. They are ideal for chat, real-time status updates, or any "push" feature:

```
subscription OnNewMessage {
messageAdded(roomId: "abc123") {
    id
    text
    author { name }
    timestamp
  }
}
```

Setting up Apollo Client

This section explains how to configure Apollo Client in a React Native application, including setting up the GraphQL endpoint, initializing the client, and connecting it to the app through an Apollo Provider.

Installation

```
npm install @apollo/client graphql
```

HTTP and WebSocket Links

To enable queries/mutations over HTTP and subscriptions over WebSocket, create two links and combine them using **split**:

```
// src/apollo/client.js
import { ApolloClient, InMemoryCache, HttpLink, split } from '@apollo/client';
import { getMainDefinition } from '@apollo/client/utilities';
import { WebSocketLink } from '@apollo/client/link/ws';

consthttpLink = new HttpLink({ uri: 'https://api.yourdomain.com/graphql' });
constwsLink   = new WebSocketLink({
uri: 'wss://api.yourdomain.com/graphql',
  options: { reconnect: true }
});

constsplitLink = split(
({ query }) => {
const definition = getMainDefinition(query);
    return (
definition.kind === 'OperationDefinition' &&
definition.operation === 'subscription'
    );
  },
wsLink,
httpLink
);

export const client = new ApolloClient({
  link: splitLink,
  cache: new InMemoryCache(),
});
```

ApolloProvider

Wrap your component tree, so that any part of the UI can use the client transparently:

```
// App.js
import { ApolloProvider } from '@apollo/client';
import { client } from './src/apollo/client';
import MainNavigator from './src/navigation';

export default function App() {
  return (
<ApolloProvider client={client}>
```

```
        <MainNavigator />
        </ApolloProvider>
          );
        }
```

Apollo Hooks

useQuery

Returns **{ data, loading, error }**. You can render a spinner while **loading === true**, show an error message if **error** is set, and display the result in **data** when available.

```
import { useQuery, gql } from '@apollo/client';

const GET_POSTS = gql`
  query GetPosts {
    posts {
      id
      title
      author { name }
    }
  }
`;

function PostsList() {
const{ data, loading, error } = useQuery(GET_POSTS);
  if (loading) return <Text>Loading posts...</Text>;
  if (error)   return <Text>Error: {error.message}</Text>;

  return data.posts.map(post => (
<Text key={post.id}>
      {post.title} – {post.author.name}
</Text>
  ));
}
```

useMutation

Provides an execution function (**mutate**) and a state object (**{ loading, error, data }**). After calling **mutate({ variables: { … } })**, you can await the response and update the UI or cache.

```
import { useMutation, gql } from '@apollo/client';

const CREATE_COMMENT = gql`
  mutation CreateComment($input: CommentInput!) {
createComment(input: $input) { id text }
  }
`;

function CommentForm({ postId }) {
const [createComment, { loading, error }] = useMutation(CREATE_COMMENT);

consthandleSubmit = async (text) => {
    await createComment({ variables: { input: { postId, text } } });
    // optional: refetchQueries or cache.modify to refresh the list
```

```
    };

    // render form UI...
  }
```

Cache Policies and Fetch Policies

The **InMemoryCache** stores query results to speed up subsequent accesses. You choose the fetch strategy with **fetchPolicy**:

- **cache-first** (default): It uses cache if available, otherwise makes a network request—great for mostly static data.
- **network-only**: It always fetches fresh data, ignoring cache—useful when immediate consistency is critical.
- **cache-and-network**: It returns cached data immediately and, in parallel, fetches from the network to update once available.

```
const{ data } = useQuery(GET_POSTS, {
fetchPolicy: 'cache-and-network',
});
```

After a mutation, you can manually update the cache using the **update** callback:

```
useMutation(CREATE_COMMENT, {
update(cache, { data: { createComment } }) {
cache.modify({
      fields: {
comments(existing = []) {
constnewRef = cache.writeFragment({
          data: createComment,
          fragment: gql`
            fragment NewComment on Comment { id text }
          `
        });
        return [...existing, newRef];
      }
    }
  });
}
});
```

With this comprehensive setup—from defining HTTP and WebSocket links to using hooks and managing cache—your React Native GraphQL application will enjoy maximum performance, flexibility, and developer experience.

Error Handling and Loading States

When your application makes network calls, communicating to the user that a process is underway and gracefully handling possible failures is just as important as the business logic itself. Clear feedback builds trust, prevents frustration, and significantly improves user experience. In the following paragraph, we detail the best practices and patterns for progress indicators, error displays, automatic retries with exponential backoff, and failure logging.

Patterns for Spinners and Progress Indicators

Not every loading scenario is the same. On a full-screen view, a centered spinner makes it clear that nothing can be interacted with until completion. In long lists or specific sections, more discreet spinners or skeleton screens cause less frustration.

- **Full-screen Spinner**: Ideal for critical actions like login or form submission. Use an **`ActivityIndicator`** inside a **`View`** that covers the entire screen, paired with a brief message such as "Submitting data...".
- **Inline List Spinner**: For infinite scrolling, use the **`ListFooterComponent`** of a **`FlatList`** or **`SectionList`**, so the user can keep scrolling while the next page loads.
- **Skeleton Screens**: Gray-shaded placeholders of the final UI—cards, lines of text—that disappear once data arrives. They remain visually stable and prevent layout shifts.

```
// Simple skeleton component
function ItemSkeleton() {
  return (
<View style={styles.skeletonCard}>
<View style={styles.skeletonAvatar} />
<View style={styles.skeletonLineShort} />
<View style={styles.skeletonLineLong} />
</View>
  );
}
```

In all cases, maintain a minimum display time (say, 300 ms) to avoid flicker when the request returns almost instantly.

Displaying Error Messages to Users

Differentiate between infrastructure failures (timeout, no connection) and business errors (form validation, access denied). Communication should be contextual:

- **Network Errors**: Show an alert modal or persistent toast with "Check your connection and try again." If your app supports offline mode, direct the user to previously downloaded content.
- **Validation Errors**: When the API returns a 400 status with details in **`error.response.data`**, highlight the related form field and display the specific message below the input.
- **Visual Fallbacks**: For non-critical content, instead of a plain error message, display a friendly illustration with a "Retry" button.

```
// Example toast with react-native-toast-message
import Toast from 'react-native-toast-message';

function showError(message) {
Toast.show({ type: 'error', text1: 'An error occurred', text2: message });
}
```

Keep messaging consistent in tone and style: use short messages, suggest an action (such as "**`Try again`**"), and avoid technical jargon in the interface.

Automatic Retry and Exponential Backoff

Temporary server failures can be mitigated with automatic retries. However, firing multiple requests back-to-back can worsen the issue. Exponential backoff addresses this by progressively increasing the delay between attempts, for example: 1 s, 2 s, 4 s, 8 s...

- **With Jitter**: Add a small random variation (± 50%) to avoid the "thundering herd" effect where many clients retry simultaneously.

  Example with `axios-retry`:

```
import axiosRetry from 'axios-retry';

axiosRetry(api, {
  retries: 3,
retryDelay: retryCount => {
const base = Math.pow(2, retryCount) * 1000;
const jitter = Math.random() * 1000;
    return base + jitter;
  },
retryCondition: error => !error.response || error.response.status>= 500,
});
```

- **Limit Attempts**: Cap the number of retries (say 3) to avoid trapping the user in a failure loop.
- **Idempotent Only**: Use automatic retry only for idempotent operations (**`GET`**, **`HEAD`**). For POST or other state-changing endpoints, prefer queuing the operation locally and syncing once the app regains connectivity.

Failure Logging for Diagnostics

Capturing and centralizing errors is vital for continuous improvement. Log not only the stack trace but also contextual data—user identity, endpoint, payload, and breadcrumb events.

Monitoring Tools: Services like Sentry, Bugsnag, and Rollbar provide SDKs to capture both native and JavaScript exceptions.

```
import * as Sentry from '@sentry/react-native';
Sentry.init({ dsn: 'https://your-dsn@sentry.io/xyz' });
```

Interceptor Integration:

```
api.interceptors.response.use(
        response => response,
        error => {
      Sentry.captureException(error, {
            extra: {
              url: error.config.url,
              method: error.config.method,
              status: error.response?.status,
            }
          });
          return Promise.reject(error);
        }
      );
```

- **Severity Levels**: Categorize logs as info, warning, or error to filter and prioritize investigations.
- **Breadcrumbs**: Record lightweight events before an error (like "**`user clicked X`**", "**`api.get('/users') started`**") to reconstruct execution flow.

In addition to third-party services, you may send logs to your own backend or store them locally (and synchronize later) for offline analysis. Having real-failure data visibility accelerates bug fixes and prevents regressions. By implementing these patterns, your app will not only inform users clearly during loading and error states but also handle failures resiliently and diagnose issues efficiently—resulting in a more robust and reliable product.

Local Data Storage

Keeping information on the device is necessary to provide a responsive experience and allow users to continue using the app even when offline. Let us explore three main approaches—simple AsyncStorage, and more structured databases like SQLite and Realm—and see how to organize a clean persistence layer (Data Access Layer).

AsyncStorage: When to Use and Its Limitations

`AsyncStorage` is an asynchronous key-value store provided by React Native. It is ideal for storing settings, authentication tokens, or small caches, but not suited for relational or large-volume data.

```
import AsyncStorage from '@react-native-async-storage/async-storage';

// Save a token
await AsyncStorage.setItem('@auth_token', token);

// Retrieve the token
const token = await AsyncStorage.getItem('@auth_token');

// Remove a value
await AsyncStorage.removeItem('@auth_token');
```

Key limitations:

- No schema or data validation.
- All access is serialized, which may cause slowdowns under heavy load.
- No support for complex queries or transactions.
- Recommended only for small data (< 6 MB on Android; iOS limits vary).

Full-Fledged Databases: SQLite and Realm

For persisting collections of objects, running queries, or using transactions, choose a full local database.

SQLite

Schema Definition

It define your tables in SQL:

```
CREATE TABLE IF NOT EXISTS users (
  id INTEGER PRIMARY KEY AUTOINCREMENT,
  name TEXT NOT NULL,
  email TEXT UNIQUE NOT NULL,
created_at TEXT DEFAULT CURRENT_TIMESTAMP
);
```

Setup and CRUD

Using **`expo-sqlite`** or **`react-native-sqlite-storage`**:

```
import * as SQLite from 'expo-sqlite';
constdb = SQLite.openDatabase('app.db');
```

```
// Create table
db.transaction(tx =>
tx.executeSql(
    `CREATE TABLE IF NOT EXISTS users (
       id INTEGER PRIMARY KEY AUTOINCREMENT,
       name TEXT, email TEXT
     )`
  )
);

// Insert
db.transaction(tx =>
tx.executeSql(
    'INSERT INTO users (name, email) VALUES (?, ?)',
    ['Alice', 'alice@example.com']
  )
);

// Query
db.transaction(tx =>
tx.executeSql(
    'SELECT * FROM users WHERE id = ?',
    [1],
    (_, { rows }) => console.log(rows._array)
  )
);

// Update
db.transaction(tx =>
tx.executeSql(
    'UPDATE users SET name = ? WHERE id = ?',
    ['Alice Smith', 1]
  )
);

// Delete
db.transaction(tx =>
tx.executeSql('DELETE FROM users WHERE id = ?', [1])
);
```

Realm

Realm offers an object-oriented database with optional sync capabilities.

Schema Definition

Create model classes:

```
import Realm from 'realm';

class User extends Realm.Object {}
User.schema = {
  name: 'User',
primaryKey: 'id',
  properties: {
```

```
    id: 'int',
    name: 'string',
    email: 'string',
    posts: { type: 'list', objectType: 'Post' }, // 1:N relation
  },
};

class Post extends Realm.Object {}
Post.schema = {
  name: 'Post',
primaryKey: 'id',
  properties: {
    id: 'int',
    title: 'string',
    content: 'string',
  },
};

const realm = new Realm({ schema: [User, Post] });
```

Basic CRUD Operations

```
// Create
realm.write(() => {
realm.create('User', { id: 1, name: 'Bob', email: 'bob@ex.com' });
});

// Read
const users = realm.objects('User').filtered('name CONTAINS[c] $0', 'bo');

// Update
realm.write(() => {
const user = realm.objectForPrimaryKey('User', 1);
  user.name = 'Robert';
});

// Delete
realm.write(() => {
const user = realm.objectForPrimaryKey('User', 1);
realm.delete(user);
});
```

Realm automatically manages change notifications, simplifying reactive UI updates.

Organizing the Data Access Layer

To keep your code clean and decoupled, create a dedicated layer that exposes clear data-access methods, hiding implementation details:

```
// src/data/userRepository.js
import api from '../services/api';
import { realm } from '../database/realm';

export constUserRepository = {
  // Local source of truth
getAllLocal: () =>realm.objects('User').sorted('name'),
```

```
saveLocal: users => {
realm.write(() => {
users.forEach(u =>
realm.create('User', u, Realm.UpdateMode.Modified)
      );
    });
  },

  // Remote source of truth
fetchRemote: async () => {
const response = await api.get('/users');
    return response.data;
  },

  // Simple sync
  sync: async () => {
constremoteUsers = await UserRepository.fetchRemote();
UserRepository.saveLocal(remoteUsers);
    return remoteUsers;
  },
};
```

In your UI, simply call **`UserRepository.sync()`** or **`UserRepository.getAllLocal()`**, without worrying whether the underlying storage is **`AsyncStorage`**, SQLite, or Realm. This abstraction makes unit testing, technology swaps, and long-term maintenance much easier.

"Offline-First" Strategies

Adopting an **Offline-First** approach means designing your application to work fully even when there is no connectivity, treating the online state as a bonus rather than an assumption. This ensures that users can view, interact with, and modify data at any time, and that all changes are synchronized transparently once the network is restored.

Principles of Offline-First

- **Local Source of Truth:** Keep a copy of essential data on the device—in memory or in a local database. The app always reads and writes against this layer, without depending on the network.
- **Reactive Synchronization:** When connectivity returns, the app automatically detects pending changes and sends them to the server, while also refreshing its local cache with the latest data of the server.
- **Failure Resilience:** Every write operation is queued locally. If synchronization fails, the app retries (using its retry strategy) without losing any user data.
- **Consistent Experience:** The user should not notice connection drops—appropriate placeholders and "stale" data keep the workflow seamless.

In-Memory Cache versus Persistent Cache

In-Memory Cache

- **Pros**: Ultra-fast access, ideal for transient session data.
- **Cons**: Cleared whenever the app closes or the device restarts.

Persistent Cache

- **Pros**: Survives app restarts, perfect for settings, critical data, and history.
- **Cons**: Higher read/write latency and storage limits.

Hybrid Strategy

1. Load initial data from a local database (Realm/SQLite).
2. Keep loaded collections in memory for fast UI operations.
3. Also write every change back to the database to guarantee persistence.

Responsive UI When Offline: Placeholders and Stale Data

- **Skeletons/Placeholders:** These show gray blocks that mimic the final UI when no data is yet loaded.
- **Cached Data:** If a local snapshot of a list or form exists, display it immediately. Add a subtle hint—like "**`Data as of [timestamp]`**" or an offline icon—to indicate that content may be out of date.
- **Visual Feedback:** When the user performs a network-dependent action (say sending a comment), show a spinner or a "Sent Locally" badge until synchronization completes.

```
{!isConnected&& (
<View style={styles.offlineBanner}>
<Text style={styles.offlineText}>
      Offline – changes will sync when you're back online
</Text>
</View>
)}

<FlatList
  data={localPosts}
ListEmptyComponent={<PostSkeleton count={3} />}
/>
```

Detecting Network Status with NetInfo

Use the **`@react-native-community/netinfo`** package to listen for connectivity changes:

```
npm install @react-native-community/netinfo
```

Creating the network status:

```
// src/hooks/useNetworkStatus.js
import { useState, useEffect } from 'react';
import NetInfo from '@react-native-community/netinfo';

export function useNetworkStatus() {
const [isConnected, setIsConnected] = useState(true);

useEffect(() => {
const unsubscribe = NetInfo.addEventListener(state => {
setIsConnected(Boolean(state.isConnected&&state.isInternetReachable));
    });
```

```
    // Initial check
NetInfo.fetch().then(state => {
setIsConnected(Boolean(state.isConnected&&state.isInternetReachable));
    });
    return unsubscribe;
  }, []);

  return isConnected;
}
```

Top-level component implementation:

```
// In your top-level component
import { useNetworkStatus } from '../hooks/useNetworkStatus';

function AppContainer() {
constisConnected = useNetworkStatus();

  return (
<>
{!isConnected&& (
<View style={styles.offlineBanner}>
<Text style={styles.offlineText}>You are offline</Text>
</View>
      )}
      {/* rest of your UI */}
</>
  );
}
```

With this hook, your service layer can:

- **Abort** network calls if **`isConnected === false`**.
- **Queue** write operations for later synchronization.
- **Notify** users with banners or toasts about connection status.

Implementing these practices ensures your app delivers a robust, fluid, and reliable experience—even in environments with unstable connectivity—fully embracing the Offline-First philosophy.

Data Synchronization on Reconnection

When the app regains Internet access after being offline, you need to reconcile all locally performed operations with the server safely and efficiently. In this section, we will detail how to implement—and organize—automatic synchronization of pending data, handle potential conflicts, and keep the user informed about progress.

Pending Operations Queue (Write Queue)

Instead of executing write requests (**`POST`**, **`PUT`**, **`DELETE`**) immediately while offline, enqueue each action in a **write queue**. Each queue entry should include:

- **Operation type** (create, update, delete)
- **Target resource or endpoint**
- **Payload data**
- **Timestamp or unique identifier**

For example, when creating a comment offline:

```
// enqueue.js
import AsyncStorage from '@react-native-async-storage/async-storage';

export async function enqueueOperation(op) {
const queue = JSON.parse(await AsyncStorage.getItem('@write_queue')) || [];
queue.push({ ...op, id: Date.now() });
  await AsyncStorage.setItem('@write_queue', JSON.stringify(queue));
}

// When adding a comment offline
enqueueOperation({
  type: 'create',
  resource: 'comments',
  payload: { postId: 42, text: 'Great post!' }
});
```

Conflict Resolution Strategies

When applying queued operations after reconnecting, conflicts may occur if the same resource was modified both locally and on the server. Two common approaches:

- **Last-Write-Wins:** The operation with the most recent timestamp overwrites the current state. Simple, but risks discarding important server-side changes.

Manual Merge

Before applying the action, fetch the latest resource from the server, compare fields, and merge:

```
// Pseudocode for manual merge
const server = await api.get(`/posts/${local.id}`);
const merged = { ...server.data, ...local.changes };
await api.put(`/posts/${local.id}`, merged);
```

For complex conflicts, present a diff view, so that the user can choose which version to keep.

Reconnection Events and Automatic Sync Triggers

Using the network-status hook (say, via **`NetInfo`**), trigger synchronization as soon as **`isConnected`** switches from **`false`** to **`true`**:

```
import NetInfo from '@react-native-community/netinfo';
import { processQueue } from './syncService';

NetInfo.addEventListener(state => {
  if (state.isConnected) {
processQueue(); // Reads and executes each pending operation
  }
});
```

In **`processQueue`**, iterate through each queue item, perform its corresponding request, and—on success—remove it from the queue. If a request fails, reschedule it according to your retry policy.

User Feedback on Sync Progress

To build user confidence, surface synchronization status:

- **Discrete banner**: "Syncing 3 of 10 operations..."
- **Toast or snackbar**: "All changes synchronized successfully."
- **Sync icon indicator**: Change color or show an animated spinner while pending.

```
function SyncStatus({ pendingCount }) {
  if (pendingCount === 0) return null;
  return (
<View style={styles.syncBanner}>
<Text>Syncing {pendingCount} items…</Text>
<ActivityIndicator size="small" />
</View>
  );
}
```

Update **pendingCount** in real time as **processQueue** advances, and hide the component once the queue is empty. By implementing this synchronization logic—with write queues, conflict-resolution strategies, reconnection triggers, and visual feedback—you ensure your users enjoy a continuous and reliable experience, even in environments with intermittent connectivity.

Testing and Best Practices

Ensuring the quality and reliability of your integration, storage, and synchronization modules requires a suite of tests and a set of patterns that keep your code healthy over time. The following are our top recommendations.

Unit Tests for API Services

This section focuses on how unit tests can be used to verify API service logic in isolation, ensuring that requests, responses, and error handling behave correctly before integration with the wider application.

Mocking Axios

Use libraries like **jest.mock('axios')** to intercept HTTP calls and simulate responses in a controlled way. This lets you test mapping logic and error handling without relying on a real server.

```
// __tests__/userService.test.js
import axios from 'axios';
import { UserService } from '../services/userService';

jest.mock('axios');

describe('UserService', () => {
it('should return a list of users', async () => {
constfakeUsers = [{ id: 1, name: 'Alice' }];
axios.get.mockResolvedValue({ data: fakeUsers });

const result = await UserService.getAll();
    expect(axios.get).toHaveBeenCalledWith('/users', expect.any(Object));
    expect(result).toEqual(fakeUsers);
  });
```

```
it('should throw on network failure', async () => {
axios.get.mockRejectedValue(new Error('Network Error'));
    await expect(UserService.getAll()).rejects.toThrow('Network Error');
  });
});
```

Mocking Apollo Client

Use the **MockedProvider** from **@apollo/client/testing** to supply fake responses to queries and mutations in React components:

```
import { render, waitFor } from '@testing-library/react-native';
import { MockedProvider } from '@apollo/client/testing';
import { GET_POSTS } from '../graphql/queries';
import PostsList from '../components/PostsList';

const mocks = [
  {
    request: { query: GET_POSTS },
    result: { data: { posts: [{ id: '1', title: 'Hello' }] } },
  },
];

it('renders posts after query', async () => {
const{ getByText } = render(
<MockedProvider mocks={mocks} addTypename={false}>
<PostsList />
</MockedProvider>
  );
  await waitFor(() => expect(getByText('Hello')).toBeTruthy());
});
```

Integration Tests in an Offline Environment

This section introduces integration of testing strategies for offline scenarios, helping verify that the application continues to behave reliably when network connectivity is limited or unavailable.

Simulating Disconnection

In Jest, spy on **NetInfo.fetch()** and **NetInfo.addEventListener()** to return **isConnected: false**, ensuring that your caching and enqueue flows run as expected.

Clearing and Restoring Storage:

Before each test, clear AsyncStorage, SQLite, or Realm to guarantee a predictable state:

```
beforeEach(async () => {
  await AsyncStorage.clear();
  // Also recreate or reset SQLite/Realm databases as needed
});
```

Typical scenarios to test:

- Reading data already saved locally when offline
- Enqueuing write operations and verifying they are persisted
- Upon "reconnection," processing the queue and clearing pending items

Monitoring: Performance and Availability Metrics

- **API Response Time:** Measure average latency and percentiles (P95/P99) using Axios interceptors or Apollo Links that record timestamps for each call.
- **Error Rate:** Count requests returning status ≥ 400 and group by endpoint. Configure alerts if rates exceed a threshold (say, 5% errors within one hour).
- **Local Resource Usage:** Monitor database size (SQLite/Realm) and write-queue length. If the queue grows too large, warn the user or trigger non-critical cleanup.

Tools: Integrate with Sentry Performance, Firebase Crashlytics, or DataDog for real-time dashboards.

Pre-Deployment Review Checklist

- **Test Coverage:**
  - Unit: ≥ 80% coverage in service and utility layers
  - Integration: key online and offline flows
- **Bundle Analysis:**
  - Check final APK/IPA size
  - Remove unused dependencies
- **Database Verification:**
  - Test migration scripts locally
  - Document backup and rollback procedures
- **Documentation:**
  - Update README/wiki with setup instructions, environment variables, and endpoints
  - Provide a tutorial for running offline tests
- **Performance:**
  - Manual testing on slow networks (using throttling tools)
  - Measure first load and sync times
- **Security:**
  - Validate token storage (such as use `SecureStore` if needed)
  - Enforce security headers on all HTTP requests

By following these testing strategies and best practices, you will reduce regressions, boost the reliability of your final product, and simplify ongoing maintenance.

Conclusion

In this chapter, we have seen how to connect your React Native app to the outside world—first by integrating with REST and GraphQL APIs using Axios and Apollo Client, then by handling the full lifecycle of network requests: from configuring instances and organizing service layers to dealing with errors, loading states, and automatic retries. Armed with interceptors and fetch policies, you can now build network flows that are both predictable and resilient.

We also explored how to persist data locally—choosing the right tool for each need, whether it is the lightweight key-value store of `AsyncStorage` or more powerful, relational/object-oriented solutions like SQLite and Realm. By structuring a clear Data Access Layer, you ensure that your UI remains agnostic of storage details, promoting maintainability and testability.

Finally, we dove into "offline-first" strategies and synchronization. With write queues, network-status detection (`NetInfo`), and well-defined conflict-resolution policies, your app can queue operations while offline and reconcile them seamlessly once connectivity returns. Coupled with visual feedback on sync progress and robust logging, these patterns guarantee a smooth, reliable user experience even under unstable network conditions.

Together, these techniques enable you to deliver React Native applications that are fast, dependable, and user-centric—whether the user is on a blazing-fast 5G connection or entirely offline. The next chapter will bring the main concepts about Accessing Native Device Features.

Self-Assessment Questions

Before consolidating what has been learned throughout this chapter, it is helpful to reflect on the key concepts of API integration, local storage, and offline synchronization. The questions below will help you review best practices, identify any remaining doubts, and reinforce your understanding of the architecture and patterns presented:

1. What are the main differences between consuming a REST API with Axios and a GraphQL API with Apollo Client?
2. How would you configure Axios interceptors to handle authentication tokens and global error handling?
3. In which scenarios would you choose to use **`AsyncStorage`** instead of SQLite or Realm, and what are the limitations of each approach?
4. Explain the "Offline First" strategy workflow: how does the application enqueue operations, detect reconnections, and synchronize pending data?
5. What are the benefits of implementing automatic retry with exponential backoff, and why should this technique be applied only to idempotent operations?
6. How would you organize a Data Access Layer to abstract local storage details and keep UI code decoupled?
7. In what ways would you provide user feedback during data synchronization, and how would you ensure visibility into failures or conflicts?
8. Which unit and integration tests would you write to validate the correct implementation of network calls and offline flows?

Answering these questions will help you assess whether the core concepts are clear and highlight any areas that may require further study before moving on to the next chapters.

Key Terms

- **REST API:** Architectural style for designing networked applications where resources are accessed via standard HTTP methods (`GET`, `POST`, `PUT`, `DELETE`) and identified by URLs.
- **GraphQL:** Query language and runtime for APIs that allows clients to request exactly the data they need in a single request, reducing over- and under-fetching.
- **Axios:** Promise-based HTTP client for JavaScript, often used in React Native to perform REST requests; supports features like interceptors, automatic JSON parsing, and request cancellation.

- **Apollo Client:** Comprehensive GraphQL client that handles queries, mutations, subscriptions, caching, and state management for React and React Native applications.
- **AsyncStorage:** Simple, asynchronous, unencrypted, persistent, key-value storage system built into React Native; suitable for small items such as tokens and user preferences.
- **SQLite:** Lightweight, file-based relational database engine that can be embedded in mobile apps via libraries like `expo-sqlite` or `react-native-sqlite-storage`; supports SQL queries, indexing, and transactions.
- **Realm:** Object-oriented mobile database with live objects, change notifications, and optional cloud sync; simplifies CRUD operations by working directly with JavaScript objects.
- **Data Access Layer (DAL):** Abstraction layer that encapsulates all interactions with local storage or remote APIs, keeping UI components decoupled from implementation details.
- **Offline First:** Design paradigm that treats the local device as the primary data source, enabling full app functionality without network, with automatic synchronization when connectivity is restored.
- **Write Queue:** In-memory or persistent queue of pending write operations (create, update, delete) that are executed later when the app regains network connectivity.
- **Exponential Backoff:** Retry strategy that increases the delay between successive retry attempts exponentially (such as 1s, 2s, 4s) to avoid overwhelming the server and handle transient failures gracefully.
- **NetInfo:** React Native community module (`@react-native-community/netinfo`) used to detect and subscribe to changes in network connectivity status.
- **Fetch Policy:** Apollo Client configuration (`cache-first`, `network-only`, `cache-and-network`, and so on) that determines how queries interact with the cache and the network.
- **Interceptor:** Axios feature that allows executing custom logic before a request is sent or after a response is received, commonly used for adding authentication headers or centralized error handling.
- **ActivityIndicator:** Core React Native component for displaying a loading spinner; used to indicate ongoing network requests or other background tasks.
- **Skeleton Screen:** Lightweight placeholder UI that mimics the structure of real content, displayed while data is loading to improve perceived performance and avoid layout shifts.

These key terms summarize some of the essential concepts covered in this chapter, helping reinforce the understanding of the ecosystem and development practices of React Native.

CHAPTER 8
Accessing Native Device Features

Introduction

Diving into native mobile device features is vital for building applications that truly stand out in the market. By integrating the camera, GPS, and notification systems directly into your JavaScript code, you can offer users richer, more engaging experiences, such as high-quality photo and video capture, real-time location tracking, and contextual alerts even when the app is running in the background. Native libraries written in Java or Kotlin for Android and Swift or Objective-C for iOS communicate directly with the APIs of each platform, ensuring lower latency and greater stability in critical operations such as image recognition or coordinate monitoring. Moreover, many of these libraries handle complex details—such as thread management, battery-consumption optimization, and adaptation to different OS versions—freeing JavaScript developers to focus on business logic.

To streamline this process, the React Native community offers mature libraries for camera access (like `` `react-native-camera` `` or `` `expo-camera` ``), geolocation (`` `react-native-geolocation-service` ``), and push notifications (via Firebase Cloud Messaging or Apple Push Notification service), which provide friendly JavaScript abstractions that mask much of the complexity involved in configuring permissions and handling app-state events. When you need functionality beyond the existing solutions, you can create custom native modules to expose specific APIs. Finally, choosing between the React Native CLI—which gives you full control over native dependencies and build configurations in Xcode; Android Studio; and the Expo Managed Workflow—which offers rapid setup and many pre-configured integrations but may require "`ejecting`" later for unsupported modules, is crucial to align your development approach, with the scope of your project for long-term flexibility.

Structure

In this chapter, we will cover the following topics:

- Camera Access
    - Popular Libraries
    - Initial Setup
    - Usage Example
    - Advanced Customizations

- Geolocation
    - Recommended Libraries
    - Permission and Manifest Configurations
    - Practical Example
    - Error Handling and Limitations
- Push Notifications
    - Local versus Remote Notifications
    - Firebase Cloud Messaging
    - Apple Push Notification Service
    - Receiving and Displaying Notifications
    - Deep Linking and Custom Actions
- Permission Management
    - Runtime Permissions
    - Requesting and Revoking on iOS
    - Supporting Libraries
    - UX Best Practices for Permissions
- Security and Privacy
    - Handling Sensitive Data
    - Responsible Use of Location and Media
    - Privacy Policies and Regulatory Compliance
- Testing and Debugging
    - Testing on Simulator/Emulator versus Real Device
    - Log Inspection Tools
    - Mocking Native APIs
- Custom Native Modules and Bridging
- Background Processing and Task Scheduling
- Future Trends and Challenges

Camera Access

Integrating image and video capture capabilities is almost mandatory in modern apps, whether for posting photos, making video calls, or enabling scanning and recognition features. In React Native, two common approaches are **`expo-camera`** (Expo ecosystem) and camera libraries used in **bare React Native** projects.

Beginner-friendly recommendation: If you are using **Expo**, start with **`expo-camera`**. It requires **no manual native configuration** in typical Expo workflows and fits the "**`config-first`**" approach, making it the fastest path to a working camera feature. You would generally switch away from **`expo-camera`** only when you need functionality that Expo does not support for your use case, or when you are moving to a workflow that includes direct native customization (for example, using a development build with custom native code or transitioning to a bare project).

For teams using the **React Native CLI (bare workflow)**, camera integration usually involves native dependencies and platform setup, but it provides maximum flexibility for advanced requirements. In the following sections, we will cover each option, how to set it up, and how to extend basic camera functionality (capture, permissions, and common UX patterns), along with guidance on when to choose one approach over the other.

Popular Libraries

To streamline access to advanced camera functionalities in your React Native applications, the community maintains several well-established libraries that simplify integration with native APIs. These solutions abstract complex processes—such as permission configuration, native callback handling, and app-state management—allowing you to add photo and video capture, barcode scanning, and even face analysis features with just a few commands. The following are two of the most popular and widely adopted options for handling camera functionality in React Native projects.

React-Native-Camera

This library has been widely used in the RN community for years. It exposes APIs for preview, photo and video capture, barcode scanning, and face detection. To install it in a project created with React Native CLI, run:

```
yarn add react-native-camera
# or
npm install react-native-camera --save
```

After installation, auto-linking should automatically add the native module to your project. Be sure, however, to verify that your **AndroidManifest.xml** (camera and audio permissions) and **Info.plist** (**NSCameraUsageDescription**, **NSMicrophoneUsageDescription**) are correctly configured.

Expo-Camera

If your app runs in an Expo-managed workflow, configuration is even simpler. Just add the package and grant permissions in your **app.json**:

```
expo install expo-camera
```

Then ensure your **app.json** contains something like:

```
{
  "expo": {
    "ios": {
      "infoPlist": {
        "NSCameraUsageDescription": "This app uses the camera to take photos."
      }
    },
    "android": {
      "permissions": ["CAMERA", "RECORD_AUDIO"]
    }
  }
}
```

Expo handles the rest—no need to touch Xcode or Android Studio.

Initial Setup

To get your React Native project ready for camera functionality, you will need to configure native permissions and rebuild the app so that the newly installed module is properly linked. Whether you are working on Android or iOS, this initial setup ensures that your app can request and handle camera and microphone access at runtime. Follow these steps to update your manifest and plist files, then rebuild your application using the React Native CLI:

React Native CLI

After running **`yarn add react-native-camera`**, open your project in Android Studio and:

In **`android/app/src/main/AndroidManifest.xml`**, add:

```
<uses-permission android:name="android.permission.CAMERA" />
<uses-permission android:name="android.permission.RECORD_AUDIO"/>
```

In iOS, open the workspace in Xcode and include in **`Info.plist`**:

```
<key>NSCameraUsageDescription</key>
<string>I need camera access to capture photos and videos.</string>
<key>NSMicrophoneUsageDescription</key>
<string>I need microphone access to record audio in videos.</string>
```

Rebuild the app:

```
npx react-native run-android
npx react-native run-ios
```

Expo Managed Workflow

In Expo, after **`expo install expo-camera`**, your component only needs to import and request permission at runtime:

```
import { Camera } from 'expo-camera';
import { useEffect, useState } from 'react';
import { Text, View } from 'react-native';

export default function CameraSetup() {
const [hasPermission, setHasPermission] = useState(null);

useEffect(() => {
    (async () => {
const{ status } = await Camera.requestPermissionsAsync();
setHasPermission(status === 'granted');
    })();
  }, []);

  if (hasPermission === null) return <View />;
  if (hasPermission === false) return <Text>Permission denied</Text>;

  return <View style={{ flex: 1 }} />;
}
```

This handles the permission prompt and user feedback if access is blocked. Here we have a common situation that may cause a mistake: always handle all three permission states (null/loading, denied, granted). Users can deny permissions permanently, so provide a way to guide them to Settings to re-enable manually.

Usage Example

Once configured, you can render a live preview and overlay buttons for capturing photos or videos:

```
import React, { useRef, useState } from 'react';
import { View, TouchableOpacity, Text } from 'react-native';
import { Camera } from 'expo-camera';

export default function CameraExample() {
constcameraRef = useRef(null);
const [type, setType] = useState(Camera.Constants.Type.back);

consttakePicture = async () => {
    if (cameraRef.current) {
const photo = await cameraRef.current.takePictureAsync({ quality: 0.7 });
console.log('Photo captured:', photo.uri);
    }
  };

  return (
<View style={{ flex: 1 }}>
<Camera ref={cameraRef} style={{ flex: 1 }} type={type}>
<View style={{ flex: 1, justifyContent: 'flex-end' }}>
<TouchableOpacity
            style={{ alignSelf: 'center', marginBottom: 20 }}
onPress={takePicture}
>
<Text style={{ fontSize: 18, color: 'white' }}>Snap</Text>
</TouchableOpacity>
</View>
</Camera>
</View>
  );
}
```

In this **expo-camera** example, the preview fills the screen, and the button calls **takePictureAsync()**. For video, instead use **recordAsync()** and **stopRecording()** .

Advanced Customizations

For finer control, you can adjust flash, zoom, and focus:

```
<Camera
  ref={cameraRef}
  style={{ flex: 1 }}
flashMode={Camera.Constants.FlashMode.auto}     // auto, on, off
  zoom={0.5}                                       // from 0 to 1
focusDepth={0.3}                                  // from 0 to 1
>
  {/* ... */}
</Camera>
```

To push further—applying a real-time color filter, for example—you can integrate **gl-react-native** and wrap **<Camera>** in a custom shader:

```
import { Node, Shaders, GLSL } from 'gl-react';

constshaders = Shaders.create({
```

```
  Sepia: {
    frag: GLSL`
      precision highp float;
      varying vec2 uv;
      uniform sampler2D camera;
      void main () {
        vec4 c = texture2D(camera, uv);
        float r = c.r * .393 + c.g * .769 + c.b * .189;
        float g = c.r * .349 + c.g * .686 + c.b * .168;
        float b = c.r * .272 + c.g * .534 + c.b * .131;
gl_FragColor = vec4(r, g, b, 1.0);
      }
    `
  }
});

export default function SepiaCamera() {
  return (
<Node shader={shaders.Sepia} uniforms={{ camera: /* reference to Camera texture */ }}
/>
  );
}
```

This pattern opens the door to augmented reality overlays, QR-code scanning with custom graphics and much more. Mastering the camera in React Native is the first step toward delivering memorable visual experiences, from a simple selfie to professional-grade computer vision applications.

Finally, it is crucial to handle device compatibility and performance considerations as you integrate these features. Always check for and gracefully handle cases where the camera hardware or permissions are unavailable, and fall back to alternative workflows (such as uploading existing images). Profile the memory of your app and CPU usage—especially when applying real-time filters or video processing—and optimize by limiting frame rates or using lower-resolution streams when appropriate. Incorporate thorough testing on a variety of physical devices to catch hardware-specific quirks, and leverage continuous integration to run automated camera-related tests. By combining robust error handling, performance tuning, and comprehensive testing, you will ensure that your camera functionality feels fluid, reliable, and polished across the full spectrum of Android and iOS devices.

Geolocation

Geolocation is an essential feature for mobile apps that need contextual information based on the position of a user, whether to show nearby places, plot routes or tailor content according to location. In React Native, you can choose specialized libraries that offer higher fidelity and robustness, or fall back on the standard browser Geolocation API when necessary, although the latter will not work if the app is completely in the background.

Recommended Libraries

For projects requiring precision and background operation support, **react-native-geolocation-service** is the preferred choice. It overcomes several limitations of built-in module of React Native—especially on modern Android devices—by handling battery optimizations and granular permission flows more effectively. If you do not need that level of complexity, you can use the Geolocation API of the browser via `navigator.geolocation` as a fallback, keeping in mind it will not function when the app is entirely backgrounded.

Permission and Manifest Configuration

On **Android**, open **android/app/src/main/AndroidManifest.xml** and declare the location permissions:

```
<uses-permission android:name="android.permission.ACCESS_FINE_LOCATION" />
<uses-permission android:name="android.permission.ACCESS_COARSE_LOCATION" />
```

To enable optional background tracking, add:

```
<uses-permission android:name="android.permission.ACCESS_BACKGROUND_LOCATION" />
```

On **iOS**, edit your **Info.plist** in Xcode, including keys that inform the user why you need location:

```
<key>NSLocationWhenInUseUsageDescription</key>
<string>This app uses your location to suggest nearby places.</string>
<key>NSLocationAlwaysAndWhenInUseUsageDescription</key>
<string>Allows tracking your position even when the app is in the background.</
string>
```

Practical Example

The following snippet uses **react-native-geolocation-service** to obtain the current position and monitor continuous updates:

```
import Geolocation from 'react-native-geolocation-service';
import { useEffect } from 'react';
import { PermissionsAndroid, Platform } from 'react-native';

async function requestLocationPermission() {
  if (Platform.OS === 'android') {
const granted = await PermissionsAndroid.request(
PermissionsAndroid.PERMISSIONS.ACCESS_FINE_LOCATION,
      {
        title: 'Location Permission',
        message: 'We need your location to provide this feature.',
      }
    );
    return granted === PermissionsAndroid.RESULTS.GRANTED;
  }
  return true;
}

export default function useLocation(onUpdate) {
useEffect(() => {
    let watchId = null;

requestLocationPermission().then(granted => {
      if (!granted) return;

   // Get a single position
Geolocation.getCurrentPosition(
pos =>onUpdate(pos.coords),
        err =>console.warn('Error getting position:', err),
{ enableHighAccuracy: true, timeout: 15000, maximumAge: 10000 }
      );

      // Watch for continuous updates
```

```
watchId = Geolocation.watchPosition(
pos =>onUpdate(pos.coords),
        err =>console.warn('Error in tracking:', err),
{ enableHighAccuracy: true, distanceFilter: 10, interval: 5000, fastestInterval: 2000
}
      );
    });

    return () => {
      if (watchId !== null) {
Geolocation.clearWatch(watchId);
      }
    };
  }, []);
}
```

Error Handling and Limitations

Even with the correct setup, the device may lack a GPS signal (for instance, when traveling through tunnels) or be in battery-saving mode. In these cases, the error callback returns codes you must interpret: **`TIMEOUT`**, **`PERMISSION_DENIED`**, or **`POSITION_UNAVAILABLE`**. It is advisable to display a friendly message suggesting the user enable GPS or grant permission, and to fall back on the browser Geolocation API when persistent errors occur. Finally, always clear watches and listeners when unmounting components to avoid memory leaks and unnecessary battery drain.

Finally, it is important to plan for real-world variability and optimize for both reliability and efficiency. Always detect and gracefully handle scenarios where location services are unavailable—whether due to disabled GPS, background restrictions, or low-power modes—and provide clear feedback or alternative workflows (for example, manual address input or coarse IP-based location). Profile the impact of your app on battery and performance, particularly when using high-accuracy, frequent updates—and adjust parameters such as **`distanceFilter`** and **`interval`** to strike the right balance.

Incorporate comprehensive testing on a range of physical devices and operating system versions to catch hardware-specific quirks, and automate your geolocation tests in CI using emulated GPS fixes or mocking libraries. Hence, by combining robust error handling, sensible defaults, and thorough testing, you will ensure that your location features remain accurate, efficient, and user-friendly across the diverse ecosystem of Android and iOS devices.

Push Notifications

Implementing notifications in a mobile app is a powerful way to keep users engaged by alerting them to important events even when the app is not in the foreground. Notifications can be **local**, triggered by the device itself at scheduled times or in response to internal events, or **remote**, sent from a server to reach clients wherever they are. Understanding these differences and the strategies for implementing them in React Native is essential to delivering a consistent, reliable experience on both Android and iOS.

Local versus Remote Notifications

Local notifications are scheduled directly on the device of the user. They do not depend on server connectivity or third-party services once configured. A typical example is a daily reminder set via an API like **`react-native-push-notification`**, which lets the app schedule a time and message for later display. Remote notifications, by contrast, require a server component that sends messages through Firebase Cloud Messaging (FCM) or Apple Push Notification Service (APNS). In this model, the server constructs the payload, specifies the target by device token, and dispatches the message—the operating system then delivers the alert to the user, even if the app is completely closed.

Firebase Cloud Messaging

To set up Firebase Cloud Messaging (FCM), start by creating a project in the Firebase Console. Register your Android and iOS apps, download **google-services.json** for Android and **GoogleService-Info.plist** for iOS, and place them in the appropriate directories of your project.

Next, install the client library:

```
yarn add @react-native-firebase/messaging
```

Follow the React Native Firebase guide to update your **android/build.gradle** and **Info.plist**. In your code, import and request permission:

```
import messaging from '@react-native-firebase/messaging';

async function requestPermission() {
constauthStatus = await messaging().requestPermission();
  if (authStatus === messaging.AuthorizationStatus.AUTHORIZED) {
console.log('Notification permission granted');
  }
}
```

Once permission is granted, obtain the unique registration token of the device:

```
const token = await messaging().getToken();
console.log('FCM Token:', token);
```

This token is essential for directing remote notifications to the correct device.

Apple Push Notification Service

In the Apple ecosystem, begin in the Apple Developer Portal by creating an App ID with Push Notifications enabled and generating an APNs certificate (or a token-based key). Export the certificate as a **.p12** file and import it into your server to authenticate requests to APNs. In Xcode, enable **Push Notifications** under **Signing and Capabilities**, and if using Firebase, include the **GoogleService-Info.plist** in your project. From there, your backend sends HTTP/2 requests to the APNs endpoint, where each JSON payload includes an **aps** object with **alert**, **badge**, and **sound** fields.

Receiving and Displaying Notifications

Within your app, you must handle notifications in three states: **foreground**, **background**, and **quit**. With React Native Firebase, you register listeners for each:

```
// App in foreground
messaging().onMessage(asyncremoteMessage => {
console.log('Foreground notification:', remoteMessage);
});

// App in background or quit—when opened via notification
messaging().onNotificationOpenedApp(remoteMessage => {
console.log('Notification opened app:', remoteMessage);
});
```

```
// App launched from a quit state
messaging().getInitialNotification().then(remoteMessage => {
  if (remoteMessage) {
console.log('App launched by notification:', remoteMessage);
  }
});
```

On iOS, remember to request alert, badge, and sound permissions via **messaging().requestPermission()**. On Android (Oreo and above), ensure you create a notification channel using:

```
import notifee from '@notifee/react-native';

await notifee.createChannel({
  id: 'default',
  name: 'Default Channel',
});
```

Deep Linking and Custom Actions

To deliver a richer experience, include routing data in your remote payload by adding a **data** field:

```
{
  "to": "<device_token>",
  "notification": { "title": "New Message", "body": "You have a new message" },
  "data": { "screen": "Chat", "conversationId": "12345" }
}
```

In your handler, read **remoteMessage.data** and navigate accordingly:

```
navigation.navigate(remoteMessage.data.screen, {
  id: remoteMessage.data.conversationId,
});
```

Additionally, you can define custom actions in your Android **AndroidManifest.xml** and iOS **UNNotificationCategory** to offer inline buttons for quick replies, marking tasks complete, or other interactions without fully opening the app.

With these techniques, your application will be fully equipped to send and receive integrated, reliable notifications, keeping users connected to your most relevant content.

Finally, it is essential to build resilience and user-friendly fallbacks around your notification workflow. Gracefully handle cases where permissions are denied or notifications are disabled—inform the user of the benefits and provide clear instructions for re-enabling alerts in system settings. Monitor delivery success and failure via server-side analytics and client-side logging, and adjust payload sizes to avoid overwhelming low-bandwidth networks or draining battery.

Incorporate comprehensive testing on both simulators and real devices—using tools such as Flipper, Reactotron, and Detox commands to simulate push events—and integrate these tests into your CI pipeline. By combining robust error handling, performance tuning, and automated end-to-end validation, you will ensure that your push notification experience remains reliable, efficient, and engaging across the full spectrum of Android and iOS environments.

Permission Management

Permission management is the foundation that ensures both security and user trust while allowing your app to access sensitive device resources without surprises. In React Native, it is crucial to understand how each platform handles granting and revoking permissions so that your application behaves predictably and delivers a smooth user experience. Let us now explore in detail the nuances of Android and iOS, the **react-native-permissions** library that unifies these flows, and some UX best practices to minimize user frustration.

Runtime Permissions

Starting with Android Marshmallow (API 23), the permission model of the system was redesigned to adopt a "just-in-time" flow. Rather than requesting all permissions at install time, the app must request each one at the moment it is needed. For example, before beginning location tracking, your code might look like this:

```
import { PermissionsAndroid } from 'react-native';

async function requestLocation() {
  try {
const result = await PermissionsAndroid.request(
PermissionsAndroid.PERMISSIONS.ACCESS_FINE_LOCATION,
      {
        title: 'Location Permission',
        message: 'We need access to your location to show your position on the map.',
buttonPositive: 'Allow',
buttonNegative: 'Deny',
      }
    );
    return result === PermissionsAndroid.RESULTS.GRANTED;
  } catch (err) {
console.warn('Error requesting permission:', err);
    return false;
  }
}
```

If the user denies and selects "Never ask again," you will receive **PermissionsAndroid.RESULTS.NEVER_ASK_AGAIN**. In such cases, you must guide the user to manually re-enable the permission in system settings, since the native dialog will no longer appear.

Requesting and Revoking on iOS

On iOS, permissions are also requested at runtime, but users can revoke them at any time via the system settings without notifying the app. To request "While In Use" or "Always" authorization, you can use native APIs or wrappers like this:

```
import { Platform } from 'react-native';
import Geolocation from 'react-native-geolocation-service';

if (Platform.OS === 'ios') {
Geolocation.requestAuthorization('always'); // or 'whenInUse'
}
```

Before each sensitive operation, your app should check the current status. If you detect that permission has been revoked, display an explanatory screen with a button that opens the iOS Settings:

```
import { Linking } from 'react-native';

function openSettings() {
Linking.openSettings();
}
```

This approach prevents silent failures by ensuring that the user understands why they need to re-enable the feature and how to do so.

Supporting Libraries

To reduce boilerplate and standardize permission handling across platforms, the React Native community offers **react-native-permissions**. This library unifies check and request calls into a single, stable API:

```
import { check, request, PERMISSIONS, RESULTS } from 'react-native-permissions';

async function ensureCameraPermission() {
const status = await check(PERMISSIONS.IOS.CAMERA);
  if (status === RESULTS.GRANTED) return true;
  if (status === RESULTS.DENIED) {
constnewStatus = await request(PERMISSIONS.IOS.CAMERA);
    return newStatus === RESULTS.GRANTED;
  }
  // RESULTS.BLOCKED or others: guide user to open settings
  return false;
}
```

With this abstraction, you handle denied, granted, blocked, and unavailable states consistently without worrying about platform-specific strings.

UX Best Practices for Permissions

Prompting for permission abruptly can startle users. Before triggering the native dialog, show a modal explaining why you need access—for example, "We need to access your camera so you can take high-quality photos to share with friends." Providing this context significantly increases acceptance rates. If the user still denies, offer a useful fallback: when location is refused, allow manual address entry; when the camera is unavailable, let users upload existing gallery images. Finally, provide step-by-step guidance on re-enabling permissions in system settings, reinforcing respect for privacy and your commitment to data security.

By following these guidelines, your app will implement a permissions flow that is robust, transparent, and aligned with modern expectations for security and user experience.

Finally, it is critical to build resilience and observability into your permission workflows. Always detect and gracefully handle cases where permission is denied or revoked—present clear feedback to the user explaining why the feature is disabled and how to re-enable it in system settings. Instrument your app to log permission requests and outcomes, so you can monitor real-world acceptance rates and pinpoint any friction points. In your CI pipeline, include automated tests—using mocks in Jest and interactive flows in Detox—that simulate permission grants, denials, and "never ask again" scenarios. By combining robust error handling, user-centric messaging, and comprehensive automated validation, you ensure that the native features of your app remain reliable, transparent, and user-friendly across every Android and iOS environment.

Security and Privacy

When working with sensitive native resources—such as user credentials, real-time location data, and captured media—adopting robust security practices is essential to protect both the information of your user, and their trust in your application. In this section, we cover secure storage of sensitive data, responsible use of location and media, and privacy policy best practices to comply with regulations such as LGPD of Brazil and the GDPR of EU.

Handling Sensitive Data

Tokens, API keys, and login credentials should **never** be stored in plain text or unprotected local storage. On iOS, the **Keychain** provides a hardware-backed, encrypted vault ideal for secrets, while **Keystore System** of Android similarly isolates cryptographic keys in a secure environment. In React Native, libraries such as **`react-native-keychain`** abstract these native APIs so your JavaScript code simply calls methods such as **`setGenericPassword`** and **`getGenericPassword`** without ever exposing raw secrets in the file system.

Beyond using secure vaults, consider applying **additional layers of encryption**. For instance, you might encrypt data client-side with a symmetric key stored in the secure enclave and then re-encrypt it server-side with your own key before writing to long-term storage. Always use proven cryptographic algorithms (say AES-GCM for encryption, HMAC-SHA256 for integrity) and rely on well-maintained libraries rather than hand-rolling your own. Finally, implement strict **key rotation policies**: periodically invalidate and renew tokens as well as encryption keys to minimize the impact of any potential compromise.

Responsible Use of Location and Media

Even when permissions are granted, developers must use location and media data **sparingly** and only for the core features of the app. For example, enable geolocation only during a guided navigation session—do not track the user continuously in the background unless strictly necessary. Likewise, capture audio or video only when the user explicitly requests it, and clearly indicate the recording status in your UI.

Transparency is the key: inform users exactly **when** and **why** you collect their data. Use contextual tooltips or a dedicated "Privacy" screen to explain each use case. If you must transmit data to your server, enforce **end-to-end encryption** (HTTPS/TLS) and consider **field-level encryption** for highly sensitive payloads. On the device, minimize local caching: remove temporary media files from caches immediately after successful upload, and offer users a one-tap "Delete all local copies" option. This not only conserves storage and battery but also demonstrates respect for user privacy.

Privacy Policies and Regulatory Compliance

Privacy laws differ by region, but universal principles such as **data minimization**, **purpose limitation**, and **informed consent** must underpin your data strategy. To comply with the LGPD (Brazil) and GDPR (EU), publish a clear, accessible privacy policy that spells out:

- **What** data do you collect (like "We collect location coordinates to provide turn-by-turn directions")?
- **Why** do you collect it (such as "Your location is used solely for routing and is not shared with third parties.")?
- **How long** do you retain it (for example, "Location data is stored for 30 days and then automatically purged")?
- **With whom** do you share it (for instance, "We share crash logs with our analytics provider under strict confidentiality agreements.")?

Your app should include a "Privacy Settings" section where users can **review and revoke** consent at any time, access logs of their own data, and initiate deletion requests. Under "right to be forgotten" of GDPR and "right to erasure" of LGPD, you must provide a straightforward mechanism—an in-app button or a linked web form—that processes data-deletion requests without undue delay. Logging these requests and their fulfillment in your backend ensures an auditable trail of compliance.

By embedding secure storage, transparent data-use policies, and user-centric privacy controls throughout your code and UX, you safeguard sensitive information, adhere to evolving regulations, and build lasting trust with your audience.

Finally, it is vital to build observability and continuous monitoring into your security posture. Instrument your app to log access attempts and encryption operations—without capturing sensitive payloads—so you can detect anomalies and audit data flows. Integrate automated security scans and dependency checks into your CI/CD pipeline to catch vulnerable libraries before they reach production. Regularly review and update your privacy policy and user-consent mechanisms to reflect changes in data handling or regulatory requirements. Conduct periodic privacy impact assessments, especially when introducing new features that process personal data. By combining secure storage, transparent communication, dynamic consent controls, and automated compliance checks, you not only protect your users' data but also foster a culture of trust that turns security and privacy into competitive advantages.

Testing and Debugging

Ensuring high quality in apps that rely on native features demands a layered testing and debugging strategy since the behavior you observe in a simulator or emulator can differ dramatically from what users experience on real hardware. In this section, we will dig deeper into approaches for validating functionality, capturing meaningful logs, and isolating native interactions in automated tests, so that you can catch issues early, iterate confidently, and deliver a rock-solid release.

Testing on Simulator/Emulator versus Real Device

While simulators and emulators are invaluable for rapid UI layout checks, navigation flows, and initial smoke tests, they often fail to capture the nuances of actual hardware. Sensors like GPS will require you to push synthetic coordinates via the emulator console—an extra step that can mask performance hiccups or permission dialogs. Similarly, camera previews are usually static placeholders, so you cannot verify autofocus, exposure, or streaming performance. Even vibration, haptic feedback, and push-notification latency can differ substantially. To bridge this gap, adopt a two-phase approach:

1. **Smoke on Emulators**: Run the headless test suite of your CI against emulated environments to catch build breaks and simple logic bugs.
2. **Sanity on Devices**: Maintain a small farm of physical devices (Android and iOS across key OS versions) in your QA lab or use cloud-based device services. Automate an overnight "device sanity" run that installs the latest build, steps through core user flows, and reports crashes or hangs. This ensures that any native-specific regressions—such as missing permissions, corrupted media streams, or AV session failures—are caught before they reach end users.

Log Inspection Tools

Native features can expose low-level errors that never bubble up to JavaScript. On Android, **Logcat** remains your best friend: filter by the custom tag of your module (say `MyCameraModule`) or look for "`ReactNativeJS`" entries to correlate bridge calls. In complex scenarios, capture full device logs (`adb logcat -v time`) and post-process them to extract patterns or error spikes over time. On iOS, the device console of XCode shows **NSLog** from Objective-C/Swift alongside JavaScript stack traces, which helps you pinpoint mismatches in threading or lifecycle events. For a unified, real-time view, tools like **Flipper**—with its Layout, Network, and React DevTools plugins—and **Reactotron** let you inspect native events, view state snapshots, and replay network calls without leaving your desktop. Instrument your app to log critical native module events (such as "`PermissionGranted`", "`CaptureStarted`", "`CaptureError`") so that you can filter and trace the exact sequence leading to a failure.

Mocking Native APIs

Unit tests should never depend on real hardware or network, so mocking is essential. With **Jest**, create comprehensive mocks for every native module your code touches: camera, geolocation, notifications, biometric sensors, and so on. This allows you to simulate success, timeouts, permission denials, and hardware errors deterministically. Structure your mocks to expose both callback-based and promise-based APIs, and include helpers to flip between modes (like `mockGeolocation.setErrorMode()`).

For **end-to-end** testing, **Detox** excels at driving real devices or emulators. Augment your test scripts with system commands:

- **iOS Simulator**: `xcrunsimctl push <device-id><bundle-id>payload.json` for notifications, or `xcrunsimctlstatus_bar` to simulate network status and battery levels.
- **Android Emulator**: `adb emu geo fix <lng><lat>`for GPS, `adb shell am broadcast` for push events, and `adb shell svc power stayon true` to disable sleep during long tests.

Embed these commands in your Detox `beforeEach` or CI pipeline, so that every PR triggers a suite of real-device scenarios: turning permissions on/off, simulating an offline network, rotating the device, and firing push notifications during background states. This not only validates your handlers but also uncovers race conditions between JS and native layers.

Putting It All Together One can put it all together by combining:

- **Emulator-based CI** for fast feedback on JavaScript logic.
- **Scheduled device sanity runs** for catching platform-specific breakages.
- **Rich log aggregation** via Flipper/Reactotron for real-time tracing.
- **Automated mocks and simulations** in Jest/Detox for comprehensive coverage.

You establish a testing ecosystem that surfaces bugs early, provides clear diagnostic information, and ensures your integration with native features remains bulletproof across the ever-changing landscape of Android and iOS devices. The result is a delivery pipeline that not only speeds development but also elevates the reliability and polish of your mobile experience.

Custom Native Modules and Bridging

Sometimes you will encounter a scenario where no existing library meets your requirements—perhaps you need to integrate with a proprietary hardware SDK, execute compute-heavy algorithms in C++ or Rust, or expose functionality that React Native has not yet wrapped. In these cases, writing your own native module is the way forward. The decision to build a custom bridge should be driven by clear business value: if the feature unlocks significant performance gains or enables unique device capabilities, the maintenance overhead of a native module is justified.

On Android, a native module consists of a Java or Kotlin class extending `ReactContextBaseJavaModule`, annotated with `@ReactMethod` for each method you want to expose to JavaScript. You bundle it in a package that implements `ReactPackage` and register that package in the `MainApplication.java` of your app. As soon as you rebuild, the methods of your module become available on `NativeModules.MyModule` allowing you to invoke them with promises or callbacks. Whether you are tapping into low-level camera APIs, performing on-device machine learning, or interfacing with a specialized Bluetooth peripheral, this pattern ensures tight integration and minimal overhead.

On iOS, the process is conceptually similar but uses Objective-C or Swift. You declare your module with the macros `RCT_EXPORT_MODULE()` and `RCT_EXPORT_METHOD()`, handling asynchronous responses via `RCTPromiseResolveBlock` and `RCTPromiseRejectBlock`. If you choose Swift, you bridge through a header file that makes the methods of your modules visible to the React Native runtime. This setup lets you call into any native framework—Core ML for AI inference, AVFoundation for custom video processing, or HealthKit for fitness data—directly from JavaScript, without detouring through web APIs or JSON RPC.

For the highest performance and lowest latency, you can adopt the newer JSI and TurboModules architecture. Instead of shipping over the classic bridge, TurboModules allow direct C++ bindings that call into JavaScriptCore or Hermes. You define your module interface in C++, generate the necessary glue code with the React Native codegen, and register it so that JavaScript can invoke methods with near-native speed. This approach is ideal for performance-sensitive tasks such as real-time image filters or audio processing, where every millisecond counts.

By mastering custom modules and bridges—whether via the tried-and-true JavaScript bridge or the cutting-edge TurboModules path—you will empower your React Native app to leverage any native feature, library, or SDK. This capability transforms your projects from "great cross-platform" toward "native-grade," giving you full control over device hardware, optimizing performance, and delivering experiences that no pure JavaScript implementation could match.

Background Processing and Task Scheduling

Mobile apps often need to perform work even when they are not in the foreground—whether it is synchronizing data, fetching location updates, or cleaning up caches. React Native provides several mechanisms to schedule and execute tasks in the background, but each platform comes with its own constraints and best practices.

On Android, **Headless JS** allows your JavaScript logic to run in a background Service when the app is closed. You register a headless task with **`AppRegistry.registerHeadlessTask('MyTaskName', () => require('./MyTaskHandler'))`**, then launch it from a native BroadcastReceiver or Service. This pattern is commonly used to handle background geofencing events or silent push notifications that carry payloads your app must process without user interaction.

In iOS, background execution is more restricted. You declare the tasks you need in Capabilities of your app, such as **Background Fetch** or **Background Processing** via **`BGTaskScheduler`**. A typical setup involves registering a fetch task in your **`AppDelegate`**:

```
BGTaskScheduler.shared.register(
forTaskWithIdentifier: "com.myapp.sync",
  using: nil
) { task in
  // Call your JS bridge to sync data
MySyncModule.performSync{ success in
task.setTaskCompleted(success: success)
  }
}
```

and scheduling it periodically:

```
let request = BGProcessingTaskRequest(identifier: "com.myapp.sync")
request.earliestBeginDate = Date(timeIntervalSinceNow: 15 * 60)
try? BGTaskScheduler.shared.submit(request)
```

For continuous location tracking or geofencing, libraries like **`react-native-background-geolocation`** abstract much of the native setup. On Android, you request **`ACCESS_BACKGROUND_LOCATION`** and start a persistent service; on iOS, you enable the "Always" location in **`Info.plist`** and configure the native **`CLLocationManager`** to deliver updates even when the app is suspended. This enables use cases such as turn-by-turn navigation or location-based reminders without the user actively keeping the app open.

To schedule simple periodic work or local notifications, you can use **react-native-background-fetch** (which bridges to WorkManager of Android and iOS Background Fetch) or `WorkManager` of Android directly. In JavaScript, you configure:

```
import BackgroundFetch from 'react-native-background-fetch';

BackgroundFetch.configure(
{ minimumFetchInterval: 15 },
asynctaskId => {
    // Your sync or notification logic
BackgroundFetch.finish(taskId);
  },
  error =>console.warn('Background fetch failed', error)
);
```

Then, when needed, schedule local reminders at intervals or specific times with the same library or with `react-native-push-notification`.

Since background tasks can drain battery and conflict with OS power-saving modes (Android Doze, iOS App Nap), it is crucial to balance frequency against necessity. Use `distanceFilter`, `timeout`, and conservative `interval` settings for location, and only enable headless JS or processing tasks when absolutely required. Monitor the power impact of your app with tools such as Battery Historian of Android or Energy Diagnostics of XCode, and adjust your scheduling policies to minimize wakeups. Group background work into as few, larger jobs as possible, and release resources promptly when tasks are complete.

By combining Headless JS, iOS background tasks, dedicated geolocation services, and scheduled fetch jobs, and by tuning your parameters for both reliability and efficiency; you will deliver background functionality that keeps your app responsive and your users happy, without draining their batteries or running afoul of platform limits.

Future Trends and Challenges

As mobile applications continue to mature, new demands and opportunities are emerging on the horizon of React Native development. In this section, we will discuss the key trends that will shape native feature access in the coming years and the challenges engineering teams must tackle to maintain quality, performance, and compliance with ever-tighter standards.

Edge Computing and On-Device AI

Shifting artificial intelligence workloads to the device itself—known as edge computing—promises to reduce latency and enhance user privacy by eliminating the need to send sensitive data to remote servers. Computer-vision and audio-processing libraries that once required a dedicated backend will increasingly ship as optimized C++ or Rust modules compiled for iOS and Android and exposed via Native Modules. The challenge will be balancing binary size (to avoid inflating initial downloads) with the need for frequent machine-learning model updates, all while ensuring compatibility across diverse chipsets (from Apple Silicon to Qualcomm and MediaTek).

Privacy, Security, and Regulation

Laws such as LGPD (Brazil), GDPR (EU), and emerging regulations such as CCPA (California) or FADP (Switzerland) now mandate that developers document—down to the code level—which libraries collect data, how it flows through the app, and where it is stored. Granular consent tools that can disable analytics or geolocation modules on demand will become standard. This shift requires software architects to design with feature flags and dependency injection, allowing sensitive components to be removed at runtime. Additionally, end-to-end encryption for captured media and push messages will become a baseline requirement in sectors such as healthcare, finance, and public safety.

API Convergence and a Unified Experience

With the rise of cross-platform frameworks such as Flutter, Kotlin Multiplatform, and Microsoft MAUI, market expectations extend beyond React Native. We will see a push toward standardized native-API specifications—potentially led by bodies such as the OpenAPI Foundation—where any JavaScript/TypeScript tool can consume the same camera, sensor, and notification interfaces regardless of runtime. Achieving this alignment will demand collaboration across open-source communities, active maintenance of interoperability bridges, and vigilance around breaking changes on each platform.

Performance, Energy Efficiency, and Offline UX

As devices become central to increasingly complex tasks—from 4K streaming to collaborative augmented reality—the pressure to optimize CPU, GPU, and networking intensifies. Video-capture libraries may offer real-time on-device transcoding, but doing so responsibly requires careful battery consumption and thermal management. At the same time, native frameworks will need to provide more sophisticated caching mechanisms for media and location data to support robust offline experiences without degrading performance when connectivity is spotty. The biggest challenge will be measuring and monitoring performance impacts in CI pipelines, incorporating battery tests and automated benchmarks as integral parts of the development workflow.

In summary, the coming decade will bring greater responsibilities—and expanded possibilities—to React Native developers. Staying abreast of hardware innovations, privacy regulations, and industry standards will be just as important as mastering the contemporary camera, GPS, and notification APIs. Only then will it be possible to deliver mobile applications that are robust, secure, and truly differentiated.

Conclusion

In this chapter, we have explored how to take a React Native app beyond its JavaScript interface by deeply integrating it with the native features of a mobile device. We saw that by accessing the camera, GPS, and push-notification system, you can deliver rich experiences—from high-quality photo and video capture to real-time location tracking and contextual alerts, even when the app runs in the background. Leveraging mature libraries such as **`react-native-camera`**, **`react-native-geolocation-service`**, and **`@react-native-firebase/messaging`** proved to be an efficient way to shorten the gap between idea and prototype.

We have also discussed the importance of handling permissions responsibly, adopting a "just-in-time" flow on Android and continuously checking the status on iOS to ensure transparency and user control. Adding security layers—such as encrypted storage in Keychain or Keystore and enforcing HTTPS traffic—reinforces user trust and safeguards sensitive data such as authentication tokens and location logs.

Furthermore, we covered testing and debugging best practices, emphasizing the need to validate on emulators and real devices, use tools such as Flipper or Logcat/Xcode console, and employ mocks in Jest or simulation commands in Detox. These techniques ensure that critical features—media capture, permission flows, and notification handlers—behave as expected in every scenario.

Finally, understanding the nuances between React Native CLI and Expo, as well as the future trends in edge computing and privacy, equips you to choose the best approach for your project. By mastering these techniques, your team will be well-positioned to build robust, secure, and highly engaging cross-platform apps that fully leverage the native capabilities of each device. In the next chapter, we are going to talk about testing and its resources, which is an important resource to validate your application.

Self-Assessment Questions

Before consolidating what we have covered in this chapter on accessing native features in React Native, it is useful to reflect on the core concepts, differing approaches and recommended best practices we have presented. The following questions will help you review the material, pinpoint any areas for deeper study, and reinforce your understanding of how to integrate cameras, geolocation, notifications, and security in cross-platform apps:

1. What are the main differences between using **`react-native-camera`** and **`expo-camera`** for media capture in React Native?
2. How does "just-in-time" permission model of Android(Android ≥ 6.0) differ from the authorization flow of iOS, and why must you treat them differently?
3. What steps are required to set up Firebase Cloud Messaging (FCM) in a React Native project, and how do you obtain and use the device registration token?
4. In which scenarios would you recommend creating a custom native module instead of relying on an existing library to access a specific feature?
5. How would you implement a notification handler using **`@react-native-firebase/messaging`** that works correctly in all three app states—foreground, background, and quit?
6. What security best practices should you follow when storing authentication tokens and location data on the device?
7. Why is it essential to test native features on real devices in addition to emulators, and which tools can help debug integrated native code?

Answering these questions will verify that you have absorbed the configuration details, code patterns, and permission flows—and that you are ready to design and maintain mobile applications that leverage the native capabilities of each platform safely and efficiently.

Key Terms

- **Camera Preview:** A live rendering of the camera feed of the device within the app, allowing users to frame photos and videos before capturing them.
- **react-native-camera / expo-camera:** JavaScript libraries that expose native camera functionality to React Native CLI projects (**`react-native-camera`**) or Expo Managed Workflow apps (**`expo-camera`**).
- **FlashMode:** A camera setting that determines flash behavior, typically with options such as **`on`**, **`off`**, and **`auto`**, controlled via a component prop.
- **Geolocation Service:** The native service for obtaining the position of the device. In React Native, this is commonly handled by **`react-native-geolocation-service`**, which provides methods such as **`getCurrentPosition`** and **`watchPosition`**.
- **AndroidManifest.xml / Info.plist:** The manifest files for Android and iOS, respectively, where you declare camera, microphone, and location permissions so that the operating system can grant access at runtime.

- **PermissionsAndroid / requestPermissionsAsync:** APIs for programmatically requesting sensitive permissions on Android (`PermissionsAndroid.request`) and Expo (`Camera.requestPermissionsAsync`, `Location.requestPermissionsAsync`) using a just-in-time flow.
- **Firebase Cloud Messaging (FCM):** The remote messaging service of Firebase that provides the infrastructure to send push notifications and data messages to Android and iOS devices, integrated into React Native via `@react-native-firebase/messaging`.
- **Apple Push Notification service (APNs):** The remote notification platform of Apple, which requires setting up certificates or token-based keys in the Apple Developer Portal and enabling Push Notifications in Xcode.
- **Notification Handlers:** Callback functions registered in the app to handle notifications in three states: foreground (`onMessage`), background (`onNotificationOpenedApp`), and quit (`getInitialNotification`).
- **Deep Linking:** A technique for embedding routing data in the payload of a notification so that tapping the notification programmatically navigates the user to a specific screen within the app.
- **react-native-permissions:** A library that unifies permission checking and requesting on Android and iOS, abstracting platform-specific methods and states (including `GRANTED`, `DENIED`, `BLOCKED`).
- **Keychain / Keystore:** Secure vaults for credentials and cryptographic keys on iOS (Keychain) and Android (Keystore), accessible in JavaScript via libraries like `react-native-keychain`.
- **LGPD / GDPR:** Lei Geral de Proteção de Dados (LGPD) of Brazil and the General Data Protection Regulation (GDPR) of EU, which define requirements for collecting, storing, and deleting user data.
- **Flipper / Reactotron:** Debugging tools that connect in real-time to a React Native app, displaying logs, Redux/Context state snapshots, and network events to simplify inspection of both native modules and JavaScript.
- **Jest Mocks / Detox:** Testing strategies in Jest, create mocks for native modules to achieve deterministic unit tests; in Detox, simulate notifications or geolocation on emulators/devices for end-to-end testing.
- **Simctl / ADB Shell:** Command-line tools (`xcrunsimctl` on iOS and `adb shell` on Android) used in CI pipelines to inject location data, trigger push notifications, or adjust emulated permissions.

These terms compile the essential concepts and tools for mastering native feature access, control, and security in React Native, serving as a quick reference throughout development.

CHAPTER 9
Testing and Debugging

Introduction

In an increasingly competitive mobile development landscape, ensuring the quality and stability of an app is just as important as delivering new features. Production bugs not only harm the user experience but can also damage the reputation of your team and incur high maintenance costs. That is why establishing a robust testing and debugging pipeline from the very start of your project is essential.

In this chapter, we will present a comprehensive approach to validate your code and monitor unwanted behavior in React Native. We shall begin by exploring unit tests with Jest, a tool that verifies the isolated behavior of functions and components, ensuring each part of your application works as expected. Next, we will be diving into integration and end-to-end tests with Detox, which simulate full usage flows on real devices or emulators, subsequently uncovering issues that only appear when multiple layers of the app interact.

We will also cover integrating Firebase Crashlytics for production crash monitoring. You will learn how to capture unhandled exceptions, log custom breadcrumbs, and set up alerts that help you pinpoint problems in real time. And to make debugging even more efficient, we will introduce the key features of React Native Debugger and Flipper—tools that let you inspect app state, analyze network logs, and even profile JavaScript performance.

Finally, we shall discuss advanced logging and continuous monitoring strategies, including best practices for structuring logs, sending them to external services, and defining performance metrics. By the end of this introduction, you will have a clear understanding of the benefits of each stage of the QA pipeline and how they work together to dramatically reduce production bugs.

Structure

In this chapter, we will cover the following topics:

- Introduction to Testing and Debugging
    - Importance of Software Quality
    - Overview of the Test Pipeline
    - Tools and Workflows Adopted in this Chapter

- Unit Tests with Jest
  - Initial Jest Configuration in React Native
  - Folder Structure and Naming Conventions
  - Writing Basic Tests
  - Mocks and Simulations (jest.mock, jest.fn)
  - Code Coverage
  - Integrating Jest into CI (GitHub Actions / CircleCI)
- Integration and End-to-End Tests
  - What E2E Tests are and When to Use Them
  - Installing and Configuring Detox
  - Setting up Devices/Emulators (iOS and Android)
  - Writing Your First Full-Flow Test
  - Synchronization and Waiting Strategies (sync)
  - Running Jest in CI
  - Best Practices and Performance Tips
- Error Monitoring with Firebase Crashlytics
  - Overview of Crashlytics
  - SDK Integration in the React Native Project
  - Capturing Unhandled Errors and Panics
  - Sending Custom Logs and Breadcrumbs
  - Report Analysis and Alert Configuration
  - Best Practices for Naming and Grouping Failures
- Real-Time Debugging
  - React Native Debugger
  - Element and Prop Inspection
  - Redux and State Debugging
  - Using Breakpoints and Watch Expressions
  - Flipper
  - Essential Plugins (Layout, Networking, Logs)
  - Database and `AsyncStorage` Inspection
  - Performance Monitor and CPU Profiler
- Continuous Logging and Monitoring Strategies
  - Structured Logging Best Practices (JSON, Severity Levels)
  - Shipping Logs to External Services (Sentry, and Loggly)
  - Performance Metrics and Tracing
  - Uptime Dashboards and Alerts
  - Feedback Cycle: From Production Error to Development Fix
- Reflections and Future Trends
  - Recapping the Testing and Debugging Pipeline

- Quality Checklist before Release
- Evolving Your QA Strategy and Future Trends

Introduction to Testing and Debugging

Software quality goes far beyond simply "making the code work." In production environments, every undetected bug represents a risk of disrupted user flows, data loss, and damage to the reputation of the development team. In mobile in particular, issues in released versions can lead users to abandon installing or updating the app.

- **User experience:** An unexpected crash or incorrect behavior undermines user trust and lowers retention rates.
- **Maintenance cost:** Fixing bugs found in production typically requires more time and investment than preventing them during development.
- **Scalability and continuous delivery:** Without a solid testing foundation, technical debt accumulates, making future releases riskier and less stable.
- **Compliance and security:** Apps handling sensitive data (some of which includes authentication, payments, or personal information) must ensure that business rules and security controls are not broken by regressions.

That is why incorporating a testing strategy (unit, integration, and end-to-end) along with debugging and monitoring tools (structured logs, crash reporting, and real-time inspection) from the very beginning makes all the difference in the health of the lifecycle of your app.

Overview of the Test Pipeline

A well-structured test pipeline should cover multiple verification layers to ensure broad coverage and early failure detection:

- **Unit Tests (Jest):**
  - Validate functions and components in isolation.
  - High execution speed—ideal to run on every code change or pre-commit hook.
- **Integration and E2E Tests (Detox):**
  - Simulate real user flows, from app launch to complete interactions.
  - Catch communication issues between screens, services, and external dependencies.
- **Quality Gate in CI/CD:**
  - Configure jobs in GitHub Actions, CircleCI, or similar to:
    - Run all tests automatically on every pull request.
    - Generate code-coverage reports.
    - Block merges if failures occur or coverage falls below the defined minimum.
- **Production Crash Monitoring (Firebase Crashlytics):**
  - Capture unhandled exceptions and failure logs after users install the app.
  - Group and prioritize fixes based on frequency and impact.
- **Local Debugging Tools (React Native Debugger, Flipper):**
  - Inspect elements, state, Redux, network requests, and performance in real time.
  - Speed up bug identification during active development.

- **Advanced Logging and Metrics:**
    - Structured logs with different severity levels (info, warn, error).
    - Ship logs to platforms like Sentry, Datadog, or Loggly for historical analysis and proactive alerts.

This sequence, from fast detection via tests to continuous production monitoring, forms a reliable workflow that drastically reduces the risk of regressions and crashes in official releases.

Tools and Workflows Used in This Chapter

To illustrate each step of the pipeline, we will use the following tools and conventions (*Table 9.1*):

Layer	Tool	Primary Use
Unit Testing	**Jest**	Isolated tests of functions and React components
Integration/E2E Testing	**Detox**	User-flow simulation on iOS/Android
CI/CD	**GitHub Actions**	Automated test runs and quality gates
Crash Reporting	**Firebase Crashlytics**	Production crash monitoring
Local Debugging	**React Native Debugger**	State, Redux, and breakpoint inspection
	Flipper	Layout, networking, and performance analysis
Logging and Monitoring	**Sentry** (example)	Structured log collection and alerts

Table 9.1: *Testing, CI/CD, Debugging, and Monitoring Tools for React Native Development*

Typical Workflow

1. **Local Development**: You write code and run unit tests (`npm test`) locally.
2. **Active Debugging**: When a bug arises, open React Native Debugger or Flipper to inspect state, network calls, and performance.
3. **Pull Request:** Upon opening the PR, GitHub Actions triggers the pipeline:
    - Install dependencies and run all Jest tests.
    - Execute Detox scenarios (on emulators or device farms).
    - Generate a coverage report and block merging if coverage is below the threshold.
4. **QA Release:** A build is distributed to the QA team; any bugs are logged in Sentry and Crashlytics.
5. **Production:** After approval, the app goes live in the stores; real-world crashes are captured by Crashlytics and flagged for prioritized fixes.

Throughout this chapter, we will follow this journey step by step, providing configuration examples, code snippets, and tips so that you can replicate and customize this pipeline in your own React Native project.

Unit Tests with Jest

Unit tests are the foundation of any software quality strategy: they validate small units of code (functions, components, utilities) in isolation, ensuring that each piece fulfills exactly its responsibility. In React Native, Jest has become the standard tool thanks to its speed, native Babel integration, and mock support. In the following paragraph, we explore in detail how to configure and use Jest to build a robust test suite.

React Native CLI projects come with **Jest preconfigured** (typically using **`babel-jest`**). While **`ts-jest`** works, it differs from the default RN testing setup and often requires extra transform configuration. For most React Native apps, it is simpler to keep **`babel-jest`** and let Babel handle TypeScript via **`@babel/preset-typescript`** (commonly available through the React Native Babel preset), since this keeps the configuration minimal. Use **`ts-jest`** mainly when you specifically need TypeScript-aware test features (such as type checking as part of the test run).

Initial Jest Configuration in React Native

Correct configuration is crucial to avoid headaches later. Start by installing the necessary dependencies:

bash

CopiarEditar

```
npm install --save-dev jest @testing-library/react-native ts-jest @types/jest
```

- **`jest`**: the test engine.
- **`@testing-library/react-native`**: Utilities to render components and interact with them.
- **`ts-jest`**: Allows running tests in TypeScript.
- **`@types/jest`**: Type definitions for Jest.

Next, add a script to your **`package.json`**:

```
"scripts": {
  "test": "jest --coverage"
}
```

Then create a **`jest.config.js`** file:

```
module.exports = {
  preset: 'react-native',
  transform: {
    '^.+\\.(ts|tsx)$': 'ts-jest',
  },
moduleFileExtensions: ['ts', 'tsx', 'js', 'jsx', 'json', 'node'],
setupFilesAfterEnv: ['@testing-library/jest-native/extend-expect'],
testPathIgnorePatterns: ['/node_modules/', '/android/', '/ios/'],
collectCoverage: true,
collectCoverageFrom: ['src/**/*.{ts,tsx,js,jsx}', '!src/**/*.d.ts'],
coverageThreshold: {
    global: { branches: 80, functions: 85, lines: 90, statements: 90 },
  },
};
```

This preset already handles transforming React Native JS/TS code. The **`setupFilesAfterEnv`** entry imports extensions that simplify platform-specific assertions, such as checking styles or component presence.

If you use TypeScript, adjust your **`tsconfig.json`** to include:

```
{
  "compilerOptions": {
    "jsx": "react",
    "types": ["jest", "react-native"]
  }
}
```

With this in place, simply run:

```
npm test
```

and Jest will discover and run all test files effortlessly.

Organization and Naming Conventions

Rather than prescribing a folder structure, adopt clear conventions: each module or feature area (like UI components, screens, utilities) should contain its own tests. Name your test files with the suffix **`.test.tsor .test.tsx`** (or **`.spec.*`** if you prefer). This way, Jest automatically finds them. Keep tests close to their corresponding source code to encourage simultaneous updates: whenever you modify a component, it should be natural to locate and update its test at the same directory level.

Also, use **`testID`** props in your React Native components whenever you need a stable selector in tests. This avoids reliance on class names or text that might change with design iterations.

Writing Basic Tests

Simple tests already provide huge value. Consider a button component:

```
// Button.tsx
export default function Button({
  title,
onPress,
}: {
  title: string;
onPress: () => void;
}) {
  return (
<TouchableOpacityonPress={onPress} testID="button">
<Text>{title}</Text>
</TouchableOpacity>
  );
}
```

A test that ensures the text renders correctly and **`onPress`** is called:

```
import { render, fireEvent } from '@testing-library/react-native';
import Button from './Button';

describe('Button', () => {
it('displays the title passed via prop', () => {
const{ getByText } = render(<Button title="Send" onPress={() => {}} />);
    expect(getByText('Send')).toBeTruthy();
  });

it('fires onPress when pressed', () => {
constfn = jest.fn();
const{ getByTestId } = render(<Button title="OK" onPress={fn} />);
fireEvent.press(getByTestId('button'));
    expect(fn).toHaveBeenCalled();
  });
});
```

The key points are illustrated as follows:

- **Isolated rendering:** No external context needed.
- **Element querying:** **getByText** and **getByTestId** locate specific components.
- **Event simulation:** **fireEvent** reproduces user interactions.

Mocks and Spies (jest.mock, jest.fn)

When your code depends on external APIs, storage, or complex modules, mocking is essential. For example, imagine a date-formatting utility:

```
// utils/formatDate.ts
export function formatDate(date: Date): string {
  // complicated logic...
}
```

In tests, simplify it:

```
jest.mock('../utils/formatDate', () => ({
formatDate: () => '01/01/2025',
}));
import { formatDate } from '../utils/formatDate';

test('formatDate uses the mock', () => {
expect(formatDate(new Date())).toBe('01/01/2025');
});
```

For callback functions, use **jest.fn()**:

```
const callback = jest.fn(arg =>arg * 2);
expect(callback(5)).toBe(10);
expect(callback).toHaveBeenCalledWith(5);
```

To "spy" on a real method without completely replacing it, use **jest.spyOn**:

```
import * as util from '../utils/formatDate';
const spy = jest.spyOn(util, 'formatDate').mockReturnValue('31/12/2024');
// ...run tests...
spy.mockRestore();
```

Mocks ensure your tests run deterministically, quickly, and independently of external factors.

Code Coverage

Coverage indicates how much of your code is actually exercised by tests. With **collectCoverage** enabled, just run:

```
npm test
```

Jest will display a summary in the terminal and generate a **coverage/** directory with detailed HTML reports. Pay attention to:

- **Statements:** Executed lines.
- **Branches:** If/Else paths.
- **Functions:** Invoked functions.
- **Lines:** Covered lines.

Define thresholds in **`jest.config.js`** to block merges when coverage falls below the minimum values. This enforces team discipline around coverage and prevents quality gate degradation over time.

Integrating Jest into CI (GitHub Actions / CircleCI)

Automating test runs on every push or pull request is essential. In GitHub Actions, a basic workflow might look like:

```
on: [push, pull_request]
jobs:
  test:
    runs-on: ubuntu-latest
    steps:
      - uses: actions/checkout@v3
      - uses: actions/setup-node@v3
        with:
          node-version: '18'
      - run: npm ci
      - run: npm test
      - uses: actions/upload-artifact@v3
        with:
          name: coverage-report
          path: coverage
```

In CircleCI, something similar:

```
jobs:
  test:
docker:
      - image: cimg/node:18
    steps:
      - checkout
      - run: npm ci
      - run: npm test
      - store_artifacts:
          path: coverage
workflows:
test_workflow:
    jobs:
      - test
```

These pipelines ensure any regressions or coverage drops fail immediately, blocking unsafe merges. Storing coverage artifacts also allows you to analyze them later or integrate with quality dashboards.

Integration and End-to-End Testing

Instead of relying on emulators and specialized E2E tools, you can use Jest itself—together with React Native Testing Library and network mocks—to run integration tests and simulate end-to-end ("light E2E") flows. This approach runs entirely in Node.js, is much faster than emulators, and catches the vast majority of UI and business-logic regressions.

What "Light E2E" Tests are and When to Use Them

- **Integration tests** validate the collaboration between multiple components, providers, and data layers within the app—for example, navigation, Redux/Context, mocked HTTP calls, and data rendering.
- We call them **"light E2E" tests** when they cover the complete flow of the user (login → dashboard → logout) but run purely in JavaScript, without involving the native runtime.

When to use

- To verify smooth navigation between critical screens.
- For actions depending on multiple hooks, providers, or side effects.
- On authentication flows, complex forms, and paginated lists.

Limitations

- Do not catch native-animation bugs, custom gestures, or real-device performance issues.
- For those, dedicated frameworks like Detox are still recommended; but for about 80–90% of business scenarios, Jest is sufficient.

Installing and Configuring the Integration Environment

Dependencies

```
npm install --save-dev jest @testing-library/react-native jest-fetch-mock
```

Jest config (`jest.config.js`)

```
module.exports = {
  preset: 'react-native',
setupFiles: ['jest-fetch-mock'],
setupFilesAfterEnv: ['@testing-library/jest-native/extend-expect'],
  transform: { '^.+\\.(ts|tsx)$': 'ts-jest' },
testPathIgnorePatterns: ['/node_modules/', '/android/', '/ios/'],
};
```

Enable Global Fetch Mock

```
// setupTests.js
import fetchMock from 'jest-fetch-mock';
fetchMock.enableMocks();
```

Common Providers

Create a helper to render your UI with all contexts:

```
// test-utils.tsx
import React, { ReactElement } from 'react';
import { render } from '@testing-library/react-native';
import { Provider as ReduxProvider } from 'react-redux';
import { NavigationContainer } from '@react-navigation/native';
import configureStore from './src/store';

export function renderWithProviders(ui: ReactElement) {
```

```
const store = configureStore();
  return {
    ...render(
<ReduxProvider store={store}>
<NavigationContainer>{ui}</NavigationContainer>
</ReduxProvider>
    ),
    store,
  };
}
```

"Emulating" Devices: Test Containers

Instead of emulators, we spin up pure-JS containers:

- **`NavigationContainer`:** Provides routing context.
- **Redux/Context:** Creates a fresh store on each test.
- **Theme, i18n, and other providers:** Minimal setup so that components render as in production.
- **Asset mocks:** Configure images and SVG imports in **`jest.config.js`** if needed.

This setup is fast and ensures that your tests faithfully reflect the structure of the app without emulator overhead.

Writing Your First Full-Flow Test

```
Imagine a login → home flow:
// __tests__/LoginFlow.test.tsx
import React from 'react';
import { fireEvent, waitFor } from '@testing-library/react-native';
import AppNavigator from '../src/navigation/AppNavigator';
import { renderWithProviders } from './test-utils';
import fetchMock from 'jest-fetch-mock';

describe('Login flow', () => {
beforeEach(() => {
fetchMock.resetMocks();
  });

it('authenticates and redirects to Home', async () => {
    // 1. Mock the login API
fetchMock.mockResponseOnce(
JSON.stringify({ token: 'xyz-token', user: { name: 'Ana' } })
    );

    // 2. Render the full app
const{ getByPlaceholderText, getByText, store } = renderWithProviders(
<AppNavigator />
    );

    // 3. User interactions
fireEvent.changeText(getByPlaceholderText('Email'), 'ana@ex.com');
fireEvent.changeText(getByPlaceholderText('Password'), 'senha123');
```

```
fireEvent.press(getByText('Entrar'));

    // 4. Wait for the UI update
    await waitFor(() => {
expect(getByText('Bem-vinda, Ana')).toBeTruthy();
    });

    // 5. Verify global (Redux) state
const state = store.getState();
    expect(state.auth.token).toBe('xyz-token');
  });
});
```

- **Mocks:** `fetchMock.mockResponseOnce` ensures a predictable response.
- **Rendering:** `renderWithProviders` avoids repetitive setup.
- **Interaction:** `fireEvent` simulates typing and taps.
- **Synchronization:** `waitFor` waits for the UI to reflect success.
- **Validation:** Asserts both UI outcomes and internal state.

Synchronization and Waiting Strategies

- `waitFor`: It waits until a condition is `Truthy` within a timeout (default 1000 ms).
- **findBy* queries:** It combines query + wait until timeout.

  ```
  const title = await findByText('Dashboard');
  expect(title).toBeTruthy();
  ```

- **Avoid fixed timeouts:** Never use `setTimeout`; rely on the async utilities of RTL.
- **Mocking slow endpoints:** You can artificially delay mocks:

  ```
  fetchMock.mockResponseOnce(
    () => new Promise(res =>setTimeout(() => res({ body: '{}' }), 100)),
  { status: 200 }
  );
  ```

Running Jest in CI

GitHub Actions

```
name: Integration Tests

on: [push, pull_request]

jobs:
  integration:
    runs-on: ubuntu-latest
    steps:
      - uses: actions/checkout@v3
      - uses: actions/setup-node@v3
        with:
          node-version: '18'
      - run: npm ci
      - run: npm test -- --runInBand
      - uses: actions/upload-artifact@v3
```

```
        with:
          name: coverage-report
          path: coverage
```

- **--runInBand** ensures tests that share global mocks do not collide.

CircleCI

```
version: 2.1

jobs:
  test:
docker:
      - image: cimg/node:18
    steps:
      - checkout
      - run: npm ci
      - run: npm test -- --runInBand
      - store_artifacts:
          path: coverage

workflows:
test_flow:
    jobs:
      - test
```

Best Practices and Performance Tips

- **Isolate mocks:** Call `fetchMock.resetMocks()` in `beforeEach` to avoid test pollution.
- **Keep tests focused:** Each should cover a single, clear flow.
- **Avoid redundant tests:** Do not repeat the same scenario across multiple specs—group related assertions.
- **Use snapshots sparingly:** It is only for stable components; prefer explicit assertions.
- **Control parallelism:** Running tests in series (`runInBand`) can be necessary when global providers are in conflict.
- **Maintain coverage above 80%:** Focus on critical routes, while ensuring broad coverage overall.
- **Inspect failures quickly:** `console.log` still works inside tests to help diagnose issues.

With Jest and React Native Testing Library, you can build a fast, maintainable suite of integration and usage-flow tests—no emulator overhead—ensuring that your most critical scenarios continue to work as expected.

Error Monitoring with Firebase Crashlytics

Firebase Crashlytics is a real-time crash-reporting solution that helps you identify, prioritize, and fix failures in mobile apps. It collects detailed crash reports—including stack traces, device info, and execution context—and automatically groups them into issues so that your team can focus on the most impactful errors.

As an alternative, many teams choose **Sentry** alongside (or instead of) Firebase Crashlytics because it has strong **JavaScript stack trace symbolication** when you upload the correct **source maps**, which can make RN issues significantly easier to debug. For **Expo-managed** projects, Sentry has **first-class Expo support** (official Expo and Sentry setup guides), while Crashlytics (typically via React Native

Firebase) requires **native code** and therefore will work in **Expo Go**—you will need a **development build / prebuild** (often via EAS Build) to include it.

Overview of Crashlytics

Crashlytics provides:

- **Automatic crash reporting:** It captures uncaught JS and native exceptions, both fatal and non-fatal.
- **Smart grouping:** Similar failures are unified into "issues" to reduce noise.
- **Device context:** App version, OS version, device model, and available memory.
- **Breadcrumbs and custom logs:** Pre-crash events that help reconstruct the execution flow.
- **Management console:** Firebase Dashboard shows metrics like crash-free user rates and regressions over time.

SDK Integration in a React Native Project

Install Dependencies

```
npm install @react-native-firebase/app @react-native-firebase/crashlytics
```

iOS native setup

Add **`GoogleService-Info.plist to ios/YourApp/`**.

In **`ios/Podfile`**:

```
platform :ios, '11.0'
target 'YourApp' do
use_frameworks!
  pod 'Firebase/Core'
  pod 'Firebase/Crashlytics'
  pod 'Firebase/Analytics'
end
```

Run:

```
cd ios&& pod install && cd ..
```

Android Native Setup

Place **`google-services.json`** in **`android/app/`**.

In **`android/build.gradle`**:

```
buildscript {
  dependencies {
classpath 'com.google.gms:google-services:4.3.15'
  }
}
```

In **`android/app/build.gradle`**:

```
apply plugin: 'com.google.gms.google-services'

dependencies {
  implementation platform('com.google.firebase:firebase-bom:32.1.0')
  implementation 'com.google.firebase:firebase-crashlytics'
}
```

Initialize in JavaScript

```
// App.js
import React from 'react';
import crashlytics from '@react-native-firebase/crashlytics';

if (__DEV__) {
  // Optional: disable automatic collection in development
crashlytics().setCrashlyticsCollectionEnabled(false);
} else {
crashlytics().setCrashlyticsCollectionEnabled(true);
}

export default function App() {
  return <YourRootNavigator />;
}
```

Capturing Unhandled Errors and Panics

By default, Crashlytics captures uncaught JS and native exceptions. To log non-fatal errors manually:

```
try {
  // Code that may throw
dangerousOperation();
} catch (error) {
  // Mark as non-fatal
crashlytics().recordError(error);
}
```

To force a test crash:

```
<Button
  title="Test Crashlytics"
onPress={() =>crashlytics().crash()}
/>
```

On Android, you can also capture native exceptions:

```
// MainApplication.java
import com.google.firebase.crashlytics.FirebaseCrashlytics;

public class MainApplication extends Application {
  @Override
  public void onCreate() {
super.onCreate();
Thread.setDefaultUncaughtExceptionHandler((thread, throwable) -> {
FirebaseCrashlytics.getInstance().recordException(throwable);
      // Hand off to the default handler
Thread.getDefaultUncaughtExceptionHandler()
.uncaughtException(thread, throwable);
    });
  }
}
```

Sending Custom Logs and Breadcrumbs

Breadcrumbs are "checkpoints" that appear in crash reports, giving context:

```
// Before a critical action
crashlytics().log('Starting user data fetch');

// Within a flow
crashlytics().setUserId(user.id);
crashlytics().setAttribute('feature_flag', 'new-home');
```

You can record up to 64 KB of logs per session. Use:

- **`log(message: string)`**: Simple flow annotations.
- **`setAttribute(key, value)`**: Metadata for context filtering.
- **`setUserId(id)`**: Associates crashes with specific users (mind privacy regulations).

Analyzing Reports and Setting Alerts

In the Firebase Console:

- **Dashboard:**
    - **Crash-free users:** Percentage of users without crashes.
    - **Recent issues:** Failure groups ordered by occurrences.
- **Issue details:**
    - Full JS and native stack traces.
    - Chronological breadcrumbs.
- **Alerts:**
    - Configure email or Slack notifications when a new issue exceeds a threshold (like rash-free rate drops by 5%).
    - Use "**`Alerts & Monitoring`**" to set conditions (version regressions, and so on).

Best Practices for Naming and Grouping

Log Message Structure

Use clear prefixes:

```
crashlytics().log('[Auth] Login started');
crashlytics().log('[Auth] Login succeeded');
```

Consistent Attributes

```
crashlytics().setAttribute(
  'env',
  __DEV__ ? 'development' : 'production'
);
crashlytics().setAttribute('screen', 'HomeScreen');
```

Versioning

Ensure each build has the correct **`versionName`** & **`versionCode`** (Android) or **`CFBundleShortVersionString`** (iOS)—Crashlytics groups issues by version.

Manual Grouping

When needed, import similar-category logs to unify issues that automatic grouping misses.

Attribute Hygiene

Avoid sensitive data (emails, IDs) in attributes; use anonymized identifiers or hashes.

By following these configurations and practices, Firebase Crashlytics becomes a powerful extension of your QA workflow, giving you real-time visibility into production failures and enabling rapid fixes that maintain user trust.

Real-Time Debugging

Real-time debugging is essential for quickly diagnosing bugs during active development. React Native Debugger and Flipper provide component inspection, state monitoring, network analysis, and performance profiling—all in a graphical interface that connects to your running app.

React Native Debugger

React Native Debugger is a desktop application that combines Chrome DevTools with extensions specifically for Redux and React Native.

Element and Prop Inspection

Element and prop inspection helps developers understand how components are rendered and how data flows through the application at runtime. By examining component hierarchies and passed properties, teams can quickly identify UI inconsistencies, unexpected behavior, and state-related issues.

Connecting

Install and launch:

```
brew install --cask react-native-debugger
open -a "React Native Debugger"
```

1. In your app, enable Remote JS Debugging (⌘D on iOS Simulator or ⌘M on Android Emulator) and choose **Debug with Chrome**.

Inspecting:

- In the **Elements** tab, select any visual component on the device.
- View its JSX/native tree and edit props in real time to test styles, text, and behavior.

Redux and State Debugging

If your app uses Redux, React Native Debugger includes **ReduxDevTools** out of the box.

Enabling

Make sure that you apply the **ReduxDevTools** middleware in your store setup:

```
import { createStore, applyMiddleware, compose } from 'redux';

constcomposeEnhancers = window.__REDUX_DEVTOOLS_EXTENSION_COMPOSE__ || compose;
const store = createStore(
```

```
rootReducer,
composeEnhancers(applyMiddleware(/* your middleware here */))
);
```

Using

- In the `Redux` tab, watch every dispatched action and view diffs between the previous and current state.
- Click on any action to "time-travel" back to that state, making it easy to reproduce bugs.

Breakpoints and Watch Expressions

Breakpoints

- In the `Sources` tab, open your `.js/.ts` files.
- Click the gutter to set a breakpoint on any line.

Step-through Execution

- When a breakpoint is hit, use `Step Over`, `Step Into`, and `Step Out` to navigate through the call stack.

Watch Expressions

- In the **Watch** panel, add expressions like `this.state.user` or `props.items.length`.
- Their values are recalculated on each pause, letting you monitor critical variables without disrupting execution.

Flipper

Flipper is an extensible debugging platform maintained by the React Native team, offering plugins for many native and JavaScript features.

Essential Plugins (Layout, Networking, Logs)

- **Layout:** Visualize the native view hierarchy and component alignment. Enable the plugin, then click **Layout** to inspect margins, padding, and background colors.
- **Networking:** Intercept all HTTP/S requests from the app. View URLs, headers, payloads, and responses—ideal for debugging APIs or CORS issues.
- **Logs:** Centralize `console.log`, `console.warn`, and native JS errors. Filter by severity or search by keyword.

Database and `AsyncStorage` Inspection

- **`AsyncStorage`:** Install the `AsyncStorage` plugin via **Manage Plugins**. Browse stored keys and values, clear test data, or edit values in real time.
- **SQLite / Realm:** If you use native databases, specific plugins let you run queries and view tables directly in Flipper.

Performance Monitor and CPU Profiler

- **Performance Monitor:** Displays FPS, frame times, and memory usage in real time—useful for pinpointing rendering bottlenecks and frame drops.

- **CPU Profiler:** Record a session and view JavaScript flame charts. Identify functions that consume excessive CPU time and optimize loops, listeners, or callbacks.

By integrating React Native Debugger and Flipper into your workflow, you gain full visibility into the UI, state, network, and performance of your app. These tools let you diagnose and fix issues far faster than relying on simple logs or **`console.log`**, elevating both app quality and developer experience.

Continuous Logging and Monitoring Strategies

To maintain the health of your app post-launch, it is essential not only to capture crashes but also to record anomalous behaviors, measure performance, and react quickly to incidents. The best practices and tools that make up a full continuous logging and monitoring workflow are discussed in the following subsection.

Structured Logging Best Practices (JSON, Severity Levels)

JSON Format

Instead of free-form text messages, emit logs as JSON objects. This makes automatic parsing and field-based searches easier.

```
console.log(JSON.stringify({
  timestamp: new Date().toISOString(),
  level: 'info',
  module: 'AuthService',
  message: 'Login attempt',
userId: user.id,
}));
```

Severity Levels

- **`debug`**: Detailed developer information.
- **`info`**: Business events (such as "**`user X completed checkout`**").
- **`warn`**: Unexpected but non-fatal conditions.
- **`error`**: Errors that affect flow but do not crash the app.
- **`fatal`**: Conditions that cause a crash or total lock-up.

Consistent Context: Include fields such as **`requestId`**, **`sessionId`**, **`version`**, and **`deviceModel`**. Use a consistent naming scheme so you can correlate logs across services.

Shipping Logs to External Services (Sentry, and Loggly)

Centralizing logs in specialized platforms enables fast search, correlation, and alerting.

Sentry

```
npm install @sentry/react-native
```

Then:

```
import * as Sentry from '@sentry/react-native';
```

```
Sentry.init({ dsn: 'https://<PUBLIC_KEY>@o0.ingest.sentry.io/0' });
```

```
Sentry.captureMessage('User clicked purchase', 'info');
Sentry.captureException(new Error('Payment failed'));
```

Loggly / Datadog

Send logs via HTTP or UDP directly from the app (consider proxying through your backend to avoid exposing keys). Many SDKs batch and flush events automatically.

Hybrid Strategy

- Keep low-level (`debug`) logs local to the console/dev environment.
- Immediately send critical (`error`, `fatal`) events to the external service.
- Batch `info`-level data to reduce network overhead.

Performance Metrics and Tracing

Beyond logs, metrics and spans help map latencies and bottlenecks:

`OpenTelemetry`

```
npm install @opentelemetry/api @opentelemetry/sdk-trace-base
```

Then:

```
import { trace } from '@opentelemetry/api';

const tracer = trace.getTracer('app-tracer');
tracer.startActiveSpan('fetch-user-data', span => {
  fetch('/user/123').then(() =>span.end());
});
```

Custom Metrics

- Screen load times.
- Event counts (like clicks, uploads).
- Memory and CPU usage (via Flipper plugins or native SDKs).

Sampling

- Collect 100% of error spans.
- Sample 5–10% of normal traffic to save resources.

Platforms like Datadog, New Relic, or Grafana Tempo ingest these traces, enabling flame-chart analysis and distributed tracing.

Uptime Dashboards and Alerts

Maintaining visibility on a central dashboard allows fast incident response:

Grafana + Prometheus:

- Prometheus scrapes health-check endpoints and custom metrics.
- Grafana visualizes response times, errors per minute, and active users.

`Alertmanager`:

- Sends emails, Slack messages, or PagerDuty alerts when metrics breach thresholds (say error rate > 1% over 5 minutes).

Uptime Robot / `StatusPage`

- External services that ping critical endpoints (login, checkout).
- In case of downtime, notify the team and publish a public status page.

Feedback Loop: From Production Error to Development Fix

This section explains how production issues are identified, analyzed, and translated into actionable fixes within the development workflow to improve stability and future releases.

1. **Detection:** Structured logs and Crashlytics raise issues in production.
2. **Investigation:** Dashboards and traces reveal root causes and context (device, session, version).
3. **Reproduction:** Write unit or integration tests that simulate the error with mocked data.
4. **Fix:** Implement the correction and cover the case with a new test to prevent regressions.
5. **Deploy:** CI/CD pipelines ensure that tests pass before releasing the fix.
6. **Validation:** Monitor the first hours post-release to confirm the error is resolved; adjust thresholds or alerts as needed.

This cycle ensures every production failure drives continuous improvement, reducing bug recurrence and boosting delivery confidence.

Reflections and Future Trends

As we mature our testing and debugging pipeline, it is important to consolidate what we have learned, document a checklist of best practices for each release, and look ahead for innovations that make our QA process even more agile and effective.

Recapping the Testing and Debugging Pipeline

- **Unit Tests (Jest):** Isolate functions and components, providing fast feedback on every code change. Minimum coverage enforced by quality gates in CI.
- **Integration and Usage-Flow Tests (Jest + RN Testing Library):** Simulate end-to-end scenarios in pure JS, including providers (Redux, Navigation) and network mocks. Offer speed and simplicity without emulator overhead.
- **Crash Monitoring (Firebase Crashlytics):** Capture fatal and non-fatal failures in production, group them into issues, and surface device context. Logs and breadcrumbs enrich reports to accelerate investigation.
- **Real-Time Debugging (React Native Debugger and Flipper):** Inspect component trees, ReduxDevTools, breakpoints, and watch expressions. Monitor layout, network, **`AsyncStorage`**, and performance live.
- **Structured Logging and Continuous Monitoring:** JSON logs with severity levels and consistent metadata. Metrics and tracing to map latencies, plus uptime dashboards and alerts.

Together, this integrated flow gives end-to-end visibility—from local code to production issues—drastically reducing bug detection and resolution cycles.

Quality Checklist before Release

Before each handoff to QA or production rollout, verify that:

- **All tests pass**: Unit, integration, and minimum coverage thresholds met.
- **Clean build**: No critical console warnings or lint errors.
- **Smoke-test manually**: Quickly exercise core flows (login, navigation, forms).
- **Crash-free rate**: Zero regressions in Crashlytics for the new version.
- **Alerts configured**: Thresholds set for errors, performance regressions, and uptime monitoring.
- **Version metadata**: versionCode/versionName (Android) and CFBundleShortVersionString (iOS) updated.
- **Test documentation**: "light" E2E scenarios and debugging guidelines up to date in the repo.

Evolving Your QA Strategy and Future Trends

- **Shift-Left Testing:** Embed tests even earlier: pre-commit hooks, PR previews in isolated environments. Incorporate automated security scans (SAST) and dependency analysis (SCA).
- **TestOps & Unified Observability:** Converged test pipelines, deployments, and monitoring in a single dashboard. Adopt lightweight chaos-engineering experiments in staging to validate resilience.
- **AI-Driven Testing:** Emerging tools that generate test cases automatically from user flows or source code. Predict flaky tests to reduce false positives.
- **Performance as Code:** Include automated performance tests in CI (component benchmarks, memory). Define performance budgets and block merges that exceed thresholds.
- **Mobile-Specific Observability:** Enhance native-module tracing and frame-drop analysis in React Native. Use mobile APMs that correlate logs, traces, and end-user metrics.
- **Culture of Continuous Quality:** Encourage test reviews in PRs and dialogue among developers, QA, and product owners. Maintain a living repository of "known issues" and "lessons learned" for collective learning.

Adopting these practices and tracking emerging trends will ensure your QA strategy evolves alongside growing complexity, scalability demands, and user-experience expectations—keeping your app secure, performant, and reliable.

Conclusion

Throughout this chapter, we have explored not only the tools and commands needed to implement a testing and debugging pipeline in React Native, but—above all—the **why** behind each step. Why write unit, integration, and "light E2E" tests? Why monitor production crashes with Crashlytics? Why invest in real-time debugging and structured logging? The answer lies in our technical maturity: the ability to anticipate consequences and shape the project with a long-term vision.

When we limit ourselves to "just making it work"—sprinkling code without structure, skipping tests, or ignoring error reports—we jeopardize reliability and scalability of the app. Mobile projects grow fast, and every shortcut taken today becomes technical debt that accrues interest in the form of subtle bugs, intermittent failures, and wasted hours in the debugger. Maturity shows itself in the conscious decision to invest time in:

- **Well-written tests** that validate code intent and prevent regressions;
- **Continuous monitoring** that turns crashes into actionable insights;
- **Proactive debugging** that speeds up diagnosis and avoids guesswork;
- **Structured logging and metrics** that provide true visibility into production behavior.

These pillars are not bureaucracy—they are acts of respect for your future self, your team, and your users. They elevate the developer from a mere "code operator" to an architect of solutions, able to traverse the bridge between JavaScript and native layers without falling into the "black-box" trap.

Ultimately, the scalability of your project depends on the intentionality you employ today. Every test you write, every alert you configure, every logging dashboard you build is an investment in the peace of mind of future releases. With a solid QA and debugging foundation, what starts as a barebones feature set transforms into a reliable, memorable product— the result of engineering that combines clarity, consistency, and empathy for the next developer who will inherit your code. As for the next chapter, we are going to work on the main concepts of Performance Optimization and Architecture Best Practices.

Questions

Before moving on to the next chapters, it is essential to consolidate the knowledge you've gained so far.

1. How does React Native differ from traditional hybrid solutions (such as WebView-based) when it comes to rendering components?
2. What is the role of the JavaScript Thread in React Native, and why can overloading it harm app performance?
3. What is the Bridge in React Native, and how does it enable communication between JavaScript code and native Android/iOS elements?
4. What are the primary responsibilities of the UI Thread and the Shadow Thread in the rendering cycle of React Native?
5. When is it necessary to resort to native modules, and how do they integrate with the architecture of React Native?
6. What are the main subdirectories inside `android/` in a React Native project, and what is each one for?
7. How is the `ios/` folder structured, and why does it remain essential even when most development happens in JavaScript?
8. Why is modular organization of the `src/` folder important, and how does it contribute to the scalability and maintainability of the project?
9. Why is it recommended to separate components, services, hooks, utilities, and styles in a React Native project?
10. What are the key criteria for choosing between Expo and the React Native CLI when starting a new project?
11. In which contexts does it make sense to use Expo, and when does migrating to the pure CLI become necessary?
12. Which tools can be used for debugging in React Native, and how do they support development and bug fixing?

13. How does the build and deploy cycle work for a React Native app—from local development through publication in app stores?
14. Why is adopting coding standards (with ESLint, Prettier, and the like) essential in projects with multiple developers?
15. How do clear documentation and regular code reviews contribute to the consistency and quality of a project?

Carefully answering these questions will not only reinforce the core concepts but also encourage critical thinking about architectural decisions, best practices, and workflows. If any answer still feels unclear, revisiting the previous topics and examples will serve as an excellent exercise to enhance your autonomy as a React Native developer.

Key Terms

This chapter introduced several core concepts for React Native development. Understanding these terms reinforces what we have learned and prepares you to deepen your mastery of architecture, performance, and organization in modern mobile apps.

- **JavaScript Thread:** Responsible for running all JavaScript code in the app—business logic, state management, and navigation. It is the JS-side core of React Native and must be used sparingly to avoid compromising UI smoothness.
- **UI Thread (Main Thread):** The native thread in charge of visually rendering the interface of the app. It handles animations, user input, and all graphical elements, ensuring a smooth experience when well managed.
- **Shadow Thread:** It is an intermediary thread that calculates layouts using the Flexbox algorithm. It processes the visual structure and sends results to the UI Thread, optimizing rendering performance.
- **Bridge:** An asynchronous communication channel between the JavaScript world and native components on Android/iOS. It enables native rendering via JS commands and integration with modules written in native code.
- **Native Module:** Platform-specific code (Java/Kotlin on Android, Swift/Objective-C on iOS) that exposes operating-system APIs to JavaScript. Used for accessing the camera, sensors, GPS, and other native functionality.
- **Modular Structure (`src/`):** The central directory where all JavaScript/TypeScript code lives. It typically includes subfolders like **`components`**, **`screens`**, **`services`**, **`hooks`**, **`utils`**, **`assets`**, and **`styles`**, each with a clear responsibility.
- **Expo:** A framework that simplifies React Native development by providing preconfigured APIs and an automated build environment. Ideal for quick projects and small teams, but with limitations on advanced native customizations.
- **React Native CLI:** The pure React Native approach, offering full control over the **`android/`** and **`ios/`** folders. Allows use of native libraries, complex plugins, and custom configurations—recommended for large, highly customized projects.
- **Eject:** The process of migrating an Expo project to a pure React Native CLI setup. It generates the native structures (**`android/`**, **`ios/`**) and requires manual configuration of dependencies for greater customization freedom.
- **`AndroidManifest.xml`:** A key file in Android projects that declares permissions, activities (screens), and metadata used by the app. Any system-resource integration must be declared here.

- **`Info.plist`:** The iOS equivalent of **`AndroidManifest.xml`**. Defines app name, requested permissions, privacy settings, and status-bar behavior.
- **React Native Debugger:** A desktop tool combining Chrome DevTools with ReduxDevTools, allowing component inspection, prop/state viewing, and step-through execution with breakpoints.
- **Flipper:** A graphical debugging platform maintained by Facebook for React Native apps. Supports log inspection, network analysis, performance monitoring, layout visualization, and more via plugins.
- **`useState/useEffect`:** Fundamental hooks in functional components are as follows:
    - **`useState`** manages local state.
    - **`useEffect`** runs side effects (requests, timers, subscriptions) in response to changes.
- **ESLint / Prettier:** Linting and formatting tools that standardize code style and prevent common errors in multidisciplinary teams.
- **Code Review:** The practice of having peers review code to ensure standards, catch bugs, and foster collective learning within the team.
- **CI/CD (Continuous Integration / Continuous Deployment):** An automated process of testing, building, and publishing apps, ensuring delivered code is stable, meets standards, and is ready for distribution.

Mastering this conceptual and practical vocabulary is essential for confidently navigating the modern mobile ecosystem and building well-structured, high-performance React Native applications ready for sustainable growth.

CHAPTER 10
Performance Optimization and Architecture Best Practices

Introduction

Performance is one of the fundamental pillars in building high-quality mobile applications. In environments where resources are limited and user expectations for instant responses are high, any delay or sluggishness can directly impact user experience and retention. In this chapter, we will explore practical techniques and architectural strategies that help keep the app responsive, even as it grows in complexity and functionality.

We will cover topics ranging from code splitting and lazy loading to the smart use of lists (FlatList, SectionList, and VirtualizedList), avoiding unnecessary renders. You will learn how to effectively apply **`useCallback`**, **`useMemo`**, and **`React.memo`** to control the component rendering cycle. Additionally, we will discuss the importance of good code organization, including folder structure, separation of concerns, and standardization. Finally, we will introduce performance analysis tools and techniques for identifying bottlenecks, ensuring that your app remains fast, scalable, and maintainable in the long run.

Structure

In this chapter, we will cover the following topics:

- Introduction to Performance Optimization
    - Importance of Performance for User Experience
    - Difference between Render Performance and Network Performance
    - The Cost of Unnecessary Re-Renders
- Code Splitting and Lazy Loading
    - What Code Splitting Means in React Native (Versus Web)
    - Lazy Loading of Heavy Components and Routes
    - Strategies For Progressive Resource Loading
- List Optimization
    - Essential Props: **`Keyextractor`**, **`Initialnumtorender`**, **`Maxtorenderperbatch`**
    - Using **`Getitemlayout`** to Improve Performance in Long Lists
    - Practical Example with **`Flatlist`** and Large Datasets

- Memoization of Components and Functions
  - Differences between Memoizing Values and Functions
  - `React.Memo` For Functional Components
  - Example Comparing Components with and without Memoization
- Code Organization and Folder Structure
  - Feature-Based Versus Type-Based Organization (Atoms, Molecules, Screens)
  - File Naming and Structuring Conventions
  - Code Standardization with Linters and Formatters (Eslint, Prettier)
- Identifying Performance Bottlenecks
  - Analysis Tools: React Devtools, Flipper, Hermes Profiler
  - Using `Console.Time`, `Why-Did-You-Render`, And Performance Hooks
- Architectural Patterns For Scalability
  - Context API versus Redux Versus Zustand: When and Why to Use Each
  - Best Practices For Layer Separation (View, State, Service, Data)
- Performance Best Practices Checklist
  - Rules to Avoid Unnecessary Re-Renders
  - Strategies For Handling Animations, Images, and Intensive Events

Introduction to Performance Optimization

Performance is an invisible aspect when everything is running smoothly – but extremely noticeable when it is not. An app that responds quickly to user actions conveys a sense of quality, professionalism, and attention to detail. On the other hand, a slow app or one that frequently lags leads to frustration, higher abandonment rates, and can even damage the reputation of the brand. In mobile development – especially with React Native – performance is not just a matter of technical optimization, but of delivering a great user experience.

A practical example illustrates this well. Imagine an e-commerce app where, while scrolling through a product list, the images load slowly and the scroll feels choppy. Even if the app is functioning correctly, the user perceives the lag as a problem – they might assume the internet connection is bad, the phone is struggling, or worse, that the app is poorly built. Often, the root cause of this issue lies in simple implementation choices, such as loading the entire product list at once or rendering each item without efficient state control.

Render Performance versus Network Performance

When optimizing app performance, it is essential to understand that there are two main types of performance to consider: **network performance** and **render performance**. The former relates to how quickly and efficiently the app retrieves data from servers, APIs, or databases. The latter concerns how the UI of the app responds and updates based on that data – in other words, how fast elements are displayed after the data is fetched.

For instance, if you are building a news reading app, you might optimize network performance by using data caching, request compression, and asynchronous calls. But even with fast data retrieval, render performance can suffer if you try to display hundreds of news articles in a single `ScrollView`, which would result in noticeable frame drops. In this case, the better approach is to use a component like `FlatList`, which implements item virtualization out of the box.

```
// Code using ScrollView (not recommended for long lists)
<ScrollView>
  {articles.map(article => (
<ArticleCard key={article.id} data={article} />
  ))}
</ScrollView>
```

While this code appears simple, it hides a major problem: all **ArticleCard** components are rendered at once, which can overload memory and cause the app to freeze. Instead, use:

```
// Code using FlatList (on-demand rendering)
<FlatList
  data={articles}
renderItem={({ item }) =><ArticleCard data={item} />}
keyExtractor={item => item.id}
/>
```

With **FlatList**, React Native only renders the elements currently visible on the screen, saving resources and ensuring smoother scrolling.

The Cost of Unnecessary Renders

Rendering a component in React Native consumes both time and processing power. When a state changes or a prop is updated, React may re-evaluate and redraw parts of the interface. This is expected behavior — it is how React works. The problem arises when these renders happen without necessity, especially in lists, animations, or screens with many components.

One common mistake that leads to unnecessary renders is constantly recreating functions inside a component. Consider this example:

```
constMyComponent = ({ onClick }) => {
consthandleClick = () => {
    console.log('Clicked');
  };

  return <Button title="Click here" onPress={handleClick} />;
};
```

The **handleClick** function is recreated every time the component re-renders. In a small app, this may not be noticeable. But in a list where each item contains similar functions, the impact quickly adds up. The solution is to use **useCallback** to memoize the function:

```
constMyComponent = ({ onClick }) => {
consthandleClick = useCallback(() => {
    console.log('Clicked');
  }, []);

  return <Button title="Click here" onPress={handleClick} />;
};
```

This small change prevents the function from being recreated unnecessarily on every render, which is especially important when child components are optimized with **React.memo**.

Another critical point is updating state that does not directly affect the UI. Changes in poorly structured global state, such as a generic context can trigger re-renders across the entire component tree. This can be avoided with strategic use of **useMemo**, **React.memo**, and properly scoped local state management.

Throughout this chapter, we will explore these techniques and more advanced strategies to help you build applications that not only work, but will also perform with excellence.

Code Splitting and Lazy Loading

Modern applications grow rapidly in size and complexity. As new features, screens, and libraries are added, the initial load time tends to increase, which can negatively impact the user experience. To mitigate this, techniques like code splitting and lazy loading are essential. They allow the app to load only what is needed at the right time, improving performance and reducing initial response time.

In web applications built with React, code splitting is widely adopted and supported by tools like Webpack. It works by breaking the main bundle into smaller chunks that are loaded on demand. This means a route, component, or library is only downloaded and executed when truly needed. React provides built-in support for this through **`React.lazy()`** and the **`Suspense`** component.

Code Splitting in React Native

In React Native, the concept of code splitting does not apply in the same way as on the web. By default, Metro bundles your JavaScript into a single production bundle (often compiled to Hermes bytecode), so **`import()`** does **not** automatically create separate "chunks" for release builds the way Webpack-style chunking does. In other words, **dynamic imports can delay evaluation/initialization of a module, but they do not necessarily reduce the size of the shipped release bundle or the amount of code delivered to the device at startup.**

That said, there are still equivalent strategies that provide real wins:

- **Lazy evaluation / deferred initialization:** Using **`React.lazy`**, conditional **`require()`**, or **`import()`** can postpone heavy module initialization until a screen is actually visited, reducing work during the first render and improving perceived startup responsiveness.
- **Render-path optimization:** Even if the code is present in the bundle, loading a heavy chart/map/editor only when needed can reduce initial render cost and memory churn on the critical path.

For example, heavier UI modules (charts, maps, rich editors) can be loaded only when the user navigates to the relevant screen—improving time-to-interactive and avoiding unnecessary work on app launch. If you truly need **separate** downloadable bundles in production (web-style splitting), that typically requires a multi-bundle approach or specialized tooling rather than relying on **`import()`** alone.

Lazy Loading Heavy Components and Routes

Lazy loading is the practice of deferring the loading of parts of the code until they are actually needed. In the context of navigation, this means certain screens (routes) are not loaded until the user navigates to them. This is essential to avoid preloading screens that may never be accessed during the current session.

In web React apps, we use:

```
import React, { Suspense, lazy } from 'react';

constChartScreen = lazy(() => import('./screens/ChartScreen'));

export default function App() {
  return (
<Suspense fallback={<LoadingIndicator />}>
<ChartScreen />
```

```
</Suspense>
  );
}
```

In the example above, the **ChartScreen** component is only loaded when the user actually navigates to it. The **Suspense** component displays a visual fallback (**<LoadingIndicator />**) while the asynchronous import is in progress.

In React Native, although **React.lazy()** and Suspense have **some** support, they are **not** a drop-in replacement for the web experience—especially for async data loading—and behavior can vary depending on your runtime (like Hermes), React Native version, and architecture. Readers should treat Suspense in RN as **environment-sensitive** and validate compatibility before adopting it broadly.

For production-grade apps, RN-first approaches are often more predictable:

- **Navigator-level lazy strategies:** Defer mounting heavy screens until the user reaches them (and consider preloading on hover/intent or after initial interaction).
- **Prefetching and warm-up:** Proactively fetch data and/or preload expensive modules after the first render or during idle time so that subsequent navigation is instant.
- **Metro/RN startup optimizations:** Focus on reducing work on the critical startup path (minimize synchronous module initialization, avoid costly side effects at import time, and keep the initial route light).

Therefore, a pragmatic alternative pattern—explicitly controlling when a heavy component is loaded—often uses **useState** and **useEffect** (or an interaction/idle callback) to defer work without relying on Suspense semantics.

```
import { useState, useEffect } from 'react';
import { ActivityIndicator, View } from 'react-native';

export default function LazyChartWrapper() {
const [ChartScreen, setChartScreen] = useState(null);

useEffect(() => {
    import('./screens/ChartScreen').then(module => {
setChartScreen(() =>module.default);
    });
  }, []);

  if (!ChartScreen) {
    return (
<View style={{ flex: 1, justifyContent: 'center' }}>
<ActivityIndicator size="large" />
</View>
    );
  }

  return <ChartScreen />;
}
```

This approach **defers** loading so the component is fetched/initialized only when needed, which can reduce work on the initial render path. However, it does not *guarantee* a faster experience overall: it may simply **shift the cost** to the moment the screen is opened, potentially causing navigation jank unless you **preload strategically** (for instance, after initial interaction or on user intent) and render an appropriate **fallback/loading state** while the module initializes.

Progressive Loading Strategies

Beyond components and routes, the concept of progressive loading can be applied to heavy assets such as high-resolution images, videos, or API data. Common techniques include:

- Showing a smaller or "preview" version of an image while the full version loads in the background
- Deferring the execution of complex animations until the screen is fully loaded
- Using temporary placeholders for network data while the actual content is fetched

For example, with images, a typical approach would be:

```
<Image
  source={isHighRes ? highResImage : lowResImage}
onLoadEnd={() =>setIsHighRes(true)}
  style={{ width: 200, height: 200 }}
/>
```

Initially, a lightweight image is shown. Once the high-resolution version finishes loading, it replaces the previous one. This strategy reduces perceived load time and provides a smoother user experience.

Even though there are differences between web and mobile environments, the core principle remains the same: avoid loading what will not be used immediately. In React Native projects, adopting lazy loading for heavy components, deferring the import of large libraries, and structuring the app to load only what is necessary are some of the key practices for consistent performance and a smoother user experience. As we move forward in this chapter, we will see how these strategies integrate with optimized lists, memoization, and performance analysis tools to build truly efficient apps.

List Optimization

Lists are among the most frequently used components in any React Native application. They appear in social media feeds, product catalogs, messaging apps, notifications—virtually any screen with dynamic content. Precisely because they are so common—and potentially heavy—optimizing lists is one of the most effective ways to ensure a smooth and responsive interface. Improper configuration can lead to choppy scrolling, slow load times, high memory usage, and low frames per second (FPS).

Fortunately, React Native provides strong primitives for rendering lists efficiently: **`FlatList`**, **`SectionList`**, and **`VirtualizedList`**. Understanding the differences between them—and tuning a small set of high-impact props—goes a long way toward maximizing performance.

`FlatList` is the most commonly used option for displaying long, homogeneous lists. It is built on top of **`VirtualizedList`**, which virtualizes rendering: only the items currently visible on screen (plus a configurable buffer around them) are mounted at any given time, reducing memory pressure and avoiding unnecessary work.

`SectionList` builds upon the same virtualization model, adding support for grouped data with per-section headers (and optional footers). It is ideal for categorized content such as contacts grouped by initial letter or products grouped by category.

`VirtualizedList` is the underlying base component behind both **`FlatList`** and **`SectionList`**. It is rarely used directly because it requires more manual configuration (say item accessors and layout assumptions). Direct usage is best reserved for highly customized, hybrid, or non-standard list implementations where the higher-level abstractions are too limiting.

High-impact FlatList configuration (essential + advanced knobs): To get the most out of FlatList, start with a small set of essentials, then selectively apply advanced tuning based on your data and UI complexity:

- **Essential Props:**
    - **`keyExtractor`:** It ensures stable item identity and reduces unnecessary re-renders.
    - **`initialNumToRender`:** It controls initial render cost; smaller values improve first paint but may show content "filling in."
    - **`maxToRenderPerBatch`:** It caps how many items render per batch; lower values reduce JS spikes but may delay content.
- **Advanced Tuning (Use Intentionally):**
    - **`windowSize`:** It controls how many "screens worth" of content are kept rendered around the viewport. Higher values reduce blank areas during fast scrolls; lower values reduce memory usage but can cause visible pop-in.
    - **`updateCellsBatchingPeriod`:** It controls the delay (ms) between rendering batches. Increasing it can smooth out spikes on slower devices; decreasing it can make content appear faster but risks frame drops.
    - **`removeClippedSubviews`:** It detaches off-screen subviews to reduce memory usage.

      Often helps with large, simple lists (especially on Android), but can cause flicker or missing content with complex layouts (for example heavy shadows/elevation, absolute positioning, animated rows, or views that rely on off-screen measurement). Because behavior can vary by platform and view hierarchy, validate carefully before enabling it broadly.

This framing makes it clear that list performance is not only about "**`using FlatList`**," but about understanding virtualization and choosing the right knobs—while acknowledging that some optimizations have real tradeoffs and should be applied selectively.

Key Props for Performance

When using `FlatList` or `SectionList`, configuring a few key properties can significantly impact performance:

- `keyExtractor`: It defines a unique key for each item to prevent unnecessary re-renders.
- `initialNumToRender`: It controls how many items are rendered initially. A number that is too high can delay the screen load; too low can cause flickering while scrolling.
- `maxToRenderPerBatch`: It sets how many items are rendered per batch, helping manage memory usage and scroll performance.

A basic example:

```
<FlatList
  data={products}
keyExtractor={(item) => item.id}
initialNumToRender={10}
maxToRenderPerBatch={8}
renderItem={({ item }) =><ProductCard data={item} />}
/>
```

With this setup, the list starts by rendering 10 items and adds 8 more in each batch as the user scrolls. This reduces the initial load impact while maintaining steady performance.

Even when only visible items are rendered, each render can be costly if the child components are complex. Ensuring that list items do not re-render unnecessarily is critical.

The main strategy is to wrap list items with **React.memo**, which prevents re-renders when props have not changed:

```
constProductCard = React.memo(({ data }) => {
  return (
<View style={{ padding: 12 }}>
<Text>{data.name}</Text>
<Text>{data.price}</Text>
</View>
  );
});
```

If **ProductCard** relies on functions or derived values, it is also important to use **useCallback** and **useMemo** to prevent function or object recreation on every render.

Boosting Performance with getItemLayout

Another crucial optimization is using the **getItemLayout** prop. It lets **FlatList** know in advance the size of each item, avoiding expensive layout calculations during scrolling – especially useful for long lists with fixed-height items:

```
<FlatList
  data={products}
keyExtractor={(item) => item.id}
renderItem={({ item }) =><ProductCard data={item} />}
getItemLayout={(data, index) => (
{ length: 80, offset: 80 * index, index }
  )}
/>
```

In this example, each item is 80 pixels tall. This allows **FlatList** to jump directly to a specific index (like with **scrollToIndex**) without measuring actual DOM elements, reducing computational cost.

Suppose you are building a product catalog with hundreds of items. Here is a realistic and optimized setup:

```
constProductList = ({ products }) => {
constrenderItem = useCallback(
({ item }) =><ProductCard data={item} />,
    []
  );

  return (
<FlatList
      data={products}
keyExtractor={(item) => item.id}
renderItem={renderItem}
initialNumToRender={12}
maxToRenderPerBatch={10}
windowSize={5}
getItemLayout={(data, index) => (
{ length: 100, offset: 100 * index, index }
      )}
    />
```

```
  );
};
```

In this setup, **useCallback** prevents **renderItem** from being recreated on each render. Initial and batch rendering settings are tuned, and **getItemLayout** allows fast, efficient scrolling through large lists.

A list might seem simple, but it has one of the greatest potentials to impact overall app performance. When using **FlatList** or **SectionList**, combining best practices like **React.memo**, well-tuned props, and virtualization strategies can be the difference between a smooth app and one that lags with every scroll. With attention and testing, your lists can scale to thousands of items without sacrificing user experience.

Memoizing Components and Functions

As your application grows in complexity, it is common to encounter performance issues caused by unnecessary re-renders. In many cases, these re-renders are triggered by minor changes in state or props that end up affecting components that, in practice, should not be updated. To handle this scenario, React provides memoization tools like **useMemo**, **useCallback**, and **React.memo**.

In this context, memoization means caching the result of a computation (whether a value, function, or component) and reusing it in future renders as long as its dependencies have not changed. This strategy avoids redundant work by React, such as recalculating or re-rendering parts of the UI that have not actually changed — saving processing time and making the app feel smoother.

The **useMemo** hook is used to memoize derived values, while **useCallback** is used to memoize functions. Both follow the same logic: if the provided dependencies remain the same between renders, the value or function will not be recreated.

Consider the following example using **useMemo**, where the computation is expensive:

```
constexpensiveCalculation = (input: number) => {
  let result = 0;
  for (let i = 0; i< 1_000_000; i++) {
    result += i * input;
  }
  return result;
};

constMyComponent = ({ number }) => {
const result = useMemo(() =>expensiveCalculation(number), [number]);

  return <Text>Result: {result}</Text>;
};
```

In this example, the calculation is only re-executed when the **number** changes, preventing the function from being called on every render.

On the other hand, **useCallback** is essential when a function is passed as a prop to child components optimized with **React.memo**:

```
constMyComponent = ({ onSave }) => {
consthandleClick = useCallback(() => {
onSave();
  }, [onSave]);

  return <Button title="Save" onPress={handleClick} />;
};
```

Without **useCallback**, **handleClick** would be recreated on every render, triggering a re-render in the child component receiving it as a prop.

Differences between Value and Function Memoization

Although **useMemo** and **useCallback** serve similar purposes, it is important to know when to use each:

- **useMemo(fn, deps)** returns the result of the function.
- **useCallback(fn, deps)** returns the function itself.

Both rely on the **deps** array to determine whether the memoized value/function can be reused. Misusing **useMemo** for functions (or **useCallback** for values) can lead to confusing behavior and even subtle bugs.

A common mistake:

```
// Incorrect usage
constmemoizedFn = useMemo(() => () => console.log('Hi'), []);
```

The correct approach is to use **useCallback** if the goal is to memoize the function:

```
constmemoizedFn = useCallback(() => console.log('Hi'), []);
```

Although powerful, these tools should not be used indiscriminately. Using **useMemo** or **useCallback** in places where the cost of recreation is low can be more harmful than helpful. That is because every memoization also introduces overhead for dependency checking and internal bookkeeping.

Use memoization when:

- The computation is expensive and depends on rarely changing data.
- The function is passed as a prop to components wrapped in **React.memo**.
- You have identified through profiling that unnecessary re-renders are affecting performance.

Avoid memoization when:

- The value or function is simple and cheap to create.
- The component is small and already fast to re-render.
- You are optimizing prematurely without measuring.

React.memo for Functional Components

React.memo is a higher-order component that wraps functional components to avoid re-renders when props have not changed. It performs a shallow comparison of props by default. Here is a practical difference:

```
// Without memoization
constInfoBox = ({ title, content }) => {
console.log('InfoBox rendered');
  return (
<View>
<Text>{title}</Text>
<Text>{content}</Text>
</View>
  );
};
```

Now applying **React.memo**:

```
constInfoBox = React.memo(({ title, content }) => {
console.log('InfoBox rendered');
  return (
<View>
<Text>{title}</Text>
<Text>{content}</Text>
</View>
  );
});
```

If neither **title** nor **content** changes, the **InfoBox** component will not re-render — even if the parent component updates.

Comparative Example: With and Without Memoization

Let us compare two practical scenarios to illustrate performance gains.

Without memoization:

```
const Parent = () => {
const [count, setCount] = useState(0);

  return (
<>
<Button title="Increment" onPress={() =>setCount(count + 1)} />
<InfoBox title="Static" content="Does not change" />
</>
  );
};
```

Every time **setCount** is called, **Parent** re-renders, and so does **InfoBox**, even though its props remain the same.

With memoization:

```
constMemoInfoBox = React.memo(({ title, content }) => {
console.log('MemoInfoBox rendered');
  return (
<View>
<Text>{title}</Text>
<Text>{content}</Text>
</View>
  );
});

const Parent = () => {
const [count, setCount] = useState(0);

  return (
<>
<Button title="Increment" onPress={() =>setCount(count + 1)} />
<MemoInfoBox title="Static" content="Does not change" />
</>
  );
};
```

In this second example, clicking the button only re-renders the **`Parent`** component. **`MemoInfoBox`** remains cached, saving resources and avoiding unnecessary re-renders.

Memoizing components and functions is one of the most effective techniques for improving performance in React Native apps, especially in components that re-render frequently or in large lists. However, like any optimization, it should be applied carefully and based on real data. By understanding when and how to apply **`useMemo`**, **`useCallback`**, and **`React.memo`**, you gain fine-grained control over the lifecycle of your components and ensure a much smoother experience for the end user.

Code Organization and Folder Structure

The structure of a project is like the foundation of a house: if poorly planned, even small changes can lead to major problems. As a React Native app evolves, adding new features or performing maintenance becomes increasingly difficult if the codebase is disorganized. A well-structured project improves readability, facilitates team collaboration, enables more accurate testing, and promotes scalability without unnecessary headaches. In this section, we will explore different ways to structure a React Native project professionally and efficiently.

Small projects often start with a few folders like **`components`**, **`screens`**, and **`assets`**. At first, this seems sufficient. However, as the project grows, this approach becomes hard to manage: files get too long, names become repetitive, and dependencies get tangled. The solution is to adopt a modular and scalable structure where each part of the app is organized by domain or functionality.

A sample structure might look like:

```
src/
├── features/
│   ├── auth/
│   │   ├── screens/
│   │   ├── components/
│   │   ├── hooks/
│   │   └── services/
│   └── products/
│       ├── screens/
│       ├── components/
│       ├── context/
│       └── services/
├── shared/
│   ├── components/
│   ├── hooks/
│   ├── utils/
│   └── types/
├── navigation/
├── assets/
└── App.tsx
```

This pattern is known as **feature-first organization** and helps encapsulate responsibilities, making it easier to locate and update specific features without affecting the rest of the codebase.

Feature-Based versus Type-Based Organization

There are two popular approaches to organizing folders:

- **Type-first organization**: Components, screens, hooks, contexts, and services are grouped by type, regardless of their feature. **Example**: **`src/components/`**, **`src/screens/`**, **`src/hooks/`**, and so on.

Pros: Easy reuse of shared resources.

Cons: Increases coupling and makes it harder to locate all parts of a specific feature.

- **Feature-first organization**: Each app feature has its own folder containing everything it needs – screens, components, hooks, and so on. **Example**: **`src/features/user/`**, **`src/features/orders/`**, and so on.

  Pros: Better encapsulation, easier maintenance and scalability.

  Cons: Can lead to duplication if shared resources are not centralized.

The most mature approach for large-scale projects is to **combine both**: use feature-first for core domains, and maintain a **`shared/`** directory for reusable components and logic.

Clear separation of concerns is essential to avoid circular dependencies, duplicated logic, and difficult-to-test code. Here is a breakdown of common roles and where they should reside:

- **`components/`**: Reusable UI parts like buttons, cards, inputs, modals.
- **`screens/`**: Full pages of the app that compose multiple components.
- **`hooks/`**: Reusable logic based on state and effects (for instance, **`useAuth`**, **`useFetch`**).
- **`context/`**: Global state management using React Context.
- **`services/`**: API calls, data caching, and business logic separated from the UI.
- **`utils/`**: Helper functions like formatters, validators, and converters.

A clear and standardized structure accelerates onboarding and improves long-term maintainability.

Naming Conventions and File Structure

Consistent naming for files and folders may seem minor, but it has a huge impact on daily development. Some good practices include:

- Use clear, descriptive file names (**`LoginScreen.tsx`**, **`useUserProfile.ts`**, **`productService.ts`**).
- Use **PascalCase** for components (**`UserCard.tsx`**) and **camelCase** for functions, hooks, and utilities (**`formatPrice.ts`**, **`useCart.ts`**).
- Avoid unnecessary abbreviations: prefer **`OrderHistoryScreen.tsx`** over **`OHScreen.tsx`**.
- Place only one main component per file, unless dealing with small, tightly related components.
- Use **`index.ts`** files to simplify imports:

```
// Instead of:
import { ProductCard } from '../../../features/products/components/ProductCard';

// You can use:
import { ProductCard } from 'features/products';
```

Standardization with Linters and Formatters

Maintaining consistent code style across team members reduces conflicts, simplifies code reviews, and improves readability. Essential tools for this include:

- **`ESLint`**: It analyzes code for errors, bad practices, and inconsistencies.
- **`Prettier`**: It automatically formats code according to defined rules (spacing, quotes, semicolons, and the like).
- **`EditorConfig`**: It sets universal formatting rules across different editors.

Example **package.json** setup:

```
"scripts": {
  "lint": "eslint . --ext .ts,.tsx",
  "format": "prettier --write \"src/**/*.{ts,tsx}\""
}
```

Additionally, tools like **Husky** and **lint-staged** can run these checks before each commit, keeping the repository clean and consistent.

A solid folder structure and clearly defined responsibilities are some of the most valuable investments you can make in the long-term health of your project. By adopting feature-based organization, applying best practices for code separation, maintaining consistent naming conventions, and using linting and formatting tools, you are laying a reliable foundation that supports growth, refactoring, and collaboration. Code is not just written for machines — it is written for humans who will read and maintain it.

Identifying Performance Bottlenecks

Before applying any kind of optimization, it is essential to identify where the actual performance bottlenecks are. Blindly optimizing code that does not impact performance can waste time — or worse, degrade the structure of the app. In React Native, many performance issues stem from unnecessary re-renders, excessive resource usage, or poor management of global state. Fortunately, there are tools and techniques available that allow you to visualize, measure, and interpret app behavior in real time, enabling evidence-based decisions.

One of the most common issues in React Native apps is the re-rendering of components that should not be updating. This typically happens when:

- Props change unnecessarily (for instance functions recreated on every render).
- Global state updates affect unrelated components.
- Child components are not wrapped with **React.memo** or **useMemo.**

A simple technique for detecting this is inserting a **console.log** directly inside the component:

```
constMyComponent = ({ title }) => {
console.log('MyComponent rendered');
  return <Text>{title}</Text>;
};
```

If this log appears even when a different part of the screen is interacted with, it means the component was re-rendered. From there, you can investigate whether the update was truly needed.

Another powerful tool is the **why-did-you-render** library, which logs to the console whenever a memoized component re-renders without actual prop changes:

```
import React from 'react';
import whyDidYouRender from '@welldone-software/why-did-you-render';

if (__DEV__) {
whyDidYouRender(React, {
trackAllPureComponents: true,
  });
}
```

This type of monitoring is extremely helpful during development for spotting inefficient behaviors.

Analysis Tools: React DevTools, Flipper, Hermes Profiler

For a more visual and in-depth analysis, several specialized tools can help pinpoint performance issues:

React DevTools

It allows real-time inspection of the component tree, including props, state, and context. By enabling the "Highlight Updates" feature, DevTools visually indicates which components are being updated – ideal for spotting excessive renders.

Flipper

It is the official debugging platform for React Native. With the right plugins, you can monitor:

- JavaScript and UI thread performance
- Navigation flows
- Network requests and logs
- Component render times

The React DevTools plugin within Flipper is especially useful when testing on physical devices, where Chrome DevTools has limited access.

Hermes Profiler

When enabled, the Hermes JavaScript engine (optional but recommended) provides detailed performance insights such as:

- Function execution time
- Memory allocation
- UI FPS (frames per second)

You can enable Hermes in the config of your project and use Flipper to analyze the generated profile, identifying function slowdowns or memory spikes.

Even without visual tools, you can extract valuable insights using **`console.log`** and manual timing. The **`console.time`** and **`console.timeEnd`** pair is excellent for measuring how long operations take:

```
console.time('renderList');
constrenderedList = data.map(renderItem);
console.timeEnd('renderList');
```

If the recorded time is high, you can start investigating the component, memoize it, or apply **`getItemLayout`** in the case of lists.

Additionally, libraries like **`@react-native-firebase/perf`** or **`expo-performances`** (if using Expo) allow you to collect real usage metrics in production. This is useful for identifying issues that only occur on real user devices with varied hardware capabilities.

Using `why-did-you-render` and `Perf` Hooks

As mentioned, the **`why-did-you-render`** package is a great way to catch unnecessary re-renders, especially when combined with **`React.memo`**. It can be enabled on specific components:

```
constExpensiveComponent = React.memo(({ value }) => {
  return <Text>{value}</Text>;
});

ExpensiveComponent.whyDidYouRender = true;
```

Additionally, React Native provides indirect performance hooks via bridges like **`PerformanceObserver`**, or through manual methods like **`requestAnimationFrame`**, which can be used to measure UI responsiveness:

```
requestAnimationFrame(() => {
constrenderTime = Date.now() - startTime;
console.log(`Render time: ${renderTime}ms`);
});
```

This approach is useful when you want to measure the time between a user action (like a button press) and the completion of an animation or screen load.

Identifying performance bottlenecks requires careful observation, controlled testing, and the use of the right tools. By combining well-placed logs with tools like React DevTools, Flipper, and Hermes Profiler, you can accurately map out critical weak points in your app and address them directly. Performance should not be treated as a final stage in development — it should be a continuous practice, especially in mobile apps where responsiveness and smooth interactions significantly impact user satisfaction.

Architectural Patterns for Scalability

As React Native applications grow and gain more features, so does the complexity of maintenance and team collaboration. In this context, well-defined architectural patterns are what ensure the codebase remains easy to understand, expand, and test. Scalability is not just about performance — it is about the ability of a project to grow safely while maintaining cohesion, predictability, and control. This section covers fundamental practices such as componentization, custom hooks, state management, and layer separation — all of which form the backbone of a solid, scalable architecture.

One of the core principles of React is reusable components. However, in larger projects, reuse must be intentional and strategic. Components should not only be copied from one screen to another — they should be generic enough to adapt to different contexts, but not so generic that they lose their purpose.

A practical approach is to follow an **atomic design pattern**, dividing components into:

- **Atoms**: These are basic UI elements like buttons, text, inputs.
- **Molecules**: These are simple combinations of atoms, such as labeled input fields with validation.
- **Organisms**: These are full functional blocks like product cards, lists, and modals.

Example:

```
// Atomic Button
export constPrimaryButton = ({ label, onPress }) => (
<TouchableOpacity style={styles.button} onPress={onPress}>
<Text>{label}</Text>
</TouchableOpacity>
);
```

This button can be reused in multiple places with different styles and labels. The key is creating clear and configurable interfaces, without coupling them to business logic.

Instead of embedding all logic directly into components or contexts, a more elegant and scalable approach is to create **custom hooks**. These allow you to encapsulate reusable behavior and separate business logic from presentation.

For example, a shopping cart hook is as follows:

```
// useCart.ts
export function useCart() {
const [items, setItems] = useState([]);

constaddItem = (item) => {
setItems((prev) => [...prev, item]);
  };

consttotalPrice = useMemo(() => {
    return items.reduce((sum, item) => sum + item.price, 0);
  }, [items]);

  return { items, addItem, totalPrice };
}
```

This hook can be reused across components (screens, modals, and so on) without duplicating logic. Over time, your hooks become a robust internal library of well-tested behaviors.

Context API versus Redux versus Zustand: When and Why

Global state management is a critical part of scalable architecture. Several solutions are available – each with its strengths and trade-offs:

Context API

- Best for static or rarely changing states (like theme, language, auth)
- Built-in and easy to configure
- Not ideal for frequently changing state or fine-grained performance control
- Can cause cascading re-renders if misused

Redux

- Suitable for complex global state with many dependencies (say cart, orders, users)
- Mature ecosystem: middlewares, DevTools, persistence, community support
- Higher learning curve, especially with Redux Toolkit
- More verbose, but excellent for well-defined business logic

Zustand

- Modern alternative, simpler than Redux
- Uses hooks to create global state with controlled mutability
- Great performance with minimal re-renders
- Ideal for apps that need reactive global state with clean and readable code

Quick Guide:

- Use **Context** for static or almost-static data
- Use **Zustand** for simplicity and performance
- Use **Redux** for large-scale apps needing flow control and robust tooling

Best Practices for Layer Separation (View, State, Service, Data)

Separation of concerns is a fundamental principle in scalable architecture. In React Native, code can be broken into four main layers:

- **View (UI):**
  - Visual components and styling
  - UI layout and design, no business logic
- **State (Logic and Control):**
  - Custom hooks, contexts, or stores (Redux/Zustand)
  - Manages transient data and app logic
- **Service (Business Rules):**
  - Validations, calculations, business flows
  - Decides *what happens* when interacting with data
- **Data (External Access):**
  - API services, local storage, database
  - Handles *how* data is retrieved and saved

Example of separation in code:

```
// View: ProductScreen.tsx
constProductScreen = () => {
const{ products, isLoading } = useProductList();

  return isLoading ?<Loading /> :<ProductList data={products} />;
};

// State: useProductList.ts
export function useProductList() {
const [products, setProducts] = useState([]);
const [isLoading, setLoading] = useState(true);

useEffect(() => {
fetchProducts().then(setProducts).finally(() =>setLoading(false));
  }, []);

  return { products, isLoading };
}

// Service: productService.ts
export function fetchProducts() {
  return api.get('/products');
}
```

With this separation, data fetching, state control, and UI rendering are clearly organized and can evolve independently.

Scaling a React Native application is not just about adding features – it is about ensuring that growth does not compromise structure. Smart componentization, effective use of custom hooks, thoughtful state management choices, and clean layer separation form the backbone of sustainable projects. These architectural patterns not only make maintenance and teamwork easier but also improve the reliability of the system over time. By adopting these practices early, you prepare your app to grow with strength and stability.

Performance Best Practices Checklist

Before publishing a React Native application, it is essential to conduct a full performance review. Many issues only surface during continuous use or on devices with limited processing power. A performance checklist serves as a practical guide to ensure all performance-sensitive areas have been reviewed and optimized. In this section, we will present a hands-on checklist focused on rendering, visual resource management, and handling intensive events — three major impact points on real-world app performance.

Use this list during the final stages of development:

- **Optimized lists using `FlatList`, `SectionList`, or `VirtualizedList`:** Avoid using **`ScrollView`** for long lists of elements.
- **Proper use of `keyExtractor`, `initialNumToRender`, `maxToRenderPerBatch`, and `getItemLayout`:** These props help control rendering and memory usage.
- **Child components optimized with `React.memo` or `useMemo` where necessary:** Prevents mass re-renders that are not needed.
- **Functions passed as props wrapped with `useCallback`:** Avoids unnecessary recreations that cause cascading re-renders.
- **Optimized images (actual size versus rendered size):** Avoid loading images at resolutions far higher than necessary.
- **Placeholders and `ActivityIndicator` for async resources:** Prevents visual freezing during loading.
- **Lazy loading for heavy components or routes using `React.lazy` or dynamic imports:** Improves initial load time.
- **Monitoring frequent global state updates:** Check if unrelated components are being affected by global changes.
- **Avoiding unnecessary state updates inside `useEffect`:** Ensure there are no redundant side effects.
- **Removing `console.log`, extra debugging, and unused dependencies in the final build:** These can bloat the bundle and hurt the performance.
- **Memory monitoring via Flipper or DevTools:** Track real-time usage and thread activity.
- **Hermes enabled (if applicable):** A more efficient JS engine with improved memory use and native profiling.

Rules to Avoid Unnecessary Re-renders

Unnecessary renders are a common cause of sluggishness and FPS drops. Follow these simple rules to prevent them:

Avoid inline function creation in props:

```
// Avoid:
<Button onPress={() =>doSomething()} />

// Prefer:
consthandlePress = useCallback(() =>doSomething(), []);
```

```
<Button onPress={handlePress} />
Use React.memo for pure and list child components:
const Item = React.memo(({ title }) =><Text>{title}</Text>);
```

Avoid updating state that does not affect the UI directly. Move internal logic to hooks or services whenever possible. Split large components into smaller parts so only what is necessary is updated.

Strategies for Animations, Images, and Intensive Events

Certain operations such as animations, image handling, or event listeners — require special attention. Here is how to manage them effectively:

Animations

- Prefer native libraries like **Reanimated** or **Lottie**, which run outside the JS thread
- Avoid long or complex animations using **`Animated`** + **`setState`** in JS

Images

- Always set **fixed dimensions** to avoid layout recalculations
- Use **optimized image sizes** that match the display resolution
- For large lists, consider libraries like **`react-native-fast-image`** for better caching and rendering

Intensive Events

- Use **`debounce`** or **`throttle`** for events like scroll, input, or resize:

  ```
  constdebouncedFn = useMemo(() =>debounce(fn, 300), []);
  ```

- Avoid listening to global events unless absolutely necessary (say window scroll)
- Clean up event listeners in **`useEffect`** properly to prevent memory leaks

A performant app is not the result of a single technique, but rather a combination of good decisions throughout development. With the right checklist in hand, you can ensure that every layer — from UI to data fetching, from animations to global state — is optimized to deliver the best possible user experience. Before every release or deployment, revisiting this checklist helps maintain product quality and stability.

Conclusion

In this chapter, we have explored essential strategies for optimizing performance and ensuring the scalability of React Native applications. We learned that the interface smoothness and response time of an app are directly linked to how we handle rendering, code organization, and resource management. With techniques like code splitting, lazy loading, and smart memoization, it is possible to significantly reduce memory usage and render time without compromising the user experience.

We also discussed how a well-defined folder structure, clear separation of concerns, and the use of custom hooks contribute to the maintainability and scalability of complex projects. To choose a state management solution — whether Context API, Redux, or Zustand — it should be based on the specific needs and performance demands of the application. And with tools like React DevTools, Flipper, and Hermes Profiler, developers can pinpoint bottlenecks with accuracy and take proactive steps to resolve them.

In the next chapter, we will expand the TypeScript usage and demonstrate how to type more complex components, interfaces, and data models, making your app more reliable and maintainable. We will also cover advanced integrations, such as using specific libraries (say Maps, QR Codes), and how to manage updates for React Native and its dependencies. You will see how to plan a gradual migration to TypeScript or start a fully TypeScript-based project from the ground up.

Questions

Before consolidating your understanding of performance optimization and architectural best practices in React Native, it is important to reflect on the strategies, tools, and techniques explored in this chapter. The questions below are designed to help you review the key topics, identify areas that may require further attention, and reinforce your ability to build responsive and scalable mobile applications:

1. What are the main benefits of using **`FlatList`** or **`SectionList`** over **`ScrollView`** when displaying long lists in React Native?
2. How do **`useCallback`** and **`useMemo`** differ in terms of what they memoize, and when should each be used to prevent unnecessary re-renders?
3. What are some indicators that a component is re-rendering unnecessarily, and which tools or techniques can help you detect and resolve those issues?
4. How does **`React.memo`** contribute to rendering optimization, and what are its limitations if props include inline functions or objects?
5. What strategies can be used to implement lazy loading and code splitting in React Native, even in the absence of traditional Webpack-based bundling?
6. Compare feature-based and type-based folder organization structures. When is it best to use each, and what are the trade-offs involved?
7. How does Zustand differ from Context API and Redux in managing global state, and in which scenarios might Zustand offer better performance or simplicity?
8. What are some best practices for handling animations, image loading, and event listeners to maintain a smooth user experience on low-end devices?
9. Why is it important to configure tools like ESLint and Prettier in a React Native project, and how do they contribute to performance and maintainability?
10. Which steps would you take during a pre-deploy performance review to ensure that your application is optimized, and what key signs would indicate performance debt?

Answering these questions will validate your grasp of the core ideas of the chapter—ranging from render optimization and code organization to architectural scalability—and prepare you to apply these best practices when building high-performance mobile apps with React Native.

Key Terms

- **`FlatList / SectionList / VirtualizedList`:** Optimized React Native components for efficiently rendering large lists. **`FlatList`** is ideal for simple lists, **`SectionList`** supports grouped data with headers, and **`VirtualizedList`** is the low-level base offering fine-grained control over on-demand rendering.
- **Memoization (`useMemo / useCallback`):** Caching strategies to prevent unnecessary recalculations or function recreations. **`useMemo`** stores the result of a function, while **`useCallback`** stores the function reference – both help prevent unwanted re-renders in child components.

- **`React.memo`:** A higher-order function that prevents re-rendering of functional components if their props have not changed, using shallow comparison to boost performance.
- **`getItemLayout`:** A **`FlatList`** prop that provides the size and position of each item ahead of time, allowing direct scrolling and avoiding expensive layout measurements for fixed-height lists.
- **`initialNumToRender` / `maxToRenderPerBatch`:** **`FlatList`** properties that control how many items are rendered initially and how many are processed per scroll batch. Crucial for balancing load time and memory usage.
- **Lazy Loading:** A technique that delays the loading of components, routes, or libraries until they are needed, reducing the initial bundle size and improving app responsiveness.
- **Dynamic Import:** A JavaScript pattern for loading modules on demand, commonly used in React Native to implement lazy loading for heavy components.
- **`why-did-you-render`:** A development library that detects unnecessary re-renders in React components, especially useful when debugging performance issues with **`React.memo`**.
- **`Flipper`:** The official React Native debugging tool, allowing real-time inspection of component state, network activity, logs, and UI performance. It integrates with the Hermes engine for advanced profiling.
- **Hermes Profiler:** A performance profiling tool built into the Hermes engine, providing detailed metrics on code execution, memory usage, and JavaScript thread behavior.
- **Feature-first / Type-first Structure:** Project organization patterns. *Feature-first* groups files by feature (including **`auth/`**, **`cart/`**), while *type-first* organizes by file type (such as **`components/`**, **`hooks/`**, **`screens/`**). This choice impacts scalability and maintainability.
- **Custom Hooks:** Functions built with **`useState`**, **`useEffect`**, and so on to encapsulate reusable logic and decouple business rules from the UI. Examples include **`useAuth`**, **`useCart`**, **`useFetch`**.
- **Context API / Redux / Zustand:** Global state management solutions. Context API is simple and built-in, Redux is robust and structured, and Zustand offers high performance with minimal boilerplate.
- **Linting / Formatting (`ESLint` / `Prettier`):** Code standardization tools. ESLint flags style and logic issues, while Prettier auto-formats code according to predefined rules.
- **console.time / console.timeEnd:** Native JavaScript functions used to measure code execution time, useful for diagnosing performance bottlenecks in async operations or large list renderings.

These terms summarize the key concepts, tools, and best practices covered in this chapter, serving as a quick reference for applying performance improvements and architectural organization in React Native projects.

CHAPTER 11

Adding TypeScript and Advanced Integrations

Introduction

This chapter aims to guide you through adopting TypeScript in React Native projects, showing how static typing can improve code quality and simplify mobile app maintenance. We will begin by presenting the motivations for gradually migrating from JavaScript to TypeScript or, alternatively, by starting a fully typed project from its bootstrap. You will also learn how to set up the environment, configure linting and build tools, and establish a solid foundation to confidently evolve your codebase.

Next, we shall explore advanced typing strategies for components, data, and external integrations. We will further dive into defining interfaces and generic types, using TypeScript utility types, and creating type declarations for libraries without official typings. To demonstrate these techniques in practice, we will be presenting real-world use cases such as modeling API responses, integrating with map libraries (like **`react-native-maps`**), and generating/reading QR Codes—highlighting how proper typing prevents compile-time errors and improves application predictability.

Finally, we will cover how to manage React Native updates and dependency upgrades in typed projects, offering tips on tools and processes for handling breaking changes without compromising your codebase. You shall discover best practices for testing in TypeScript, documenting types, and implementing gradual rollout strategies—ensuring your TypeScript adoption or migration is safe, scalable, and well-planned.

Structure

In this chapter, we will cover the following topics:

- Introduction to TypeScript in React Native
  - Gradual Migration Scenarios versus 100% TypeScript Projects
  - Benefits of Strong Typing for Maintainability and Scalability
- Preparing the Project for TypeScript
  - Configuring ESLint and Prettier for TS Projects
  - Adjustments to the Metro Bundler and Build Configuration Files

- Incremental Migration from JavaScript to TypeScript
  - "File-by-File" versus "Whole-Project" Strategies
  - Handling Modules Without Official Type Definitions
- Creating a Fully TypeScript React Native Project
  - Folder Structure and Naming Conventions
  - Best Practices for Code Organization in TS
- Advanced Typing in React Native Components
  - Generic Components with `React.FC<…>` and Generics
  - TypeScript Utility Types (Partial, Pick, Omit, Record, and so on)
  - Higher-Order Components (HOC) and Typing Higher-Order Functions
- Data Modeling and Interfaces
  - API Response Types: DTOs and Schemas
  - Using interface vs. type for Domain Entities
  - Integration with Validation Libraries (Zod, Yup) and Type Generation
- Typings for External Libraries
  - Creating Module Declarations (`.d.ts`) for Untyped Libraries
  - Maintaining and Versioning of Custom Typings
- Advanced Integrations
  - QR Code Reading and Generation (like, `react-native-qrcode-svg`)
  - Other Integrations: Camera, Sensors, and BLE, with Native Plugin Typing
- Managing React Native and Dependency Updates
  - Handling Breaking Changes and Typing Conflicts
  - Automating Regression Testing after Upgrades
- Best Practices and Migration Patterns
  - Documenting Types: Using TSDoc and Generating Docstrings
  - Gradual Rollout Strategies and Error Monitoring in Production

Introduction to TypeScript in React Native

This chapter aims to demonstrate why adopting TypeScript in React Native projects is a key step toward building more robust and predictable applications. You will see how static typing can catch errors early—errors that, in plain JavaScript, would only surface at runtime—and how this positively impacts the development workflow. Our goal is to provide both a strategic perspective—when to migrate and how to plan the transition—and a set of practical examples and coding techniques that you can immediately apply in your day-to-day work.

Adding TypeScript to your React Native project gives you a "safety net" throughout the app development process. Imagine you have a function that calculates the subtotal of an order:

```
function calculateSubtotal(items: { price: number; quantity: number }[]): number {
  return items.reduce((sum, { price, quantity }) => sum + price * quantity, 0);
}
```

If someone accidentally calls **calculateSubtotal([{ price: "20", quantity: 3 }])**, the compiler will immediately flag that the **price** type is incorrect—preventing a silent failure. Additionally, interface and type declarations enhance the autocomplete of your editor, turning each function and component into a living, always up-to-date documentation source.

Gradual Migration versus 100% TypeScript Projects

It is not always feasible to convert an entire codebase all at once. For teams with an existing and mature JavaScript foundation, a "file-by-file" strategy is often the most practical. Setting **"allowJs": true** in your **tsconfig.json** allows **.js** files to coexist with **.ts** and **.tsx** files, which enables you to progressively introduce types starting from the most critical modules. On the other hand, brand-new or early-stage projects can benefit from a fully typed template right from the start:

```
npx react-native initMyApp --template react-native-template-typescript
```

In this case, the entire app skeleton, from folder structure to linter settings, is already prepared for TypeScript, offering consistency from the very first commit.

Benefits of Strong Typing for Maintenance and Scalability

For teams managing codebases over months or even years, strong typing is a major ally during refactoring. If you rename a field in an API response interface, any outdated references will immediately trigger compilation errors, clearly indicating where updates are needed. This makes large-scale changes safer and more predictable. Furthermore, by defining clear data contracts, communication between front-end and back-end becomes more transparent, reducing misunderstandings. Over time, typed projects make onboarding new developers easier, as interfaces and types serve as a guide for navigating the codebase.

With these foundational concepts in place, you will be well-prepared to move on to the following sections, where we shall explore how to set up your environment, migrate the existing code, define advanced typings, and integrate with libraries such as maps, QR Codes, and more—fully leveraging the benefits TypeScript brings to React Native development.

Preparing the Project for TypeScript

Before diving into writing typed components, it is essential to configure your development environment to fully support TypeScript. In this stage, you will be installing the necessary dependencies, setting up your linter and formatter, and be making small adjustments to the build configuration of React Native.

To begin with, install the TypeScript compiler along with the type definitions for React and React Native. In your project directory, run:

```
yarn add -D typescript @types/react
```

Next, create a **tsconfig.json** file at the root of your project. A balanced starting configuration might look like this:

```
{
  "compilerOptions": {
    "target": "ESNext",
    "module": "ESNext",
    "jsx": "react-native",
    "strict": true,
    "allowJs": false,
```

```
    "esModuleInterop": true,
    "skipLibCheck": true,
    "forceConsistentCasingInFileNames": true,
    "moduleResolution": "node",
    "resolveJsonModule": true,
    "baseUrl": "./src"
  },
  "include": ["src/**/*"],
  "exclude": ["node_modules", "babel.config.js", "metro.config.js"]
}
```

This **tsconfig.json** enables strict checks, supports JSON imports, and organizes your code in the **src/** directory. From here, you can start using **.ts** and **.tsx** extensions for your files.

Configuring ESLint and Prettier for TypeScript Projects

Maintaining code style and consistency becomes even more important with type safety. Use ESLint with TypeScript support along with Prettier:

```
yarn add -D eslint @typescript-eslint/parser @typescript-eslint/eslint-plugin eslint-config-prettier eslint-plugin-prettier prettier
```

In your **.eslintrc.js** file, combine **ESLint** rules with TypeScript and Prettier plugins:

```
module.exports = {
  root: true,
  parser: '@typescript-eslint/parser',
  plugins: ['@typescript-eslint', 'prettier'],
  extends: [
    'eslint:recommended',
    'plugin:@typescript-eslint/recommended',
    'prettier',
    'plugin:react-native/all',
  ],
parserOptions: {
ecmaFeatures: { jsx: true },
ecmaVersion: 2020,
sourceType: 'module',
  },
  rules: {
    'prettier/prettier': 'error',
    '@typescript-eslint/no-unused-vars': ['warn', { argsIgnorePattern: '^_' }],
    'react-native/no-unused-styles': 'warn',
  },
  settings: {
    react: { version: 'detect' },
  },
};
```

Then, add a simple **.prettierrc** to centralize your style guide:

```
{
  "singleQuote": true,
  "trailingComma": "all",
```

```
  "printWidth": 100
}
```

Now, running **eslint . --ext .ts,.tsx** and **prettier --check .** will help ensure quality and consistency across your codebase.

Adjustments to the Metro Bundler and Build Configuration Files

Finally, a few small tweaks to the Metro bundler will ensure that React Native handles TypeScript correctly. Create or update your **metro.config.js**:

```
const{ getDefaultConfig } = require('metro-config');

module.exports = (async () => {
const {
    resolver: { sourceExts, assetExts },
  } = await getDefaultConfig();
  return {
    transformer: {
babelTransformerPath: require.resolve('react-native-typescript-transformer'),
    },
    resolver: {
assetExts,
sourceExts: [...sourceExts, 'ts', 'tsx'],
    },
  };
})();
```

If you are using Babel directly, make sure your **babel.config.js** includes the preset **module:metro-react-native-babel-preset**. No additional changes are typically required, but it is important to confirm that **.ts**and **.tsx** extensions are properly resolved to avoid bundling errors.

With these configurations in place, your project will be ready to support TypeScript components and modules—offering full type checking and seamless integration with your React Native development workflow.

Incremental Migration from JavaScript to TypeScript

When adopting TypeScript in an existing codebase, it rarely makes sense to convert everything all at once—especially in mature projects. The incremental approach allows you to gradually introduce typings into **.js** files, reducing risks and spreading the effort of the team over time. In this section, we shall explore "file-by-file" versus "whole-project" migration strategies, how to configure key flags in **tsconfig.json**, and how to handle packages that lack official typings.

"File-by-File" versus "Whole-Project" Strategies

The "file-by-file" migration starts by keeping the project running in JavaScript, installing TypeScript, and configuring **tsconfig.json** so that **.js** files are still accepted. Then, you select critical modules—such as API services or core components—and rename them to **.ts** or **.tsx**, gradually adding types. This approach decouples deployments, preventing regressions in areas that have not yet been migrated.

On the other hand, migrating the "whole-project" can make sense for small squads or apps with low test coverage, especially when there is a dedicated maintenance window. In this case, a migration branch is created, the entire codebase is converted at once, and each module is reviewed under strict rules. While more demanding initially, this approach results in a fully typed project without legacy JavaScript coexistence.

To enable **.js** files without removing them right away, configure your **tsconfig.json** like this:

```
{
  "compilerOptions": {
    "allowJs": true,    // includes .js files in the compilation process
    "checkJs": false,   // doesn't enforce type checks in .js files by default
    "noEmit": true,
    "strict": true,
    "jsx": "react-native",
    "moduleResolution": "node"
  },
  "include": ["src/**/*"]
}
```

With **allowJs: true**, your editor will seamlessly recognize both **.js** and **.ts** imports. As you convert each file, simply rename it to **.ts**or **.tsx**. You can optionally enable **checkJs: true** for selected files—or for the entire project once most of the migration is complete.

Handling Modules without Official Typings

Not every library comes with **@types** declarations. To fill these gaps, you can create a global typings file at **src/types/globals.d.ts**:

```
// src/types/globals.d.ts
declare module 'some-untyped-library' {
  // define the main APIs here, or use `any` as a placeholder
  export function doSomething(arg: any): any;
  export const VERSION: string;
}
```

In simpler cases, using **// @ts-ignore** above a problematic import or function call can serve as a temporary measure. However, the recommended approach is to write your own declaration files—even if basic at first—and refine them over time based on real usage. This way, you maintain type safety and gradually reduce the scope of **any** in your code, reaping the long-term benefits of a strongly typed codebase.

Creating a 100% TypeScript React Native Project

In this section, you will be learning how to start a fully typed React Native application from scratch using the official template, adopting folder structures and naming conventions that make your codebase easier to maintain and scale.

Starting with **React Native 0.71** (January 2023), **TypeScript is the default** for new projects created with the React Native CLI. That means you no longer need to pass **--template react-native-template-typescript** to get a TypeScript setup—running the standard command will generate a project that already includes **App.tsx** and a preconfigured **tsconfig.json**.

To create a new TypeScript project today, use:

```
npx react-native initMyApp
```

You only need the **--template react-native-template-typescript** flag when targeting **older React Native versions** that predate 0.71. The standalone TypeScript template is now **deprecated** because the base template already includes first-class TypeScript support.

Folder Structure and Naming Conventions

A clear structure helps keep the codebase organized as the app grows. A domain-based or "feature-based" pattern works well:

```
MyApp/
├─ src/
│  ├─ components/     # generic components (buttons, inputs)
│  ├─ screens/        # app screens (login, profile, home)
│  ├─ navigation/     # route and stack configuration
│  ├─ services/       # API calls and business logic
│  ├─ types/          # global type declarations and interfaces
│  ├─ hooks/          # custom hooks
│  └─ utils/          # utility functions and helpers
├─ App.tsx
└─ tsconfig.json
```

Each component file should use the **.tsx** extension and follow naming conventions such as **MyButton.tsx** for components and **useAuth.ts** for hooks. Use plural names for folders to indicate collections of items. Submodules can follow the **index.ts** pattern to centralize exports and simplify imports:

```
// src/components/Button/index.ts
export { default } from './Button';
```

This allows for clean imports like:

```
import Button from '@/components/Button';
```

When you configure **"baseUrl": "./src"** in your **tsconfig.json**.

Best Practices for Organizing Code in TypeScript

When writing TypeScript code, aim to centralize your types and interfaces under **src/types**. For example, API responses can have their DTOs (Data Transfer Objects) defined in dedicated files:

```
// src/types/Product.ts
export interface Product {
  id: string;
  title: string;
  price: number;
}
```

Then, services that consume these APIs can use the type directly, ensuring that any change in the response format is flagged throughout the application:

```
// src/services/productService.ts
import { Product } from '@/types/Product';

export async function fetchProducts(): Promise<Product[]> {
const response = await fetch('https://api.example.com/products');
  return response.json();
}
```

Avoid mixing presentation logic with business logic. Keep components "pure," and offload API calls to the **services** folder, while global state and custom hooks should live in **hooks** or a global context (say **src/context**). This reinforces separation of concerns, enabling safer refactoring and easier testing.

Lastly, standardize formatting and import alignment using ESLint and Prettier so that the entire team adheres to a consistent style.

Advanced Typing in React Native Components

In this section, you will learn how to harness the full power of TypeScript when typing React Native components. You shall gradually see how to define contracts for props and state, create generic components that accept different data formats, use TypeScript utility types to quickly transform existing types, and even build fully typed Higher-Order Components (HOCs).

When a component needs to receive external data, defining a clear interface for its props helps TypeScript ensure nothing unexpected gets passed in. For example, in a product card component:

```
interface ProductCardProps {
  id: string;
  name: string;
  price: number;
onAddToCart: (productId: string) => void;
}

export constProductCard: React.FC<ProductCardProps> = ({
  id,
  name,
  price,
onAddToCart,
}) => (
<View style={styles.card}>
<Text>{name}</Text>
<Text>R$ {price.toFixed(2)}</Text>
<Button title="Add" onPress={() =>onAddToCart(id)} />
</View>
);
```

If you also need internal state, you can explicitly type it using **useState**. By specifying a generic type, TypeScript provides autocomplete and ensures that you do not assign the wrong value type:

```
export function QuantitySelector() {
const [quantity, setQuantity] = useState<number>(1);

  function increase() {
setQuantity(prev =>prev + 1);
  }

  return (
<View>
<Text>Quantity: {quantity}</Text>
<Button title="+" onPress={increase} />
</View>
  );
}
```

Generic Components with `React.FC<...>` and Generics

To create reusable components that work with various data types, you can leverage Generics. Imagine a generic **`List`** component that renders any kind of item:

```
interface ListProps<T> {
  items: T[];
renderItem: (item: T) =>React.ReactNode;
}

export function List<T>({ items, renderItem }: ListProps<T>) {
  return (
<View>
      {items.map((item, idx) => (
<View key={idx}>{renderItem(item)}</View>
      ))}
</View>
  );
}
```

In practice, when using this component, TypeScript automatically infers the type of **`T`**:

```
<List
  items={[{ id: '1', name: 'Shirt' }]}
renderItem={(product) =><Text>{product.name}</Text>}
/>
```

This ensures safe typing without duplicating code for each data structure.

TypeScript Utility Types (`Partial`, `Pick`, `Omit`, `Record`)

Utility types are powerful tools for modifying the existing types without manual effort. Suppose you have a complete **`User`** model:

```
interface User {
  id: string;
  name: string;
  email: string;
isAdmin: boolean;
}
```

If you need to represent only the fields that can be updated, use **`Partial<User>`**. This creates a type where all properties of **`User`** are optional:

```
function updateUser(id: string, changes: Partial<User>) {
  // changes can contain any combination of User fields
}
```

To extract only the **`email`** and **`name`**, **`Pick`** makes it simple:

```
type UserContact = Pick<User, 'name' | 'email'>;
```

Meanwhile, **`Omit<User, 'isAdmin'>`** removes the **`isAdmin`** property, and **`Record<string, User>`** creates a user map indexed by a string key. These utilities save time and reduce code repetition.

Higher-Order Components (HOCs) and Typing Higher-Order Functions

Higher-Order Components let you add functionality to existing components. To type them correctly, you will need to handle generics and preserve the original props:

```
function withLoading<P>(Component: React.ComponentType<P>) {
  return function WrappedWithLoading(props: P & { isLoading: boolean }) {
const{ isLoading, ...rest } = props;
    if (isLoading) {
      return <ActivityIndicator />;
    }
    return <Component {...(rest as P)} />;
  };
}
```

When applying **withLoading**, TypeScript ensures that the resulting component accepts all the original props plus the new **isLoading** prop:

```
constProductListWithLoading = withLoading(ProductList);
// ProductListWithLoading expects all ProductList props + isLoading: boolean
```

With these advanced typing techniques, your React Native components gain superior safety, reusability, and clarity—making them ready to handle complex scenarios and evolve sustainably over time.

Data Modeling and Interfaces

When working with APIs in React Native, it is essential to define clear contracts for the data structures exchanged between the front end and back end. Instead of using loose objects and guesswork, we create Data Transfer Objects (DTOs) or schemas that describe exactly which fields we expect, including their types and formats. For example, when fetching a user, we can define a DTO like this:

```
// src/types/UserDTO.ts
export interface UserDTO {
  id: string;
  name: string;
  email: string;
avatarUrl?: string;    // optional
createdAt: string;     // ISO date
}
```

This DTO will serve as the return type for our service functions:

```
async function fetchUser(id: string): Promise<UserDTO> {
const res = await fetch(`https://api.example.com/users/${id}`);
constjson = await res.json();
  return json as UserDTO;
}
```

API Response Types: DTOs and Schemas

While a DTO describes the raw network format, a schema—whether manually written or generated—can validate and transform data on the client side. For example, using Zod, we define a schema that ensures **createdAt** is parsed as a **Date**:

```
import { z } from 'zod';

export constUserSchema = z.object({
  id: z.string(),
  name: z.string(),
  email: z.string().email(),
avatarUrl: z.string().url().optional(),
createdAt: z.string().transform(s => new Date(s)),
});

// In a service:
async function fetchAndParseUser(id: string) {
const res = await fetch(`/users/${id}`);
const raw = await res.json();
  return UserSchema.parse(raw); // throws an error if schema validation fails
}
```

This guarantees that the resulting object not only has the correct fields but also comes with proper typing (like **createdAt** as **Date**), reducing the need for manual runtime checks.

Using Interface versus Type for Domain Entities

In TypeScript, both **interface** and **type** can describe the shape of objects, but there are subtleties that influence your design choices:

- **interface is extensible:** You can merge declarations, which is useful for augmenting third-party libraries or module declarations.
- **type is more flexible:** It supports intersections, unions, and conditional types, making it ideal for complex compositions.

For instance, for our **Product** domain entity, we might use **type** to represent mutable or partial states:

```
export type Product = {
  id: string;
  title: string;
  price: number;
description?: string;
};

// To represent an editable product:
export type EditableProduct = Partial<Product>&{ id: string };
```

If we want other modules to extend **Product** by adding methods, **interface** is more appropriate:

```
export interface Product {
  id: string;
  title: string;
  price: number;
}

declare module '@/types/Product' {
  interface Product {
calculateDiscountedPrice(discount: number): number;
  }
}
```

Integration with Validation Libraries (Zod, Yup) and Type Generation

Libraries like **Zod** and **Yup** offer two main advantages: client-side data validation at the point of consumption and automatic generation of TypeScript types based on the schema itself. With Zod, we have already seen how to use **`z.object()`**. Using Yup follows a similar pattern:

```
import * as yup from 'yup';

export constProductSchema = yup.object({
  id: yup.string().required(),
  title: yup.string().required(),
  price: yup.number().positive().required(),
  description: yup.string().optional(),
});

// Inferring the type from the schema:
export type ProductFromSchema = yup.InferType<typeofProductSchema>;
```

In both cases, validation is done on the client before populating state or sending data forward. This helps prevent unexpected crashes and reinforces your initial DTO definitions. As business rules evolve, simply updating the schemas ensures your app continues to respect strict contracts, generating updated types and catching inconsistencies automatically.

Typings for External Libraries

When you add third-party libraries to your TypeScript project, you will not always find ready-to-use official type definitions. In this section, we will be exploring how to take advantage of the existing declaration packages, when to install them, and how to create and maintain your own typings to ensure that your entire codebase adheres to the type rules of the TypeScript.

Many popular packages already have community-maintained type definitions via the DefinitelyTyped project. For example, to use the React Navigation package, you just need to install its corresponding **`@types`** package:

```
yarn add -D @types/react-navigation
```

After installation, TypeScript will automatically recognize the module and provide autocomplete and type checking for all imports. Whenever you add a new library, be sure to search for a **`@types/libraryname`** package first. If it exists, install it right away. Otherwise, you will likely encounter a "Cannot find module" error during import, indicating that you will need to write your own module declaration.

Creating `.d.ts` Module Declarations for Untyped Libraries

When there is no official typing available, the solution is to create a declaration file in your project, such as **`src/types/custom.d.ts`**. There, you declare the module and describe only the parts of the API that you actually use:

```
// src/types/custom.d.ts
declare module 'awesome-untyped-lib' {
  interface ConfigOptions {
    endpoint: string;
```

```
timeout?: number;
  }

  export function initialize(options: ConfigOptions): void;
  export function fetchData(id: string): Promise<any>;
}
```

With this declaration, you immediately gain a basic level of type safety when calling:

```
import { initialize, fetchData } from 'awesome-untyped-lib';
```

If you later use more APIs from the library, simply extend this **.d.ts** file with new functions or types—avoiding excessive use of **any** in your codebase.

Maintaining and Versioning Custom Typings

It is important to version your custom typings directory alongside your source code. Whenever you update the third-party dependency, review your **.d.ts** file to ensure nothing has broken or changed. A good strategy is to create a subfolder like **src/types/libs/libraryname/** and store all related declarations there. This way, when updating the library version, you will know exactly where to look.

For stricter control, add a script to your **package.json** that runs **tsc --noEmit** in your CI pipeline to catch any type inconsistencies before merging. If the library evolves and adds new features, you can create update branches for your type declarations that run compilation tests and ensure compatibility. This helps your team maintain a clear history of changes to typings, avoiding surprises when consuming new versions of dependencies without official types.

Advanced Integrations

In this section, we shall explore how to incorporate native features and specialized libraries into your typed React Native app, ensuring that each integration respects type contracts and minimizes runtime errors.

To display maps, the most commonly used package is **react-native-maps**. After installing it:

```
yarn add react-native-maps
```

Define an interface for geographic coordinates:

```
// src/types/MapTypes.ts
export interface LatLng {
  latitude: number;
  longitude: number;
}
```

Then use this type in your map component:

```
import MapView, { Marker } from 'react-native-maps';
import { LatLng } from '@/types/MapTypes';

interface MapProps {
initialRegion: {
    latitude: number;
    longitude: number;
latitudeDelta: number;
longitudeDelta: number;
  };
```

```
  markers: LatLng[];
}

export function GeoMap({ initialRegion, markers }: MapProps) {
  return (
<MapView style={{ flex: 1 }} initialRegion={initialRegion}>
      {markers.map((coord, idx) => (
<Marker key={idx} coordinate={coord} />
      ))}
</MapView>
  );
}
```

This typing ensures that valid **latitude** and **longitude** values are always provided for each marker.

QR Code Generation and Scanning (react-native-qrcode-svg)

To generate QR codes, **react-native-qrcode-svg** offers a simple component:

```
yarn add react-native-qrcode-svg
```

Usage:

```
import QRCode from 'react-native-qrcode-svg';

interface QRProps {
  value: string;
size?: number;
}

export function QRGenerator({ value, size = 150 }: QRProps) {
  return <QRCode value={value} size={size} />;
}
```

For scanning QR codes, you can pair it with **react-native-camera** and type the scan result callback:

```
// src/types/CameraTypes.ts
export interface BarcodeScanResult {
  data: string;
  type: string;
}

import { RNCamera } from 'react-native-camera';
import { BarcodeScanResult } from '@/types/CameraTypes';

export function QRScanner({ onRead }: { onRead: (result: BarcodeScanResult) => void
}) {
  return (
<RNCamera
      style={{ flex: 1 }}
onBarCodeRead={({ data, type }) =>onRead({ data, type })}
    />
  );
}
```

Other Integrations: Camera, Sensors, and BLE with Typed Native Plugins

For access to the camera, sensors, or Bluetooth LE, libraries such as **react-native-camera**, **react-native-sensors**, and **react-native-ble-plx** are commonly used. In each case, you create types for the returned data:

```
// src/types/SensorTypes.ts
export interface AccelerometerData {
  x: number;
  y: number;
  z: number;
  timestamp: number;
}
```

Accelerometer example:

```
import { accelerometer, SensorTypes } from 'react-native-sensors';
import { AccelerometerData } from '@/types/SensorTypes';

export function useAccelerometer(onData: (data: AccelerometerData) => void) {
React.useEffect(() => {
const subscription = accelerometer.subscribe((data: SensorTypes) => {
onData({ ...data } as AccelerometerData);
    });
    return () =>subscription.unsubscribe();
  }, [onData]);
}
```

For BLE (Bluetooth Low Energy), define the device and service types:

```
// src/types/BleTypes.ts
export interface BleDevice {
  id: string;
  name: string;
rssi: number;
}
```

React Native requires explicit permissions for accessing sensitive resources. To handle this in a typed way:

```
// src/types/PermissionTypes.ts
export type PermissionStatus = 'granted' | 'denied' | 'blocked' | 'unavailable';
```

Example: Checking Camera Permission:

```
import { request, PERMISSIONS, RESULTS } from 'react-native-permissions';
import { PermissionStatus } from '@/types/PermissionTypes';

export async function checkCameraPermission(): Promise<PermissionStatus> {
const status = await request(PERMISSIONS.IOS.CAMERA);
  return status as PermissionStatus;
}
```

When dealing with native callbacks, always use clear typings:

```
interface GeolocationPosition {
coords: {
    latitude: number;
```

```
    longitude: number;
    accuracy: number;
  };
  timestamp: number;
}

export function getCurrentLocation(): Promise<GeolocationPosition> {
  return new Promise((resolve, reject) => {
navigator.geolocation.getCurrentPosition(resolve, reject, {
enableHighAccuracy: true,
    });
  });
}
```

Thus, by following these practices, every advanced integration in your app retains the same level of type safety as the rest of your code—preventing runtime surprises and making the system easier to maintain.

Managing React Native and Dependency Updates

Keeping your React Native app and its dependencies up to date is essential to benefit from security patches, performance improvements, and new platform features. However, version updates can introduce significant API changes, adjustments in the Metro bundler, or modifications in how typings are provided by libraries. Below, we present the main tools and best practices for performing these updates in a controlled and safe manner.

The command **`npx react-native upgrade`** is the official starting point for updating React Native. It analyzes your **`package.json`** and suggests changes to configuration files (such as **`App.js`**, **`android/`**, **`ios/`**) according to the targeted version. In general, it is recommended to run:

```
git checkout -b upgrade-rn-0.70
npx react-native upgrade 0.70.0
```

By default, the script displays an interactive diff, allowing you to accept or reject each change. However, to better understand what has changed between versions, the Upgrade Helper shows side-by-side file comparisons for the "before" and "after" states. Simply select your current and target versions to get a complete diff. This is especially helpful for resolving merge conflicts and manually adapting build scripts or customizations in **`AndroidManifest.xml`** and **`Info.plist`**.

Handling Breaking Changes and Typing Conflicts

Breaking changes may occur in native APIs, navigation packages, or even TypeScript updates. When upgrading, always refer to the changelog and migration guide for the version. If a function in **`react-native-gesture-handler`** changes its signature, or if **`ViewStyle`** receives new properties, the TypeScript compiler will flag affected locations, enabling quick fixes:

```
// Before (v1): onGestureEvent receives GestureEventType
function onGestureEvent(event: GestureEventType) { /* ... */ }

// After (v2): the signature has changed
function onGestureEvent(event: NativeSyntheticEvent<PanResponderGestureState>) { /*
... */ }
```

To resolve typing conflicts in dependencies, configure the **`paths`** field in **`tsconfig.json`** or provide augmentation modules (**`.d.ts`**) that point to the new APIs. In extreme cases, a temporary fork of the package may be necessary, redirecting the import to a local version while waiting for an upstream fix.

Automating Regression Testing after Upgrades

To ensure that the update has not introduced bugs, it is crucial to have an automated test suite covering both unit tests (with Jest) and key UI flows (using Detox, Appium, or React Native Testing Library). In your CI pipeline, configure a job that runs:

```
yarn install &&npx react-native run-android --variant=release
jest --coverage
detox test --configuration android.emu.release
```

Any failure signals a regression before the code is merged. Additionally, storing Jest snapshots for components helps detect unexpected visual changes after the update. Lastly, establish a routine (say monthly) to review and align dependencies, ensuring your app stays on the latest possible version of React Native and critical libraries—reducing the risk and effort of future "big bang" upgrades.

Best Practices and Migration Patterns

For your migration to TypeScript to be sustainable and continuously valuable to your React Native project, it is essential to apply well-established practices in testing, documentation, and rollout. Below are detailed guidelines for each step.

Writing tests in a typed codebase provides feedback from both the compiler and the test suites themselves. Set up Jest with TypeScript support by adding the following to your **`package.json`**:

```
"jest": {
  "preset": "react-native",
  "transform": {
    "^.+\\.(ts|tsx)$": "ts-jest"
  },
  "moduleFileExtensions": ["ts", "tsx", "js", "jsx", "json", "node"]
}
```

Then, write your tests using the types defined in your domain. For example, a test for the product service:

```
// __tests__/productService.test.ts
import { fetchProducts } from '@/services/productService';
import { Product } from '@/types/Product';

jest.mock('node-fetch', () => require('fetch-mock').sandbox());
import fetchMock from 'node-fetch';

describe('productService', () => {
it('should return a list of products typed correctly', async () => {
constmockProducts: Product[] = [
{ id: '1', title: 'Shirt', price: 49.9 },
{ id: '2', title: 'Pants', price: 99.9 },
    ];
fetchMock.get('https://api.example.com/products', mockProducts);

const products = await fetchProducts();
    expect(products[0].price).toBeCloseTo(49.9);
    // TypeScript ensures that .price is a number, not a string
  });
});
```

With **ts-jest**, type errors in the test suite itself are caught at compile time, making your tests more reliable.

Documenting Types: Using TSDoc and Generating Docstrings

Keeping your interfaces and functions well-documented makes onboarding easier for new developers. Use TSDoc-style comments to describe each element:

```
/**
 * Returns all available products from the API.
 * @returns {Promise<Product[]>} A list of products with id, title, and price.
 */
export async function fetchProducts(): Promise<Product[]> {
  // ...
}
```

Tools like **TypeDoc** can generate HTML documentation from these comments, creating a live reference for your types. In **tsconfig.json**, enable:

```
{
  "compilerOptions": {
    "declaration": true,
    "emitDeclarationOnly": true
  }
}
```

And add a script:

```
"scripts": {
  "docs": "typedoc --out docs src/types"
}
```

Whenever you modify a type or interface, be sure to update the TSDoc comments to keep your documentation in sync.

Gradual Rollout Strategies and Production Error Monitoring

Even in typed projects, changes can introduce subtle bugs. To minimize impact, deploy updates in small batches (using feature flags or short-lived branches)—for example, start by migrating only the authentication module before moving on to payment logic.

Combine this approach with production monitoring using tools like **Sentry** or **Bugsnag**, configured to capture exceptions and breadcrumbs:

```
import * as Sentry from '@sentry/react-native';

Sentry.init({ dsn: 'https://<key>@sentry.io/<project>' });

function handleError(err: unknown) {
Sentry.captureException(err);
}
```

When releasing a migration, monitor the error rates of the affected modules and set alerts for unexpected regressions. If something goes wrong, you can quickly disable the feature flag or apply a hotfix before it affects end users. This ensures your migration follows a controlled, safe path with full visibility into the health of the application.

Conclusion

To conclude this chapter, we revisited the key benefits of adopting TypeScript in React Native—from early error detection to continuous improvements in code readability and maintainability. We covered how to configure your project—either through incremental migration or by creating a fully TypeScript-based template—and explored advanced typing practices for components, data, and native integrations. With utilities like **`Partial`**, **`Pick`**, and Generics, along with strongly typed HOC patterns, you now have the tools to build robust internal APIs and highly reusable components.

In the second half, we demonstrated how to model your DTOs and schemas, validate them with Zod or Yup, and maintain typings for external libraries by creating your own declarations when necessary. We also covered advanced integrations—maps, QR codes, camera, sensors, and BLE—always with explicit type contracts and proper permission handling. To wrap up, we discussed strategies for updating React Native and its dependencies, automating regression tests, and implementing gradual rollout patterns, ensuring that your typed codebase evolves safely.

With this foundation in place, your React Native project becomes more predictable, scalable, and aligned with mature CI/CD workflows. In the next chapter, we shall dive into Internationalization (i18n) and Accessibility.

Self-Assessment Questions

Before moving on to hands-on practice, take a moment to reflect on the concepts and techniques covered in this chapter. The following questions will help you review key topics such as TypeScript typing, migration strategies, data modeling, and advanced integrations—while also preparing you to apply this knowledge in real-world projects:

1. What are the advantages of starting a React Native project with the TypeScript template instead of gradually migrating an existing JavaScript codebase?
2. How does **`allowJs`** combined with **`checkJs`** in **`tsconfig.json`** facilitate a "file-by-file" transition, and at what point would you recommend disabling `allowJs`?
3. Describe a strategy for typing a library without official type declarations (`@types`). What should you include in a minimal **`.d.ts`** declaration file?
4. When does it make sense to use `interface` instead of `type` to define your domain entities, and vice versa? Provide an example for each case.
5. How can utility types (**`Partial`**, **`Pick`**, **`Omit`**, **`Record`**) speed up the creation of DTOs and state models in a React Native app?
6. Explain how you would type a generic component that receives a list of items of any type and a `renderItem` function. What generics and constraints would be necessary?
7. What precautions should you take when integrating **`react-native-maps`**, especially regarding the typing of coordinates and management of region deltas?
8. In a scenario involving QR code generation and scanning, how would you define safe types for scan callbacks and the configuration props of the generator component?
9. Name two native libraries (for example, camera, sensors, or BLE) and explain how you would create types for the data returned by the plugin, ensuring compatibility with React Native and TypeScript.

10. What steps and tools would you use to automate regression tests after migrating your project to TypeScript, ensuring nothing breaks during future dependency upgrades?

Answering these questions will strengthen your ability to design a well-typed React Native foundation, with advanced integrations and clearly defined update processes.

Key Terms

- **TypeScript:** A superset of JavaScript that adds optional static typing, allowing developers to catch errors at compile time and providing automatic documentation in the editor.
- **tsconfig.json:** The TypeScript compiler configuration file, where options like **strict**, **allowJs**, **checkJs**, **jsx: "react-native"**, and **paths** for absolute imports are defined.
- **allowJs / checkJs:** Flags in **tsconfig.json** that control whether or not **.js** files are included in the compilation process (**allowJs**) and whether they receive type checking (**checkJs**), enabling incremental migrations.
- **React.FC<Props>:** A generic type for functional components, allowing you to explicitly define prop structures and ensure consistent use of JSX.
- **Generics:** Type parameters (like **<T>**) used to build reusable components and functions that adapt to different data structures without sacrificing type safety.
- **Utility Types:** Built-in TypeScript tools like **Partial<T>**, **Pick<T, K>**, **Omit<T, K>**, **Record<K, T>**, and **Required<T>** that help transform existing types and reduce repetitive code.
- **Data Transfer Object (DTO):** Interfaces or types that precisely represent the shape of data exchanged with the API, serving as clear contracts between front-end and back-end.
- **Validation Schemas (Zod, Yup):** Libraries used to define and validate object structures at runtime, which can also generate TypeScript types and perform data transformations (such as string → Date).
- **Module Declarations (.d.ts):** Files where you define types for libraries without official typings, declaring functions, classes, and interfaces to avoid using **any** throughout your code.
- **Interface Merging:** The ability of TypeScript to "merge" interface declarations, allowing you to extend third-party types without modifying their original definitions.
- **React Native Template TypeScript:** The command **npx react-native initMyApp --template react-native-template-typescript** generates a project preconfigured for TypeScript, including **App.tsx**, **index.js**, **tsconfig.json**, and ESLint/Prettier presets.
- **Metro Bundler:** The default bundler of React Native, which requires configuration in **metro.config.js** to recognize **.ts** and **.tsx** extensions and use appropriate transformers.
- **Higher-Order Components (HOC):** Functions that receive a component and return a new one with added functionality; when typing HOCs, Generics are used to preserve the original props and add new ones.
- **react-native-maps / LatLng:** A mapping library for React Native; the **LatLng** type (with **latitude** and **longitude**) ensures correct values are provided for markers and regions.
- **react-native-qrcode-svg / onRead:** A component for generating QR codes with a **value: string** prop; when implementing scanners (such as with **react-native-camera**), the **onRead** callback is typed as **{ data: string; type: string }**.

- **Native Plugins (Camera, Sensors, BLE):** Libraries like `react-native-camera`, `react-native-sensors`, and `react-native-ble-plx` that require typed data structures (including `AccelerometerData`, `BleDevice`) and typed `subscribe/unsubscribe` callbacks.
- **`react-native-permissions` / `PermissionStatus`:** Manages native permissions (for instance, Camera, Location); the `PermissionStatus = 'granted' | 'denied' | 'blocked' | 'unavailable'` type standardizes results and simplifies handling.
- **React Native Upgrade / Upgrade Helper:** Tools for version migration: `npx react-native upgrade` and the Upgrade Helper website display configuration diffs between releases to help resolve upgrade conflicts.
- **Breaking Changes and Type Augmentation:** The process of handling API signature changes; use module augmentation (`declare module`) or type overrides to maintain compatibility until the official update is available.
- **Testing in TypeScript (Jest + ts-jest):** Jest setup to compile `.ts/.tsx` via `ts-jest`, allowing you to write tests that leverage domain typings and catch type errors within the test suite itself.
- **`TSDoc` and `TypeDoc`:** A documentation style (`/** … */`) for functions, interfaces, and types, used to generate docstrings and automatic HTML documentation with TypeDoc.
- **Gradual Rollout and Monitoring (`Sentry`, `Bugsnag`):** A strategy of releasing changes via feature flags and observing production error metrics to quickly roll back or fix issues.
- **Typing CI:** A pipeline that runs `tsc --noEmit`, `eslint`, and `jest` to validate types, enforce code style, and run tests before every merge, ensuring that your typed codebase remains consistent and regression-free.

These terms summarize the key concepts, tools, and best practices covered in this chapter, serving as a quick reference for applying performance improvements and architectural organization in React Native projects with Typescript.

CHAPTER 12
Internationalization (i18n) and Accessibility

Introduction

To build mobile applications that reach a global audience, it is not enough to rely solely on strong technical capabilities—it is equally important to consider cultural diversity and the specific needs of users. In this context, internationalization (i18n) emerges as a vital set of practices and techniques that ensure your app can be easily adapted to different languages, date formats, numbers, and currencies. More than simply translating text, internationalization involves delivering user experiences that respect local customs, creating a sense of familiarity and inclusion for users around the world.

Alongside internationalization, accessibility stands as another fundamental pillar in crafting inclusive applications. Ensuring that people with different abilities can fully use a mobile app is not just a best practice—it is an ethical and social responsibility for developers. By adopting accessibility practices and following standards such as the WCAG (Web Content Accessibility Guidelines) and WAI-ARIA, we can adapt components and interfaces to be fully usable by users with visual, auditory, or motor impairments—especially through assistive technologies like screen readers.

In this chapter, you will learn practical steps to configure and implement internationalization in React Native projects using TypeScript, leveraging well-established libraries such as i18n-js and react-intl. We will also explore the key techniques required to make components accessible to major assistive tools like VoiceOver of iOS and TalkBack of Android, following inclusive design principles and best practices. By the end, you will be equipped to develop applications that not only cross language barriers but also provide a dignified, accessible, and welcoming experience for all users.

Structure

In this chapter, we will cover the following topics:

- Core Concepts of Internationalization
- Setting Up i18n Libraries in React Native
    - Installing and Configuring `i18n-js` with TypeScript
    - Organizing Translation JSON Files
    - Using react-intl for More Advanced Needs
    - Choosing Between i18n-js and react-intl

- Translating Text and Components
  - Dynamic Language Switching
  - Formatting Dates, Numbers, and Currencies
  - Internationalized Date Formatting with react-intl
  - Displaying Numbers Across Cultures
  - Proper Currency Display and Monetary Formatting
- Managing Internationalization State
  - Example: Persisting Language Preference with Context API and AsyncStorage
  - Integrating i18n with Global State Managers (Zustand and Redux)
- Introduction to Accessibility in Mobile Apps
  - Making Components Accessible
  - Basic Accessibility: Making Components Readable by Screen Readers
  - Describing Dynamic States with `accessibilityState`
  - Improving Focus Navigation
  - Testing with VoiceOver and TalkBack
- Inclusive Design in React Native Applications
  - Color and Contrast Accessibility
  - Font Scaling and Readability
  - Supporting Dark Mode
  - High Contrast Mode Support
- Best Practices and Advanced Tips
  - Translation Management in Collaborative Environments
  - Automating Translations with External Platforms
  - Accessibility Audits and Continuous Testing
  - Improving Complex Components

Core Concepts of Internationalization

Internationalization, often abbreviated as **i18n**, is the process of preparing an application from the ground up to be easily adapted to different languages, regions, and cultures without requiring major structural changes. The abbreviation "i18n" comes from the word *internationalization*, where the number "18" represents the number of letters between the first "i" and the last "n." The primary goal of internationalization is to ensure that an app can support varied translations and formatting (dates, numbers, currencies) in a simple and efficient way, allowing for quick expansion into global markets.

Internationalization (**`i18n`**) is often confused with **localization (`l10n`)**, but while the two are related, they are distinct and complementary concepts. Internationalization refers to the technical preparation of a project to support multiple languages and cultures. Localization, on the other hand, is the actual process of adapting the product for a specific region or language. Localizing an app goes beyond translating text—it includes adapting date and time formats, currency symbols, measurement units, imagery, and even color schemes that might carry cultural significance. In essence, internationalization is a broader and strategic process, while localization is more targeted and operational, tailored to the needs of a specific locale.

To quickly illustrate these concepts, imagine an e-commerce app initially developed in Brazil. You would first internationalize (i18n) the app by setting up its infrastructure to support multiple languages. Later, when launching it in Japan, you would perform localization (l10n) by translating text into Japanese, adjusting number and currency formats for Yen, and modifying layouts or images where culturally relevant.

Here is a simple example of internationalization using the **i18n-js** library in a React Native project with TypeScript:

```
// i18n.ts
import i18n from 'i18n-js';

i18n.translations = {
en: { welcome: 'Welcome!' },
pt: { welcome: 'Bem-vindo!' },
};

i18n.locale = 'pt'; // User-selected language
i18n.fallbacks = true;

export default i18n;
```

And in your React Native component, you can easily use it like this:

```
import React from 'react';
import { Text, View } from 'react-native';
import i18n from './i18n';

export default function App() {
  return (
<View>
<Text>{i18n.t('welcome')}</Text>
</View>
  );
}
```

Beyond internationalization, another essential concept is **accessibility**, which focuses on ensuring that all individuals—regardless of their physical or cognitive abilities—can fully use a mobile application. In mobile contexts, this means enabling users with visual, auditory, motor, or cognitive impairments to navigate and interact with content effectively and efficiently. Accessibility is not just a set of tweaks—it is a mindset and an ethical approach to design and development that aims to create truly inclusive digital experiences.

A widely recognized method for ensuring accessibility is adhering to international standards such as the **WCAG** (Web Content Accessibility Guidelines). Developed by the W3C, these guidelines provide a framework of principles and criteria for making digital content accessible to everyone. They are structured in three levels of conformance: A, AA, and AAA. Additionally, the **WAI-ARIA** specification (Web Accessibility Initiative - Accessible Rich Internet Applications) defines attributes that improve the interaction between dynamic content and assistive technologies such as screen readers.

Here is a simple React Native example demonstrating how to apply accessibility attributes to support screen readers like iOS's VoiceOver and Android's TalkBack:

```
import React from "react";
import { TouchableOpacity, Text } from "react-native";

export default function AccessibleButton({
```

```
isSubmitting = false,
}: {
isSubmitting?:boolean;
}) {
  return (
<TouchableOpacity
      // `accessible` is redundant here—Touchables are accessible by default.
accessibilityRole="button"
accessibilityLabel="Submit form"
accessibilityHint="Submits your form data"
accessibilityState={{ disabled: isSubmitting, busy: isSubmitting }}
      disabled={isSubmitting}
onPress={() => {
        /* submit */
      }}
>
<Text>{isSubmitting ? "Submitting…" : "Submit"}</Text>
</TouchableOpacity>
  );
}
```

In this example, the **`accessible={true}`** attribute ensures the element is picked up by screen readers. **`accessibilityLabel`** provides a clear description of the element's purpose, and **`accessibilityRole`** clarifies its function within the interface.

Ensuring that both accessibility and internationalization is not just beneficial for product reach and reputation—it represents a firm ethical commitment to diversity and inclusion. Applications that adhere to international best practices such as WCAG and WAI-ARIA deliver superior experiences for all users and stand out as responsible, user-centered products capable of adapting to a wide range of global contexts.

Setting Up i18n Libraries in React Native

One of the first steps when internationalizing a React Native application is choosing the library that best fits your needs. Two of the most popular and well-established solutions in the ecosystem are **`i18n-js`** and **`react-intl`**. Both aim to support multilingual applications, but they differ slightly in their approaches and features—ranging from lightweight setups for simple apps to robust solutions for more complex projects.

In addition to **`i18n-js`**, many React Native teams use **`react-i18next`** (i18next + React bindings) because it integrates cleanly with the broader React ecosystem and supports features like **namespaces** (splitting translations by feature/screen) and **lazy loading** of translation resources for larger apps. If you choose **`i18n-js`**, be aware that **v4 introduced significant breaking changes compared to v3**, so ensure your code examples match the **v4 documentation** (do not assume the older v3 API). For **Expo** projects, it is common to pair your **`i18n`** library with **`expo-localization`** to detect the device's locale and language settings and initialize your app's default language accordingly.

`i18n-js` is widely adopted due to its simplicity and minimal footprint. It enables direct translations with support for variable interpolation, pluralization, and language fallbacks. On the other hand, **`react-intl`** provides more advanced features such as formatting for dates, numbers, currencies, and support for complex conditional messages. Because of this, it is often preferred for projects that require greater flexibility in handling international content.

Let us begin by configuring **`i18n-js`** in a React Native project using TypeScript.

Installing and Configuring i18n-js with TypeScript

Start by installing the required dependencies:

```
npm install i18n-js @react-native-async-storage/async-storage
npm install --save-dev @types/i18n-js
```

It is common to use **AsyncStorage** to persist the user's language preference.

After installation, create a configuration file called **i18n.ts** at the root of your project or inside a dedicated folder (for example, **src/i18n/i18n.ts**). In this file, configure your i18n instance with basic translations:

```
// src/i18n/i18n.ts
import I18n from 'i18n-js';
import { getLocales } from 'expo-localization'; // Use react-native-localize if not
using Expo

// Import translation files
import pt from './translations/pt.json';
import en from './translations/en.json';

// Define available translations
I18n.translations = { pt, en };

// Set default locale and fallback
I18n.fallbacks = true;
I18n.defaultLocale = 'en';

// Automatically detect device language
const locales = getLocales();
I18n.locale = locales[0].languageCode;

export default I18n;
```

In this setup, we use **expo-localization** to detect the device's locale automatically. If you are not using Expo, you can use **react-native-localize** as an alternative.

Organizing Translation JSON Files

A good practice is to keep translations separated in JSON files for easy maintenance and scalability. A typical structure would look like:

```
/src
  /i18n
    - i18n.ts
    /translations
      - en.json
      - pt.json
```

Example of en.json:

```
{
  "welcome": "Welcome!",
  "login": {
    "title": "Login",
    "button": "Sign In"
```

```
  },
  "home": {
    "greeting": "Hello, {{name}}!"
  }
}
```

Example of `pt.json`:

```
{
  "welcome": "Bem-vindo!",
  "login": {
    "title": "Entrar",
    "button": "Acessar"
  },
  "home": {
    "greeting": "Olá, {{name}}!"
  }
}
```

To use these translations inside a React Native component:

```
// Example usage
import React from 'react';
import { Text, View, Button } from 'react-native';
import I18n from '../i18n/i18n';

export default function HomeScreen() {
  return (
<View>
<Text>{I18n.t('welcome')}</Text>
<Text>{I18n.t('home.greeting', { name: 'Felipe' })}</Text>
<Button title={I18n.t('login.button')} onPress={() => {}} />
</View>
  );
}
```

Note how dynamic interpolation is used to insert values into the translated strings.

Using react-intl for More Advanced Needs

If your project requires more advanced features, you might prefer `react-intl`. To set it up with TypeScript:

```
npm install react-intl
npm install --save-dev @types/react-intl
```

The basic setup for `react-intl` involves creating a global context to provide translations across the app.

```
// src/App.tsx
import React from 'react';
import { IntlProvider } from 'react-intl';
import messages_en from './i18n/translations/en.json';
import messages_pt from './i18n/translations/pt.json';
import { getLocales } from 'expo-localization';
```

```
const messages: Record<string, Record<string, string>> = {
en: messages_en,
pt: messages_pt,
};

const locale = getLocales()[0].languageCode;

export default function App() {
  return (
<IntlProvider locale={locale} messages={messages[locale]}>
      {/* Your root component here */}
</IntlProvider>
  );
}
```

Then in your components, use the **`react-intl`** API to access translations:

```
import React from 'react';
import { Text } from 'react-native';
import { useIntl } from 'react-intl';

export default function Greeting() {
constintl = useIntl();

  return (
<Text>
      {intl.formatMessage({ id: 'home.greeting' }, { name: 'Felipe' })}
</Text>
  );
}
```

The JSON translation structure for **`react-intl`** is similar to **`i18n-js`**, making it easy to switch between libraries if needed.

Choosing between `i18n-js` and `react-intl`

Both libraries are excellent choices, but generally:

- **`i18n-js`** is better suited for smaller projects or when you need a fast, lightweight, and straightforward implementation.
- **`react-intl`** is ideal for larger, more complex apps that require advanced formatting of dates, numbers, currencies, or conditional messages.

Choose the one that best fits the complexity and scalability your project needs—always keeping in mind that the ultimate goal is to deliver a smooth, culturally aware, and user-friendly experience to a global audience.

Translating Text and Components

When implementing internationalization in React Native applications, translating static text is only the beginning. Real-world applications require more dynamic and flexible approaches—for example, variable interpolation within messages and proper handling of pluralization. Additionally, giving users the ability to switch languages dynamically is essential for any app aiming to serve a diverse global audience.

Let us start by translating simple text using the **i18n-js** library. Consider the following Portuguese translation file (**pt.json**):

```
{
  "home": {
    "title": "Páginainicial",
    "greeting": "Olá, {{name}}!",
    "notifications": {
      "zero": "Vocênãopossuinotificações",
      "one": "Vocêpossui {{count}} notificação",
      "other": "Vocêpossui{{count}} notificações"
    }
  }
}
```

Note the use of special syntax (**{{ }}**) to indicate where dynamic variables will be inserted.

Now, here is how to implement these dynamic translations in a React Native component using TypeScript:

```
import React from 'react';
import { Text, View } from 'react-native';
import I18n from '../i18n/i18n';

interface HomeProps {
userName: string;
notificationCount: number;
}

export default function Home({ userName, notificationCount }: HomeProps) {
  return (
<View>
<Text>{I18n.t('home.title')}</Text>
<Text>{I18n.t('home.greeting', { name: userName })}</Text>
<Text>{I18n.t('home.notifications', { count: notificationCount })}</Text>
</View>
  );
}
```

In this example, interpolation is handled directly via the **I18n.t()** function, by passing an object with the dynamic values. Pluralization is automatically handled by `i18n-js` based on the `count` value. For instance, if `count` is 0, the message will be "**Vocênãopossuinotificações**"; if it's 1, the singular form is used; otherwise, the plural form is applied.

The library automatically determines the correct pluralization rule based on the current locale. This approach greatly simplifies adapting your app to various languages, while ensuring grammatical correctness and enhancing the user experience.

Dynamic Language Switching

It is common and highly recommended to offer users the ability to change the app's language in real time. To enable this, you'll need a structure that allows the selected language to be changed dynamically and reflected instantly throughout the app.

Consider creating a simple global context using React's Context API to manage the language state:

```
// LanguageContext.tsx
import React, { createContext, useState, ReactNode } from 'react';
```

```
import I18n from './i18n/i18n';

interface LanguageContextProps {
  locale: string;
setLocale: (locale: string) => void;
}

export constLanguageContext = createContext<LanguageContextProps>({
  locale: I18n.locale,
setLocale: () => {},
});

export function LanguageProvider({ children }: { children: ReactNode }) {
const [locale, setLocaleState] = useState(I18n.locale);

constsetLocale = (newLocale: string) => {
    I18n.locale = newLocale;
setLocaleState(newLocale);
  };

  return (
<LanguageContext.Provider value={{ locale, setLocale }}>
      {children}
</LanguageContext.Provider>
  );
}
```

Wrap your application with this `LanguageProvider`:

```
// App.tsx
import React from 'react';
import { LanguageProvider } from './LanguageContext';
import Home from './screens/Home';

export default function App() {
  return (
<LanguageProvider>
<Home />
</LanguageProvider>
  );
}
```

Now, in any component, you can access the context and change the language dynamically. Here is a practical example using a simple language **toggle** button:

```
import React, { useContext } from 'react';
import { View, Button, Text } from 'react-native';
import { LanguageContext } from '../LanguageContext';
import I18n from '../i18n/i18n';

export default function LanguageSwitcher() {
const{ locale, setLocale } = useContext(LanguageContext);

consttoggleLanguage = () => {
constnewLocale = locale === 'en' ? 'pt' : 'en';
setLocale(newLocale);
  };

  return (
```

```
<View>
<Text>{I18n.t('home.title')}</Text>
<Button title="Change Language" onPress={toggleLanguage} />
</View>
  );
}
```

In this example, when the "**Change Language**" button is pressed, the app switches between English and Portuguese, and the displayed messages update immediately. This approach provides a responsive and user-friendly experience for international users.

By implementing dynamic translations, variable interpolation, and real-time language switching, your React Native app becomes more robust, scalable, and enjoyable for international audiences—delivering a truly global and inclusive user experience.

Formatting Dates, Numbers, and Currencies

Beyond translating text and adapting language, a crucial part of internationalization is ensuring that dates, numbers, and monetary values are displayed according to the cultural conventions of each region. For example, users in the United States expect to see dates formatted as MM/DD/YYYY, while users in Brazil are accustomed to DD/MM/YYYY. Similarly, thousands and decimal separators—as well as currency symbols—differ from country to country. The `react-intl` library is particularly powerful for handling these aspects.

When using `react-intl`, you gain access to several methods for international formatting, such as:

- `formatDate()` for dates
- `formatNumber()` for numbers
- `formatNumber({ style: 'currency' })` for currencies

Internationalized Date Formatting with `react-intl`

Let us start with formatting dates correctly based on the locale of the user. Make sure your component is wrapped in an **IntlProvider**, as previously shown. Then, format dates dynamically like this:

```
import React from 'react';
import { Text, View } from 'react-native';
import { useIntl } from 'react-intl';

export default function DateExample() {
constintl = useIntl();
constcurrentDate = new Date();

  return (
<View>
<Text>
        {intl.formatDate(currentDate, {
          year: 'numeric',
          month: 'long',
          day: 'numeric',
        })}
</Text>
<Text>
        {intl.formatDate(currentDate, {
          weekday: 'long',
          year: 'numeric',
```

```
          month: 'short',
          day: '2-digit',
        })}
</Text>
</View>
  );
}
```

For users with English locale settings, the output might be:

```
July 10, 2025
Thursday, Jul 10, 2025
```

Whereas for Brazilian Portuguese, it would appear as:

```
10 de julho de 2025
quinta-feira, 10 de jul. de 2025
```

Displaying Numbers across Cultures

Number formatting can vary significantly by region. For instance, **1,234.56** in the U.S. would be represented as **1.234,56** in Brazil. **react-intl** makes this easy:

```
import React from 'react';
import { Text, View } from 'react-native';
import { useIntl } from 'react-intl';

export default function NumberExample() {
constintl = useIntl();
const value = 1234567.89;

  return (
<View>
<Text>
        {intl.formatNumber(value)}
</Text>
<Text>
        {intl.formatNumber(value, { style: 'unit', unit: 'kilometer-per-hour' })}
</Text>
</View>
  );
}
```

In en-US locale, the output would be:

```
1,234,567.89
1,234,567.89 km/h
```

In pt-BR locale:

```
1.234.567,89
1.234.567,89 km/h
```

Proper Currency Display and Monetary Formatting

Monetary values are especially sensitive to localization—not just in terms of the currency symbol, but also how the numbers themselves are formatted. **react-intl** offers robust support for formatting currency values according to regional standards.

Here is how to format currencies:

```
import React from 'react';
import { Text, View } from 'react-native';
import { useIntl } from 'react-intl';

export default function CurrencyExample() {
constintl = useIntl();
const price = 3499.99;

  return (
<View>
<Text>
        {intl.formatNumber(price, { style: 'currency', currency: 'USD' })}
</Text>
<Text>
        {intl.formatNumber(price, { style: 'currency', currency: 'BRL' })}
</Text>
<Text>
        {intl.formatNumber(price, { style: 'currency', currency: 'EUR' })}
</Text>
</View>
  );
}
```

For the `en-US` locale, the result would be:

```
$3,499.99
R$3,499.99
€3,499.99
```

For the `pt-BR` locale:

```
US$ 3.499,99
R$ 3.499,99
€ 3.499,99
```

Notice how the library automatically formats the numeric values and places the currency symbol appropriately according to local conventions. By using these advanced formatting techniques offered by **`react-intl`**, you significantly simplify the process of ensuring that your application delivers a culturally appropriate and comfortable experience for users worldwide. This not only enhances usability but also elevates the perceived quality and professionalism of your React Native application.

Managing Internationalization State

In a robust and user-friendly React Native application, enabling dynamic language selection is only the first step. It is equally important to keep the language preference of the user persistent so that it is remembered every time the app is reopened. Additionally, integrating internationalization into the global state of your app makes your architecture more scalable and maintainable—especially as the project grows in complexity.

To persist the selected language, a common and effective approach is to use `AsyncStorage`, a native local storage solution available in React Native. With it, you can easily store and retrieve simple key-value data, ensuring that the language choice of the user is preserved between sessions.

Example: Persisting Language Preference with Context API and AsyncStorage

First, install **AsyncStorage**:

```
npm install @react-native-async-storage/async-storage
```

Now, create a language context that combines the Context API with AsyncStorage to persist the user's selection:

```
// LanguageContext.tsx
import React, { createContext, useState, useEffect, ReactNode } from 'react';
import I18n from './i18n/i18n';
import AsyncStorage from '@react-native-async-storage/async-storage';

interface LanguageContextProps {
  locale: string;
setLocale: (locale: string) => void;
}

export constLanguageContext = createContext<LanguageContextProps>({
  locale: I18n.locale,
setLocale: () => {},
});

export function LanguageProvider({ children }: { children: ReactNode }) {
const [locale, setLocaleState] = useState(I18n.locale);

useEffect(() => {
async function loadLocale() {
conststoredLocale = await AsyncStorage.getItem('@app_locale');
      if (storedLocale) {
        I18n.locale = storedLocale;
setLocaleState(storedLocale);
      }
    }
loadLocale();
  }, []);

constsetLocale = async (newLocale: string) => {
    I18n.locale = newLocale;
setLocaleState(newLocale);
    await AsyncStorage.setItem('@app_locale', newLocale);
  };

  return (
<LanguageContext.Provider value={{ locale, setLocale }}>
      {children}
</LanguageContext.Provider>
  );
}
```

In this example, whenever the user changes the language, the new preference is saved to AsyncStorage. When the app restarts, the previously selected language is automatically restored and applied.

Integrating i18n with Global State Managers (Zustand and Redux)

If your application already uses a global state manager like Zustand or Redux, integrating internationalization can offer additional benefits—especially for larger, more complex apps.

Example with Zustand

Zustand is a lightweight and intuitive state manager that simplifies this task. Here is a basic store for managing language:

```
// languageStore.ts
import { create } from 'zustand';
import I18n from './i18n/i18n';
import AsyncStorage from '@react-native-async-storage/async-storage';

interface LanguageState {
  locale: string;
setLocale: (locale: string) => void;
loadStoredLocale: () => void;
}

export constuseLanguageStore = create<LanguageState>((set) => ({
  locale: I18n.locale,
setLocale: async (locale: string) => {
    I18n.locale = locale;
set({ locale });
    await AsyncStorage.setItem('@app_locale', locale);
  },
loadStoredLocale: async () => {
conststoredLocale = await AsyncStorage.getItem('@app_locale');
    if (storedLocale) {
      I18n.locale = storedLocale;
set({ locale: storedLocale });
    }
  },
}));
```

Now you can use this store in any component:

```
import React, { useEffect } from 'react';
import { Button, View, Text } from 'react-native';
import { useLanguageStore } from './languageStore';
import I18n from './i18n/i18n';

export default function LanguageSwitcher() {
const{ locale, setLocale, loadStoredLocale } = useLanguageStore();

useEffect(() => {
loadStoredLocale();
  }, []);

consttoggleLanguage = () => {
setLocale(locale === 'en' ? 'pt' : 'en');
  };
```

```
  return (
<View>
<Text>{I18n.t('welcome')}</Text>
<Button title="Change Language" onPress={toggleLanguage} />
</View>
  );
}
```

Example with Redux

For apps using Redux, language can be managed through a reducer and actions:

First, define an action:

```
// actions/languageActions.ts
export const SET_LOCALE = 'SET_LOCALE';

export constsetLocale = (locale: string) => ({
  type: SET_LOCALE,
  payload: locale,
});
```

Then the corresponding reducer:

```
// reducers/languageReducer.ts
import{ SET_LOCALE } from '../actions/languageActions';
import I18n from '../i18n/i18n';

interface LanguageState {
  locale: string;
}

constinitialState: LanguageState = {
  locale: I18n.locale,
};

export default function languageReducer(state = initialState, action: any) {
  switch (action.type) {
    case SET_LOCALE:
      I18n.locale = action.payload;
AsyncStorage.setItem('@app_locale', action.payload);
      return { ...state, locale: action.payload };
    default:
      return state;
  }
}
```

Now connect your component to Redux and update the language:

```
import React, { useEffect } from 'react';
import { View, Button, Text } from 'react-native';
import { useDispatch, useSelector } from 'react-redux';
import { setLocale } from '../actions/languageActions';
import I18n from '../i18n/i18n';
import AsyncStorage from '@react-native-async-storage/async-storage';
```

```
export default function LanguageSwitcher() {
const dispatch = useDispatch();
const locale = useSelector((state: any) =>state.language.locale);

useEffect(() => {
async function loadLocale() {
conststoredLocale = await AsyncStorage.getItem('@app_locale');
      if (storedLocale) {
        dispatch(setLocale(storedLocale));
      }
    }
loadLocale();
  }, []);

consttoggleLanguage = () => {
constnewLocale = locale === 'en' ? 'pt' : 'en';
    dispatch(setLocale(newLocale));
  };

  return (
<View>
<Text>{I18n.t('welcome')}</Text>
<Button title="Change Language" onPress={toggleLanguage} />
</View>
  );
}
```

No matter which solution you choose—Context API with AsyncStorage, Zustand, or Redux—the main goal remains the same: to provide a seamless user experience where language preferences are respected, persisted, and integrated in a simple and efficient way. These approaches ensure your app is well-structured and ready to grow while delivering a consistent and high-quality experience to users around the world.

Introduction to Accessibility in Mobile Apps

Digital accessibility aims to ensure that products and services can be easily used by everyone, including people with visual, auditory, motor, or cognitive impairments. In mobile applications, implementing accessibility is especially critical due to the wide diversity of users and the global reach of these platforms. Following international standards and guidelines is therefore essential to guarantee an inclusive and respectful experience for all users.

One of the most important references for accessibility is the **Web Content Accessibility Guidelines (WCAG)**, developed by the W3C. WCAG organizes its recommendations into three levels of compliance:

- **Level A**: The most basic and mandatory level, addressing critical issues that, if unaddressed, completely block access to content. Examples include providing alternative text for images and enabling keyboard or screen reader navigation.
- **Level AA**: Considered the standard minimum in many legal and corporate contexts, this intermediate level introduces more rigorous criteria, such as sufficient color contrast, clarity in interactive elements, and enhanced screen reader support.
- **Level AAA**: The highest and strictest level, recommended for applications requiring maximum accessibility—such as government platforms or essential services. It includes advanced criteria like enhanced legibility, precise control over animations, detailed audio alternatives, and highly adaptable interfaces.

Although WCAG was originally designed for web content, its principles are widely applied to mobile apps as well, due to their clarity and universal applicability. Another key standard is **WAI-ARIA** (Web Accessibility Initiative - Accessible Rich Internet Applications), also developed by the W3C. WAI-ARIA provides a technical specification focused on defining extra attributes that help describe interface elements more accurately, so assistive technologies like screen readers can properly interpret dynamic interfaces.

In React Native, accessibility attributes follow principles similar to WAI-ARIA. For example, properties like **`accessibilityLabel`**, **`accessible`**, and **`accessibilityRole`** provide additional context for screen readers, making navigation and interaction clearer for users with visual or motor impairments.

Here is a practical example of these attributes in use:

```
import React from 'react';
import { TouchableOpacity, Text } from 'react-native';

export default function AccessibleButton() {
  return (
<TouchableOpacity
      accessible={true}
accessibilityLabel="Submit contact form"
accessibilityRole="button"
>
<Text>Submit</Text>
</TouchableOpacity>
  );
}
```

In this example, we clearly define the component's role as a "**`button`**" and provide a readable description for screen readers, helping visually impaired users interact with greater clarity and confidence.

Beyond following best practices and international standards, it is essential to perform **accessibility testing regularly** throughout development. Fortunately, both major mobile platforms include built-in tools to support this:

- **VoiceOver (iOS)**: It is the native screen reader of Apple that allows users to navigate apps using specific gestures or a keyboard. It can be enabled via **`Settings`** > **`Accessibility`** >**`VoiceOver`**.
- **TalkBack (Android)**: It is the standard assistive technology on Android devices, functioning similarly to VoiceOver. It can be activated via **`Settings`** > **`Accessibility`** >**`TalkBack`**.
- **Accessibility Inspector (iOS Simulator)**: It is a tool built into Xcode that helps developers check accessibility properties of UI elements during development.
- **Accessibility Scanner (Android)**: It is an official Google app that automatically analyzes UI components and provides actionable suggestions to improve accessibility.

Regularly testing your app with these tools ensures that serious accessibility issues do not go unnoticed and helps foster a genuinely inclusive user experience. Implementing accessibility in mobile applications should not be seen as secondary or optional—it is an ethical responsibility and a critical feature that expands your user base while significantly improving the overall user experience. By following clear guidelines like WCAG and WAI-ARIA and leveraging the right testing tools, you'll be equipped to build accessible, equitable, and effective apps for a broad and diverse audience.

Making Components Accessible

Adapting your React Native components for screen readers is essential for building a truly inclusive application. Screen readers like VoiceOver (iOS) and TalkBack (Android) assist users with visual impairments by converting visual content into audio or Braille. For this technology to function properly, it is crucial to clearly communicate what elements are on the screen and what their purpose is.

React Native provides several accessibility-specific properties to define the behavior and role of each component in the interface. The most important ones include: `accessible`, **`accessibilityLabel`**, **`accessibilityRole`**, and **`accessibilityState`**.

Basic Accessibility: Making Components Readable by Screen Readers

Starting with the most fundamental property, **`accessible`** determines whether a component should be exposed to screen readers. By default, native components like buttons have this set to **`true`**, but you will need to explicitly set it for custom components to ensure accessibility.

Here is a simple example of making a custom button accessible:

```
import React from 'react';
import { TouchableOpacity, Text } from 'react-native';

export default function CustomButton() {
  return (
<TouchableOpacity
      accessible={true}
accessibilityLabel="Add item to cart"
accessibilityRole="button"
>
<Text>Add</Text>
</TouchableOpacity>
  );
}
```

In this example:

- **`accessible={true}`** ensures the component is recognized by screen readers.
- **`accessibilityLabel`** provides a clear, descriptive label that will be read aloud by VoiceOver or TalkBack.
- **`accessibilityRole="button"`** helps the screen reader announce that the element is a button, guiding the user's interaction.

Describing Dynamic States with `accessibilityState`

Interface elements often have dynamic states such as "**`selected`**," "**`disabled`**," or "active/inactive." Use **`accessibilityState`** to convey these states to screen readers effectively:

```
import React, { useState } from 'react';
import { TouchableOpacity, Text } from 'react-native';

export default function SelectableOption() {
const [selected, setSelected] = useState(false);

  return (
<TouchableOpacity
      accessible={true}
accessibilityLabel="Credit card payment option"
accessibilityRole="checkbox"
```

```
accessibilityState={{ checked: selected }}
onPress={() =>setSelected(!selected)}
>
<Text>{selected ? 'Selected' : 'Not selected'}</Text>
</TouchableOpacity>
  );
}
```

In this example, pressing the button updates the screen reader with the new state—"**checked**" or "**unchecked**"—improving clarity and helping users understand the component's behavior.

Improving Focus Navigation

An essential part of accessibility is ensuring smooth, logical navigation through component focus. This is especially important for users who rely on external keyboards, switch controls, or screen reader navigation gestures.

In React Native, you can enhance focus navigation using:

- **importantForAccessibility** (Android)
- **accessibilityElementsHidden** (iOS)
- **accessibilityViewIsModal** (iOS)

These properties help define how users interact with your UI in specific contexts. Here is a practical example using **accessibilityViewIsModal**:

```
import React from 'react';
import { View, Text, TouchableOpacity } from 'react-native';

export default function ModalExample() {
  return (
<View
      accessible={true}
accessibilityViewIsModal={true}
>
<Text>You need to confirm this action.</Text>

<TouchableOpacity
        accessible={true}
accessibilityLabel="Confirm action"
accessibilityRole="button"
>
<Text>Confirm</Text>
</TouchableOpacity>

<TouchableOpacity
        accessible={true}
accessibilityLabel="Cancel action"
accessibilityRole="button"
>
<Text>Cancel</Text>
</TouchableOpacity>
</View>
  );
}
```

Setting **`accessibilityViewIsModal={true}`** ensures that the screen reader keeps focus within this modal until the interaction is complete, preventing distractions from unrelated UI elements and improving user comprehension of the current task.

Testing with VoiceOver and TalkBack

Once accessibility properties are in place, it is highly recommended to test your components using actual screen readers:

- On **iOS**, activate **`VoiceOver`** via:

  `Settings → Accessibility → VoiceOver`

- On **Android**, activate **`TalkBack`** via:

  `Settings → Accessibility → TalkBack`

Testing with these tools allows you to catch issues and unclear interactions, helping you refine labels, roles, and states to deliver the best possible experience for users with disabilities.

By making your React Native components accessible in this way, you are not only meeting technical requirements— but you also are creating a more dignified, more usable, and inclusive experience for everyone. This enhances the overall usability of your app and broadens its reach to a more diverse and global user base.

Inclusive Design in React Native Applications

Building truly inclusive applications means thoughtfully considering the many different ways users may interact with your app from the very beginning. Inclusive design is an approach focused on embracing user diversity by ensuring interfaces are accessible, understandable, and enjoyable for all people—regardless of their abilities, contexts, or limitations.

The first core principle of inclusive design is to view human diversity as the starting point for interface development. Instead of creating isolated solutions for specific groups, the goal is to design a single, flexible, and welcoming system that serves everyone. This requires empathy, research, continuous testing, and a clear understanding of how different people interact with technology.

Color and Contrast Accessibility

One of the most critical aspects of inclusive design is the mindful use of **colors and contrast**. Approximately 8% of the global population has some level of color vision deficiency, with color blindness being one of the most common. That's why it's essential to ensure sufficient contrast between text and background, icons, and visual elements—so that users with visual limitations can clearly understand the content.

There are practical tools like the **WebAIM Contrast Checker** to help verify contrast ratios. According to WCAG (Level AA), a minimum contrast ratio of **4.5:1** is recommended for normal text. In React Native, always aim for high-contrast color combinations when styling components. Here is a basic example using Tailwind-like styles:

```
import React from 'react';
import { View, Text } from 'react-native';

export default function AccessibleText() {
  return (
<View style={{ backgroundColor: '#ffffff', padding: 16 }}>
<Text style={{ color: '#111827', fontSize: 16 }}>
        Text with adequate contrast for readability.
```

```
</Text>
</View>
  );
}
```

Font Scaling and Readability

Another key principle is respecting **text size scaling**. Many users adjust font sizes on their mobile devices for comfort or necessity. To accommodate this, React Native supports **`allowFontScaling`**, allowing text to automatically adapt to system preferences.

Avoid fixed font sizes and instead use relative or scalable units to ensure readability:

```
import React from 'react';
import { Text, View } from 'react-native';

export default function ScalableText() {
  return (
<View>
<Text allowFontScaling={true} style={{ fontSize: 18 }}>
        This text scales based on the user's font size preferences.
</Text>
</View>
  );
}
```

Scalable components improve accessibility and enhance reading comfort for users with low vision or other visual needs.

Supporting Dark Mode

Today, many applications support **dark mode**, which helps reduce eye strain and provides a more comfortable viewing experience for users sensitive to light. React Native includes the **`useColorScheme`** hook to detect the current theme of the system and apply appropriate styles:

```
import React from 'react';
import { useColorScheme, View, Text, StyleSheet } from 'react-native';

export default function DarkModeExample() {
constcolorScheme = useColorScheme();

  return (
<View style={colorScheme === 'dark' ? styles.darkContainer : styles.lightContainer}>
<Text style={colorScheme === 'dark' ? styles.darkText : styles.lightText}>
        Automatic dark mode support
</Text>
</View>
  );
}

const styles = StyleSheet.create({
darkContainer: {
backgroundColor: '#121212',
    padding: 16,
  },
lightContainer: {
```

```
backgroundColor: '#ffffff',
    padding: 16,
  },
darkText: {
    color: '#ffffff',
fontSize: 16,
  },
lightText: {
    color: '#000000',
fontSize: 16,
  },
});
```

Using this technique ensures your app respects user preferences and offers a smoother, more adaptive experience.

High Contrast Mode Support

While mobile operating systems natively support **high contrast modes**, well-designed applications can go a step further by offering their own high contrast theme. This can be implemented using context or global state management:

```
import React, { useState } from 'react';
import { View, Text, Button, StyleSheet } from 'react-native';

export default function HighContrastExample() {
const [highContrast, setHighContrast] = useState(false);

  return (
<View style={highContrast ? styles.highContrast : styles.normal}>
<Text style={highContrast ? styles.highContrastText : styles.normalText}>
        Text with high contrast support
</Text>
<Button
        title="Toggle High Contrast"
onPress={() =>setHighContrast(prev => !prev)}
      />
</View>
  );
}

const styles = StyleSheet.create({
highContrast: {
backgroundColor: '#000000',
    padding: 16,
  },
  normal: {
backgroundColor: '#ffffff',
    padding: 16,
  },
highContrastText: {
    color: '#FFFF00', // Bright yellow
fontSize: 18,
  },
```

```
normalText: {
    color: '#333333',
fontSize: 18,
  },
});
```

This feature allows users to switch to a high contrast view, benefiting especially those with low vision or visual processing difficulties.

Adopting **inclusive design principles** in React Native means crafting a user experience that is clear, flexible, and comfortable for a broad range of people. By intentionally designing for color contrast, font scalability, dark mode, and high contrast themes, you not only comply with international accessibility standards—rather, you build an app that is truly welcoming, empathetic, and at the same time, inclusive.

Best Practices and Advanced Tips

When implementing internationalization and accessibility in large and complex React Native projects, it becomes essential to adopt advanced practices and effective strategies to ensure ongoing quality and scalability. In this context, several best practices can significantly simplify your workflow—especially in collaborative teams—by helping maintain updated translations and regularly audited accessibility features.

Translation Management in Collaborative Environments

In collaborative teams, it is critical to establish a clear methodology for managing translations. This ensures consistency, organization, and ease of updates. A recommended best practice is to store all translation files in a standardized format (such as JSON), organized in a well-structured directory that is easily accessible by all team members.

Use clear naming conventions for translation keys—grouping them by context (like, **`home.title`**, **`profile.editButton`**, and so on)—to maintain clarity and avoid redundancy or conflict. Git-based version control with platforms like GitHub or GitLab is also highly effective for tracking changes and resolving translation file conflicts during parallel development.

Automating Translations with External Platforms

For projects with a large volume of translations, automation through external localization platforms like **Crowdin**, **Lokalise**, or **Phrase** can be extremely valuable. These platforms integrate directly with your Git repository and allow professional translators or community contributors to manage translations independently.

This lets your development team focus on code while translators update the text remotely via the platform, maintaining a streamlined and consistent translation workflow. A common pattern is to configure **continuous integration (CI)** to sync translation files automatically whenever updates are pushed to the main repository—minimizing manual work and reducing the risk of outdated or missing translations.

Accessibility Audits and Continuous Testing

Regarding accessibility, it is recommended to **conduct regular audits** throughout the development lifecycle of the app. Use native screen readers like **`VoiceOver`** (iOS) and **`TalkBack`** (Android), along with automated tools like **Accessibility Scanner** (Android) and **Accessibility Inspector** (iOS/Xcode).

It is also valuable to schedule **external accessibility audits**, especially at critical project milestones, to ensure compliance with international standards (such as **WCAG AA or AAA**), uncover usability barriers, and receive actionable feedback.

To optimize this process, include **accessibility checklists in pull request reviews**, where developers or QA testers validate key criteria such as color contrast, accessibility labels, navigation clarity, and screen reader compatibility.

Improving Complex Components

When working with complex UI components—like extensive forms, navigation menus, or dynamic lists—it is important to follow specific recommendations to enhance accessibility and localization.

For forms, ensure that each input field has a meaningful **`accessibilityLabel`**, so screen reader users can understand the purpose of the field clearly:

```
import React from 'react';
import { View, TextInput, Text } from 'react-native';

export default function AccessibleForm() {
  return (
<View>
<Text>Full Name:</Text>
<TextInput
        accessible={true}
accessibilityLabel="Field to enter your full name"
        placeholder="Enter here"
      />
</View>
  );
}
```

For complex navigation patterns, use **`accessibilityRole="navigation"`** and define clear roles for all interactive elements.

For dynamic lists, use native components like **`FlatList`** or **`SectionList`**, which are optimized for performance and accessibility. Avoid overly long lists without pagination, scroll markers, or grouping aids.

Example with `FlatList`:

```
import React from 'react';
import { FlatList, Text, TouchableOpacity } from 'react-native';

const items = [
{ id: '1', label: 'Settings' },
{ id: '2', label: 'Notifications' },
{ id: '3', label: 'Profile' },
];

export default function AccessibleList() {
  return (
<FlatList
      data={items}
keyExtractor={(item) => item.id}
renderItem={({ item }) => (
```

```
<TouchableOpacity
          accessible={true}
accessibilityRole="button"
accessibilityLabel={`Option: ${item.label}`}
>
<Text>{item.label}</Text>
</TouchableOpacity>
      )}
    />
  );
}
```

By adopting these advanced strategies and best practices, you go beyond technical compliance to deliver an intuitive, scalable, and inclusive experience for a global and diverse user base. With efficient translation management, automated localization workflows, continuous accessibility testing, and special attention to complex UI components, your React Native app will be well-positioned to provide a professional, accessible, and user-centered experience across all markets.

Conclusion

To conclude this chapter, we have reviewed the key concepts and techniques required to implement internationalization (**i18n**) and accessibility in React Native applications using TypeScript. We also explored how to prepare your app to reach a global audience—from basic configurations to advanced strategies—ensuring support for multiple languages and cultures. This included the use of libraries like `` `i18n-js` `` and `` `react-intl` `` for dynamic translations, variable interpolation, and proper formatting for dates, numbers, and currencies, as well as techniques for dynamic language switching with persistent user preferences.

In the second part of the chapter, we focused specifically on accessibility, emphasizing its ethical and practical importance in building inclusive interfaces. We, in the sections ahead, further covered how to adapt components for screen readers like VoiceOver and TalkBack, and explored core inclusive design principles such as sufficient color contrast, scalable typography, and support for dark mode and high-contrast themes. We also highlighted best practices for continuous accessibility auditing and efficient translation management—including the use of external platforms to streamline collaboration within large teams.

By applying these practices, your React Native project will be better equipped to serve diverse users, providing an accessible, comfortable, and culturally appropriate experience. In the next chapter, we will dive deeper into advanced performance and optimization strategies to ensure an even smoother and faster experience with build automation and CI/CD.

Self-Assessment Questions

Before diving into practical implementation, take a moment to reflect on the concepts covered in this chapter. The questions below are designed to reinforce your understanding of internationalization and accessibility in React Native applications—and to help you internalize best practices for real-world scenarios that involve localization, inclusive design, and global readiness.

1. What is the difference between internationalization (**i18n**) and localization (**l10n**), and why is it important to plan for both from the start of your project?
2. How do libraries like **i18n-js** and **react-intl** differ in terms of setup and functionality? In which type of project would you choose one over the other?

3. Describe how interpolation and pluralization work in i18n systems. How do you structure translation keys and values to support these features?
4. What are some effective strategies for persisting the user's language preference across app sessions in React Native?
5. How can you use the Context API, Zustand, or Redux to manage and switch app languages globally? What are the benefits and trade-offs of each approach?
6. What are the WCAG levels (A, AA, AAA), and how do they guide the development of accessible mobile applications?
7. What is the role of **`accessibilityLabel`**, **`accessibilityRole`**, and **`accessibilityState`** in making components usable for screen reader users?
8. How would you ensure that your app supports both **`VoiceOver`** (iOS) and **`TalkBack`** (Android)? What kinds of testing procedures would you follow?
9. What considerations must be made when formatting dates, numbers, and currency values across multiple locales? How does **`react-intl`** simplify this task?
10. What design adjustments help improve readability and accessibility in terms of font sizes, color contrast, and dark mode support?
11. How can collaborative teams manage large translation files efficiently? What external tools or platforms support automated translation workflows?
12. How do you audit accessibility in a React Native app? What tools and testing habits help you catch and fix potential issues early?
13. What accessibility and i18n concerns are common when building more complex components like forms, dynamic lists, or navigation systems? How would you address them?

Answering these questions will deepen your understanding of inclusive and global application design. You will be better prepared to create user experiences that are not only technically robust, but also universally accessible and culturally relevant.

Key Terms

- **Internationalization (`i18n`):** The process of preparing an application to support multiple languages, cultures, and regional formats by separating textual content and locale-specific rules from application logic.
- **Localization (`l10n`):** The adaptation of an internationalized application for a specific language or a region, including text translation, currency formatting, date formatting, and cultural adjustments.
- **`i18n-js`:** A lightweight internationalization library for React Native and general JavaScript. Supports interpolation, pluralization, and automatic language fallbacks. Ideal for simple to mid-size projects.
- **`react-intl`:** A robust library based on the ECMA-402 standard, used for advanced formatting of messages, dates, numbers, and currencies. Recommended for projects with multiple locales and complex formatting needs.
- **`accessibilityLabel`:** A React Native property used to provide a clear text description that is read aloud by screen readers like **`VoiceOver`** and **`TalkBack`**.
- **`Accessible`:** A boolean property that determines whether a component (or a group of components) should be exposed to screen readers as an accessible element.

- **`accessibilityRole`:** Defines the semantic role of an element (for example, `'button'`, `'link'`, `'header'`), helping assistive technologies provide functional context to users.
- **`accessibilityState`:** An object that describes a component's current state (for example, `{ checked: true }`), allowing screen readers to announce statuses like selected, disabled, or expanded.
- **`VoiceOver` / `TalkBack`:** Native screen readers for iOS (`VoiceOver`) and Android (`TalkBack`) that convert visual interfaces into audio output—essential tools for accessibility testing.
- **WCAG (Web Content Accessibility Guidelines):** A global set of standards designed to make digital content accessible to all. Levels A, AA, and AAA represent increasing levels of compliance and rigor.
- **WAI-ARIA:** A specification that provides additional attributes to make rich web interfaces more accessible, allowing developers to define roles and states in a semantic and functional way.
- **`allowFontScaling`:** A React Native property that enables automatic text resizing based on the user's system-level accessibility preferences.
- **`useColorScheme()`:** A native React Native hook that detects whether the system is using light or dark mode, enabling dynamic theming based on user preferences.
- **Dark Mode and High Contrast:** Visual modes provided by operating systems to improve readability, reduce eye strain, and support users with light sensitivity or low vision.
- **`AsyncStorage`:** A local storage solution in React Native used to persist user preferences, such as selected language, between app sessions.
- **`Crowdin` / `Lokalise` / `Phrase`:** External platforms for collaborative translation management, supporting Git integration and automated syncing via CI/CD pipelines.
- **Accessibility Inspector (iOS) / Accessibility Scanner (Android):** Native tools for identifying accessibility issues in mobile UIs and suggesting fixes directly within the development environment.
- **Context API / Zustand / Redux:** Global state management solutions in React Native. All can be used to control and dynamically switch the application's language.
- **Internationalized Formatting:** The process of displaying dates, numbers, and currencies according to regional standards, like., 10/07/2025 (BR) vs. 07/10/2025 (US).
- **Pluralization and Interpolation:** Techniques for adapting messages with dynamic values and quantities (say, "1 notification" versus "5 notifications") to preserve linguistic accuracy and natural flow.
- **Inclusive Design:** A design approach that considers user diversity from the start, prioritizing legibility, clarity, adequate contrast, and sensory accessibility.
- **Accessible Components:** Components structured with accessibility best practices, including navigable focus, clear states, and descriptive labels for screen readers and assistive navigation.
- **Accessibility Auditing:** A continuous process of reviewing and validating accessibility within the app, involving manual testing, automated tools, and user validation.

These terms summarize the core concepts, practices, and tools covered in this chapter, serving as a quick reference to help ensure your React Native applications are truly global, accessible, and ready to serve a diverse and inclusive user base.

CHAPTER 13
Build Automation and CI/CD

Introduction

Speed and quality in mobile app delivery have now become one of the competitive advantages in the current market of the day. To achieve this level of excellence, it is essential to adopt Continuous Integration (CI) and Continuous Delivery (CD) practices that automate every stage of the software lifecycle — from committing to the repository to making builds available for testing or production.

In this chapter, we will introduce the fundamental concepts of CI/CD and show how to structure efficient pipelines that ensure consistent builds, thorough testing, and fast deployments.

We will further explore in detail how to configure workflows in GitHub Actions to trigger validations on every push, preventing regressions and detecting failures early in the development process. Next, we shall dive into build automation with **Fastlane**, which is a tool that simplifies the generation of iOS and Android packages, management of signing profiles, and automatic publishing to TestFlight and Google Play Internal Testing.

Additionally, we will be covering **EAS (Expo Application Services)** as a modern alternative for Expo projects, making it easy to configure builds and deliver artifacts without complex infrastructure.

Finally, we will discuss branching strategies; comparing **GitFlow** and **trunk-based development;** and presenting a macro view of the build → test → deploy workflow. By adopting these processes and tools, your mobile team will gain agility, predictability, and robustness, minimizing human errors and accelerating the release cycle with greater confidence.

Structure

In this chapter, we will cover the following topics:

- CI/CD Fundamentals and Pipeline Structure
  - Branching Strategies: GitFlow versus Trunk-Based Development
  - End-to-End Flow: Build → Test → Deploy
- GitHub Actions and Test Automation
  - Job and Step Structure
  - Test Integration

    - Coverage Reports and Status Badges
- Fastlane: Automating Builds and Releases for iOS and Android
    - Defining Lanes for iOS and Android
    - Secure Certificate and Profile Management
    - Fully Automated Release in CI/CD Pipelines
- EAS (Expo Application Services) para Build e Deploy
    - Integrating EAS Build with CI (GitHub Actions + Secrets)
    - Submitting Automatically with EAS Submit
    - Comparison: EAS CLI versus Fastlane (and How to Combine Them)
- Secure Key and Certificate Management
    - Apple Certificates: Creation and Import in Fastlane / EAS
    - Secure Credential Storage
    - Security Best Practices and Key Rotation
- Optimizations, Monitoring, and Next Steps
    - Job Parallelization and Artifact Cleanup
    - Build Notifications
    - Evolving Your Pipeline: Advanced Strategies

CI/CD Fundamentals and Pipeline Structure

Continuous Integration (CI) is a foundational software engineering practice where developers regularly integrate their code changes into a shared repository, often multiple times a day. Each integration triggers an automated process that includes building the application and running a suite of tests, ensuring that code changes are immediately verified and that defects are identified early in the development cycle. This creates a consistent rhythm of validation and fosters a culture of collaboration and accountability across the team.

Continuous Delivery (CD) builds upon CI by ensuring that the software is not only integrated and tested but is always in a deployable state. That means every successful build is potentially ready for release to staging or even production environments. This enables teams to deliver updates faster and more safely, with minimal manual intervention.

Going a step further, **Continuous Deployment** fully automates the final step of the release process: pushing new versions directly to production whenever the pipeline passes all necessary validations. This approach is especially valuable in fast-paced environments, where releasing new features, bug fixes, or improvements rapidly can provide a critical competitive edge.

Implementing CI/CD brings transformational benefits to mobile development teams, helping them overcome common pain points such as platform fragmentation, long build times, and manual deployment errors. Here is how:

- **Accelerated Delivery:** By automating build and test processes, teams reduce the time between writing code and delivering value to users. Whether it is releasing a new feature or patching a bug, automation shortens the feedback loop and enables faster iteration.
- **Improved Reliability:** Running automated test suites on every commit or pull request helps catch regressions and broken functionality early — before they affect production builds. This level of consistency reinforces trust in the stability of the app.

- **Minimized Human Error:** Manual build steps, such as compiling source code or uploading artifacts, are prone to oversight and inconsistencies. With CI/CD, these tasks are handled through repeatable scripts, ensuring deterministic outcomes and clean environments.
- **Cross-Platform Consistency:** Mobile apps often need to be released across Android and iOS. CI/CD pipelines help maintain uniformity in build and test processes, regardless of the target platform.

For React Native pipelines, build time and reliability often hinge on a few operational practices beyond "run tests + build":

- **Aggressive Caching (Biggest Win):** Cache `node_modules` (or your package manager store), Metro/TypeScript caches, and **CocoaPods** assets to cut iOS build times significantly. Common targets include the `npm/yarn/pnpm` cache directory, `Pods/`, and the CocoaPods download cache (plus `XcodeDerivedData` if your CI environment supports it safely). The key is to cache based on lockfiles (such as `package-lock.json/yarn.lock/pnpm-lock.yaml`) and `Podfile.lock` so caches invalidate correctly.
- **Matrix builds for compatibility:** Use **matrix builds** to validate against multiple environments in parallel—including different Node versions, Android API levels, and (when relevant) multiple React Native versions for shared libraries/SDKs. This is especially useful for monorepos or teams shipping internal packages used by multiple apps.
- **Self-hosted runners for iOS:** iOS builds require macOS. If you routinely hit hosted macOS minute limits or need more predictable performance, **self-hosted macOS runners** can be cost-effective and faster (especially when paired with persistent caches and preinstalled toolchains).
- **Artifact management and retention policies:** Treat build artifacts (APKs/AABs/IPAs, dSYMs, source maps, test reports) as first-class outputs. Store them with clear naming (commit/branch/version), **set expiration/retention rules**, and keep security in mind (avoid leaking signing material). Retain crash-symbolication assets (dSYMs/source maps) longer than binaries, since you may need them well after release.

Branching Strategies: GitFlow versus Trunk-Based Development

Selecting the right branching model is critical to optimizing your CI/CD strategy. Two widely adopted models are:

- **GitFlow:** It is a more traditional branching model that introduces long-lived branches such as `develop`, `release/*`, `hotfix/*`, and `feature/*`. It provides fine-grained control over versioning, making it suitable for teams with strict release processes or enterprise-level applications. However, it comes with increased complexity due to frequent merges and branch synchronizations.
- **Trunk-Based Development:** It is a modern approach where all developers commit directly to the main branch (`main` or `master`) or short-lived branches that are merged back quickly. Feature flags are commonly used to manage incomplete features. This strategy encourages continuous integration and keeps codebase deployable at all times, reducing merge conflicts and facilitating faster feedback.

Each model has its merits, and the right choice depends on your team size, release cadence, and need for stability versus agility.

End-to-End Flow: Build → Test → Deploy

A typical CI/CD pipeline in mobile development follows a three-phase flow:

1. **Build Phase:** Whenever code is pushed to the repository or a pull request is opened, the pipeline begins by cloning the project, installing dependencies, and compiling the application. This results in build artifacts such as APKs for Android or IPAs for iOS, ensuring that the codebase compiles correctly in a clean environment.
2. **Test Phase:** Automated tests are executed next. These typically include unit tests to validate individual components or functions, as well as optional integration and UI tests to ensure that the system behaves as expected. Code coverage reports and error logs are generated at this stage to help assess the quality of the changes.
3. **Deploy Phase:** If all validations pass, the generated artifacts are stored on a centralized artifact server (say GitHub Packages, Firebase App Distribution, or custom storage). Depending on the branch or environment configuration, the build may be deployed to:
   - **Staging environments** for internal QA.
   - **TestFlight** for iOS beta testing.
   - **Google Play Internal Testing** for Android preview distribution.

This automated sequence guarantees that every change undergoes a rigorous validation process before being released, minimizing risk and increasing confidence with each deployment. A well-structured CI/CD pipeline transforms how mobile apps are developed and delivered. By integrating frequently, testing thoroughly, and deploying consistently, development teams can deliver high-quality applications at speed which is a necessity in the current competitive mobile ecosystem. Whether working in a startup or an enterprise, CI/CD is no longer optional; it is the backbone of modern mobile engineering.

GitHub Actions and Test Automation

Test automation lies at the heart of any successful CI/CD pipeline. When each push automatically triggers builds, test execution, and report generation, every code change is consistently validated, helping prevent regressions and ensuring continuous quality. In this section, we will be building a complete build → testflow using GitHub Actions to orchestrate triggers, jobs, and steps, integrate different types of tests, and publish coverage metrics.

A GitHub Actions workflow is defined in **`.github/workflows/ci.yml`**. Inside this file, we specify the events that trigger the pipeline:

```
name: CI Pipeline

on:
  push:
    branches:
      - main
      - develop
pull_request:
    branches:
      - main
      - develop
  release:
    types:
      - created
```

```
  schedule:
    - cron: '0 3 * * *'        # runs daily at 3 AM UTC
workflow_dispatch: {}        # allows manual trigger
```

- **push**: Validates every commit pushed to **main** or **develop**.
- **pull_request**: Blocks merges if tests fail.
- **release**: Runs only when a new release tag (like **v1.2.0**) is created.
- **schedule** and **workflow_dispatch**: Enables scheduled or manual runs, and is useful for nightly builds or ad hoc testing.

These triggers ensure your pipeline covers all necessary scenarios, from feature development to production readiness.

Job and Step Structure

Workflows are composed of **jobs**, which contain **steps**. Jobs can run in parallel or sequentially, while each step executes a shell command or a reusable action. Here is a complete example:

```
jobs:
  build-and-test:
    name: Build & Test
    runs-on: ubuntu-latest

    steps:
      - name: Checkout code
        uses: actions/checkout@v3

      - name: Set up Node.js
        uses: actions/setup-node@v3
        with:
          node-version: '18'
          cache: 'npm'

      - name: Install dependencies
        run: npm ci

      - name: Build application
        run: npm run build

      - name: Run unit tests
run: npm run test:unit -- --coverage

      - name: Upload coverage to Coveralls
        uses: coverallsapp/github-action@v2
        with:
github-token: ${{ secrets.GITHUB_TOKEN }}

      - name: Save coverage report as artifact
        uses: actions/upload-artifact@v3
        with:
          name: coverage-report
          path: coverage/
```

Explanation of key steps:

- **actions/checkout**: Clones the repository.
- **actions/setup-node**: Sets up Node.js and caches npm dependencies.

- **`npm ci`**: Installs dependencies cleanly.
- **`npm run build`**: Compiles the app (web, Metro, and the like.).
- **`npm run test:unit`**: Runs unit tests with coverage.
- **`coverallsapp/github-action`**: Uploads coverage results to Coveralls.
- **`upload-artifact`**: Makes coverage reports available for download.

In advanced setups, **job matrices** can be used to test multiple Node versions or Android/iOS SDKs in parallel, increasing test coverage and feedback speed without duplicating code.

Test Integration

Unit tests validate isolated functions or components. In JavaScript/TypeScript projects, common tools include **Jest** and **Mocha + Chai**.

Jest:

```
// package.json
{
  "scripts": {
    "test:unit": "jest --config jest.config.js"
  }
}
```

```
// jest.config.js
module.exports = {
  preset: 'ts-jest',
testEnvironment: 'node',
collectCoverage: true,
coverageDirectory: 'coverage/'
};
```

```
- name: Run unit tests (Jest)
  run: npm run test:unit -- --coverage
```

Mocha + Chai:

```
{
  "scripts": {
    "test:unit": "mocha --recursive 'src/**/*.spec.ts'"
  }
}
```

```
- name: Run unit tests (Mocha)
  run: npm run test:unit
```

E2E / UI Tests

End-to-end (E2E) tests simulate real user interactions, ensuring the application behaves correctly on actual devices or emulators.

Detox (React Native):

```
- name: Build Android for Detox
  run: |
    cd android
./gradlewassembleDebugassembleAndroidTest -DtestBuildType=debug
```

```
- name: Run Detox tests
  run: npm run test:e2e
// package.json
{
  "scripts": {
    "test:e2e": "detox test --configuration android.emu.debug"
  }
}
```

Cypress (Web/PWA):

```
- name: Install Cypress
  run: npm ci

- name: Run Cypress
  run: npx cypress run --record --key ${{ secrets.CYPRESS_RECORD_KEY }}

// cypress.json
{
  "baseUrl": "http://localhost:3000",
  "video": true,
  "screenshotsFolder": "cypress/screenshots"
}
```

Appium: Use WebDriver to test both Android and iOS from a single test suite. Separating **unit test** and **E2E test jobs** helps isolate failures and allocate runners more efficiently (like using macOS runners only when required for Detox or Appium).

Coverage Reports and Status Badges

Publishing test coverage metrics and build status directly in the repository increases visibility and encourages developers to maintain high quality standards.

Upload coverage report:

```
- name: Save coverage report
  uses: actions/upload-artifact@v3
  with:
    name: coverage-report
    path: coverage/
```

Add status badges to README:

```
<!-- Build Status -->
[![CI Status](https://github.com/YOUR_USER/YOUR_REPO/actions/workflows/ci.yml/badge.
svg)](https://github.com/YOUR_USER/YOUR_REPO/actions/workflows/ci.yml)

<!-- Coverage -->
[![Coverage](https://coveralls.io/repos/github/YOUR_USER/YOUR_REPO/badge.
svg?branch=main)](https://coveralls.io/github/YOUR_USER/YOUR_REPO?branch=main)
```

Quality Gates / Fail Fast: To prevent low-quality code from being merged, you can enforce a minimum coverage threshold:

```
- name: Check minimum coverage
  run: |
    COVERAGE=$(npx coverage-summary | grep lines | awk '{print $2}' | sed 's/%//')
```

```
  if [ "$COVERAGE" -lt80 ]; then
    echo "Coverage below 80% ($COVERAGE%)"
    exit 1
  fi
```

Checks Integration: GitHub Checks surface failures directly in the Pull Request UI, making reviews easier and ensuring only verified changes are merged.

With this GitHub Actions setup, your repository gains a robust pipeline that builds the app, runs unit and E2E tests, publishes reports, and keeps the README updated with real-time status badges. In the next chapter, we will take automation even further using **Fastlane** to orchestrate mobile build lanes and automate deployments to TestFlight and Google Play.

Fastlane: Automating Builds and Releases for iOS and Android

In mobile development, delivering builds quickly, securely, and consistently across platforms is often a challenging and time-consuming task, especially when dealing with signing certificates, provisioning profiles, build variants, and app store submissions. **Fastlane** addresses these challenges by providing a powerful set of tools for automating the entire release process for iOS and Android apps, including React Native projects.

Fastlane allows mobile teams to streamline every step, from code signing and build generation to distribution on platforms like **TestFlight** and **Google Play Console**. In this section, we shall explore how to set up and configure Fastlane in a React Native monorepo, define custom lanes, and manage credentials safely, both locally and in CI pipelines.

To begin with, initialize Fastlane in the iOS and Android directories of your project:

```
cd ios
fastlaneinit

cd ../android
fastlaneinit
```

This creates a **`fastlane/`** directory in each subproject, containing a **`Fastfile`** and **`Appfile`**. The **`Fastfile`** defines workflows (called **lanes**), while the **`Appfile`** stores metadata such as the **`app_identifier`**, **`apple_id`**, or **`package_name`**.

In React Native projects, it is a common practice to **centralize the `Fastfile`** at the root of the repository to coordinate both iOS and Android builds from a single place:

```
# fastlane/Fastfile

default_platform(:ios)

platform :ios do
  # iOS lanes go here...
end

platform :android do
  # Android lanes go here...
end
```

This structure promotes reusability, simplifies CI integration, and enables conditional logic for cross-platform releases.

Defining Lanes for iOS and Android

Lanes define the sequence of actions Fastlane should perform, from building to deploying. Let us explore platform-specific examples.

iOS Lane: Build and Upload to TestFlight

```
platform :ios do
desc "Build and upload to TestFlight"
lane :beta do
match(type: "appstore")                                # Syncs provisioning profiles
and certificates
gym(scheme: "MyApp", export_method: "app-store")       # Builds the .ipa
pilot(skip_submission: true)                           # Uploads to TestFlight
end
end
```

Key actions:

- **`match`**: It securely manages certificates and provisioning profiles using a Git-based repository.
- **`gym`**: It invokes Xcode to build the app using the specified scheme (**`MyApp.xcworkspace`**).
- **`pilot`**: It handles TestFlight uploads, including internal test group assignment or automatic submission.

This lane encapsulates the entire release process, ensuring consistency and eliminating human error in certificate management or App Store Connect configuration.

Android Lane: Build and Upload to Google Play

```
platform :android do
desc "Assemble release and upload to Internal Testing"
lane :beta do
gradle(
      task: "assembleRelease",
project_dir: "android/",
      properties: {
        "android.injected.signing.store.file" => ENV["KEYSTORE_PATH"],
        "android.injected.signing.store.password" => ENV["KEYSTORE_PASSWORD"],
        "android.injected.signing.key.alias" => ENV["KEY_ALIAS"],
        "android.injected.signing.key.password" => ENV["KEY_PASSWORD"]
      }
    )
supply(
      track: "internal",
apk: Dir["android/app/build/outputs/**/*.apk"].first,
package_name: "com.myapp.package"
    )
  end
end
```

Key actions:

- **`gradle`**: It builds the release version of the app using a signing configuration from environment variables.

- **supply**: It uploads the resulting APK or AAB to the specified track (**internal**, **alpha**, **beta**, or **production**) in Google Play Console.

This lane ensures Android builds are signed, versioned, and published in a fully automated pipeline — removing the need to manually interact with Android Studio or the Play Console UI.

Secure Certificate and Profile Management

Fastlane simplifies iOS code signing with several auxiliary tools:

- **match**: Stores provisioning profiles and certificates in a private Git repository, syncing them during builds.
- **cert**: Creates new certificates (if needed).
- **sigh**: Downloads or renews existing provisioning profiles.

A typical **Matchfile** might look like this:

```
git_url("git@github.com:my-org/certificates.git")
type("appstore")                           # or "development", "adhoc"
app_identifier(["com.myapp.ios"])
username("apple@mycompany.com")
```

In your CI environment (GitHub Actions, Bitrise, CircleCI, etc.), set the following environment variables securely:

```
export MATCH_PASSWORD="your_repo_password"
export FASTLANE_USER="apple@mycompany.com"
export FASTLANE_APPLE_APPLICATION_SPECIFIC_PASSWORD="your_app_specific_password"
```

Fastlane will then authenticate with Apple services, pull the necessary profiles/certs, and build your app without requiring manual keychain access.

Fully Automated Release in CI/CD Pipelines

You can integrate Fastlane lanes into GitHub Actions to trigger automatic publishing after each merge or release:

```
- name: Publish iOS to TestFlight
  run: fastlaneios beta
  working-directory: ./fastlane

- name: Publish Android to Google Play
  run: fastlane android beta
  working-directory: ./fastlane
```

By combining this with proper workflow triggers (**on: push**, **on: release**, etc.), your pipeline will:

1. Sync certificates and provisioning profiles (via **match**).
2. Build the app for iOS (**gym**) and Android (**gradle**).
3. Publish directly to **TestFlight** or **Google Play Internal Testing**.

This enables a true **"push-to-release"** workflow, thereby allowing teams to move faster, ship more confidently, and drastically reduce manual errors and delays in the release cycle.

Fastlane is not just a build automation tool — it is a foundation for **mobile DevOps**. By integrating Fastlane into your CI/CD pipelines, you empower your development team to automate critical steps in the release process, enhance traceability, and ship updates consistently across platforms. Whether you are a solo developer or a part of a large-scale team, adopting Fastlane will bring immediate and long-term benefits: faster feedback loops, fewer production issues, and a streamlined path from code to users' devices.

EAS (Expo Application Services) para Build e Deploy

EAS Build and **EAS Submit** offer a lightweight, zero-configuration alternative to Fastlane for Expo and React Native projects. These tools allow developers to offload the build and deployment process to the cloud and publish artifacts directly to app stores with minimal setup. For teams that value speed, simplicity, and cross-platform efficiency, EAS provides an elegant solution for managing CI/CD pipelines without needing local macOS or Android environments.

EAS Build is a hosted service, so it **requires an Expo account** and is subject to **plan limits/usage-based pricing**. On the current pricing page, the **Free** plan includes **15 Android + 15 iOS builds per month** in a low-priority queue, while paid tiers add build credit and higher-priority capacity. For teams planning sustained CI/CD throughput (multiple branches, PR builds, nightly builds), it is worth to explicitly budget for build volume and queue priority rather than discovering limits mid-release.

EAS Build is not limited to "**`managed Expo`**" apps: the docs state of Expo supports building binaries for **Expo and React Native projects**, and Expo also documents how its tooling/services can be used in **existing (bare) React Native apps**, but bare projects typically require more manual configuration (credentials/signing, native project settings, and ensuring the app includes the necessary Expo modules for the features you want).

In this section, we shall walk through configuring the **`eas.json`** file with multiple build profiles, integrating EAS with GitHub Actions, automating store submission via **`eas submit`**, and understanding when to use EAS alone or in combination with Fastlane.

At the root of your Expo project, create an **`eas.json`** file to define various build environments (profiles) with tailored configurations:

```
{
  "build": {
    "development": {
      "distribution": "internal",
      "android": { "buildType": "apk" },
      "ios": { "simulator": true }
    },
    "preview": {
      "distribution": "internal",
      "android": { "buildType": "app-bundle" },
      "ios": { "scheme": "myapp-preview" }
    },
    "production": {
      "distribution": "store",
      "android": { "buildType": "app-bundle" },
      "ios": {
        "scheme": "myapp",
        "enterpriseProvisioning": "adhoc"
      }
    }
  }
}
```

- **`development`**: Fast builds for internal testing, accessible via QR codes or the Expo dev client.
- **`preview`**: Staging builds that closely resemble production, intended for internal testers or QA.
- **`production`**: Fully signed and store-ready builds for Google Play and the App Store.

Each profile can override default configurations, such as using different SDK versions, keystores, provisioning strategies, or Xcode schemes — giving teams control over how builds are prepared for different contexts.

Integrating EAS Build with CI (GitHub Actions + Secrets)

To run builds automatically in your CI/CD pipeline, such as after every push to **`main`** or a release tag, you can add a dedicated GitHub Actions job:

```
jobs:
  expo-build:
    name: EAS Build
    runs-on: ubuntu-latest
    steps:
      - uses: actions/checkout@v3

      - name: Set up Node and Yarn
        uses: actions/setup-node@v3
        with:
          node-version: '18'
          cache: 'yarn'

      - name: Install Expo CLI and EAS CLI
        run: npm install -g expo-cli eas-cli

      - name: Authenticate with Expo
env:
          EXPO_TOKEN: ${{ secrets.EXPO_TOKEN }}
        run: eas login --token $EXPO_TOKEN

      - name: Run EAS Build (production)
env:
          EXPO_TOKEN: ${{ secrets.EXPO_TOKEN }}
        run: eas build --platform all --profile production --non-interactive
```

Required secrets:

- **`EXPO_TOKEN`**: Created via **`eastoken:create`**, this token allows CI environments to trigger builds securely.

You can also set optional secrets like:

- **`EAS_BUILD_PROFILE`** (to specify build type dynamically)
- **`EAS_PROJECT_ID`**
- Custom environment variables for Android/iOS keystore credentials if not using the credential management system of Expo.

Submitting Automatically with EAS Submit

Once your APK, AAB, or IPA is built, you can automate the submission to the app stores using **`eas submit`**. The following example job handles this process:

```
expo-submit:
    name: EAS Submit
    runs-on: ubuntu-latest
    needs: expo-build
    steps:
      - uses: actions/checkout@v3

      - name: Install EAS CLI
        run: npm install -g eas-cli

      - name: Authenticate with Expo
env:
          EXPO_TOKEN: ${{ secrets.EXPO_TOKEN }}
        run: eas login --token $EXPO_TOKEN

      - name: Submit to App Store and Play Store
env:
          EXPO_TOKEN: ${{ secrets.EXPO_TOKEN }}
          FASTLANE_APPLE_APPLICATION_SPECIFIC_PASSWORD: ${{ secrets.APP_SPECIFIC_
PASSWORD }}
          GOOGLE_APPLICATION_CREDENTIALS: ${{ secrets.GOOGLE_CREDENTIALS_JSON }}
        run: |
eas submit --platform ios --latest --non-interactive
eas submit --platform android --latest --non-interactive
```

- **`--latest`**: It submits the most recently built artifact from the Expo servers.
- **Credentials must be configured depending on your authentication method:**
    - **iOS**: It requires **`APP_SPECIFIC_PASSWORD`** (Apple ID)
    - **Android**: It requires the **`GOOGLE_CREDENTIALS_JSON`** service account key

Comparison: EAS CLI versus Fastlane (and How to Combine Them)

Aspect	EAS CLI	Fastlane
Initial Setup	Minimal — **`easinit`** + **`eas.json`**	Requires **`fastlaneinit`** and configuration of Ruby lanes
Environment	Expo Cloud (no need for local macOS)	Requires macOS for iOS, Linux/ macOS for Android
Credential Management	Automated via Expo Credentials Manager	Manual or via **`match`**, **`cert`**, **`sigh`**
Flexibility	Focused on Expo/React Native only	Works with any iOS/Android project, native or hybrid
Customization	Simple, opinionated commands	Fully customizable Ruby DSL (snapshots, metadata, etc.)

***Table 13.1**: Comparison between EAS CLI and Fastlane*

When to Combine EAS and Fastlane

In many hybrid React Native projects, it is common and **recommended** to use both tools together:

- Use **EAS Build** for fast, infrastructure-free compilation and artifact delivery.
- Use **Fastlane** for advanced workflows such as:
  - Capturing and uploading **screenshots.**
  - Managing **localized metadata.**
  - Automating **release notes.**
  - Running **native UI tests** or custom deployment lanes.

By using both in your CI pipeline, you can take advantage of **the simplicity and cloud power of EAS**, while relying on **the depth and extensibility** of Fastlane for full-scale release management.

EAS CLI radically simplifies mobile app builds for Expo and React Native developers. It enables teams to build, sign, and submit apps using a fully cloud-based solution, significantly reducing setup time and eliminating the need for platform-specific hardware.

When paired with tools like GitHub Actions, it becomes a powerful force for release automation. And when combined with Fastlane, it offers the best of both worlds: ease of use for standard operations, and fine-grained control for specialized needs. Whether you are shipping daily updates or managing complex enterprise apps, EAS can help you deliver confidently and at scale.

Secure Key and Certificate Management

Managing signing keys and certificates securely is a critical component of a reliable mobile CI/CD pipeline. Leaking a keystore or letting a certificate expire unnoticed can halt your release flow, expose your app to tampering, or even require republishing under a new identity. In this section, we will explore best practices for generating, versioning, and using Android keystores, managing Apple certificates, securely storing credentials, and rotating them periodically to ensure your pipeline remains safe and operational.

Generating a Keystore

You can generate your Android signing keystore using the following command:

```
keytool -genkeypair \
  -v \
  -keystoremyapp.keystore \
  -alias myapp_alias \
  -keyalg RSA \
  -keysize 2048 \
  -validity 10000
```

Be sure to choose a **strong password** and securely store the **`alias`**, **`keystore path`**, and credentials. Never share this file publicly or commit it to version control unencrypted.

Secure Versioning

Avoid storing your keystore in plaintext in a Git repository. Instead, choose one of the following secure storage methods:

- A **separate private Git repository**, encrypted **`usinggit-crypt`** or BlackBox.

- A secure **artifact store** such as AWS S3 with Server-Side Encryption (SSE).
- A **secure secrets manager of CI/CD provider.**

Example with **`git-crypt`**:

```
git-crypt init
git-crypt add-gpg-user --trusted ${GPG_KEY_ID}
git-crypt lock
git add myapp.keystore
git commit -m "Add encrypted keystore"
```

Usage in CI (GitHub Actions)

To use your keystore in GitHub Actions securely, follow this pattern:

```
steps:
  - name: Download Keystore
    uses: actions/download-artifact@v3
    with:
      name: android-keystore

  - name: Set Signing Environment Variables
    run: |
     echo "REACT_NATIVE_KEYSTORE_PASSWORD=${{ secrets.KEYSTORE_PASSWORD }}" >> $GITHUB_
ENV
      echo "REACT_NATIVE_KEY_ALIAS=${{ secrets.KEY_ALIAS }}" >> $GITHUB_ENV
      echo "REACT_NATIVE_KEY_PASSWORD=${{ secrets.KEY_PASSWORD }}" >> $GITHUB_ENV

  - name: Build Android Release
    run: |
      cd android
./gradlewassembleRelease \
        -Pandroid.injected.signing.store.file=$GITHUB_WORKSPACE/android/myapp.keystore \
        -Pandroid.injected.signing.store.password=$REACT_NATIVE_KEYSTORE_PASSWORD \
        -Pandroid.injected.signing.key.alias=$REACT_NATIVE_KEY_ALIAS \
        -Pandroid.injected.signing.key.password=$REACT_NATIVE_KEY_PASSWORD
```

Apple Certificates: Creation and Import in Fastlane / EAS

This section outlines how Apple certificates are created and securely imported into Fastlane or EAS to support automated iOS signing and deployment.

Creating a Certificate in Apple Developer Console

Navigate to Certificates, Identifiers and Profiles, then:

1. Click "+" to add a new certificate.
2. Choose **`App Store and Ad Hoc`** for production.
3. Follow the instructions to generate a Certificate Signing Request (**`.certSigningRequest`**).
4. Download the resulting **`.cer`** file.

Importing Certificates in Fastlane with `match`

In your **`Matchfile`**:

```
git_url("git@github.com:your-org/certificates.git")
storage_mode(:git)
type("appstore")  # or "development", "adhoc"
app_identifier(["com.myapp.*"])
username("apple@example.com")
```

In your lane:

```
match(type: "appstore")
```

Fastlane will automatically create, download, and sync the certificates and provisioning profiles using Git encryption.

Importing into EAS

To manage credentials with Expo, you can use either **Expo Credentials Manager** or import them manually.

Automatic Setup:

```
eas credentials
eascredentials:manager --platform ios
```

Manual Import:

```
eascredentials:import --platform ios --type distribution \
  --path ./certs/distribution.p12 \
  --password ${{ secrets.APPLE_P12_PASSWORD }}
```

Secure Credential Storage

GitHub Secrets

Ideal for sensitive values such as:

```
env:
  EXPO_TOKEN: ${{ secrets.EXPO_TOKEN }}
  KEYSTORE_PASSWORD: ${{ secrets.KEYSTORE_PASSWORD }}
  APPLE_P12_PASSWORD: ${{ secrets.APPLE_P12_PASSWORD }}
```

Secrets are encrypted at rest and scoped per repository.

EAS Credentials Manager

Expo offers built-in, centralized credential storage for:

- Android keystores.
- iOS distribution certificates.
- Provisioning profiles.

These are managed securely in the cloud and scoped to your project and team.

External Vaults

For large teams or compliance-heavy environments, consider:

- **HashiCorp Vault**
- **AWS Secrets Manager**

- **Azure Key Vault**
- **GCP Secret Manager**

These tools provide:

- Fine-grained access policies.
- Automatic key rotation.
- Audit logs and change tracking.

Security Best Practices and Key Rotation

Principle of Least Privilege

- Each CI job should access only the secrets it needs.
- Separate credentials by **environment**: development, staging, production.

Key and Certificate Rotation

- Establish rotation schedules (like in every 90 days).
- Automate alerts for expired or soon-to-expire certificates and profiles.
- Revoke old or unused credentials to reduce the attack surface.

Auditing and Monitoring

- Use logging tools to track all access to secrets.
- Enable alerts for unusual behavior or authentication failures.

Encrypted Backups

- Maintain off-site, encrypted backups of all keys and provisioning profiles.
- Use strong passphrases and store them in password vaults such as **`1Password`**, **`Bitwarden`**, or **`LastPass`**.

By implementing strong credential management practices, your React Native CI/CD pipeline becomes significantly more resilient and secure, and you reduce the risk of:

- Credential leakage.
- App signing key loss.
- Unexpected build failures due to expired certificates.
- Accidental exposure of sensitive files in version control.

Proactively managing keys, automating access, and monitoring usage ensures not only compliance with industry best practices but also a smoother development and release experience for your entire team.

Optimizations, Monitoring, and Next Steps

To maintain a CI/CD pipeline that is fast, reliable, and scalable, it is essential to apply continuous optimizations, establish proper monitoring, and plan for future enhancements. React Native projects—due to their cross-platform complexity—can especially benefit from strategic improvements in caching, parallelization, and proactive feedback. This section outlines best practices using GitHub Actions and highlights paths for scaling your pipeline further.

Installing packages can be one of the slowest parts of the build process, particularly in clean CI environments. Caching package managers and native build tools is one of the easiest wins in terms of build speed.

Example: GitHub Actions Caching Setup

```
jobs:
  build:
    runs-on: ubuntu-latest
    steps:
      - uses: actions/checkout@v3

      # Cache npm dependencies
      - name: Cache npm
        uses: actions/cache@v3
        with:
          path: ~/.npm
          key: ${{ runner.os }}-node-${{ hashFiles('**/package-lock.json') }}
          restore-keys: |
            ${{ runner.os }}-node-

      - name: Install dependencies
        run: npm ci

      # Cache CocoaPods (iOS)
      - name: Cache CocoaPods
        uses: actions/cache@v3
        with:
          path: ios/Pods
          key: ${{ runner.os }}-pods-${{ hashFiles('ios/Podfile.lock') }}

      - name: Install Pods
        run: |
          cd ios
          pod install

      # Cache Gradle (Android)
      - name: Cache Gradle
        uses: actions/cache@v3
        with:
          path: |
            ~/.gradle/caches
            ~/.gradle/wrapper
          key: ${{ runner.os }}-gradle-${{ hashFiles('**/*.gradle*', '**/gradle-
wrapper.properties') }}

      - name: Build Android
        run: cd android && ./gradlewassembleRelease
```

These cache layers significantly reduce setup time in CI, especially on macOS runners or when rebuilding on every commit.

Job Parallelization and Artifact Cleanup

Parallelization helps accelerate testing and linting by running multiple configurations at the same time using a **job matrix**:

```
strategy:
  matrix:
    node-version: [14, 16, 18]
os: [ubuntu-latest, macos-latest]
```

```
runs-on: ${{ matrix.os }}
steps:
  - uses: actions/setup-node@v3
    with:
      node-version: ${{ matrix.node-version }}
```

This approach is ideal for validating against multiple environments (Node versions, OSs, toolchains) with minimal additional configuration. To prevent disk space exhaustion or cost overages due to unused artifacts, add a cleanup step:

```
- name: Cleanup old artifacts
  run: |
gh run artifacts \
      | tail -n +3 \
      | awk '{print $1}' \
      | xargs -n1 gh run artifact delete --yes
env:
    GITHUB_TOKEN: ${{ secrets.GITHUB_TOKEN }}
```

This command uses GitHub CLI to remove previous build artifacts after they have been used, helping maintain a clean workspace.

Build Notifications

Proactive communication with your team ensures faster responses to failures. Automated Slack alerts can be integrated into the workflow:

```
- name: Notify Slack on failure
  if: failure()
  uses: slackapi/slack-github-action@v1.25.0
  with:
    payload: |
      {
        "channel": "#ci-alerts",
        "attachments": [
        {
            "color": "danger",
            "text": "The *${{ github.workflow }}* build failed on `${{ github.ref }}`.
<${{ github.run_url }}|View details>"
          }
        ]
      }
env:
    SLACK_BOT_TOKEN: ${{ secrets.SLACK_BOT_TOKEN }}
```

You can also integrate with Microsoft Teams, Discord, or even SMTP to send build notifications via email.

Evolving Your Pipeline: Advanced Strategies

Canary Releases: Gradually roll out new app versions to a small percentage of users, monitor performance or crashes in production, and expand rollout only when confidence is high.

Automatic Rollbacks: Monitor production error rates using tools like **Sentry** or **Datadog**. When a threshold is exceeded, trigger automated rollback scripts via GitHub Actions or cloud function hooks.

Static Analysis and Security Scanning

Include quality gates and security checks as part of your pipeline:

```
- name: Lint code
  run: npm run lint
- name: Run static type checks
  run: tsc --noEmit
- name: Security audit
  run: npm audit --audit-level=high
```

For enterprise security, integrate **OWASP Dependency-Check** to detect known vulnerabilities in your dependencies.

Performance Testing: Define baseline thresholds for bundle size or app startup time, and fail builds if those thresholds are exceeded:

```
- name: Check Bundle Size
  run: node ./scripts/check-bundle-size.js
```

This keeps app performance consistent and prevents regressions from sneaking into production.

By continuously applying optimizations, monitoring pipelines, and integrating advanced controls, your CI/CD infrastructure evolves into a robust, developer-friendly system. These practices ensure:

- Faster feedback loops.
- Early detection of regressions and security issues.
- Higher confidence during deployments.
- Better collaboration and transparency across teams.

A well-optimized pipeline is more than just automation — it is a core pillar of delivering high-quality mobile apps at scale, safely and predictably.

Conclusion

In this chapter, we have explored the essential principles, tools, and best practices for implementing a robust CI/CD pipeline in React Native applications. We began by establishing the foundations of Continuous Integration and Continuous Delivery/Deployment, explaining how automating build and test processes not only accelerates delivery but also improves reliability and reduces manual errors.

We then examined how to integrate GitHub Actions to automate every stage of the pipeline—from code validation with unit and E2E tests to the generation of coverage reports and deployment status badges. The use of tools like **`Fastlane`** and **`EAS CLI`** allowed us to fully automate build and release processes for both Android and iOS, including secure certificate management, internal distribution, and store submissions. By combining these tools, mobile teams can strike a balance between simplicity and full control over complex release workflows.

The final sections emphasized the importance of optimizing pipeline performance through dependency caching, job parallelization, and artifact cleanup, as well as adopting proactive monitoring strategies such as Slack alerts and error-based rollbacks. We also discussed forward-looking improvements like static code analysis, security auditing, and performance thresholds, thereby empowering teams to maintain code quality and release velocity at scale.

By implementing these practices, your mobile development workflow becomes faster, safer, and more scalable—enabling teams to ship confidently and frequently. In the next chapter, we will explore strategies for advanced publishing on the App Store and Google Play, Maintenance, and Future Updates.

Questions

Before moving on to implementation or more advanced topics, take a moment to reflect on the key practices and decisions involved in setting up a reliable CI/CD pipeline for mobile development. The questions below are designed to help solidify your understanding of automated workflows, cloud-based build systems, and DevOps strategies, so you can confidently apply them in real-world React Native projects.

1. What are the core differences between Continuous Integration (CI), Continuous Delivery (CD), and Continuous Deployment? Why is it important to distinguish between them when designing a mobile pipeline?
2. How does automating build and test processes improve the speed, reliability, and scalability of a mobile development workflow?
3. What are the advantages of using GitHub Actions for CI/CD in a React Native project? How would you trigger builds for pull requests, tags, or scheduled jobs?
4. How do Fastlane and EAS (Expo Application Services) differ in terms of setup, flexibility, and target use cases? In what situations would you combine both tools?
5. Describe how signing credentials (Android keystores and iOS certificates) are managed securely in a CI environment. What are the risks of poor key management, and how can they be mitigated?
6. What caching strategies can be used in GitHub Actions to reduce build times for dependencies like **`npm`**, **`CocoaPods`**, and **`Gradle`**?
7. How can job matrices be used to test against multiple versions of Node.js or operating systems? What are the performance benefits of parallel job execution?
8. Why is it important to send notifications (like Slack, email) when a build fails? How can real-time alerts help reduce downtime and improve team coordination?
9. What is a canary release, and how can it be implemented in a CI/CD pipeline for mobile apps?
10. How does automated rollback work, and what kind of production monitoring tools (such as Sentry, Datadog) can trigger it?
11. What static analysis and security tools can be integrated into a pipeline to prevent regressions and vulnerabilities before deployment?
12. How can you enforce bundle size limits or startup performance budgets in your CI workflow to ensure your app remains fast and responsive?
13. When storing secrets like tokens, keystore passwords, and Apple credentials, what are the trade-offs between GitHub Secrets, EAS credentials, and external secret managers like AWS Secrets Manager or **`HashiCorpVault`**?
14. What steps can be taken to rotate credentials periodically and maintain a secure build environment across different teams or organizations?
15. How would you evolve a simple CI workflow into a mature, production-grade pipeline? What metrics and monitoring tools would you introduce to track performance and maintain visibility?

Answering these questions will strengthen your command of modern mobile DevOps workflows and help you design CI/CD systems that are not only automated, but secure, observable, and maintainable, supporting the ability of your team to ship faster, safer, and with greater confidence.

Key Terms

- **Continuous Integration (CI):** The practice of automatically integrating and validating code changes from multiple developers into a shared repository. CI ensures that each commit triggers automated builds and tests, helping detect issues early.
- **Continuous Delivery (CD):** The process of automatically preparing and verifying code changes for release, ensuring that the application is always in a deployable state—even if the final push to production is manual.
- **Continuous Deployment:** An extension of CD in which code changes that pass all stages of the pipeline are automatically deployed to production, eliminating manual intervention entirely.
- **CI/CD Pipeline:** A sequence of automated steps (build, test, deploy) triggered by events such as commits or pull requests, designed to ensure consistent integration and delivery of software.
- **GitHub Actions:** A workflow automation service native to GitHub, allowing developers to define and run CI/CD pipelines using YAML syntax and community-built or custom actions.
- **`Fastlane`:** A powerful automation tool for building and deploying iOS and Android apps. It supports certificate management, app signing, store submissions, screenshots, metadata, and more—ideal for native and hybrid apps.
- **EAS CLI (Expo Application Services):** A cloud-based build and deployment toolset for Expo and React Native projects. Offers zero-config builds, internal distribution, and app store submission via **`eas build`** and **`eas submit`**.
- **`eas.json`:** A configuration file used by EAS CLI to define multiple build profiles (development, preview, production), allowing customized settings for different stages of the release process.
- **`match` / `cert` / `sigh`:** Fastlane tools for managing iOS certificates and provisioning profiles. `match` centralizes credentials using a Git repository, while **`cert`** and **`sigh`** create and download certificates and profiles.
- **Keystore (Android):** A secure file used to sign Android apps. It includes a private key and must be stored securely and referenced during the release build process.
- **Provisioning Profile (iOS):** A file issued by Apple that links the certificate of a developer with an app ID and devices or distribution type, required for building and deploying iOS apps.
- **GitHub Secrets:** Encrypted environment variables stored in GitHub repositories. Used to securely manage tokens, credentials, and sensitive data in CI workflows.
- **Artifact:** A file generated during a build process (including **`.apk`**, **`.ipa`**, coverage reports) that can be stored, uploaded, or used in later stages of the pipeline.
- **Caching:** A strategy to store previously computed or downloaded dependencies (npm, Pods, Gradle) to speed up future builds by avoiding redundant work.
- **Job Matrix:** A feature in GitHub Actions that allows running the same workflow across multiple combinations of environments (like Node.js versions, OS types) in parallel.
- **Slack Notifications:** Automated messages sent from CI/CD workflows to Slack channels, alerting teams of build failures, deployment completions, or other critical events.
- **Canary Release:** A gradual rollout strategy where a new app version is released to a small subset of users before full deployment, reducing risk in production.

- **Rollback:** An automated or manual process that reverts an app to a previous version in response to critical errors or performance issues in production.
- **Static Analysis:** The practice of analyzing code without executing it, used to enforce style, detect bugs, and identify security vulnerabilities before deployment.
- **Bundle Size / Startup Time:** Key performance metrics for mobile apps. CI workflows can track and enforce thresholds to prevent regressions in user experience.
- **Sentry / Datadog:** Monitoring platforms that track app performance, errors, and crashes. Can be integrated into CI pipelines for alerting and rollback automation.
- **OWASP Dependency-Check:** A security tool that scans project dependencies for known vulnerabilities, enabling proactive remediation during the build process.
- **EAS Credentials Manager:** A feature of EAS CLI that handles keystore and certificate management for Android and iOS in a centralized and secure way.
- **Secrets Rotation:** A best practice involving periodic updates to sensitive credentials (tokens, passwords, certificates) to reduce exposure and meet compliance standards.
- **Accessibility of the Pipeline:** The ability of CI/CD systems themselves (like dashboards, logs) to be navigable and readable by all team members, regardless of ability, reinforcing inclusion even within DevOps tooling.

These terms summarize the essential components, tools, and concepts discussed throughout this chapter. Use this list as a reference to reinforce your understanding of mobile DevOps practices and to help build CI/CD pipelines that are not only powerful and automated, but also secure, maintainable, and aligned with real-world production demands.

CHAPTER 14
App Store Publishing and Maintenance

Introduction

In this chapter, you will gain a comprehensive understanding of the process involved in publishing, updating, and maintaining your React Native applications on both the Apple App Store and Google Play. Publishing an app is an exciting milestone; but it is also a process that requires careful preparation, adherence to platform-specific guidelines, and continuous follow-up.

We will explore how to package your React Native app for distribution, manage the review processes of both app stores, and efficiently handle updates and user feedback. Additionally, you will learn how to interpret usage metrics to improve your application continuously, ensuring long-term success.

Understanding this publishing and maintenance cycle is especially crucial for React Native developers, as cross-platform frameworks introduce unique considerations regarding builds, app optimization, compliance, and performance tracking. By mastering these concepts, you will be able to confidently deliver high-quality, continuously evolving apps that meet the expectations of your user.

Structure

In this chapter, we will cover the following topics:

- Creating Developer Accounts
    - Apple Developer Program
    - Google Play Developer Account
- Preparing Your React Native App for Submission
    - App Icons and Assets
    - Build Configuration
- Submission and Review Process
    - Submitting to the App Store (iOS)
    - Submitting to Google Play (Android)

- App Updates and Versioning
  - Semantic Versioning Strategies
  - Submitting Incremental and Major Updates
  - Forced versus Optional Updates for Users
- Analyzing App Usage and Metrics
  - Understanding Metrics in App Store Connect and Google Play Console
  - Integrating Analytics with React Native
- Handling User Feedback
  - Collecting and Interpreting Reviews and Feedback
  - Store-Integrated Feedback Tools
  - Continuous Improvement from Real Feedback
- Maintenance and Continuous Evolution Strategies
  - Bug Fixing and Codebase Maintenance
  - Adding New Features
  - Staying Compliant with Store Policies

Creating Developer Accounts

Publishing your React Native application requires setting up developer accounts on both the Apple App Store and Google Play Store. These accounts grant you access to tools necessary for publishing, testing, and maintaining your applications. In this section, we will dive into the specifics of creating and configuring developer accounts for both platforms.

Apple Developer Program

Before you can submit apps to the App Store, you will have to enroll in the Apple Developer Program. Apple requires this membership to verify your identity, manage app distribution, and maintain a secure and trusted app ecosystem.

Creating an Apple ID and Enrolling in the Program

If you do not have an Apple ID, you will have to first create one. You can do this directly on the Apple ID webpage. Make sure to use a valid email address, as Apple will use it to communicate important updates and review status notifications.

Once your Apple ID is ready, you can head over to the Apple Developer Portal and begin the enrollment process. Apple charges an annual fee (currently $99 USD) to join the Apple Developer Program. Choose carefully between an individual or organizational account:

- **Individual** accounts are quicker to set up but limit collaboration features. Your name will appear as the publisher of your app.
- **Organization** accounts require additional documentation, such as proof of business registration (say a D-U-N-S number), but they allow multiple team members and more flexible roles.

After completing enrollment and making the payment, Apple usually approves the account within a few days.

Certificates and Provisioning for iOS

Once enrolled, you need to handle certificates and provisioning profiles—an essential step before submitting your React Native app to the App Store. Certificates prove your identity as a developer, while provisioning profiles define how your apps can run on physical devices or be distributed via the App Store.

To manage certificates and provisioning, follow these steps:

1. **Certificate Creation:** Using Xcode, you can generate signing certificates. Open Xcode and navigate to **`Xcode > Settings > Accounts`**. After signing in with your Apple ID, select **Manage Certificates** and create the required certificates (typically, Apple Distribution and Apple Development certificates).
2. **Provisioning Profiles:** Provisioning profiles tie together the unique identifier of your app, devices (for development or testing), and the associated certificates. You'll manage these profiles in the **`Apple Developer`** portal under the **`Certificates, Identifiers & Profiles`** section.

Here is an example of creating a provisioning profile in the developer portal:

1. Sign in to your Apple Developer account.
2. Navigate to **`Certificates,` Identifiers & Profiles > Profiles**.
3. Click **+** to create a new provisioning profile.
4. Choose **App Store** as the distribution method for a profile used in publishing your application.
5. Select the app identifier you previously created for your application.
6. Select the appropriate certificate.
7. Name and download the provisioning profile, and then double-click it to install automatically in Xcode.

Properly managing certificates and provisioning profiles ensures smooth submission and updates of your React Native apps on the App Store.

Google Play Developer Account

Creating and managing your Google Play Developer Account is comparatively straightforward and involves fewer initial technical requirements. Still, it is essential for distributing Android apps built with React Native.

Setting up Your Google Play Developer Account

To publish Android apps, first, you will need a standard Google Account (for example, a Gmail account). Afterward, visit the Google Play Developer Console to begin enrollment. Google requires a one-time fee (currently $25 USD) for lifetime membership.

Upon creating the account and paying the registration fee, your account will typically be activated immediately. Google might occasionally require additional information to verify your identity, but this is less common.

Once your account is active, you can access the Developer Console dashboard, from where you'll upload your app bundles, manage app listings, and track analytics.

Managing Subscriptions and Payments

Google Play Developer Console allows you to manage subscriptions and payments with ease. It is crucial if your React Native app uses a subscription model or offers in-app purchases.

For payment management, navigate to **Monetize > Products > Subscriptions** in the Google Play Console. Here, you can configure subscription products, prices, and subscription periods. Additionally, payment profiles—where Google transfers your app revenue—are configured under **Setup > Payments profile**.

Here is a simple example illustrating how you might define a subscription in React Native using the billing library of Google:

```
// Example using react-native-iap library
import RNIap, { requestSubscription } from 'react-native-iap';

const subscriptionSku = 'com.yourapp.premium_subscription';

async function subscribeToPremium() {
  try {
    await RNIap.initConnection();
    await requestSubscription(subscriptionSku);
  } catch (error) {
    console.error('Subscription failed', error);
  } finally {
    await RNIap.endConnection();
  }
}
```

This snippet leverages the popular **react-native-iap** library to handle subscription payments smoothly in React Native apps. Setting up developer accounts is an essential administrative step on your journey to publishing successful React Native applications. While it may seem tedious at first, carefully following these initial steps will pave the way for smooth app submission, effective maintenance, and trouble-free updates. It is crucial to ensure your accounts and certifications remain up-to-date, as any disruptions in account validity or provisioning can directly affect the availability of your app to end-users.

Preparing Your React Native App for Submission

Before publishing your app to the App Store or Google Play, it is essential to properly package and configure your React Native project. This preparation involves creating high-quality app assets, configuring your build settings for a production-ready release, and generating the appropriate files (.IPA for iOS and .APK or .AAB for Android). Let us explore each of these steps in detail.

App Icons and Assets

The visual assets of your app, particularly the app icon, significantly impact the success of your application by making a strong first impression on users. Both Apple and Google have specific guidelines for icon and asset design, requiring adherence to detailed specifications.

Specifications and Recommended Tools

Both platforms require multiple sizes and resolutions of your app icon and splash screen. React Native simplifies this process through various tools:

- **Icon Specifications:**
    - **Apple (iOS):** App icons should be provided in PNG format with square dimensions and no rounded corners. You must provide multiple resolutions, typically ranging from `20x20` pixels up to `1024x1024` pixels (used on the App Store).

- **Google (Android)**: Icons should also be PNG files, with recommended sizes from `48x48` up to `512x512` pixels for Play Store listings.

- **Recommended Tools:**
  - **App Icon Generator**: appicon.co or makeappicon.com can automatically generate all necessary sizes from a single high-resolution image.
  - **Figma & Sketch Templates**: These popular design tools provide templates tailored to Android and iOS guidelines, making the design process smoother and more compliant.

Once generated, place your icons and assets in the following directories within your React Native project:

For iOS: `ios/YourAppName/Images.xcassets/AppIcon.appiconset/`

For Android: `android/app/src/main/res/`

Proper organization ensures seamless build and submission processes.

Build Configuration

Configuring your build for a production environment is critical. React Native provides straightforward mechanisms to switch between development and release modes, optimizing your app's performance, stability, and security.

Configuration for Production (Release Builds)

In development mode, React Native apps include extra debugging tools, logs, and warnings. In production mode, these are stripped away to enhance performance and reduce file size.

For **Android**, you need to configure signing keys for app security and identification. Edit your **`android/app/build.gradle`** file to reflect release settings:

```
android {
  ...
  signingConfigs {
    release {
      storeFile file('my-release-key.keystore')
      storePassword 'yourStorePassword'
      keyAlias 'yourKeyAlias'
      keyPassword 'yourKeyPassword'
    }
  }

  buildTypes {
    release {
      signingConfig signingConfigs.release
      minifyEnabled true
      shrinkResources true
      proguardFiles getDefaultProguardFile('proguard-android-optimize.txt'),
'proguard-rules.pro'
    }
  }
}
```

For **iOS**, configure your build settings using Xcode. Set the **Scheme** to "**`Release`**" when archiving your app. Additionally, update the project settings to ensure proper signing with your distribution certificates.

Generating APK/AAB (Android) and IPA (iOS)

React Native apps are distributed as APK or AAB (Android App Bundle) for Android and IPA for iOS.

Android: Generate your Android release build with the following commands: `cd android`

```
./gradlew assembleRelease  # generates APK
./gradlew bundleRelease    # generates AAB
```

- The resulting files will be located in:
    1. APK: `android/app/build/outputs/apk/release/app-release.apk`
    2. AAB: `android/app/build/outputs/bundle/release/app-release.aab`
- **iOS:** Use Xcode for generating your IPA file:
    1. Open your project (`ios/YourApp.xcworkspace`) in Xcode.
    2. Select "**`Generic iOS Device`**" as the build target.
    3. From the top menu, select **`Product`** → **`Archive`**.
    4. Once archiving completes, an organizer window appears. Select the archive and choose "Distribute App" to generate and export the IPA file.

Using Tools such as Expo EAS or Fastlane

While manual builds are effective, automation tools greatly simplify and speed up the build process, particularly for React Native projects. Two widely used solutions are **Expo Application Services (EAS)** and **Fastlane**.

Expo EAS: Expo provides EAS Build, a cloud-based service that handles complex configurations automatically. If you are using Expo-managed workflows or Expo prebuild (Bare workflow), EAS simplifies build generation:

```
eas build -p android --profile production
eas build -p ios --profile production
```

- Expo manages signing certificates, provisioning profiles, and optimizations, providing ready-to-submit APK/AAB and IPA files.
- **Fastlane**: Fastlane is a powerful open-source toolkit that automates tedious release tasks and integrates seamlessly with React Native:

Android example (`fastlane/android/build_release`):

```
lane :build_release do
  gradle(task: "bundleRelease")
end
```

iOS example (`fastlane/ios/build_release`):

```
lane :build_release do
  build_app(scheme: "YourApp", export_method: "app-store")
end
```

Execute these lanes using:

```
fastlane android build_release
fastlane ios build_release
```

Fastlane saves significant time during releases by automating version management, build signing, and uploads.

Preparing your React Native app for submission involves careful attention to detail, from visual assets to release-ready configurations. By adhering strictly to platform-specific guidelines and utilizing tools like Expo EAS or Fastlane, you streamline this critical phase of the journey of your app to production. Investing time in these preparations will lead to smoother submissions and fewer obstacles during the review processes for both App Store and Google Play.

Submission and Review Process

After successfully preparing your React Native app, the next crucial step is submitting it to the app stores. Each platform, the App Store of Apple and of Google Play, has its unique submission procedures, review guidelines, and beta-testing options. Understanding these differences is essential to streamline your publishing process and get your app approved without unnecessary delays.

Submitting to the App Store (iOS)

The App Store submission process of Apple involves multiple steps to ensure apps meet high-quality standards. Let us explore each step clearly and sequentially.

Configuring Your Application in App Store Connect

First, log in to App Store Connect. App Store Connect is the dedicated platform of Apple for managing your apps. Here, you will define the metadata of your app, upload screenshots, add descriptions, configure pricing, and specify availability.

To create a new app:

1. Click on "`My Apps`" and then select the "`+`" icon.
2. Fill in basic information such as the name, primary language, bundle identifier (which must match your Xcode project), and SKU (an internal identifier).
3. Provide detailed app metadata:
    - **Screenshots**: Provide accurate screenshots for each supported device type (such as iPhone, iPad).
    - **App Icon**: Should match the specifications previously discussed.
    - **Description and Keywords**: Write clear, engaging descriptions and relevant keywords for better discoverability.

Always double-check your metadata, as mistakes here often result in rejection during the review of Apple.

TestFlight for Beta Testing and Internal Distribution

Before officially publishing your app, Apple provides **`TestFlight`**, a powerful beta-testing tool built into App Store Connect. It allows you to distribute your app to testers, gather early feedback, and fix critical issues prior to release.

To use TestFlight:

- After creating your app entry, navigate to **`TestFlight`** from App Store Connect.
- Click "**`Internal Testing`**" or "**`External Testing`**" to configure beta tests.
- Internal testing lets you invite up to 100 team members immediately, while external testing requires quick approval of Apple but can accommodate thousands of external testers.

- Upload your build through Xcode by archiving and selecting "**`Distribute App`**" to **`TestFlight`**. Testers receive invitations and provide valuable insights directly via built-in feedback mechanism of TestFlight.

Here is a simplified workflow to upload your build using Xcode:

1. **`Product`** → **`Archive`** from Xcode.
2. After the archive completes, click "**`Distribute App`**", and choose "**`App Store Connect`**" → "**`Upload`**".
3. After uploading successfully, your build appears in the **`TestFlight`** tab of App Store Connect, ready for internal or external testing.

Detailed Review Process of Apple

When you feel your app is production-ready, submit your build for official review:

- Select your uploaded build under the "**`App Store`**" tab in App Store Connect.
- Confirm the metadata of your app and then click "**`Submit for Review`**".
- The team of Apple thoroughly reviews each submission, typically within 24 to 48 hours. They assess compliance with their strict App Store Review Guidelines.

The review covers areas like:

- **Functionality and Stability**: Your app must be stable, without significant bugs or crashes.
- **Privacy and Security**: Clear disclosure of user data usage.
- **App Completeness**: App must not feel unfinished or provide placeholders or broken features.

Apple communicates via email and App Store Connect notifications about approval status or any necessary changes. Address any feedback promptly to expedite the approval of your app.

Submitting to Google Play (Android)

Google Play submission tends to be slightly more flexible but equally demands attention to detail and compliance with its policies.

Initial Setup in Google Play Console

Access the Google Play Console and start by creating a new app:

1. Click "**`Create App`**" and fill out details, including the app name, default language, and type (app or game).
2. Specify if your app is free or paid.
3. Complete app metadata, screenshots, and feature graphics. Remember, accurate information improves your visibility and user trust.

Google strongly emphasizes clear and accurate Play Store listings, including localized descriptions, to help reach global audiences effectively.

Internal, Closed, and Open Beta Testing with Google Play

Google provides several beta-testing channels to help refine your app before final release:

- **Internal Testing**: Allows rapid deployments to up to 100 testers without a formal review by Google, enabling quick feedback loops.
- **Closed Testing**: A more controlled testing phase for select user groups. Requires a brief review of Google, providing flexibility and expanded feedback options.

- **Open Testing**: Broad beta testing open to the general public. Excellent for wider usability tests before a full release.

Uploading a build to any testing channel involves:

- Navigating to **Testing** → selecting your preferred channel.
- Uploading an **AAB (App Bundle)** or **APK** file.
- Configuring testers by sharing testing links or email invitations.

This multi-layered beta-testing approach helps resolve critical issues early and greatly enhances app quality prior to full production launch.

Detailed Review Process of Google

When ready, you will submit your app for full production release. The review of Google focuses on compliance with their Google Play Policies:

- Ensure your app aligns with their guidelines regarding content, data privacy, permissions, and security practices.
- Clearly disclose your data handling practices in the mandatory **`Data Safety`** section.
- Adhere to the security and performance standards of Google, avoiding crashes and harmful behaviors.

To submit your app for production:

1. Select the **`Production`** track in Google Play Console.
2. Upload your final, tested AAB or APK file.
3. Provide necessary metadata and confirm all required sections (including privacy policy link, content rating, and data safety).
4. Click "**`Review and Roll Out Release`**".

Google typically completes reviews within hours, but it can sometimes take up to a few days, especially for new apps or significant updates. Any policy violations or required changes are clearly communicated in the Google Play Console and via email. Quickly addressing these helps ensure swift approval.

Common App Store / Play Store pitfalls for React Native Apps

- **"Thin wrapper" / minimum functionality (iOS):** Apple frequently rejects apps that feel like a **minimal WebView wrapper** (that is the app mainly mirrors a website with little native value), often under the umbrella of **minimum functionality** concerns. Ensure your React Native app delivers an app-like experience with meaningful native UX and functionality beyond simply rendering web content.

- **Startup time and perceived performance (bundle size and initialization work):** Large JS bundles and heavy initialization can increase **startup time**, which harms user experience and can surface as quality issues in store-facing tooling. On Android, **Play Console / Android vitals** explicitly tracks and flags **excessive startup times** (like cold start ≥ 5s). Treat bundle size reduction, lazy-loading, and startup work minimization as release hygiene, not afterthoughts.

- **Unnecessary permissions (iOS review and user trust):** iOS reviewers and users are sensitive to apps requesting permissions that do not clearly map to user-facing features. In React Native, this often happens when libraries add permission keys to **`Info.plist`** that you are not actually using. Audit permissions and remove anything unnecessary; keep your permission prompts and purpose strings tightly aligned to real features. The privacy guidance of Apple emphasizes not pushing users toward **unnecessary data access**.

- **Privacy policy URL requirements (Google Play):** Google Play requires a **privacy policy link** (and in-app access to it) especially for apps that request **sensitive permissions/data** under user data policies. If you use sensitive permissions, treat the privacy policy URL as mandatory release metadata.
- **Data privacy disclosures (both platforms):** Both stores enforce strict disclosure requirements:
    - **iOS (App Privacy Details / "nutrition label"):** You must accurately disclose what data your app and embedded SDKs collect and how it is used.
    - **Android (Data Safety section):** You must declare how data is collected, shared, and protected, including data handled by third-party SDKs.

Practical RN checklist before submission

- Verify your app is not "just a website in a shell" (native navigation, offline handling where relevant, meaningful native UX).
- Measure startup and reduce early work; watch Android vitals thresholds.
- Audit permissions (`Info.plist`, Android manifest) and remove unused ones.
- Add/verify privacy policy URL (Play Console + in-app).
- Keep iOS App Privacy and Android Data Safety declarations consistent with your code and SDK inventory.

Successfully navigating the review processes of both, Apple and Google respectively, involves understanding their distinct guidelines and leveraging their provided beta-testing tools. Utilizing **TestFlight** and **Google Play's testing tracks** significantly enhances your chances of publishing a robust, polished React Native app that meets user expectations and platform requirements. Stay patient, detail-oriented, and proactive in communication with reviewers to ensure a smooth and rewarding submission experience.

App Updates and Versioning

Keeping your React Native app updated regularly is vital to ensure continuous improvement, fix bugs, introduce new features, and comply with ever-changing app store policies. Effective app versioning and a clear update strategy help maintain user trust, engagement, and satisfaction. In this section, we'll explore semantic versioning strategies, approaches to incremental and major updates, forced versus optional updates, and best practices for writing engaging release notes tailored for React Native apps.

OTA Updates

Over-the-Air (OTA) updates let you ship **JavaScript bundle + asset** changes to users without waiting for App Store / Play Store review, which makes them a strong complement to regular binary releases. In React Native, the two most common approaches are **EAS Update** (Expo, via expo-updates) and **CodePush** (React Native integration).

- **When OTA is a great fit:** OTA is ideal for **bug fixes, UI tweaks, copy changes, and other non-native logic changes**, because users receive updates quickly (often on next app launch) without a full store update cycle.
- **Critical limitation (must be explicit in the book):** OTA updates **cannot change native code**. Any change that requires rebuilding the native app—new/updated native modules, native

dependency changes, or platform configuration changes—still requires a normal App Store / Play Store submission.

- **Policy/compliance guardrails (do not "bypass review"):** Both platforms allow certain forms of shipping interpreted code and updates, but they draw a clear line: you must not use remote updates to **fundamentally change the primary purpose** of the app or **hide features from review**. The guidance of Apple on interpreted code emphasizes not changing the core purpose of the app via downloaded code, and Google Play warns against dynamically downloading/executing code that introduces functionality not present during review.

Operational best practices (update UX)

- Use **silent/background updates** for small fixes and low-risk UI adjustments.
- Use **prompted updates** (release notes + "Restart to update") for significant changes where user context matters.
- Keep a clear separation between **native releases** (store) and **JS releases** (OTA), and document what types of changes are allowed in each lane.

Semantic Versioning Strategies

Versioning is crucial for communicating the extent of changes in each app release. A widely adopted standard across software development—and strongly recommended for React Native projects—is **Semantic Versioning (`SemVer`)**. SemVer follows the format:

```
MAJOR.MINOR.PATCH
```

Each number indicates the level of change in your app:

- **MAJOR:** Incremented when introducing significant changes that might break compatibility or drastically alter user experience. Examples include major UI overhauls, significant changes in app behavior, or breaking API updates.
- **MINOR:** Incremented when introducing new features without breaking existing functionality. For example, adding new screens, performance improvements, or new integrations.
- **PATCH:** Incremented for minor changes, including bug fixes, security patches, and small performance enhancements.

For instance:

- Version `1.2.3` would become `1.2.4` after a bug fix.
- Version `1.2.3` would become `1.3.0` when adding a new feature.
- Version `1.2.3` would become `2.0.0` after major changes, such as a complete redesign or breaking API change.

Clearly communicating version changes helps users and developers set appropriate expectations about updates.

Submitting Incremental and Major Updates

App updates typically fall into two categories: incremental (smaller improvements) and major releases (substantial feature updates or redesigns).

Incremental Updates usually focus on stability and small improvements. They typically include:

- Bug fixes and stability improvements.
- Small performance enhancements.
- Security patches.

These updates should be frequent to maintain high app quality and user satisfaction. Regular incremental updates convey active maintenance and responsiveness to user feedback.

Major Releases involve significant changes and enhancements, such as:

- New features or large functionality upgrades.
- Major UI/UX redesigns.
- Significant changes in the underlying React Native version or key dependencies.

Major releases require thorough testing, extensive beta feedback, and careful planning. Utilize beta-testing tools (TestFlight or Google Play Beta) to validate these substantial updates before general availability.

Forced versus Optional Updates for Users

An essential strategic decision is determining whether updates are optional or forced.

- **Optional Updates:** Most updates are optional, allowing users to upgrade at their convenience. Users typically receive app-store notifications indicating an available update. Optional updates are suitable for incremental releases, minor feature improvements, or non-critical bug fixes.
- **Forced Updates:** Occasionally, forcing an update becomes necessary, such as addressing severe security vulnerabilities, major breaking changes, or ensuring compliance with app store requirements.

In React Native, you can implement forced updates through a simple remote configuration using services like Firebase Remote Config or custom server-side checks. Here is a conceptual example in React Native:

```
// Example pseudocode for forced updates
import { Alert, Linking } from 'react-native';

const MINIMUM_APP_VERSION = '2.0.0';

function checkAppVersion(currentVersion) {
  if (currentVersion < MINIMUM_APP_VERSION) {
    Alert.alert(
     'Update Required',
     'Please update to continue using the app.',
     [{ text: 'Update Now', onPress: () => Linking.openURL(appStoreUrl) }],
     { cancelable: false }
    );
  }
}
```

Use forced updates judiciously, as overuse may frustrate users. Clearly communicating the necessity of these updates will enhance user understanding and acceptance.

Best Practices for Release Notes in React Native

Effective release notes are a vital channel of communication with your users, providing transparency about updates, generating excitement, and clearly stating the value of each release. Consider these best practices for writing engaging, informative release notes:

- **Clear and Concise:** Write briefly but clearly. Highlight key changes without technical jargon that users may not understand.

Categorize Changes: Divide notes into sections like "New Features," "Improvements," and "Bug Fixes." Users can quickly identify what matters most to them. `What's New (v1.5.0):`

```
New Features:
- Dark mode support
- New profile screen

Improvements:
- Improved loading speed on home screen

Bug Fixes:
- Fixed login issue affecting some users
```

React Native Specificity: When applicable, clearly indicate performance improvements or bug fixes related to platform-specific issues, such as:

```
- Fixed Android-specific crash on camera launch
- Improved scroll performance on iOS devices
```

Include a Human Touch: Engage users with friendly, approachable language: `"We've squashed pesky bugs and added exciting new features—check them out!"`

- **Consistency and Regularity:** Maintain consistent formatting and frequency. Users appreciate predictability and clarity.

A well-planned versioning and update strategy significantly impacts the user experience of React Native app and retention rates. Using SemVer, carefully balancing forced and optional updates, and providing clear, engaging release notes ensure users understand the value of keeping your app up to date. Thoughtful app maintenance, paired with effective communication, encourages user loyalty and helps your app remain successful long-term.

Analyzing App Usage and Metrics

Launching your React Native app is just the beginning—ensuring its success requires actively monitoring how users interact with it. Effective analysis of usage metrics provides insights into the performance of your app, user satisfaction, retention, and areas for improvement. This section covers the essential metrics available in the App Store Connect and Google Play Console, along with integrating powerful analytics tools into your React Native project.

Understanding Metrics in App Store Connect and Google Play Console

Both Apple and Google offer comprehensive dashboards that deliver valuable insights into app performance and user behavior. Mastering these analytics helps identify strengths, weaknesses, and opportunities for ongoing improvement.

Downloads, Active Users, and Retention Rates

These are core metrics to gauge the popularity and user engagement of your app:

- **Downloads and Installs:** Reflects the attractiveness and marketing effectiveness of your app. Monitoring trends in downloads after releases helps measure impact from new features or marketing campaigns.
- **Active Users:** Indicates how many users are actively engaging with your app. Active user counts are typically segmented as daily active users (DAU), weekly active users (WAU), or monthly active users (MAU).

- **Retention Rate:** Measures the percentage of users who continue using your app over time. Higher retention rates demonstrate strong user satisfaction and app value.

App Store Connect clearly visualizes these metrics under the **Analytics** tab, while Google Play Console provides them under **Statistics** and **Engagement** sections.

Crash Reports and Performance Monitoring

Monitoring the stability and performance of your app is equally important. Frequent crashes negatively impact user experience, reviews, and overall ratings.

Both App Store Connect and Google Play Console offer built-in crash-reporting tools:

- **App Store Connect:** The **Crashes** tab provides detailed crash logs, affected devices, iOS versions, and occurrence frequencies. Investigate these reports closely to pinpoint problematic code or third-party dependencies.

- **Google Play Console:** Navigate to `Quality → Android Vitals → Crashes and ANRs` (Application Not Responding). Google highlights crashes with affected Android versions, device models, stack traces, and user impact.

While native analytics help identify issues, leveraging specialized third-party tools significantly enhances your ability to monitor performance and proactively fix problems.

Integrating Analytics with React Native

Integrating analytics libraries into your React Native app empowers you with deeper, real-time insights into specific user behaviors, event tracking, and custom metrics tailored to the goals of your app. Here are several recommended tools and best practices for integration.

Recommended Analytics Tools for React Native

Popular analytics solutions suited to React Native projects include:

- **Firebase Analytics:** It is the robust and easy-to-integrate analytics platform of Google, offering real-time event tracking, demographic data, and user-behavior analytics.

- **Amplitude:** It is a powerful tool for product analytics, especially effective for tracking detailed user interactions, funnel analyses, and behavioral segmentation.

- **Sentry:** It proves to be exceptional for error tracking, crash reporting, and performance monitoring, providing detailed stack traces, real-time alerts, and issue-resolution workflows.

For most React Native projects, a combination of these tools, such as Firebase Analytics for general user behavior and Sentry for error tracking provides comprehensive insights.

Monitoring Specific User Behaviors and Events

Integrating these tools into your React Native app involves straightforward configuration and strategic event tracking:

Example: Integrating Firebase Analytics into React Native:

```
npm install @react-native-firebase/app @react-native-firebase/analytics
```

After that:

```
import analytics from '@react-native-firebase/analytics';

// Track a custom event
```

```
async function trackUserSignup(method) {
  await analytics().logEvent('user_signup', {
  signup_method: method,
  });
}

// Tracking screen views
import { useEffect } from 'react';
import { useNavigation } from '@react-navigation/native';

function HomeScreen() {
  const navigation = useNavigation();

  useEffect(() => {
    analytics().logScreenView({
      screen_name: 'Home',
      screen_class: 'HomeScreen',
    });
  }, [navigation]);

  return (
    // Your Home screen component
  );
}
```

This setup logs key user interactions—such as registrations, button clicks, or purchases—helping you better understand user behaviors and app usage patterns.

Example: Error Tracking with Sentry:

```
npm install @sentry/react-native
```

Initialize Sentry in your app entry point (`index.js` or `App.js`):

```
import * as Sentry from '@sentry/react-native';

Sentry.init({
  dsn: 'your-sentry-dsn-here',
});

// Capture custom errors
try {
  // your problematic code
} catch (error) {
  Sentry.captureException(error);
}
```

Sentry captures crashes and errors with detailed context, allowing rapid debugging and proactive stability improvements.

Proactively analyzing app metrics helps you make informed decisions, prioritize future updates, and enhance user experiences. While the native analytics provided by Apple and Google are beneficial starting points, integrating specialized analytics and crash-reporting tools into your React Native app takes your monitoring capabilities further. This practice empowers you to build a consistently engaging, reliable, and successful application, ensuring users remain satisfied and loyal long-term.

Handling User Feedback

User feedback is a living pulse of the health of your application. It tells you what is working, what is broken, and what users want next. For a React Native app that spans both iOS and Android, feedback arrives through store reviews, in-app reports, support channels, and indirect signals (like drop-off patterns tied to frustration). This section walks through collecting that feedback intelligently, leveraging the built-in tooling of App Store Connect and Google Play Console, and turning real feedback into a disciplined continuous improvement loop.

Collecting and Interpreting Reviews and Feedback

Collecting feedback is partly about providing the right channels and partly about listening with structure. Passive feedback—store reviews and complaints—is valuable, but you can also solicit proactive feedback at moments when users are most satisfied (such as after a successful transaction or task completion) while avoiding interrupting frustrated users.

A common pattern in React Native apps is to delay a review prompt until the user has performed a few meaningful actions. Libraries like **`react-native-in-app-review`** wrap the native in-app review APIs on iOS and Android so you can ask without sending users out of the app:

```
npm install react-native-in-app-review
```

After that:

```
import InAppReview from 'react-native-in-app-review';

function promptForReview() {
  if (InAppReview.isAvailable()) {
    InAppReview.RequestInAppReview()
      .then((hasFlowFinishedSuccessfully) => {
        // Optional: record that you asked, to avoid asking too often
      })
      .catch((err) => {
        console.warn('Review prompt failed', err);
      });
  }
}
```

Trigger this after a positive signal—for example, user completed onboarding, achieved a milestone, or used a core feature several times. Avoid triggering it on errors or during first launch when users have not formed an opinion yet. For more detailed or critical feedback, embed a lightweight in-app feedback form. Example structure:

```
// Simplified feedback form component
import { useState } from 'react';
import { View, TextInput, Button, Alert } from 'react-native';

export default function FeedbackForm() {
  const [message, setMessage] = useState('');

  const submitFeedback = async () => {
    try {
      await fetch('https://your.api/feedback', {
        method: 'POST',
        headers: { 'Content-Type': 'application/json' },
        body: JSON.stringify({ message, timestamp: new Date().toISOString() }),
```

```
      });
      Alert.alert('Thanks!', 'Your feedback has been sent.');
      setMessage('');
    } catch (e) {
      Alert.alert('Error', 'Failed to send feedback. Please try again later.');
    }
  };

  return (
<View>
<TextInput
        placeholder="Tell us what you think..."
        value={message}
        onChangeText={setMessage}
        multiline
        style={{ borderWidth: 1, padding: 8, minHeight: 100 }}
      />
<Button title="Submit Feedback" onPress={submitFeedback} disabled={!message.trim()}
/>
</View>
  );
}
```

Once you have feedback flowing in, interpretation becomes critical. Do not treat each review or comment in isolation. Aggregate and categorize: bugs, feature requests, performance complaints, usability issues, and praise. Look for trends; if multiple users mention sluggish scrolling on a specific screen, prioritize diagnosing and optimizing that interaction. Consider lightweight sentiment analysis (even simple keyword tagging) to surface negative feedback versus praise. Maintain a feedback backlog that is triaged with severity, frequency, and effort to address.

Store-Integrated Feedback Tools

Both Apple and Google provide built-in interfaces to view, respond to, and act on feedback submitted via their stores. These are not just visibility dashboards—properly used, they become part of your maintenance workflow.

In **App Store Connect**, reviews appear under the "Ratings and Reviews" section of your app. You can:

- See ratings broken down by version and region.
- Read the text of reviews and view associated metadata (such as device, iOS version).
- Respond publicly to reviews. Thoughtful responses can mitigate negative sentiment and show users you're listening, especially for issues already resolved in newer versions ("Thanks for the feedback! This was fixed in v1.3.2—please update and let us know if you still see it.").

In **Google Play Console**, review management is under the "`User Feedback`" area. Features include:

- Filtering reviews by star rating, app version, country, and language.
- Replying to reviews directly.
- Viewing trends in review volume and average rating over time.

A disciplined cadence is valuable: for example, allocate a weekly "review triage" session where recent store reviews are reviewed, categorized, and linked to your issue tracker (such as GitHub Issues, Jira, and so on). High-impact complaints (crashes, payment failures, onboarding blockers) get immediate attention; lower-priority suggestions feed into future roadmap planning.

Continuous Improvement from Real Feedback

Collecting and seeing feedback is only useful if it triggers action. Build a feedback loop that ties reviews to development cycles:

1. **Capture and Tag**: Pull reviews from both stores and internal feedback forms. Tag them (bug, UX, feature, performance).
2. **Triage and Prioritize**: Use criteria like user impact, frequency, and alignment with your product strategy to prioritize.
3. **Plan and Act**: Slot the highest-priority items into your sprint or release plan. Couple rough estimates with expected user value.
4. **Release and Communicate**: When fixing an issue or adding a requested feature, mention it in release notes or directly respond to the original review if appropriate.
5. **Close the Loop**: If a user raised a complaint and you released a fix, reply to their review thanking them and noting the resolution. This increases trust and can sometimes turn a negative review into a positive one.

You can also integrate feedback signals into internal dashboards. For example, combine rating trends with crash analytics (from Sentry or similar) to see if a spike in one-star reviews aligns with a backend regression or recent update. Use this data to roll back, hotfix, or explain what is being done transparently to users.

Finally, expose a lightweight "What's new / Feedback" screen in the app where you highlight recent improvements that came from user input. Framing updates as community-driven ("You asked, we delivered") reinforces engagement and makes users feel heard.

Handling user feedback is not a one-off task; it is an ongoing, structured practice that differentiates apps that stagnate from those that evolve. By collecting feedback proactively, using store tools to manage and respond to reviews, and building a closed loop where real feedback informs real changes, you turn users into partners in your app's growth.

Maintenance and Continuous Evolution Strategies

A successful React Native app is not something you ship once and forget; it is a living product that needs ongoing care, adaptation, and strategic evolution. This section lays out how to keep codebase healthy, how to introduce new capabilities without chaos, and how to stay ahead of changing platform requirements so your app does not suffer sudden disruptions.

Bug Fixing and Codebase Maintenance

Fixing bugs quickly and safely while keeping the codebase sustainable requires deliberate process and tooling. An ad hoc "find and patch" approach leads to regressions, technical debt, and developer fatigue. Instead, establish a repeatable maintenance workflow:

1. **Efficient Correction and Deployment Pipeline:** Every bug report—whether from crash monitoring, automated tests, or user feedback—should flow into a triage system. Assign severity, reproduce it in a controlled environment (locally or in a staging build), and create a small scoped fix. Use feature branches, peer code reviews, and automated CI checks (linting, unit/integration tests, smoke tests) before merging. Once merged, deploy to a canary or beta track first (TestFlight/internal Google Play testing) to validate the fix before a full release. For

critical issues, have a documented hotfix path that bypasses long cycles but still includes a minimal sanity check.

2. **Dependency Management in React Native:** React Native projects pull in many JavaScript and native dependencies, and outdated or conflicting versions are a common source of bugs and security exposure. Automating updates while retaining control is crucial. Tools like Renovate (or alternatives such as Dependabot) can continuously scan your `package.json`, native pods, and Gradle/Maven dependencies, opening curated update merge requests that include changelog context, version bump rationale, and impact assessment. Following the best practices recommended by Renovate maintainers—running the tool regularly, using its "best-practices" preset, reviewing changelogs, and updating major versions in a planned way—keeps the surface of outdated, vulnerable libraries small. Integrations and case studies specifically for React Native show how these tools reduce manual overhead and surface-breaking changes early, letting teams react before users do.

3. **Regular Upgrades of React Native and Core Libraries:** The React Native framework itself evolves frequently, delivering bug fixes, security patches, performance improvements, and compatibility updates. Skipping too many versions makes future migrations harder and can leave you exposed to deprecated APIs or platform mismatches. Use the official React Native Upgrade Helper and documentation to plan and execute upgrades; it shows differences between versions and guides which files need manual reconciliation. Adopt a cadence—either aligning with LTS-like milestones or scheduling periodic reviews—so upgrades are incremental rather than traumatic. Always couple framework upgrades with a burst of regression testing, since changes can surface in native modules, layout behavior, or underlying bridge contracts.

Adding New Features

Evolving the app means balancing user value, technical effort, and strategic direction. Without discipline, feature requests accumulate into a noisy backlog, and teams lose focus.

- **Prioritization and Planning**: Not all ideas are equal. Effective prioritization frameworks help distinguish high-impact work from distractions. Structured approaches such as MoSCoW (Must/Should/Could/Won't), RICE (Reach, Impact, Confidence, Effort), and hybrid combinations give you objective lenses to rank and sequence features. For example, using RICE scoring, a new onboarding flow might outrank a cosmetic tweak because the calculated "reach × impact × confidence / effort" yields a higher value, ensuring the team focuses on improvements that move key metrics. MoSCoW can be layered on top to define what must exist for a minimal viable iteration versus what can wait, helping shape releases under time constraints.

- **Maintaining the Evolutionary Roadmap**: The roadmap is your communication and coordination artifact. It should reflect prioritized features, anticipated timelines, and how new work links to user feedback, metrics, or strategic aims. Keep it living: revisit it after major releases, fold in validated user requests, and retire items that no longer fit. A well-maintained roadmap allows product, design, and engineering to align on what is next, what is deferred, and why—reducing rework and managing stakeholder expectation. Use the roadmap in tandem with your feedback loop (previous section) so that high-frequency, high-value signals from real users feed directly into the prioritization process.

Staying Compliant with Store Policies

Both Apple and Google regularly update their platform rules and enforcement emphasis; failure to adapt can result in rejections, takedowns, or degraded discoverability. Compliance is not a once-per-release checkbox—it is ongoing vigilance.

Proactive Policy Change Management

Subscribe to and monitor official update channels. Apple publishes changes to the App Store Review Guidelines and posts detailed announcements when guidelines are revised—such as the May 2025 updates related to external links and purchases, reflecting evolving legal landscapes. Google surfaces policy changes through its Play Console announcements, PolicyBytes updates, and the Developer Policy Center, including time-bound deadlines for compliance (for example the July 2025 policy updates and periodic transparency requirements). Maintain an internal changelog of relevant policy shifts, track which of the features of your app touch sensitive areas (data collection, financial services, health content, and the like), and schedule reviews ahead of enforcement windows to avoid rush remediations. When a policy touches your app (for example, inaccuracies in the Data Safety section have led to compliance flags), ensure your disclosures accurately reflect real behavior to prevent soft rejections or forced remediation.

Ensuring Continuous Compliance

Embed compliance into your development workflow. Build a lightweight checklist per release that includes items such as: review of data collection disclosures, validation of required privacy/security disclosures, audit of third-party SDKs for policy-allowed usage, and verification of content categories. Use automated linting or preflight scripts where possible to catch obvious violations (for instance missing privacy policy links or unauthorized user data access patterns). For more nuanced compliance (like emerging requirements around transparency, content moderation, or in-app purchase flows), pair automated signals with periodic manual audits by a team member who reconciles the current app state against the latest official guidelines.

When policy changes affect the business model of your app or UI (such as new requirements for disclosure or payment handling), plan these as part of your roadmap and communicate early in release notes or in-app messaging so users understand impacts, rather than surprising them post-deployment.

Sustainable maintenance and evolution require aligning technical rigor with product discipline and compliance awareness. Efficient bug-fixing pipelines, automated dependency and framework upgrades, disciplined feature prioritization, and a vigilant stance toward platform policies create the scaffolding upon which a React Native app can grow confidently. When these practices are institutionalized—not treated as ad hoc—the app remains resilient, responsive to users, and well-positioned for long-term success.

Conclusion

In this chapter, we have walked through the full lifecycle that takes a React Native app from a finished build to a sustainable, evolving product in the wild. You began with the foundational administrative work: creating and configuring developer accounts the App Store of Apple and Google Play, handling the nuances of certificates, provisioning, and payment/subscription setup. From there, you learned how to prepare the app itself—designing compliant assets, configuring release builds, and generating production artifacts—while leveraging automation tools like Expo EAS and Fastlane to reduce friction and human error.

We then navigated to the submission and review pipelines for both iOS and Android, including how to structure metadata, run meaningful beta tests via TestFlight and Google Play testing tracks, and anticipate the criteria and common pitfalls during official review. Once the app is live, the attention shifts to lifecycle management: versioning with SemVer to communicate change intent clearly, balancing incremental versus major releases, and deciding when to prompt users for optional updates or enforce critical ones.

Metrics and feedback from the feedback loop that keeps the app aligned with real user needs. You now know how to interpret downloads, active user counts, retention, crashes, and performance signals from store dashboards, and how to augment those with rich, custom analytics and error tracking through tools such as Firebase, Amplitude, and Sentry. That insight feeds directly into a structured feedback-handling process—collecting, categorizing, triaging, closing the loop with users, and incorporating learning into your roadmap.

Finally, maintaining and evolving the app responsibly requires discipline. You have seen how to build efficient bug-fix pipelines, keep dependencies and the React Native core up to date without disruption, prioritize and plan new features with objective frameworks, and stay ahead of shifting platform policies through proactive compliance practices embedded in your workflow.

By combining these elements—correct account setup, polished submission, disciplined versioning, data-informed iteration, user-centered feedback loops, and vigilant maintenance—you transform a one-time release into a resilient product that can grow, adapt, and retain trust over time. In the next chapter, we will build on this foundation by exploring advanced strategies for real-world case studies and collaboration best practices.

Questions

Before moving on, take a moment to reflect on the decisions, trade-offs, and practices you have seen in this chapter. These questions are meant to help you internalize the workflow around publishing, updating, observing, and evolving a React Native mobile app. Write brief answers, sketch how you would apply them in your own project, or discuss with a teammate.

1. What are the key differences between an individual and an organization Apple Developer account, and when would you choose one over the other?
2. What are the required steps to enroll in the Google Play Developer Console, and what common pitfalls should you avoid during setup?
3. Why is correct management of certificates, provisioning profiles (iOS), and keystores (Android) critical before the first submission? What happens if they are misconfigured?
4. What are the minimum asset and metadata requirements for a successful submission to App Store Connect and Google Play Console?
5. How does beta testing differ between TestFlight (iOS) and the internal/closed/open tracks of Google Play, and how would you structure a pre-release validation plan using them?
6. Describe the typical reasons for rejection during the review process on each platform, and how proactive preparation can reduce the chance of rejection.
7. In what scenarios would you automate submission versus perform it manually, and what safeguards would you build into an automated submission pipeline?
8. How does semantic versioning (SemVer) help communicate what has changed between releases to both users and internal stakeholders?
9. When would you choose to enforce a forced update versus leaving an update optional, and how would you implement and communicate each in a React Native app?
10. What makes release notes effective for end users, and how would you structure them differently for a minor bug fix versus a major feature rollout?
11. Which usage metrics from App Store Connect / Google Play Console are most indicative of product-market fit and retention, and how would you prioritize investigating anomalies in those metrics?
12. How would you combine store-native crash reporting with third-party tools (say Sentry) to get a fuller picture of stability issues?
13. What events or user behaviors would you instrument in a React Native app to feed analytics that help you decide what to improve next?

14. Describe a feedback loop that starts with a user review and ends with a code change being shipped and acknowledged. What tooling and touchpoints are involved?
15. How would you keep dependencies (including React Native itself) up to date without introducing regressions, and what is your strategy for scheduling and validating those upgrades?
16. What frameworks or criteria would you apply to prioritize new features or bug fixes for upcoming releases?
17. How does maintaining a public or internal roadmap help align engineering, product, and user expectations during continuous evolution?
18. What mechanisms would you put in place to stay ahead of changes in App Store and Google Play policies, and how would you audit your app for compliance regularly?
19. Explain the purpose of a canary or staged rollout for mobile apps. How would you design one to limit blast radius while still gathering meaningful validation?
20. Under what conditions would you trigger a rollback, and how would production monitoring signals (for example, spike in errors from Sentry or degraded performance metrics) feed into that decision?
21. If you were starting from a single successful release, what three changes would you make next to move toward a more resilient, observability-driven publishing and maintenance process?
22. What key indicators (metrics, feedback patterns, and release stability) would you track over time to judge whether or not is your publishing and update strategy healthy and improving?

Answering these questions will strengthen your command of modern mobile DevOps workflows and help you design CI/CD systems that are automated, secure, observable, and maintainable—empowering your team to ship faster and with greater confidence.

Key Terms

- **Apple Developer Program:** Enrollment program required to publish on the App Store; includes identity verification, access to certificates/provisioning, and app management.
- **Google Play Developer Account:** One-time-paid account required to publish on Google Play; provides access to app listings, subscriptions, and analytics.
- **App Store Connect:** The dashboard of Apple for configuring, submitting, testing (via TestFlight), and managing iOS apps, metadata, and reviews.
- **Google Play Console:** The dashboard of Google for configuring, submitting, testing, and managing Android apps, including listings, policies, and user feedback.
- **Developer Account:** General term for the authenticated account (Apple or Google) that owns and controls app publication, billing, and access.
- **Certificate (iOS):** Digital identity proving the authenticity of the developer; used to sign iOS builds.
- **Provisioning Profile (iOS):** File binding certificates, app identifiers, and distribution method or devices; required to build and distribute iOS apps.
- **Keystore (Android):** Secure file containing private keys for signing Android application packages (`.apk`/`.aab`); essential for updates and identity.
- **TestFlight:** The beta distribution system of Apple for internal and external testers to preview and validate iOS builds before full release.
- **Beta Testing Channels:** Controlled release tracks (internal, closed, and open) on both stores used to validate releases with limited audiences before production.

- **App Submission:** The act of uploading a build, providing metadata, and initiating the review process of the platform for a release.
- **Review Process:** Platform-specific automated/manual evaluation of the compliance, stability, and policy alignment of the app prior to approval.
- **App Store Review Guidelines:** The published rules of Apple that apps must adhere to in order to be approved for distribution.
- **Data Safety / Policy Compliance:** Declarations and configurations (especially on Google Play) about how user data is handled, and required for transparent and compliant distribution.
- **Semantic Versioning (SemVer):** Versioning scheme using `MAJOR.MINOR.PATCH` to signal breaking changes, new features, and fixes.
- **Incremental Update:** Small, frequent releases focused on bug fixes, minor improvements, or performance tweaks.
- **Major Release:** A substantive update introducing new features, redesigns, or significant changes that may affect compatibility or behavior.
- **Forced Update:** A mechanism requiring users to upgrade (such as for critical fixes or policy compliance), often enforced via remote configuration.
- **Optional Update:** Standard updates that users may install at their discretion without blocking continued use.
- **Release Notes:** Descriptions exposed to users explaining what changed in a version: new features, fixes, improvements, and context.
- **Downloads:** Count of installations, reflecting reach and acquisition effectiveness.
- **Active Users (DAU/WAU/MAU):** Metrics that represent how frequently and how many users engage with the app on daily, weekly, or monthly bases.
- **Retention Rate:** Percentage of users who return over time; a key indicator of sustained value.
- **Crash Reports:** Diagnostics collected when the app fails or crashes, used to identify stability issues.
- **Performance Monitoring:** Observing app responsiveness, startup time, and resource usage to maintain quality.
- **Analytics:** Collection and analysis of behavioral data to inform decisions (like feature usage, funnels).
- **Firebase Analytics:** The event-based analytics platform of Google for tracking user behavior in mobile apps.
- **Amplitude:** Product analytics tool specialized in behavioral segmentation, funnels, and user journeys.
- **Sentry:** Error and performance monitoring platform capturing exceptions, crashes, and contextual telemetry.
- **Remote Config:** Mechanism (for instance via Firebase) to change app behavior or enforce policies (like forced updates) without resubmitting.
- **Feedback Loop:** Structured process of capturing user feedback, triaging, and acting, communicating changes, and closing the loop.
- **Roadmap:** Living plan that aligns upcoming features, fixes, and strategic goals with user feedback and metrics.

- **Feature Prioritization:** Frameworks (including RICE, MoSCoW) to rank and sequence work based on impact, effort, and strategic value.
- **Continuous Evolution:** Ongoing process of improving, extending, and adapting the app in response to real usage and changing context.
- **CI/CD Pipeline:** Automated sequence (build → test → deploy) enabling consistent, safe software delivery.
- **GitHub Actions:** Native GitHub automation platform used to define workflow triggers, job matrices, and pipeline steps in YAML.
- **Fastlane:** Automation tool for mobile release tasks (building, signing, metadata, screenshots, submission) for iOS/Android.
- **EAS CLI (Expo Application Services):** Cloud-enabled build and submission tool for Expo/React Native projects, handling credentials, builds, and uploads.
- **`eas.json`:** Configuration file for EAS defining build profiles, environment settings, and behavior per release type.
- **Credential Management:** Secure handling and retrieval of signing keys, certificates, and secrets used in automated builds.
- **Key Rotation:** Periodic replacement of secrets and credentials to minimize risk from compromise or stale access.
- **Canary Release:** Gradual rollout to a small subset of users to validate stability before full-scale deployment.
- **Rollback:** Reverting to a previous stable version in response to critical failures or regressions detected post-release.
- **Compliance Monitoring:** Ongoing validation against platform policies to avoid takedowns or rejections.
- **Dependency Management:** Process of keeping third-party libraries (JS/native) up to date safely (for example via Renovate or **`Dependabot`**).
- **Upgrade Helper:** Tools or processes (like React Native Upgrade Helper) to plan and apply framework/library version migrations.
- **Static Analysis:** Pre-execution code checks (linting, type checks, security scans) to catch issues early.
- **Bundle Size / Startup Time:** Performance budgets enforced to prevent regressions in app size or initial load latency.
- **In-App Review Prompt:** Contextual trigger within the app to solicit store reviews when the user has a positive signal.
- **User Feedback Channels:** Mechanisms (store reviews, in-app forms, replies) for collecting qualitative input from users.
- **Build Notifications:** Alerts (such as Slack, email) sent when pipelines succeed/fail to keep stakeholders informed and responsive.
- **Monitoring Tools:** Platforms like Sentry or Datadog used to observe runtime health, trigger alerts, and feed automation logic (say rollbacks).

These terms serve as a working glossary to anchor your implementation and conversations about publishing, evolving, and maintaining React Native mobile applications.

CHAPTER 15

Case Studies and Collaboration Best Practices

Introduction

Throughout this book, we have explored the fundamentals, best practices, and advanced features of React Native. We have covered everything from initial environment setup to complex integrations, passing through state management, performance optimization, accessibility, and build automation. However, no matter how complete a theoretical approach is, it cannot replace the value of seeing how all of this comes together in a real-world project.

This chapter was created precisely with therefore, a similar purpose: to connect the accumulated knowledge up to this point with the reality of production development. Moving from theory, to concrete cases, we can observe the real impact of technical decisions, understand why certain patterns were adopted, and analyze how different teams responded to challenges in architecture, deadlines, and scope changes.

The goal is not only to show that "it works in practice," but also, to deconstruct these experiences, identifying which choices led to success, which trade-offs were necessary, and which mistakes could have been avoided. In the end, the objective for you is to be not only more technically confident but also better prepared to navigate the human and organizational aspects of a React Native project.

Structure

In this chapter, we will cover the following topics:

- From Theory to Practice
  - How Collaboration Impacts Project Success
- Real-World Case Studies
  - Case 1 — Cross-Platform E-commerce Application
  - Case 2 — Health and Wellness App with Native Integrations
  - Case 3 — Interactive Education Platform
  - Mini-Case — The Cost of Speed: When Expo Was Not Enough
  - Mini-Case — Performance That Pays Off: Early Optimization
- Architectural Decisions and Trade-offs

  - Criteria for Choosing an Architecture
  - Monorepo versus Multiple Repositories
  - Modularization and Component Reuse
  - Sacrificing Performance for Delivery Speed
- Team Collaboration Best Practices
  - Version Control and Git Workflows
  - Code Reviews and Constructive Feedback
  - Code Standards and Quality Tools
  - Communication and Alignment
  - Continuous Integration and Continuous Delivery (CI/CD)
- Risk Management and Contingency Planning in React Native Projects
  - Common Risk Categories
  - Risk Management Cycle
- Lessons Learned and Recommendations
  - Common Mistakes to Avoid
  - Strategies to Speed Up New Member Onboarding
  - Practices to Ensure Long-Term Maintainability

From Theory to Practice

Real case studies bring a dimension that no tutorial, sample project, or controlled example can fully replicate: they expose the context. While code snippets and playground apps are useful for grasping syntax and basic patterns, they rarely show the messy realities of production systems. A large-scale application is never built in a vacuum; it emerges from a complex interplay of business pressures, technical constraints, team dynamics, market timing, and user expectations.

In the controlled world of a tutorial, assumptions are made to simplify the learning path: APIs are always available and fast, dependencies are stable, and requirements are frozen in time. In the real world, deadlines shift, APIs break, requirements evolve mid-development, and new devices or OS versions can appear overnight, forcing architectural adjustments on the fly. This is why transitioning from theory to practice is not just about writing more code, but about adapting that code to fit a constantly changing environment.

When we analyze a project that has gone through all lifecycle stages; conception, development, testing, publishing, maintenance, and continuous improvement, we begin to see how technical decisions are inseparably linked to external factors:

- **Business alignment:** Any team may choose Redux for state management not purely because of its scalability features, but because it allows sharing patterns and even some logic with a pre-existing web application, reducing the cognitive load for developers who work across platforms.
- **Platform requirements**: The decision between React Native CLI and Expo often comes down to the depth of native integrations required. A team building a proof-of-concept in two weeks might lean on Expo for its rapid setup, while another integrating a proprietary video codec or payment SDK will likely opt for CLI or eject from Expo to gain full control over native modules.
- **Time-to-market constraints:** An architectural decision that knowingly sacrifices some degree of performance. For example, using a ready-made WebRTC library instead of building

a custom native video layer, might be entirely justified if it enables a critical launch before a major marketing event, securing funding or market share.

In each of these examples, the technical choice is the result of balancing trade-offs between performance, maintainability, cost, delivery speed, and long-term scalability. Understanding this balancing act is one of the core skills that separate an experienced developer from someone who has only worked on isolated exercises.

Studying real scenarios allows us to develop the ability to evaluate risks and benefits with greater maturity. We can see how a "perfect" architectural pattern in theory might fail in practice due to organizational bottlenecks, or how a less elegant but pragmatic solution can lead to faster delivery and better business results.

Decision Point	Option A – *Pros / Cons*	Option B – *Pros / Cons*	Real-World Example
Project Initialization	**Expo Managed Workflow** **Pros:** Fast setup, large ecosystem of prebuilt modules, OTA updates. **Cons:** Limited native integration, possible need to eject later.	**React Native CLI** **Pros:** Full control over native code, easier to integrate with custom SDKs. **Cons:** Longer setup, more responsibility for native configurations.	A startup used Expo Managed to build an MVP in 3 weeks; later ejected to CLI when adding a custom video streaming library.
State Management	**Redux Toolkit** **Pros:** Predictable state flow, devtools, scalability for large apps. **Cons:** Boilerplate overhead for small projects.	**Context API + Hooks** **Pros:** Simpler for small/ medium apps, less boilerplate. **Cons:** Performance issues if not optimized (for example, memoization, splitting contexts).	An e-commerce app chose Redux to share patterns with its web frontend; a small productivity app stayed with Context API for faster delivery.
Codebase Organization	**Monorepo** **Pros:** Code reuse, centralized dependency management, shared UI components. **Cons:** Risk of excessive coupling, slower builds in large projects.	**Multi-repo** **Pros:** Isolated changes, faster builds, independent versioning. **Cons:** Harder to sync changes across services, duplicated code.	A health app with shared UI across web and mobile used a monorepo; a logistics platform with separate teams opted for multiple repos.
Data Storage Strategy	**SQLite / Realm (Local DB)** **Pros:** Complex queries offline, strong data persistence. **Cons:** Additional native setup, potential sync conflicts.	**AsyncStorage / MMKV** **Pros:** Simple key-value storage, easy to implement. **Cons:** Not ideal for complex relational data.	An education platform used SQLite to store large offline course content; a news app used AsyncStorage for simple article caching.
Offline Capability	**Full Offline-First** **Pros:** Works without internet, higher reliability. **Cons:** Complex sync logic, larger storage footprint.	**Online-First with Caching** **Pros:** Simpler implementation, smaller storage usage. **Cons:** Reduced usability without internet.	A delivery tracking app required offline GPS logging; a social media app prioritized online-first due to constant real-time interactions.

Decision Point	Option A – Pros / Cons	Option B – Pros / Cons	Real-World Example
Feature Delivery Approach	**Feature Flags** **Pros:** Gradual rollout, safe testing in production. **Cons:** Requires flag management infrastructure.	**Direct Release** **Pros:** Simpler release flow. **Cons:** Higher risk of introducing critical bugs to all users at once.	A fintech used feature flags for new payment flows; a weather app opted for direct releases due to low-risk feature changes.
Performance Optimization Priority	**Ahead-of-Time Optimization** **Pros:** Avoids bottlenecks in production, smoother UX. **Cons:** More upfront dev time.	**On-Demand Optimization** **Pros:** Faster initial delivery. **Cons:** Risk of performance debt if not revisited.	A streaming app optimized lists and caching early; an internal HR tool only optimized after feedback from first release.

Table 15.1: *Comparison between Expo and React Native*

Moreover, these case studies expose patterns of common pitfalls that can derail a project if not addressed early:

- **Library overload**: Integrating too many dependencies without considering maintenance cost, API stability, or long-term compatibility with React Native upgrades.
- **Overly complex architectures**: Prematurely implementing micro-frontends, elaborate dependency injection frameworks, or abstracting business logic too aggressively, which increases onboarding time and debugging complexity.
- **Inefficient communication**: Teams that lack clear decision documentation often re-discuss the same topics or make conflicting changes, leading to merge conflicts, duplicated work, or delayed releases.

The real value in moving from theory to practice is in internalizing these lessons. By learning from both, the success and mistakes of others, we can shorten our own learning curve; avoid repeating unnecessary errors, and gain confidence in making architectural and organizational decisions. Ultimately, the goal is not just to "build an app that works" but to build an app that can survive and thrive under the pressures of the real world – where delivery timelines, evolving requirements, and the need for a cohesive team strategy are constant realities.

How Collaboration Impacts Project Success

One of the most evident point when observing successful projects is that they are not sustained solely by clean code or well-thought-out architecture—they are the result of efficient collaboration. In a React Native project, where the team often involves specialists in different areas (mobile, backend, design, QA), integration among these roles is critical to the quality and speed of deliveries.

Collaboration goes far beyond "working together." It involves:

- **Organized version control**: Using strategies Such as Git Flow or Trunk-Based Development to avoid conflicts and maintain predictable release cycles.
- **Structured code reviews**: Ensuring that improvements are suggested constructively and, that quality standards are upheld.
- **Clear communication standards**: Where technical decisions are documented, preventing repetitive discussions or misunderstandings.
- **Continuous Integration/Continuous Deployment (CI/CD) tools:** Automating tests, builds, and deployments, reducing friction between teams and avoiding the infamous "works on my machine" problem.

In practice, efficient collaboration reduces rework, accelerates problem-solving, and increases both client and user confidence in the final product.

Real-World Case Studies

Although, theory provides the foundation for learning React Native, nothing compares to seeing how principles, tools, and best practices come together in actual production environments. Real-world projects reveal the complexity behind decision-making, where technical considerations must be balanced with business goals, deadlines, and resource constraints.

In the following case studies, we will explore three distinct React Native projects from different sectors – e-commerce, health and wellness, and education. Each example highlights:

- **The Project Context**: The specific needs, constraints, and objectives that shaped the development process.
- **Key Architectural Decisions**: The technologies, frameworks, and patterns chosen, along with the reasoning behind them.
- **Challenges and Solutions**: The obstacles encountered during development and how they were addressed.
- **Results**: Measurable outcomes in performance, user engagement, and business impact.

These scenarios are not meant to serve as rigid templates, but rather as practical insights into the trade-offs, optimizations, and collaboration practices that can help you make more informed choices in your own React Native projects.

Case 1: Cross-Platform E-commerce Application

Project Context

A national retail chain sought to replace its hybrid application (built with Ionic) with a more performant solution that offered a better user experience. The goal was to maintain a single codebase for both Android and iOS while delivering native-like performance and feel. The deadline: 6 months to launch before Black Friday.

Key Architectural Decisions

- React Native CLI instead of Expo, due to the need for deep integrations with native payment modules (Apple Pay, Google Pay).
- Redux Toolkit for global state management, ensuring predictability and data integrity for cart, wishlist, and authentication.
- Axios for integration with the existing REST API, using interceptors for JWT authentication and error handling.
- `FastImage` for optimizing catalog image loading.

```
// Authentication interceptor example
api.interceptors.request.use(config => {
  const token = store.getState().auth.token;
  if (token) config.headers.Authorization = `Bearer ${token}`;
  return config;
});
```

Challenges and Solutions

- **Large list performance:** Used FlatList with **`getItemLayout`** and tuned **`windowSize`** to reduce re-renders.
- **Offline experience:** Implemented caching with **`AsyncStorage`** for the catalog and purchase history.
- **Frequent deliveries:** CI/CD pipeline with GitHub Actions + Fastlane for automated builds and regression testing.

Results (Example Outcomes; Measured Post-Launch)

The following figures are **illustrative example outcomes** to show the kind of impact teams often track. In a real project, report the exact metrics and measurement methodology:

- **Startup time:** Example reduction from ~8s to ~2.5s, measured via startup instrumentation (like app start traces / performance tooling) on a defined device set and build type (release), comparing before/after baselines.
- **Engagement:** Example +25% daily engagement, measured via analytics (say DAU, sessions/user, conversion funnel) over a consistent time window, controlling for campaign effects where possible.
- **Stability:** Improved crash detection and faster remediation using Firebase Crashlytics; crash-rate changes should be reported as **crash-free users/sessions** over time and tied to specific fixes released after monitoring surfaced the top offenders.

Case 2: Health and Wellness App with Native Integrations

Project Context

It is about a mental health startup offering video consultations, daily tracking, and integration with wearable devices. The solution should run smoothly on both Android and iOS, integrating Bluetooth and custom notifications.

Key Architectural Decisions

- **Expo Bare Workflow**: Quick project setup, but ejected to implement native Bluetooth Low Energy (BLE) modules.
- **Context API** for smaller, session-specific states, and Redux for global data such as user profile and activity history.
- **`react-native-webrtc`** for video calls integrated with a Node.js backend.

```
// Hook to monitor a wearable device
export function useHeartRateMonitor(deviceId: string) {
  useEffect(() => {
    BLEManager.connect(deviceId);
    BLEManager.onUpdate(data => setHeartRate(data.value));
    return () => BLEManager.disconnect(deviceId);
  }, [deviceId]);
}
```

Challenges and Solutions

- **Video streaming reliability**: Optimized bitrate with a fallback to audio-only for unstable connections.
- **Sensitive permissions management**: Used **`react-native-permissions`** to handle camera, microphone, and location access.
- **Wearable synchronization**: Implemented an offline event queue to prevent data loss.

Results

- 40% reduction in data consumption during video calls.
- 100% reliable heart rate data synchronization, even with connection drops.
- App store rating increased from 3.2 to 4.6.

Case 3: Interactive Education Platform

Project Context

A private university needed to develop an app that unified multimedia content, interactive quizzes, and progress tracking, with multilingual support and offline functionality for areas with unstable internet access.

Key Architectural Decisions

- **React Native + TypeScript** from the start for better safety and maintainability.
- **i18n-js** for internationalization, with dynamic loading of translations.
- **SQLite** for storing progress and downloaded study materials offline.

```
// i18n configuration
i18n.translations = {
  en: { welcome: "Welcome" },
  pt: { welcome: "Bem-vindo" },
};
i18n.locale = Localization.locale;
```

Challenges and Solutions

- **Offline/online progress synchronization**: Implemented a background service to update the backend once the connection was restored.
- **Accessibility**: Full support for **`VoiceOver`** and **`TalkBack`**, with adapted buttons and captions.
- **Video compatibility**: Used **`react-native-video`** with multiple formats to support older devices.

Results

- 30% increase in daily platform usage.
- Course completion rate increased from 42% to 67%.
- University recognized for inclusive practices in educational technology.

Mini-Case — The Cost of Speed: When Expo was Not Enough

An urban mobility startup needed to quickly launch an application for trip monitoring and QR code payments. The development team chose the Expo Managed Workflow to accelerate the MVP, leveraging ready-made modules for geolocation and camera functionality.

Decision: With only four weeks before the official marketing campaign launch, the team ruled out using the React Native CLI, assuming that native configuration would delay the project too much.

Consequences: In the final testing phase, the team discovered that the payment SDK integrating with the national banking system required a native module not supported by Expo Managed. The solution was to eject to the Bare Workflow under tight deadlines, refactoring a significant portion of the integration code and adjusting build pipelines.

Lessons Learned:

- **Ignored trade-off:** Native integration limitations were not considered in the initial decision.
- **Impact:** Two extra weeks of rework, delaying delivery and reducing the marketing window.
- **Improvement for the future:** Create a technical requirements matrix from the start, including planned integrations and stack limitations.

Mini-Case — Performance That Pays Off: Early Optimization

An educational streaming platform decided to create a React Native app for accessing offline video lessons and live streaming. The team knew that smooth scrolling and fast loading were essential for maintaining user retention.

Decision: Instead of focusing solely on rapid delivery, the team invested time in early optimization by:

- Implementing FlatList with windowing and lazy loading.
- Preloading thumbnails with intelligent caching.
- Setting up image compression on the backend before sending them to the app.

Consequences: Even with a slightly longer release timeline, the app received positive reviews from the first month. Average session time was 35% higher than competitors, and the drop-off rate during the first week decreased significantly.

Lessons Learned:

- **Well-calculated trade-off:** Delaying the launch by 10 days to optimize performance paid off.
- **Impact:** Less rework later and a better NPS from the very beginning.
- **Improvement for the future:** Document performance budgets as a non-functional requirement before starting development.

Architectural Decisions and Trade-offs

In software development, particularly in React Native projects that often span both iOS and Android ecosystems, there is no single “perfect” architectural path. Real-world products operate in an environment where business urgency, budgetary constraints, team skill sets, and market timing shape — and sometimes distort — technical decisions.

In theory, architectural design could be a purely rational exercise: evaluate all possible options, select the one that optimizes for scalability, maintainability, and performance, and follow it until the end. In practice, however, the reality is far messier. Decisions are often made under incomplete information, with changing requirements, and in the face of competing priorities. This is where trade-offs become unavoidable — every choice optimizes for some aspects while sacrificing others.

The three case studies analyzed in this chapter demonstrate how each architectural decision is a balancing act, and how these decisions, while technical in nature, are always deeply connected to the context in which the project is developed.

Criteria for Choosing an Architecture

Before diving into comparisons, it is important to understand the most common criteria influencing architectural decisions in a React Native project:

- **Delivery speed:** Short deadlines tend to favor solutions with a large base of ready-to-use libraries (for example, Expo Managed Workflow).
- **Critical native integrations:** When the project requires specific native modules, such as payment or Bluetooth, it may be necessary to opt for React Native CLI or eject from Expo.
- **Long-term maintainability:** Large teams often prefer more standardized architectures with strong typing (TypeScript).
- **Scalability:** When anticipating an increase in features or integration with multiple systems, code modularization becomes a priority.
- **User experience:** Apps requiring smooth animations, fast loading, and low latency demand optimization starting at the architectural design phase.

Monorepo versus Multiple Repositories

In the analyzed cases, we saw different approaches to code organization:

- **E-commerce:** Choose multiple repositories (frontend, backend, and separate microservices) to enable specialized teams to work autonomously. This reduced version control conflicts but increased continuous integration efforts.
- **Health/Wellness:** Used a monorepo with Yarn Workspaces, centralizing frontend and shared libraries. This sped up the evolution of reusable components but required greater discipline in code reviews to prevent unrelated changes from impacting other areas.
- **Education:** Maintained a single repository for the mobile app, keeping the backend separate. This simplified management for a small team but limited code reuse between web and mobile.

Main trade-off: Monorepos increase reuse and consistency but also raise the risk of excessive coupling and slower builds.

Modularization and Component Reuse

Modularization was a key point in all three projects but applied at different levels:

- **E-commerce:** Invested heavily in creating isolated modules for cart, authentication, and catalog, facilitating maintenance and unit testing.
- **Health/Wellness:** Focused on modules for critical integrations, such as Bluetooth and WebRTC, as they were the most vital components.
- **Education:** Modularized only essential features (authentication, video player, quizzes), keeping the rest more integrated for simplicity.

Main trade-off: The greater the level of modularization, the more robust and scalable the application becomes, but the initial development cost, and build complexity also increases.

Performance Optimizations

Each project faced specific performance bottlenecks:

- **Large lists (E-commerce)**: Advanced use of FlatList with **`getItemLayout`**, optimized **`initialNumToRender`**, and **`shouldComponentUpdate/memo`** to avoid unnecessary re-renders.
- **Video streaming (Health/Wellness)**: Dynamic bitrate adjustment with automatic fallback to audio on unstable networks.
- **Offline content (Education)**: Selective preloading with SQLite and incremental synchronization to avoid overloading the first login.

Technical example — FlatList optimization:

```
<FlatList
  data={products}
  renderItem={renderProduct}
  keyExtractor={(item) => item.id}
  getItemLayout={(_, index) => ({
    length: ITEM_HEIGHT,
    offset: ITEM_HEIGHT * index,
    index,
  })}
  initialNumToRender={10}
  windowSize={5}
/>
```

Main trade-off: Optimizations increase code complexity and require more rigorous testing, but they significantly reduce user-perceived slowdowns.

Sacrificing Performance for Delivery Speed

Not every choice prioritizes maximum performance. Two of the analyzed projects opted for trade-offs:

- **Health/Wellness**: Gave up a fully custom video player in favor of using the ready-made **`react-native-webrtc`** implementation, accelerating the launch by 2 months, even though memory consumption was slightly higher.
- **Education**: Chose not to implement real-time synchronization in the initial release, focusing only on uploading progress when reconnecting, in order to meet the deadline of the first class.

These choices show that, in real-world environments, achieving business goals often takes precedence over technical ideals. The key is ensuring these compromises are conscious and planned, avoiding "technical debt" that never gets repaid.

Team Collaboration Best Practices

Efficient collaboration in software development goes far beyond the idea of "working together" — it is about engineering an ecosystem in which communication, decision-making, and delivery operate in a consistent, predictable, and measurable manner. In React Native projects, where frontend, backend, and native layers intersect, the absence of well-defined collaborative practices almost always results in friction, delays, and costly misunderstandings.

From the three case studies analyzed, one point became clear: teams that succeed do not rely solely on individual talent; they rely on structured processes that make that talent scalable. These teams create an environment where any developer, regardless of when they joined the project, can quickly understand the current status, contribute effectively, and make decisions aligned with the goals of the project.

Well-structured collaboration starts with clear versioning rules, continues with enforced coding standards, and is sustained by consistent, transparent communication – both synchronous and asynchronous. Let us explore these pillars in depth.

Version Control and Git Workflows

Version control is the backbone of any collaborative project. The analyzed teams adopted different strategies:

- **E-commerce:** Classic **Git Flow**, with **`main`** (production), **`develop`** (pre-production), **`feature/*`**(new features), **`release/*`**, and **`hotfix/*`**branches. This structure worked well for a large team, enabling planned releases and urgent fixes.
- **Health/Wellness: Trunk-Based Development**, maintaining a single main branch and using feature flags to control what is released to production. This sped up continuous delivery but required discipline to prevent incomplete code from impacting users.
- **Education:** Simplified **GitHub Flow**, with short-lived branches and small PRs merged directly into **`main`**, ideal for a small team.

Example of Git Flow branch naming convention:

```
feature/payment-integration
release/1.2.0
hotfix/cart-discount-bug
```

Technical recommendations:

- Use small, frequent pull requests to make reviews easier.
- Configure CI/CD to run automated tests before any merge.
- Standardize commit messages (for example, Conventional Commits) to keep history clean.

Code Reviews and Constructive Feedback

In all successful projects, code review was not treated as a mere formality but as a tool for collective learning.

PR checklist: Before submitting a PR, developers ensured: tests were updated, lint passed with no errors, documentation for new components was added, and minimum coverage requirements were met.

Centralized technical discussions: Comments and decisions were recorded directly in the PR, avoiding the loss of information in isolated chat messages.

Example of a GitHub PR checklist:

```
### Checklist
- [ ] Code follows ESLint/Prettier standards
- [ ] Unit tests cover new functionality
- [ ] Documentation updated
- [ ] PR reviewed by at least 1 team member
```

Code Standards and Quality Tools

Maintaining code consistency reduces onboarding time for new members and minimizes errors.

Common tools:

- **ESLint:** Static analysis to prevent common mistakes.
- **Prettier:** Automatic code formatting.
- **Husky + lint-staged:** Running checks before each commit.

Adopted conventions:

- PascalCase for component files (`ProductCard.tsx`) and camelCase for utilities (`formatPrice.ts`).
- Clear separation of layers: `/components`, `/screens`, `/services`, `/store`.

Example Husky configuration:

```
"husky": {
  "hooks": {
    "pre-commit": "lint-staged"
  }
}
```

Communication and Alignment

Effective communication avoids rework and ensures everyone is aware of priorities.

Adopted rituals:

- Short daily stand-ups (maximum 15 minutes) to align progress and blockers.
- Bi-weekly planning to prioritize backlog and define deliverables.
- Monthly retrospectives to evaluate what worked and what needs improvement.

Tools used:

- Jira or Trello for task management.
- Slack or Microsoft Teams for asynchronous communication.
- Centralized documentation in Notion or Confluence.

Observed practice in the Education app: The team recorded all technical decisions in an **Architecture Decision Record (ADR)** document, providing history and traceability.

Continuous Integration and Continuous Delivery (CI/CD)

Automating tests and builds was the key to maintaining quality in all analyzed cases.

- **E-commerce:** GitHub Actions + Fastlane for automated builds, unit tests, and publishing to TestFlight/Google Play Internal.
- **Health/Wellness:** CI/CD integrated with security checks (`Dependabot`, `npm audit`) and end-to-end tests before each release.
- **Education:** Simpler pipeline but with automatic deployment to a staging environment.

Example of a basic GitHub Actions workflow:

```
name: CI
                                                       on:
```

```
    pull_request:
      branches: [ main ]
  jobs:
    build:
      runs-on: ubuntu-latest
      steps:
        - uses: actions/checkout@v3
        - uses: actions/setup-node@v3
          with:
            node-version: 18
        - run: npm ci
        - run: npm run lint
        - run: npm test
```

The most efficient teams were not necessarily the most technically experienced but those that established clear processes, consistent standards, and fluid communication. In React Native, where integrations, multiple platforms, and multidisciplinary collaboration are the norm, the disciplined application of these practices can make the difference between a scalable, high-quality project and one that becomes a chaotic, hard-to-maintain system.

Risk Management and Contingency Planning in React Native Projects

Even in the best-structured teams, with solid architecture and well-defined collaboration processes, projects can encounter unexpected challenges. These can range from technical issues, such as breaking API changes or performance bottlenecks, to organizational and market factors such as team turnover or sudden scope changes.

Managing risks proactively is not just about *reacting* when things go wrong; it is about identifying potential threats early and having clear, tested contingency plans in place.

Common Risk Categories

- **Technical Risks**
    - **Dependency Breakage**: Libraries or SDKs may stop being maintained or change APIs in a breaking way.
    - **Platform Changes**: New iOS or Android versions introducing changes in permissions, APIs, or UI patterns.
    - **Performance Regression**: A feature causing degraded FPS or higher memory usage in production.
- **Organizational Risks**
    - **Team Turnover**: Key developers leaving without proper handover.
    - **Knowledge Silos**: Critical know-how concentrated in a single person or squad.
- **Operational Risks**
    - **Deployment Failures**: App updates rejected by app stores due to guideline changes.
    - **Service Downtime**: Backend outages affecting mobile functionalities.
- **Market and External Risks**
    - **Regulatory Changes**: New compliance requirements (for example, privacy, payments).
    - **Competitive Pressure**: Need to accelerate delivery to respond to a competitor launch.

Risk Management Cycle

1. **Identification**
    a. Create a risk register early in the project.
    b. Use retrospectives, code reviews, and ADR discussions to surface potential risks.
2. **Assessment**
    a. Estimate *impact* (High, Medium, or Low) and *likelihood* (Frequent, Occasional, and Rare).
3. **Mitigation**
    a. Adopt *feature flags* to disable incomplete or unstable functionalities in production.
    b. Maintain *forked versions* of critical dependencies.
    c. Establish *cross-training* to prevent knowledge silos.
3. **Contingency Planning**
    a. Define rollback procedures (for example, revert app store release, disable flag, hotfix).
    b. Keep a *"last known good build"* tagged in CI/CD.
    c. Simulate incident responses during low-pressure periods.

Example: Risk Scenario in Practice

Scenario: An e-commerce team relies on a third-party payment SDK for in-app purchases.

Risk: SDK could introduce breaking changes or be discontinued.

Mitigation: Abstract payment logic into an internal module with a defined interface.

Contingency: Maintain a documented fallback flow (web-based checkout) ready for activation if the SDK fails in production.

Tools and Practices for Risk Management

- **Documentation**: Maintain a *Risk Register* in Notion, Confluence, or GitHub Wiki.
- **Automation**: Configure CI to run smoke tests against staging after dependency updates.
- **Monitoring and Alerts**: Use Sentry, Crashlytics, and backend monitoring tools to detect anomalies early.
- **Release Strategy**: Combine staged rollouts with feature flags for safe deployments.

Key Takeaways

- Risks in React Native projects can be technical, organizational, operational, or market-driven.
- Early identification and clear contingency plans reduce the impact of unexpected events.
- Embedding risk management into your architecture and collaboration practices increases project resilience.
- A prepared team can turn potential failures into opportunities for trust-building with stakeholders.

Lessons Learned and Recommendations

After analyzing the three case studies and the architectural and collaboration practices adopted, it is possible to identify recurring patterns that emerge regardless of industry, target audience, or team size. These patterns are not just academic observations — they represent **practical lessons** that can directly guide the development of more efficient, sustainable, and higher-quality React Native projects.

The findings below synthesize both **technical best practices** and **collaboration principles** into a set of actionable recommendations.

Common Mistakes to Avoid

Ignoring Business Context and Objectives: In all successful cases, architectural and tooling decisions aligned closely with **deadlines**, **budget constraints**, and **end-user expectations**. A common failure pattern occurs when teams attempt to adopt "every promising technology" without assessing its compatibility with business needs.

- **Example:** Choosing a microservices-based backend when the project scope only requires a simple monolith, wasting valuable development time.
- **Consequence:** Increased complexity, slower iterations, and inflated costs.

Over-Engineered Architecture: Modules, design patterns, and third-party libraries should be introduced **in response to actual problems** — not simply because they are trending or popular in the community.

- **Example:** Adopting a multi-layered architecture with repository, use case, and service layers for a simple CRUD mobile app.
- **Consequence:** Extra code maintenance, longer onboarding, and diminished agility in early-stage releases.

Lack of Clear Coding Standards: Without **linters**, **automatic formatting tools** (for example, Prettier), and **naming conventions**, teams quickly lose consistency, making code harder to maintain, refactor, or debug.

- **Example:** Inconsistent file naming (`UserList.tsx` versus `user_list.js`) creates friction in cross-platform builds and searchability.

Unrecorded Informal Communication: Decisions made only through chat tools or verbal discussions are easily lost, leading to misaligned implementations.

- **Recommendation:** Use lightweight documentation approaches such as decision records (ADR) or concise wiki entries to preserve the rationale behind choices.

Strategies to Speed up New Member Onboarding

- **Minimum Required Documentation:**
    - Keep an **up-to-date README** with environment setup, dependencies, and build instructions.
    - Provide **setup scripts** for first-time environment configuration, including .env templates.
- **Practical Examples in the Repository:**
    - Include **reusable components** (buttons, modals, list items) and **custom hooks** (API requests, authentication).
    - Provide **API integration templates** showing standard request/response handling.
- **Initial Mentorship:**
    - Assign an **experienced developer** to guide newcomers through their first pull requests and architecture overview.
- **Ready-to-Use Development Environment:**
    - Use **Docker** or automated scripts to eliminate OS-specific setup issues and version conflicts.

Practices to Ensure Long-Term Maintainability

Semantic Versioning (SemVer)

Apply strict rules for **major**, **minor**, and **patch** updates — ensuring that any breaking changes are predictable and documented.

Automated Tests as Part of the Delivery Flow

- **Unit tests** for business logic.
- **Integration tests** for API interactions.
- **End-to-end (E2E) tests** for critical workflows, such as authentication or payment flows.

Continuous Monitoring

Integrate tools such as **Crashlytics**, **Sentry**, or **Datadog** to capture runtime errors and monitor performance metrics in production.

Conscious Dependency Management

- Evaluate the **maintenance frequency** and **community activity** of libraries before adoption.
- Establish quarterly dependency audits to remove outdated or vulnerable packages.
- Real-world success comes from **balancing technical excellence with business viability**.
- Architectural decisions must **factor in deadlines, integrations, scalability needs, and team capabilities**.
- **Structured collaboration:** With consistent versioning, code reviews, documented communication, and agreed-upon coding standards — is as vital as the code itself.
- **Maintenance discipline** ensures long-term scalability and prevents technical debt from accumulating unnoticed.

The following table highlights key lessons and collaboration practices, their real-world impact, and the tools or methods that help teams apply them effectively.

Lesson / Practice	Real-World Impact	Recommended Tools / Methods
Align architecture with business goals	Avoids overengineering and reduces time-to-market	Business requirement matrix, ADR (Architecture Decision Records)
Avoid over-engineered architecture	Minimizes maintenance overhead and improves agility	YAGNI principle, iterative design reviews
Enforce clear coding standards	Improves team collaboration and code maintainability	ESLint, Prettier, Stylelint
Document decisions and communication	Preserves decision rationale and reduces rework	Project wiki, Notion, Confluence
Provide minimum onboarding documentation	Speeds up integration of new team members	README.md, setup scripts, .env templates

Table 15.2: *Continuous Monitoring Analysis*

By adopting these recommendations from the very start of a project, teams can create an environment where **technology is an enabler rather than a bottleneck**. Sustainable success in React Native development is not just about writing functional code — it is about building **solutions that can evolve** with changing requirements, user feedback, and market conditions.

The true measure of a successful project is its ability to **withstand time, change, and complexity** while continuing to deliver value to both the business and the end user.

Conclusion

In this chapter, we walked through the complete cycle that transforms a set of React Native concepts and tools into a functional, sustainable product capable of evolving continuously in the real market. We began by connecting theory to practice, exploring how real-world case studies reveal nuances that go far beyond academic examples — from deadline and budget constraints to integration requirements with complex systems and specific platforms.

From there, we have delved into three concrete projects; e-commerce, health and wellness, and interactive education. We have, further analyzed their architectural decisions, performance optimizations, and creative solutions in the face of both business and technical challenges. We have also seen how each choice, whether adopting a monorepo or prioritizing fast delivery over maximum performance, involves conscious trade-offs that shape the final outcome.

We also discussed the collaboration practices that sustain these projects over the long term: well-defined Git workflows, consistent code reviews, quality standards reinforced by automated tools, clear and documented communication, and CI/CD pipelines that ensure predictable deliveries. These practices not only maintain technical quality but also create an environment where the team can quickly respond to change and remain aligned even in high-pressure scenarios.

Finally, we have consolidated the lessons learned and recommendations that emerged from these cases. You have seen how to avoid common pitfalls, such as overly complex architectures or lack of documentation, and how to adopt processes that accelerate onboarding, increase maintainability, and keep the project healthy even in the face of team or market changes.

By combining these elements; critical analysis of real cases, balanced architectural decisions, solid collaboration practices, and lessons drawn from concrete experiences, you can transform a simple React Native application into a resilient product, capable of growing, adapting, and maintaining user trust over time.

In the next chapter, we will build upon this foundation by exploring emerging trends and the future of React Native, preparing you to position yourself strategically for the next waves of innovation in mobile development.

Questions

Before moving forward, take a moment to reflect on the decisions, trade-offs, and practices discussed in this chapter. The questions below will help you internalize how to turn theory into practice while balancing architecture, performance, and collaboration in React Native teams. Answer briefly, sketch how you would apply them to your project, or discuss them with a teammate.

1. In which context would you choose Expo (Managed/Bare) or React Native CLI? What impact does this have on native integrations, time-to-market, and maintainability?
2. Given your current project, monorepo or multiple repositories, how does this choice affects change isolation, build speed, versioning, and module reuse?
3. Where will you set module boundaries like, auth, catalog, payments, and media? Also, what criteria would you use (volatility, external dependencies, and business domains)?
4. Which state management strategy best fits your case (Redux Toolkit/RTK Query, Context API, Zustand, React Query/Apollo)? What are the signals that indicate the need to migrate or combine approaches?
5. How would you prove that your virtualized list implementation (**`FlatList/SectionList`**) is optimized? Which parameters (for example, **`getItemLayout`**, **`windowSize`**, **`initialNumToRender`**, **`keyExtractor`**) would you adjust and why?

6. Which RN-specific performance metrics would you track (frame drops in JS/UI thread, TTI, startup time, memory usage)? How would you instrument and interpret each one?
7. Does your app need to operate offline-first? What cache/sync design (**`AsyncStorage/SQLite/Realm`**, event queues, conflict resolution) would you adopt and how would you validate reconnection scenarios?
8. What performance versus delivery speed trade-offs would you accept in your project (for example, using a prebuilt player with a larger footprint to meet a deadline)? How would you document and plan to "pay down" this technical debt?
9. Which Git workflow best fits your team today (Git Flow, GitHub Flow, Trunk-Based + feature flags)? What would change if the team size doubled?
10. How would you ensure small PRs and effective reviews? What minimum checklist would you adopt (tests, lint/format, docs, screenshots/recordings)? How would you avoid **`bikeshedding`** during code review?
11. Which coding standards and quality tools would you standardize (ESLint, Prettier, strict TypeScript, Husky + lint-staged)? Where and how would you document these rules (conventional commits, ADRs)?
12. What communication practices reduce rework in your team (short dailies, weeklies, ADRs, RFCs, decision records in PRs)? How would you ensure decision traceability?
13. How would you design a minimal viable CI/CD pipeline for RN (lint, unit tests, build, E2E on device farm/emulator, tester distribution)? Which "gates" will prevent regressions?
14. When will you use feature flags and experiments (A/B)? How shall you isolate incomplete code in production and plan for flag removal?
15. What is your production observability strategy (**`Crashlytics/Sentry`**, structured logs, custom UX metrics)? What alerts should you configure (thresholds and notification channels)?
16. Describe a feedback loop: from user review to delivered and communicated code change. What tools/touchpoints are involved (store review, help desk, board, PR, release notes)?
17. How do you decide between refactoring and quick fixes? What signals (cyclomatic complexity, bug hotspots, mean time to fix, test coverage) guide that choice?
18. Which automated tests are critical in your context (unit, integration, E2E, API contract tests)? Where do you have gaps and how would you prioritize filling them?
19. Would your team adopt a design system and shared component library? How would this impact consistency, accessibility, and speed? What governance would you apply to evolve it without breaking apps?
20. Which security/privacy risks are most likely (sensitive permissions, token storage, BLE/Health data)? How would you mitigate and audit them (reviews, SAST/DAST scanners, targeted pentests)?
21. In what situations would you do a staged rollout/canary release? What metrics/thresholds determine progression, pause, or rollback?
22. When would you trigger a rollback? What signals (crash spikes, ANRs, latency, conversion drop) and what operational plan would you follow (disable feature flag, revert version, hotfix)?
23. How would you keep dependencies (including RN) up to date without breaking things? What update window, dedicated branches, smoke tests, and staging environments would you establish?
24. What prioritization criteria would you use for bugs/features (RICE/ICE, impact versus effort, severity SLAs)? How would you communicate decisions to stakeholders?

25. How can a public/internal roadmap improve alignment between engineering, product, and support? What level of granularity and timeline would you maintain?
26. Considering the three case studies, which decisions would you adopt in your project and which would you avoid? What in your context makes those choices appropriate?
27. If you started from a single successful release, what three changes would you make to evolve toward a more resilient, observability-driven process?
28. What continuous indicators will you track to judge the health of your strategy (cycle time, PR approval rate, crash-free sessions, retention, NPS, incident recovery speed)?

Answering these questions reinforces your mastery of modern architecture and collaboration flows in React Native projects, helping you build automated, observable, and sustainable teams and systems — capable of delivering faster and with greater confidence.

Key Terms

- **Architecture Trade-off:** A technical decision where certain benefits (for example, delivery speed) are prioritized over others (for example, performance), directly impacting the evolution of the project.
- **Monorepo:** A single-repository structure containing multiple modules/projects, promoting reuse and consistency but potentially increasing build time and coupling.
- **Multi-repo:** A structure with separate repositories for each service or component, enabling autonomy and isolation but requiring more integration and synchronization.
- **Module Boundary:** The logical delimitation of a code module (for example, authentication, catalog, payments) to facilitate maintenance, testing, and reuse.
- **State Management:** Strategies for controlling application state, such as Redux Toolkit, Context API, Zustand, React Query/Apollo, chosen based on complexity and scalability needs.
- **Offline-First:** An architecture that prioritizes operation without a network connection, storing data locally (`AsyncStorage`, `SQLite`, `Realm`) and syncing changes when the network is available.
- **Performance Budget:** A predefined limit for metrics such as load time, bundle size, and memory usage, preventing regressions.
- **Virtualized List:** Components like `FlatList/SectionList` that render only visible content, optimizing memory and performance in large lists.
- **Feature Flag:** A mechanism to enable/disable features dynamically, allowing safe deployment of incomplete code or A/B testing.
- **Debt Register:** A documented record of technical debt, including reason, impact, and resolution plan, to prevent unmanaged accumulation.
- **Git Flow:** A versioning strategy with `main`, `develop`, `feature/*`, `release/*`, and hotfix/* branches to manage predictable releases.
- **Trunk-Based Development:** A strategy with frequent commits to the main branch and heavy use of feature flags to control feature exposure.
- **Pull Request (PR):** A merge request reviewed by other team members to ensure quality and consistency.
- **Code Review Checklist:** A list of mandatory criteria (for example, tests, linting, documentation) to be verified before approving a PR.

- **Linting/Formatting:** Tools (ESLint, Prettier) that automate code standards, ensuring consistency and preventing common errors.
- **Husky / lint-staged:** Git hooks that run automated checks (lint, tests, build) before commits to prevent invalid code from entering the repository.
- **Architecture Decision Record (ADR):** A document that records relevant architectural decisions, their context, evaluated alternatives, and justifications.
- **RFC (Request for Comments):** A formal proposal for a significant change, open for review and discussion by the team before implementation.
- **Daily Stand-up:** A short meeting for daily alignment on progress, blockers, and priorities.
- **Retrospective:** A recurring meeting to evaluate what went well, what needs improvement, and defines actions for team evolution.
- **CI/CD Pipeline:** An automated flow that compiles, tests, and distributes the application, ensuring frequent and safe releases.
- **End-to-End Testing (E2E):** Tests that simulate real application usage, covering multiple layers (UI, logic, API) to validate the complete flow.
- **Observability:** The ability to monitor and understand system behavior in production through logs, metrics, and distributed tracing.
- **Crash Reporting:** Real-time automatic monitoring of application crashes (for example, Sentry, Firebase Crashlytics) to detect, prioritize, and fix issues.
- **User Feedback Loop:** A continuous process that captures user feedback, prioritizes improvements, implements changes, and communicates results.
- **Roadmap:** A living document organizing future features, fixes, and strategic objectives, aligning team, product, and users.
- **Feature Prioritization:** Techniques (RICE, ICE, and MoSCoW) to rank features and fixes according to impact and effort.
- **Staged Rollout / Canary Release:** Gradual release of a new version to a subset of users, validating stability before full rollout.
- **Rollback:** Reverting to a stable previous version in case of critical production failures.
- **Dependency Management:** Practices to keep libraries and frameworks up to date safely (for example, Renovate, **Dependabot**).
- **Upgrade Helper:** A tool or guide (such as React Native Upgrade Helper) to migrate the project between framework versions.
- **Static Analysis:** Automated code verification before execution, covering style, typing, and security.
- **Onboarding Guide:** Documentation describing environment setup, standards, and processes to quickly integrate new team members.
- **Design System:** A set of components, visual standards, and UX guidelines that ensure consistency and efficiency in development.
- **Team Retention:** Practices and culture that maintain motivation, productivity, and low turnover within the development team.

These terms serve as a working glossary to anchor your implementation and conversations about publishing, evolving, and maintaining React Native mobile applications.

CHAPTER 16

Emerging Trends and the Future of React Native

Introduction

Throughout its journey, React Native has established itself as one of the leading frameworks for cross-platform mobile app development, offering a unique balance between productivity, flexibility, and closeness to the native experience. However, the sustainability of any technology in the contemporary digital ecosystem depends on its ability to evolve in the face of new paradigms and to respond to the growing demands of users and organizations. In this context, understanding the emerging trends and future directions of React Native becomes essential for professionals and companies that want to remain relevant and competitive in the industry.

In recent years, a structural transformation has been observed at the core of the framework, which is marked by the introduction of features such as Fabric, TurboModules, and the JavaScript Interface (JSI), which redesign the way communication occurs between JavaScript code and the native environment. At the same time, the community has played a decisive role in maintaining and expanding the ecosystem, driving the emergence of libraries, tools, and practices that broadens the scope of React Native. This combination of technical innovation and collective collaboration projects a future in which the technology becomes increasingly robust, interoperable, and prepared to face new challenges.

The relevance of React Native should also be analyzed in light of its position relative to competing frameworks such as Flutter and Kotlin Multiplatform, which compete for space in the cross-platform arena with different approaches. The comparison reveals that although each solution has its specific advantages, the maturity of React Native, its natural integration with the React ecosystem, and its wide adoption by global companies reinforce the perception that it will continue to be a strategic choice in the medium and long term.

Finally, while new libraries and APIs emerge to expand the technical capabilities of the framework, the market signals significant changes in the expected profile of mobile developers. Emerging skills such as AR/VR integration, development for wearables, expertise in accessibility, and collaboration in open-source ecosystems are becoming increasingly relevant. Thus, this chapter explores not only recent advances and the technical roadmap of React Native but also discusses its future viability and the role of professionals who build and maintain solutions within this constantly evolving ecosystem.

Structure

In this chapter, we will cover the following topics:

- Evolution of the Ecosystem and New Libraries
  - Advanced Development Tools
  - Support Frameworks and Integration
- Integration with Emerging Technologies (AR, VR, and Wearables)
  - Development for Smartwatches and Wearable Devices
  - Technical Challenges and Solutions for Integration with Innovative Hardware
- New Features and API Proposals
  - Proposals Under Discussion and the Community Roadmap
  - Impacts on Performance, Interoperability, and Enterprise Adoption
- Security, Privacy, and Compliance in React Native
- Server-Driven UI, Superapps, and Multi-Experience Orchestration
- Cross-Platform Beyond Mobile: React Native for Desktop and Web
- Integration of Artificial Intelligence with React Native
  - Technical Integration Strategies
  - Challenges, Ethics, and Best Practices
  - Future Directions
- Community Contributions and Open Source
  - How to Collaborate with Libraries, Documentation, and RFCs
  - Examples of Successful Collective Contribution Initiatives
- Sustainability and Longevity of React Native
  - Factors that Reinforce the Permanence of React Native in the Market
  - Adoption by Major Companies as an Indicator of Long-term Viability
- The Future of the Mobile Developer
  - The Profile of the Cross-Platform Developer in Evolving Market Scenarios
  - How to Prepare for Career Trends and New Opportunities

Evolution of the Ecosystem and New Libraries

The React Native ecosystem is in a constant process of maturation, reflecting both the strength of the open-source community and the growing market pressure for more performant, scalable, and interoperable mobile solutions. Since its creation, the technology has evolved from a basic set of tools into a sophisticated environment that enables the development of high-level applications, often indistinguishable from their native counterparts. This evolution is marked by three central axes: the emergence of new libraries that expands the capabilities of the platform, the maturation of build, debugging, and profiling tools, and the consolidation of support frameworks that provide more integrated and efficient workflows.

In recent years, some libraries have taken on a central role in building advanced interfaces and managing complex resources. A notable example is React Native Reanimated 3, which introduced a declarative model for animations based on the concept of worklets. This model offloads a significant portion of the processing from the JavaScript layer to the native level, eliminating long-standing bottlenecks and enabling smooth animations even on lower-end devices. Another essential component is React Native Gesture Handler, whose latest version provides a robust system for handling multitouch gestures, replacing the limited `PanResponder` approach and enabling modern interactions such as swipe cards, bottom sheets, and dynamic contextual menus.

Beyond libraries focused on user interface and experience, there has been a growing adoption of solutions aimed at asynchronous data management, such as React Query (TanStack Query), which simplifies caching logic and synchronization with REST and GraphQL APIs, reducing coupling between the presentation layer and data services. At the same time, lightweight state management libraries like Zustand and Jotai have emerged as alternatives to Redux in small- and medium-sized applications, showcasing the diversity of options that now make up the toolkit of React Native developer. The overall trend points clearly toward reducing complexity in the bridge between JavaScript and native code, offering abstractions that make the development experience closer to that of React for the web, without sacrificing the performance required in mobile environments.

The New Architecture Remains the Defining Platform Shift

In **React Native 0.83**, the biggest long-term story of the ecosystem is still the **New Architecture**—a foundational redesign that continues to be hardened and expanded, while tooling (notably DevTools) improves around it. The release of RN 0.83 highlights major DevTools upgrades, and the New Architecture remains the baseline direction for modern apps.

- **Fabric (The Modern Renderer): Fabric** is the new rendering system of React Native. It modernizes how UI work is scheduled and committed, enabling more reliable handling of high-priority UI events and smoother interaction-heavy experiences. The key takeaway for readers is that rendering behavior and scheduling differ materially between the legacy renderer and Fabric, especially under complex, gesture-driven UIs.

- **TurboModules (Modern Native Module System): TurboModules** replace the legacy Native Modules design with a typed, codegen-driven approach and **lazy initialization** (modules are created on first access). This can reduce startup overhead in apps that previously paid an upfront cost to load many modules at launch (actual gains vary by app and dependency graph).

- **JSI (JavaScript Interface) as the Foundation: JSI** removes the legacy asynchronous Bridge model and enables direct JS↔C++ interop (without JSON serialization overhead by default). This makes "near-native" performance patterns feasible for certain categories of libraries—especially storage and databases.

  Examples commonly cited in the RN ecosystem include **`react-native-mmkv`** (JSI-backed key/value storage) and **`react-native-quick-sqlite`** (SQLite with JSI bindings), which explicitly document their JSI-based design.

- **Codegen (Type-Safe Native Interfaces):** The New Architecture formalizes a spec-first workflow: you define a typed interface (TypeScript/Flow), and **Codegen** generates the native bindings for **Turbo Native Modules** (and Fabric components). This shifts many integration mismatches earlier in the lifecycle (build-time) and improves long-term maintainability of native interfaces.

Advanced Development Tools

The maturity of the ecosystem can also be observed in the sophistication of tools that support the software lifecycle. Among them, Flipper stands out, having become the de facto standard for real-time inspection of React Native applications. It enables developers to analyze logs, inspect layouts, monitor network traffic, and even check resource consumption in an integrated manner. Its plugin-based architecture ensures extensibility, accommodating use cases ranging from simple debugging to complex scenarios in large teams.

Another crucial advancement is the Hermes engine, optimized specifically for executing JavaScript code on mobile devices. Hermes significantly reduces application startup time (time-to-interactive) while lowering memory consumption through strategies such as ahead-of-time compilation. In parallel, the Metro bundler, already part of the ecosystem, has received important improvements in code splitting and dynamic loading, contributing to smaller initial bundle sizes and faster user interface delivery.

Performance analysis tools such as react-native-performance and integrations with Chrome DevTools also allow developers to identify dropped frames, bottlenecks in virtual lists, and memory allocation issues. This level of observability, increasingly integrated into the development flow, brings React Native closer to the best practices of critical software engineering systems, where quality and reliability are non-negotiable.

Support Frameworks and Integration

The third pillar of this evolution is the consolidation of frameworks that act as "umbrella" solutions for different development processes. Expo is perhaps the most representative example. Initially seen only as a prototyping tool, it is now positioned as a robust solution for production projects, mainly due to Expo Dev Client and Expo Application Services (EAS), which simplify everything from building native packages to publishing on official app stores. This shift has transformed the perception of Expo, making it a strategic choice for teams seeking to balance delivery speed with production reliability.

Another relevant example is the combination of Reanimated + Gesture Handler, which has become the de facto standard for implementing advanced interface experiences in React Native. This synergy demonstrates that hybrid solutions are already capable of achieving usability and performance levels once reserved only for pure native applications. Similarly, the arrival of React Native Skia represents a true expansion of the boundaries of the technologies, enabling low-level graphics rendering based on the same engine used in browsers such as Chrome. This innovation opens new possibilities for interactive visualizations, custom graphics, and even applications in the gaming field.

Taken together, these advances demonstrate that the React Native ecosystem is moving toward greater professionalization, where libraries, tools, and frameworks converge to reduce development friction and expand the potential of the platform. The focus is no longer just on the feasibility of building a cross-platform app but rather on how to deliver mobile experiences with quality equivalent to native ones, without compromising deadlines and costs. This ongoing evolution positions React Native as a strategic solution for the future of mobile development, addressing not only current demands but also emerging needs for innovation.

Integration with Emerging Technologies

The trajectory of React Native goes beyond the creation of traditional mobile applications. With the popularization of **Augmented Reality (AR)**, **Virtual Reality (VR)**, and **Wearable** devices such as smartwatches and fitness trackers, demand has grown for solutions that expand the boundaries of cross-platform development. These emerging technologies not only diversify the scope of React Native but also reinforce its role as a bridge between the JavaScript ecosystem and innovative hardware available on the market.

The integration of React Native with AR and VR libraries opens the door to immersive experiences across a variety of sectors, including education, healthcare, entertainment, and retail. Frameworks such as **ViroReact** allow rendering of 3D objects in real time, enabling augmented reality features on mobile devices without the need for a dedicated native graphics engine. Similarly, **Expo AR** provides basic support for manipulating augmented environments, allowing developers to create immersive experiences within the familiar React development flow.

AR/VR in React Native (Current Landscape)

- **Camera-first AR (most common "RN AR" today): VisionCamera + frame processors:** For many production "AR-like" experiences in React Native (face filters, hand tracking overlays, live object detection), **react-native-vision-camera** is the practical foundation because its **Frame Processors** let you run per-frame analysis as **JS worklets**. Frame processors are invoked for each camera frame, and docs and examples of Vision Camera emphasize real-time processing—community plugins can reach **60+ FPS** when optimized.
- Performance caveat worth stating explicitly: frame processors run on every frame and must finish quickly (say ~16ms budget at 60 FPS) or frames will be dropped, which is why heavy pipelines often require native optimization.
- **On-device ML (MediaPipe / TensorFlow Lite) via frame-processor plugins:** A common pattern is pairing VisionCamera with **native frame processor plugins** that call into **MediaPipe** or **TensorFlow Lite** models (face detection, hand landmarks, pose, and object recognition) and return compact results to JS for rendering overlays. The plugin model of VisionCamera is designed for this style of native-per-frame processing, and community write-ups demonstrate MediaPipe-based implementations inside frame processors.
- **"True AR" (world tracking, planes, anchors) usually requires ARKit/ARCore bridges:** If you need real AR features like **plane detection, anchors, hit testing, world tracking**, most teams end up relying on **native ARKit/ARCore** and bridging into React Native, because those capabilities are platform SDK-centric. Community ARKit bridges exist (with the usual maintenance/compatibility caveats), and many production-grade AR apps still drop to native for the core tracking/rendering loop.
- **3D rendering with Three.js: feasible, but AR support varies by runtime:** For Three.js-style 3D scenes in RN, **expo-three** (with Expo GL) is a common integration path for rendering and scene management. Note that AR support has historically been separated (the expo-three repo explicitly notes AR moved to expo-three-ar), and "full AR" remains more robust when backed by ARKit/ARCore rather than relying on web-only standards.
- **WebXR in React Native is an experimental territory:** WebXR is fundamentally a **web platform** API; attempting "WebXR-like" behavior inside a React Native app tends to be experimental, with community prototypes and engine-specific approaches (for example, Babylon React Native discussions around WebXR features). Treat these as exploration rather than a default recommendation for shipping AR.
- **Apple Vision Pro / visionOS: emerging, still early:** Support for building visionOS apps with React Native is emerging via **Callstack's `react-native-visionos`** fork and docs. This is best framed as **`experimental/early-stage`**; promising for exploration and prototypes, but do expect platform gaps and a faster-moving toolchain.
- **Wearables; health data via bridges and watchOS apps are separate:** For health data access, libraries like **`react-native-health`** (HealthKit) and **`react-native-google-fit`** (Google Fit) are commonly used bridges into platform health stores.

In practice, these integrations range from educational applications—such as the visualization of three-dimensional anatomical models—to corporate systems that use augmented reality for technical training and equipment maintenance. In entertainment and marketing, AR has gained relevance through virtual try-on features or interactive catalogs, demonstrating how React Native can enhance user engagement. Although still at an early stage, these implementations highlight the ability of the framework to adapt to paradigms that go beyond conventional two-dimensional interfaces.

Development for Smartwatches and Wearable Devices

Another expanding area is development for wearables, including smartwatches, fitness bands, and medical monitoring devices. While most of these platforms offer native SDKs (such as The **WatchKit** of Apple and **Wear OS SDK** of Google), hybrid solutions have emerged to simplify integration with React Native applications.

The main goal in this context is to create a continuous ecosystem in which the main React Native application communicates directly with the wearable device, either to collect sensor data (such as heart rate and steps) or to send notifications and commands. Technologies such as **Bluetooth Low Energy (BLE)** and synchronization APIs are frequently employed, enabling scenarios where a central mobile application acts as a data hub for multiple devices.

Practical applications include digital health systems capable of monitoring metrics in real time and sending alerts to doctors and patients, as well as productivity solutions such as calendar notifications and quick replies directly on smartwatches. By integrating with these architectures, React Native enables development teams to deliver consistent experiences across different screens and device formats.

Technical Challenges and Solutions for Integration with Innovative Hardware

Despite the opportunities, integrating with AR, VR, and wearables introduces a series of technical challenges. The first is **graphics performance**. AR and VR experiences require real-time rendering, demanding low latency and high frame rates. In this regard, the reliance on intermediate layers of React Native can become a bottleneck. Hybrid solutions often need to rely on optimized native bridges, such as the **JavaScript Interface (JSI)** and **TurboModules**, to reduce communication latency between JavaScript code and native modules.

Another challenge is **device and API fragmentation**. Each wearable manufacturer or AR/VR platform provides its own kits and APIs, often with significant differences in permissions, data formats, and available features. This diversity increases maintenance complexity and hinders the standardization of universal libraries. A common approach has been the use of open-source abstraction layers that encapsulate APIs of multiple vendors, thereby enabling developers to interact through a single interface.

Security and privacy concerns also become central, particularly in the case of body-monitoring devices. The handling of sensitive data, such as medical information, requires compliance with regulations like **LGPD** and **GDPR**, as well as the implementation of best practices in encryption and consent management.

Despite these obstacles, there is active community engagement in developing solutions that bridge the gap between React Native and emerging technologies. Open-source projects, collaborative documentation, and initiatives from major companies (such as Meta and Microsoft) have helped turn integration with AR, VR, and wearables into a promising field, significantly expanding the scope of cross-platform development.

Integration with emerging technologies confirms the potential of React Native as a development platform that not only keeps pace with mobile industry trends but also projects itself into the future. Whether in creating immersive AR/VR experiences or in building integrated ecosystems with wearable devices, the framework demonstrates adaptability and scalability. Although technical challenges still present significant barriers, the continuous evolution of libraries, APIs, and best practices signals a scenario in which React Native will play a central role in the convergence of mobility, immersion, and connectivity.

New Features and API Proposals

The evolution of the core of React Native in recent years has been driven by a deep architectural redesign, aimed at reducing long-standing bottlenecks in the communication between the JavaScript and native layers. This transformation is supported by three fundamental pillars: **Fabric**, **TurboModules**, and the **JavaScript Interface (JSI)**. These initiatives represent more than just simple code updates; they signal a paradigm shift in how React Native handles rendering, interoperability, and extensibility.

The first element in this renewal is **Fabric**, the new rendering engine. Unlike the previous model, where communication between JavaScript code and native elements was managed by an asynchronous bridge based on JSON serialization, **Fabric** introduces a more direct and efficient rendering process. By adopting the concept of concurrency and aligning with the evolution of React (notably React 18 and Concurrent Rendering), Fabric allows for faster updates, better control over rendering priorities, and greater consistency between Android and iOS platforms. In practice, this translates into more responsive interfaces with lower latency perceptible to the end user.

In parallel, **TurboModules** redefine the way native APIs are accessed. Previously, each native module relied on the JSON-based bridge system, which created overhead and performance limitations. With **TurboModules**, integrated with JSI, synchronous direct calls between JavaScript and native code are possible, significantly reducing communication costs and enabling more complex operations without perceptible degradation of the user experience.

The **JavaScript Interface (JSI)**, in turn, forms the foundation of this renewed architecture. Unlike the traditional bridge, JSI is a flexible interoperability layer that connects the JavaScript engine (whether Hermes, V8, or JavaScriptCore) to the native code without the need for intermediate serialization. This approach opens new possibilities, such as integrating multiple JavaScript engines, supporting C++-written modules more transparently, and enabling more efficient execution of critical tasks on mobile devices.

Proposals under Discussion and the Community Roadmap

The React Native community roadmap, led by the React Native Core Contributors Working Group and the Meta teams, reflects an ongoing effort toward ecosystem stabilization and modernization. Among the proposals under discussion, the following stand out:

- Enhanced **Codegen** for TurboModules and Fabric, which automates the creation of bindings between JavaScript and native modules, reducing the risk of inconsistencies and increasing productivity.
- Support for multiple JavaScript engines, consolidating the possibility of choosing between Hermes, V8, and others, depending on performance or compatibility needs.
- Deeper integration with React 18+, leveraging features such as Suspense and Concurrent Mode in mobile scenarios, with a direct impact on the smoothness of transitions and the loading of asynchronous data.
- Extensibility of **DevTools** for unified debugging, allowing developers to inspect applications with more granularity, subsequently including detailed memory analysis, concurrent execution, and native threads.

This set of proposals reveals an effort to make React Native not only competitive against alternatives like Flutter or Kotlin Multiplatform but also more predictable and robust for enterprise-level use.

Impacts on Performance, Interoperability, and Enterprise Adoption

The structural changes brought by Fabric, TurboModules, and JSI have a direct impact on application performance. The reduction of latency between layers and the adoption of concurrent rendering contribute to smoother interfaces, even on devices with limited resources. This aspect is crucial for emerging markets, where entry-level hardware still represents a significant portion of the user base.

In terms of interoperability, the new architecture brings React Native closer to ecosystems previously considered out of reach. The possibility of direct integration with C++ modules or the adoption of different JavaScript engines broadens the configuration options depending on the project profile. This is particularly relevant for companies needing to integrate React Native into legacy systems, optimized low-level libraries, or more complex cross-platform architectures.

Finally, regarding enterprise adoption, these changes offer greater predictability and security for organizations considering React Native as the foundation for their mobile applications. The stability of the architecture, combined with the ability to closely follow the official roadmap and community RFCs (Request for Comments), strengthens the perception that React Native is a technology not only for the short term but also for the long lifecycle. Large companies, seeing practical performance and scalability gains, find stronger justification to invest in specialized teams for the platform.

The innovations in the core of React Native are not limited to incremental improvements; they represent a fundamental reconstruction of the technological base of the framework. The trio of **Fabric**, **TurboModules**, and **JSI** symbolizes the transition from an architecture based on asynchronous bridges to a more direct, modern, and performant model. Along with the dynamism of the proposals under discussion by the community, this evolution projects a future in which React Native will become increasingly competitive, interoperable, and capable of meeting both independent projects and large-scale enterprise demands.

Security, Privacy, and Compliance in React Native

As React Native applications grow in scale and begin to handle increasingly sensitive data, concerns around security and privacy shift from being an afterthought to becoming central architectural priorities. Protecting user trust, complying with regulatory frameworks, and ensuring that security practices can be maintained across long-lived projects are now just as important as delivering performant and visually polished applications.

Security begins with a clear understanding of the risks of the system. Teams benefit from lightweight threat modeling exercises that identify assets, potential attack surfaces, and realistic threats. By classifying data—whether public, internal, confidential, or restricted—developers can define clear rules for how information should be stored, transmitted, and retained. On the device side, this often means relying on secure storage mechanisms provided by the operating system, such as iOS Keychain or Android Keystore, instead of defaulting to solutions like AsyncStorage for sensitive tokens. Where persistent storage is unavoidable, database encryption solutions such as SQLCipher or Realm with encryption enabled can help reduce exposure.

At the network level, best practices like enforcing TLS 1.2+ connections, rotating API keys, and adopting OAuth with PKCE flows ensure that communication between the mobile client and backend is resilient against interception. Beyond encryption, developers must also consider how to enforce least-privilege principles by scoping backend permissions carefully, validating inputs server-side, and avoiding assumptions that the client alone can guarantee integrity.

A particular challenge in modern mobile development is supply chain integrity. React Native projects often depend on hundreds of third-party packages, making dependency hygiene essential. Automated tools such as Renovate or Dependabot can keep libraries up to date and mitigate vulnerabilities. Static and dynamic analysis pipelines, along with mobile-specific scanning tools, reduce the risk of inadvertently shipping insecure code. Similarly, careful review of third-party SDKs—for analytics, ads, or payments—is essential, not only to minimize attack surfaces but also to comply with increasingly strict privacy regulations.

Privacy-by-design must also become part of the React Native workflow. Developers are encouraged to request permissions just-in-time, provide clear explanations for why access is needed, and avoid collecting unnecessary data. In applications that process sensitive domains like health or financial information, compliance with regulations such as GDPR and LGPD demands transparent consent management, anonymization where possible, and robust encryption for data both in transit and at rest.

Compliance, however, is not merely a checklist—it requires auditable processes. Documenting key architectural decisions through ADRs (Architecture Decision Records), establishing clear incident response playbooks, and tracking release histories that note which SDKs and libraries were included all contribute to transparency and accountability. Continuous monitoring is equally important: metrics like time-to-patch for vulnerabilities, crash-free user rates after security updates, and user acceptance rates for permission prompts offer concrete feedback on whether security practices are effective.

In this light, security and privacy should not be seen as burdens but as features in their own right, designed, tested, and iterated with the same rigor as performance or user experience. React Native teams that embed these practices into their culture will be better positioned to deliver trustworthy applications that endure in highly regulated, competitive markets.

Server-Driven UI, Superapps, and Multi-Experience Orchestration

Another significant trend in the evolution of React Native is the growing adoption of server-driven user interfaces and the rise of superapps that consolidate multiple experiences into a single container. Instead of treating the mobile application as a static binary that requires an app store update for every UI change, organizations are increasingly using React Native as a runtime capable of rendering layouts, flows, and behaviors defined by server-side configurations.

The rationale is straightforward: business requirements change faster than mobile release cycles allow. Companies want to update copy, layouts, and even feature availability instantly, without waiting for store approvals. By representing screens through schemas delivered from the backend, React Native clients can render content dynamically, cache assets for offline use, and gracefully handle fallbacks when network conditions are poor. This model has proved particularly effective for applications that need to serve multiple markets, where regulations, languages, and branding requirements may vary.

Yet this approach brings its own technical challenges. Rendering remote payloads requires a carefully designed component registry on the client side, ensuring that server instructions map safely to predictable React Native primitives. Validation layers are essential to prevent corrupted or malicious payloads from causing failures, and performance budgets must be enforced to avoid overloading devices with deeply nested layouts or heavy assets. Server-driven design must balance flexibility with guardrails, ensuring that user experience remains smooth while updates remain fast.

Superapps take this concept further by combining multiple independent modules—often called mini-apps—within a shared container. In such architectures, React Native provides the shell, navigation, and design system, while each domain team develops and maintains its own vertical, such as payments, chat, or marketplace features. This modular approach distributes ownership, allowing teams to release independently while maintaining consistent branding and performance across the platform. However, the benefits of autonomy and rapid iteration come at the cost of additional governance: clear contracts must be defined between the shell and modules, testing strategies must ensure compatibility, and robust monitoring must be in place to trigger rollbacks or kill switches when issues are detected.

Observability plays a crucial role in this paradigm. It becomes important not only to track traditional metrics like crashes or network failures, but also to correlate which server-defined schema version was rendered on which client and how it affected performance or engagement. This granularity allows organizations to roll out features gradually, validate them in real time, and withdraw them seamlessly if problems arise.

Despite the operational overhead, server-driven UI and superapp architectures represent a powerful evolution for React Native. They extend the role of the framework from being simply a development tool to becoming a dynamic delivery platform, enabling global products to adapt instantly to changing business conditions. While not every project needs this level of complexity, for enterprises managing multiple markets or high-frequency updates, the flexibility of React Native makes it an ideal foundation for orchestrating multi-experience ecosystems.

Cross-Platform beyond Mobile: React Native for Desktop and Web

The boundaries of React Native are no longer confined to mobile development. With initiatives like React Native for Windows and macOS, as well as React Native Web, the framework has extended its reach into desktop and browser environments. This shift aligns with the broader industry trend of converging experiences across devices, where users expect seamless transitions between mobile, desktop, and web platforms.

React Native Web, in particular, demonstrates the adaptability of the framework. By mapping React Native components to standard web primitives, teams can reuse large portions of their codebase across iOS, Android, and browsers. This approach reduces duplication, accelerates delivery, and ensures that updates reach all platforms simultaneously. In enterprise contexts, it enables consistent branding and interaction models across internal dashboards, customer-facing portals, and mobile applications.

On the desktop side, the support of Microsoft for React Native Windows and macOS has created a viable ecosystem for building native desktop apps using React Native principles. Applications such as Microsoft Office products and third-party enterprise tools have adopted this approach to unify their development pipelines. The challenge here lies in handling desktop-specific paradigms—such as multiple windows, system tray interactions, and advanced keyboard shortcuts—that differ significantly from mobile UX. Still, the ability to target multiple device classes with a shared knowledge base underscores the position of React Native as a true cross-platform development paradigm.

This convergence beyond mobile points toward a future where React Native is less about iOS and Android specifically, and more about delivering experiences across a wide spectrum of form factors. Developers who embrace these capabilities will be able to design for an ecosystem of devices rather than isolated platforms.

Cloud-Native Integration and Edge Computing

Another transformative trend for React Native is its growing relationship with cloud-native architectures and edge computing. Modern applications are rarely self-contained; they depend on scalable backends, real-time data pipelines, and intelligent services delivered through the cloud. For React Native developers, the challenge is to build mobile clients that integrate seamlessly with this distributed infrastructure while still providing responsive and reliable experiences on devices.

The rise of serverless computing—through platforms such as AWS Lambda, Azure Functions, and Google Cloud Functions—has reshaped the way APIs and event-driven interactions are designed. React Native applications can consume lightweight endpoints that scale dynamically with user demand, enabling startups and enterprises alike to deliver global solutions without managing complex server fleets. At the same time, GraphQL APIs have become increasingly popular, particularly when paired with tools like Apollo or Relay, as they offer flexible and efficient data fetching tailored to mobile environments where bandwidth is limited.

Edge computing introduces another dimension. By moving computation closer to the user—whether at telecom data centers or IoT hubs—applications can achieve lower latency and better reliability even under poor connectivity. React Native apps that integrate with edge services can offer real-time capabilities, such as multiplayer gaming, AR streaming, or predictive analytics in industrial environments, without relying exclusively on centralized cloud endpoints.

This evolution suggests that the role of the mobile developer is expanding into cloud-native thinking. Designing for scalability, fault tolerance, and distributed architectures is no longer optional—it is an expected part of delivering modern React Native applications. The adaptability of framework ensures that it can act as the front-end bridge to increasingly sophisticated backend and edge ecosystems.

Observability, Monitoring, and Data-Driven Improvement

As applications grow in complexity, the ability to monitor, analyze, and improve them based on real-world data has become a defining factor for long-term success. Observability in React Native projects goes far beyond simple crash reporting; it now encompasses comprehensive monitoring of performance, resource usage, user flows, and even business KPIs, all integrated into the development lifecycle.

Tools like Sentry, Firebase Crashlytics, and Bugsnag have made it easier to detect and prioritize issues in production. Beyond crash detection, however, modern teams increasingly rely on telemetry pipelines that integrate logging, tracing, and metrics collection into centralized dashboards, often backed by systems like Datadog, Grafana, or Elastic Stack. These platforms provide insights into frame rates, memory consumption, network latency, and the behavior of virtualized lists, enabling teams to diagnose subtle performance degradations before they affect the majority of users.

Equally important is the feedback loop between users and developers. Collecting and analyzing user behavior data—such as navigation flows, feature adoption rates, and session duration—allows teams to refine UX and prioritize features based on evidence rather than assumptions. When combined with A/B testing powered by feature flags and staged rollouts, this creates a continuous cycle of experimentation, validation, and improvement.

Data-driven improvement is not only about enhancing performance but also about aligning applications with business outcomes. Metrics such as conversion rates, retention, and churn provide critical signals for whether the technical decisions being made are supporting organizational goals. For React Native teams, cultivating a culture of observability ensures that applications are not just functional at launch, but continuously evolving to deliver better user experiences over time.

Integration of Artificial Intelligence with React Native

The incorporation of Artificial Intelligence (AI) into mobile applications is no longer a differentiator but a competitive requirement across multiple industries. From e-commerce and healthcare to education and entertainment, intelligent features now shape the way users interact with digital services. Capabilities such as virtual assistants, personalized recommendations, voice and image recognition, fraud detection, and predictive analytics are already embedded in large-scale applications, redefining expectations around usability and engagement. React Native, thanks to its flexible and cross-platform foundation, provides fertile ground for integrating AI solutions, whether through JavaScript/ TypeScript libraries or through interoperability with specialized native modules.

AI integration in mobile development is not just about convenience; it is about enabling applications to adapt, learn, and evolve in real time. For instance, financial apps employ machine learning models to detect fraudulent behavior by analyzing spending patterns, while health platforms rely on AI-powered image recognition to interpret medical scans or wearable data. Education apps, on the other hand, are beginning to integrate adaptive learning systems that customize the pace and difficulty of lessons based on individual progress, offering a tailored experience that traditional static apps cannot replicate.

Common areas where AI has proven highly impactful in React Native applications include:

- **Natural Language Processing (NLP):** Chatbots and virtual assistants integrated with services like Dialogflow, Rasa, or the OpenAI API enable users to interact with applications conversationally. These assistants can handle customer service, task automation, and even voice-driven navigation, reducing friction and improving accessibility.
- **Image recognition and computer vision:** Libraries such as TensorFlow.js or native integrations with CoreML (iOS) and ML Kit (Android) allow detection of objects, faces, and text in real time. This capability is particularly valuable in sectors like retail (virtual try-on solutions), logistics (barcode scanning), and healthcare (diagnosis support).
- **Personalized recommendations:** Recommendation engines, powered by backend machine learning models, help applications suggest products, content, or features tailored to the behavior of each user. React Native serves as the front-end layer consuming APIs that deliver these recommendations, directly influencing engagement and revenue.
- **Sentiment analysis and feedback interpretation:** By analyzing reviews, comments, and even voice tone, applications can proactively adjust services or trigger support interventions, enhancing overall user satisfaction.

These examples illustrate how AI extends the potential of React Native, allowing developers to create applications that move beyond static interfaces into adaptive, intelligent systems capable of anticipating user needs.

Technical Integration Strategies

Developers have multiple pathways to integrate AI into React Native projects, each with trade-offs in terms of performance, scalability, and complexity.

The **most common approach** is consuming **external AI APIs** from providers such as AWS AI Services, Google Cloud AI, or Azure Cognitive Services. These cloud platforms expose pre-trained models for vision, speech, translation, or text analysis, which can be consumed via REST or GraphQL. This method lowers entry barriers, as teams can leverage highly optimized services without building models from scratch.

A more advanced strategy involves **embedding models directly on the device** using libraries like TensorFlow Lite or ONNX Runtime. Running inference locally provides two advantages: reduced dependency on network connectivity and improved privacy since data does not leave the device. However, this approach requires careful performance optimization, as heavy models can drain battery and slow down low-end devices. Techniques such as quantization, pruning, and model distillation are often applied to make these models mobile-friendly.

For scenarios demanding maximum performance or deeper control, **native bridges** become essential. By developing custom modules in Swift or Kotlin and connecting them to React Native via

TurboModules and JSI, developers can integrate directly with CoreML, PyTorch Mobile, or specialized GPU frameworks. This hybrid approach enables efficient communication between JavaScript and the native AI runtime, ensuring smooth execution of complex tasks like augmented reality object tracking or live speech translation.

Challenges, Ethics, and Best Practices

While the promise of AI in React Native is compelling, implementation introduces a unique set of challenges. The most immediate concern is **real-time performance**. Running complex models on entry-level devices often results in lag or poor responsiveness, undermining user experience. To mitigate this, developers should balance local and server-side inference, relying on edge-optimized models where possible and offloading heavy computation to backend services when necessary.

Data privacy is another critical challenge. Many AI-driven applications process sensitive data such as voice recordings, biometric information, or health metrics. Ensuring compliance with regulations like GDPR, LGPD, and HIPAA is non-negotiable. Secure data handling, transparent consent flows, and user controls for opting in or out of AI features must be designed from the start.

Beyond compliance, developers must consider **ethical dimensions**. Bias in AI models can lead to unfair or discriminatory outcomes, particularly in areas like hiring, lending, or healthcare recommendations. Integrating bias detection tools, ensuring diverse training datasets, and communicating clearly with users about how AI-driven decisions are made are all part of responsible AI development.

Another ongoing challenge is the **rapid pace of evolution in AI frameworks**. Libraries like TensorFlow.js, PyTorch Mobile, and ONNX Runtime are updated frequently, sometimes introducing breaking changes or deprecating features. Teams must commit to continuous monitoring and regular updates to ensure compatibility and security. This also implies that developers need to cultivate a culture of ongoing learning, staying ahead of shifts in AI technology.

Future Directions

Looking ahead, the convergence of React Native and AI will continue to reshape the mobile landscape. Emerging techniques such as **federated learning** promise to enable collaborative model training across devices without centralizing user data, addressing both privacy concerns and personalization needs. Similarly, advances in **on-device neural acceleration**—through the Neural Engine of Apple or AI processors of Qualcomm—will expand the feasibility of executing sophisticated models on smartphones and wearables.

AI-driven features will also intersect with other trends highlighted in this chapter, such as AR/VR and wearables. For example, AR applications can integrate AI-based object recognition to create interactive learning tools, while fitness wearables can combine AI and React Native to provide predictive insights about user health. In e-commerce, blending AI with server-driven UI may enable apps that dynamically reconfigure shopping experiences in real time, adapting not only to market changes but also to individual behavior.

The integration of AI with React Native transforms applications from static interfaces into adaptive ecosystems that learn, predict, and personalize experiences at scale. By leveraging a spectrum of strategies, from consuming cloud APIs to deploying embedded models or building native bridges developers can tailor AI integration to their specific business and technical requirements. At the same time, addressing challenges around performance, privacy, and ethics ensures that these innovations are sustainable and trustworthy.

Ultimately, the flexibility of React Native positions it as an ideal vehicle for bringing AI-driven experiences to millions of users across platforms. As mobile technology continues to converge with artificial intelligence, the framework will play a central role in shaping the digital future, where applications are not only responsive but also intelligent, predictive, and deeply personalized.

Community Contributions and Open Source

One of the key factors for the longevity and relevance of React Native is its open and collaborative nature. Unlike closed-source frameworks, whose evolution depends exclusively on internal corporate decisions, React Native has an ecosystem built and maintained collectively, where the community plays a central role not only in maintaining the source code but also in defining strategic guidelines for the future of the project. This characteristic ensures continuous innovation, rapid problem resolution, and the creation of solutions that reflect the real needs of developers in different contexts.

The core of React Native is coordinated by the Meta team (formerly Facebook), but its practical support depends on hundreds of independent contributors and organizations that actively participate in the development cycle. The community is responsible for opening issues, submitting pull requests, reviewing changes to codebase, and maintaining satellite libraries that complement the main framework.

This distributed governance reflects the model of modern open-source projects: leading companies provide infrastructure and strategic direction, while the community contributes creative energy and diverse use cases. The result is an innovation cycle that would be difficult to replicate in closed environments, as each new library or bug fix often originates from a practical problem faced by developers in production.

How to Collaborate with Libraries, Documentation, and RFCs

The React Native ecosystem is organized around multiple repositories distributed on GitHub, each with its own scope. Collaboration can occur at different levels:

- **Libraries**: Developers can create extensions for functionalities not covered by the core, such as integration with sensors, cameras, or native operating system APIs. Many of these packages start as personal projects and, over time, become essential parts of the ecosystem.
- **Documentation**: The official documentation is collaborative in nature, and improvements in clarity, translations into other languages, or the inclusion of code examples are highly valued contributions. Since React Native is adopted globally, internationalization efforts have a significant impact on the spread of the technology.
- **RFCs (Request for Comments)**: Inspired by governance models from languages such as Rust or projects like ReactJS, RFCs serve as formal proposals for changes to the core of the framework. Through this process, any community member can suggest improvements, discuss technical feasibility, and take part in decision-making about the future of the project.

Together, these mechanisms ensure not only code quality but also transparency and legitimacy in architectural decisions.

Examples of Successful Collective Contribution Initiatives

Several initiatives illustrate the positive impact of community contribution within the React Native ecosystem. A notable example is the migration of critical libraries to the **react-native-community** organization on GitHub, which centralizes essential projects such as *react-native-camera*, *react-native-device-info*, and *react-native-maps*. This initiative reduced fragmentation and facilitated collaborative governance, allowing packages once maintained by isolated individuals to benefit from continuous support by multiple maintainers.

Another emblematic case is **Expo**, which, although developed by a specific company, maintains a strong connection with the community and evolves through open contributions. The same applies to the **React Native Directory**, a collaboratively maintained catalog of libraries that helps developers quickly identify reliable solutions for their projects.

In addition, the creation of tools such as **Flipper**, widely adopted for debugging, and the engagement around the **Hermes Engine** demonstrate how collaboration between companies (Meta, Microsoft, Shopify) and the open-source community drives advancements that benefit the entire user base.

Community contributions and the open-source model are not just accessories to React Native but constitute the backbone of its evolution. Without this collective effort, it would be unlikely to sustain the pace of innovation required to keep up with the demands of the mobile market. The possibility for any developer, regardless of geographical location or institutional affiliation to directly influence the future of the framework reinforces the inclusive and democratic nature of the technology. More than just a development tool, React Native emerges as a living ecosystem shaped by the ongoing interaction between companies, independent developers, and local and global communities.

Sustainability and Longevity of React Native

The question of technological sustainability is one of the decisive factors for organizations considering the adoption of a cross-platform development framework. The choice involves not only immediate technical aspects but also an analysis of long-term viability: will the technology continue to be maintained, evolve, and meet market demands in the coming years? In this scenario, React Native has established itself as a stable and promising option, even in the face of strong competitors such as Flutter and Kotlin Multiplatform Mobile (KMM).

Flutter, maintained by Google, is perhaps the most direct competitor of React Native. Its main advantage lies in the use of the **Skia graphics engine**, which ensures full control over interface rendering and visual standardization across different platforms. This results in high aesthetic consistency as well as stable performance, especially in complex animations. However, this same level of control comes at a higher cost of updates: Flutter applications ship with the rendering engine, which can increase the size of the final package. Moreover, the relative youth of the ecosystem still limits the availability of mature libraries widely tested in production, compared to the vast repository accumulated by React Native since 2015.

Kotlin Multiplatform Mobile (KMM), an initiative by JetBrains with support from Google, adopts a different strategy. Instead of fully abstracting the UI layer, as React Native and Flutter do, KMM focuses on sharing business logic, while graphical interfaces are implemented natively in Swift (iOS) and Kotlin/Java (Android). This approach ensures native performance and full freedom in the interface layer but, at the same time, reduces productivity gains for teams seeking a single codebase for the entire application.

React Native, by positioning itself between these two approaches, seeks balance: it abstracts the interface layer to allow code reuse while preserving the ability to integrate with native components when necessary. This flexibility distinguishes it both from the highly controlled model of Flutter and from the partial focus of KMM.

Factors that Reinforce the Permanence of React Native in the Market

Several elements sustain the longevity of React Native. First is the **maturity of its community and ecosystem**: with millions of developers, thousands of maintained libraries, and a vast learning base available through courses, videos, and documentation, the framework has reached a level of consolidation that is difficult to replicate quickly by newer competitors.

Another relevant factor is its **alignment with the evolution of React**, which continues to be one of the most widely used libraries in web development. The synergy between React for the web and React Native for mobile creates a smoother learning curve and ensures that innovations launched in the React ecosystem (such as hooks, concurrent rendering, and server components) are incorporated into the mobile environment relatively naturally.

In addition, **technological adaptability** has proven to be a central characteristic of React Native. The transition from the old bridge-based architecture to the new structure with **Fabric, TurboModules, and JSI** demonstrates not only a commitment to technical evolution but also the ability of the community and Meta to redesign core components without losing backward compatibility. This technological plasticity contributes to the perception of security for companies that require long-term stability.

Adoption by Major Companies as an Indicator of Long-Term Viability

The sustainability of a technology can also be measured by its adoption at an enterprise scale. React Native is used in globally impactful applications such as **Facebook, Instagram, Walmart, Bloomberg, Discord, Shopify, and Microsoft** (through products like Office Lens and parts of Teams). These examples not only demonstrate the ability of the framework to handle high-traffic and complex demands but also serve as implicit guarantees of continuity: it is unlikely that a technology central to the products of major corporations would be abandoned in the short term.

Another highlight is the use of React Native in fast-growing digital product companies such as **Airbnb** (in earlier phases), **UberEats**, and **Pinterest**, which have explored or continue to explore the framework to accelerate development. This diversity of cases shows that React Native can be applied both in robust corporate contexts and in startups that prioritize delivery speed.

The commitment of **Meta**, the original maintaining company, also reinforces the future viability of the framework. Even though part of the maintenance is in the hands of the community, the presence of a large organization ensures ongoing investment in research, infrastructure, and strategic roadmap planning.

The comparative analysis with Flutter and Kotlin Multiplatform reveals that React Native occupies a unique position in the cross-platform framework landscape: mature enough to support large-scale applications, yet flexible enough to keep up with new market trends. Its sustainability is based not only on technical characteristics but also on the size of its community, its synergy with the React ecosystem, and the trust placed in it by global companies.

In terms of longevity, React Native has already demonstrated resilience against waves of technological hype and remains one of the most solid choices for cross-platform mobile development. By balancing productivity, flexibility, and robustness, the framework reinforces its position as a strategic technology that will continue to play a central role in the future of mobile development.

The Future of the Mobile Developer

The mobile development landscape is in constant transformation, driven by the evolution of frameworks, the spread of smart devices, and the growing expectation of users for immersive, personalized, and high-performance digital experiences. In this context, the role of the mobile developer is no longer restricted to mastering a specific operating system (iOS or Android) but increasingly requires a multidisciplinary profile, capable of working across different platforms, languages, and development paradigms. For professionals specialized in React Native, this shift represents both challenges and opportunities, reinforcing the need for emerging skills and continuous adaptation strategies.

The future of the React Native developer demands competencies that go beyond mastery of the framework itself. First, a deep understanding of software architecture becomes essential, including concepts such as modularization, separation of concerns, and integration with distributed services. The complexity of modern applications requires developers to structure scalable, resilient, and sustainable solutions over the long term.

Additionally, knowledge of native languages (Swift, Objective-C, Kotlin, and Java) is becoming increasingly important. Although React Native abstracts much of the interaction with the operating system, integration with native modules will remain a necessity in complex projects. Developers capable of building custom bridges or optimizing specific resources will hold a significant competitive advantage.

Another set of emerging skills involves user experience (UX) and accessibility. With the growing demand for inclusive and globally accessible applications, mastery of standards such as WCAG and inclusive design best practices is becoming a valuable differentiator. Similarly, familiarity with augmented reality (AR), virtual reality (VR), and wearable devices broadens the opportunities for React Native developers to operate in innovative fields.

The Profile of the Cross-Platform Developer in Evolving Market Scenarios

The current market increasingly values cross-platform developers capable of building consistent solutions that transcend operating system barriers. This profile is defined by three main characteristics:

- **Technological versatility**: The modern developer must be able to work across React Native, competing frameworks (Flutter, KMM), and complementary technologies (such as Node.js on the backend), adapting according to the demands of each project.
- **Product-oriented vision**: More than just coding, professionals are expected to understand business objectives and propose technical solutions aligned with the strategic goals of the organization.
- **Collaboration in distributed ecosystems**: With teams that are increasingly remote and multicultural, the ability to contribute in open-source environments, adopt DevOps practices, and integrate CI/CD workflows is now part of the expected routine of a cross-platform developer.

In this sense, the future of the mobile developer is less about mastering a single tool and more about cultivating transversal competencies that allow for agile responses to market changes and the rapid pace of technological obsolescence.

Preparing for Career Trends and New Opportunities

Preparing for the future of a career in mobile development requires a combination of continuous learning and strategic positioning. The first step is to stay updated on the React Native roadmap and the most relevant libraries in the ecosystem, ensuring that practices adopted in projects are aligned with innovations brought by Fabric, TurboModules, and JSI.

Furthermore, active participation in open-source communities and contributions to collaborative projects are ways to establish technical authority and expand professional networks. This engagement not only strengthens professional reputation but also provides early access to emerging trends and opportunities.

Another key aspect is investing in adjacent skills such as mobile application security, real-time data analysis, and integration with cloud services (AWS, Firebase, and Azure). The convergence of mobile development, cloud computing, and artificial intelligence is expected to define the future of the industry, and professionals prepared to operate across these domains will be better positioned.

Finally, continuous development of soft skills—such as communication, problem-solving, and teamwork—complements technical expertise and enhances employability in a globalized market. The mobile developer of the future will not only be a code executor but also a professional capable of articulating technological solutions aligned with the needs of users, businesses, and society.

The future of the React Native developer—and, by extension, the cross-platform mobile developer—is intrinsically linked to their ability to adapt to emerging technologies and evolving market demands. The expected profile is that of a hybrid professional who combines advanced technical knowledge in React Native and native languages, product vision, community engagement, and continuous preparation for innovations such as AR, VR, wearables, and AI integrations.

Thus, more than ensuring employability, this set of competencies positions the mobile developer as a key player in digital transformation, operating in an ecosystem that will continue to grow in importance and global impact.

Conclusion

In this chapter, we have explored the emerging trends and the future of React Native, broadening the perspective beyond immediate technical practices and projecting possible scenarios for the coming years. We began with an analysis of the evolution of the ecosystem, observing how libraries, support frameworks, and debugging and optimization tools have been transforming cross-platform development into a more mature and professional discipline. We then examined the integration with emerging technologies—ranging from augmented and virtual reality to wearable devices—that reposition mobile applications as part of intelligent, connected ecosystems.

We also looked at the structural advancements in the core of React Native, with the arrival of Fabric, TurboModules, and JSI, which redefine the architecture and usher in a new cycle of performance and interoperability. Alongside this, we considered the central role of the open-source community in this process, from maintaining essential libraries to proposing RFCs and building collaborative solutions that sustain the growth of the framework. The comparison with competitors such as Flutter and Kotlin Multiplatform reinforced the perception that React Native holds unique characteristics that ensure its longevity: maturity, flexibility, and widespread adoption by global companies.

However, more than just a technical analysis, this chapter also reflected on the future of the mobile developer. We saw that the profile of this professional is no longer limited to mastering a single framework but requires a skill set that spans multiple domains: integration with native modules, expertise in accessibility and inclusive UX, collaboration in distributed environments, and increasingly, the ability to integrate AI-based solutions. This last point is particularly noteworthy: the convergence of React Native and AI opens a horizon of possibilities for creating applications that learn, adapt, and deliver personalized experiences at scale.

We have now reached the conclusion of this journey. Throughout the chapters, you progressed from environment setup and the fundamentals of React Native to publishing complete applications in official stores, passing through architecture, optimization, testing, CI/CD, and finally, the trends shaping the future of cross-platform development. The aim has always been to offer not only a technical guide but also a strategic roadmap that connects practice, theory, and long-term vision.

If there is a final message this book conveys, it is that React Native should not be seen merely as a set of tools but as a living ecosystem, sustained by community collaboration and constant technological reinvention. The future of mobile applications will depend on the ability to integrate innovation, sustainability, and adaptability—three qualities that React Native has already been demonstrating.

By completing this reading, you are now prepared not only to develop high-quality cross-platform applications but also to actively contribute to the evolution of this ecosystem. Whether by building new libraries, contributing to the community, integrating AI, or exploring frontiers such as AR, VR, and wearables, your work can directly shape the future of technology. The next step is no longer within these pages—it is in your hands, in the code you will write, the products you will launch, and the contributions you will make to a constantly evolving market.

Questions

Before closing this chapter—and also the book—it is important to reflect on how emerging trends, new technical features, and the role of the community can influence your own project decisions. The questions below were designed to help you transform concepts into practice, evaluating how to position yourself strategically within the React Native ecosystem in the coming years.

1. How would you assess the adoption of new emerging libraries (including Reanimated, Skia, and Zustand)? What criteria would you use to decide between the stability of mature packages and the innovation of more recent tools?
2. When faced with a project that requires digital immersion, how would you design the integration of AR/VR or wearables in React Native? What technical and performance limitations would you anticipate, and how would you mitigate them?
3. In what ways would the adoption of Fabric, TurboModules, and JSI impact your architecture of the application? How would you validate the performance gains compared to the traditional bridge model?
4. What would be your strategy for contributing to the React Native community? Would you collaborate on libraries, documentation, or RFC proposals? How could this practice strengthen your career and your professional network?
5. When comparing React Native with Flutter and Kotlin Multiplatform, which factors would be decisive for your choice in a real project (available team, native integration, time-to-market, long-term maintenance)?
6. How would you prepare, as a developer, for the future of cross-platform mobile development? Which new competencies (such as accessibility, AI, data security, native integrations) would you prioritize in your learning path?
7. In what scenarios would it make sense to incorporate artificial intelligence into your React Native application? Would you opt for cloud services (AWS, Azure, GCP), embedded models (TensorFlow Lite, ONNX), or native bridges with CoreML/PyTorch?
8. What technological sustainability indicators would you monitor to ensure the longevity of your React Native project (library adoption, community support, API stability, production performance metrics)?
9. How would you balance innovation and stability when adopting emerging features? What processes (testing, canary releases, feature flags) would you implement to reduce risks when experimenting with new APIs or libraries in production?
10. What long-term vision do you have for your role as a React Native developer? How would you position yourself not only to use the framework but also to contribute to shaping its future?

Answering these questions will help consolidate the learning from this chapter, enabling you to envision not only how to apply React Native today but also how to sustain your relevance in an ecosystem that is constantly evolving.

Key Terms

- **Architecture Trade-off:** A technical decision where certain benefits (for instance delivery speed) are prioritized over others (say performance), directly impacting the evolution of the project and its ability to adapt to new demands.
- **Monorepo:** A single repository structure containing multiple modules/projects, promoting reuse and consistency but potentially increasing build time and coupling between system components.

- **Multi-repo:** A structure with separate repositories for each service or component, allowing greater autonomy and isolation but requiring more integration and synchronization between them.
- **Module Boundary:** A logical boundary of a code module (for example authentication, catalog, payments) to facilitate maintenance, testing, and reuse across multiple projects or teams.
- **State Management:** Strategies for managing application state, such as Redux Toolkit, Context API, Zustand, and React Query/Apollo, chosen based on scalability, complexity, and performance needs.
- **Offline-First:** An architecture that prioritizes operation without network connection, storing data locally (`AsyncStorage`, `SQLite`, `Realm`) and synchronizing changes when the network is available.
- **Performance Budget:** A predefined limit for metrics such as load time, bundle size, and memory usage, preventing performance regressions throughout the lifecycle of the application.
- **Virtualized List:** Components such as `FlatList/SectionList` that render only visible content, optimizing memory and performance in large lists, essential for developing applications with large data volumes.
- **Feature Flag:** A mechanism for dynamically enabling/disabling features, allowing for the safe deployment of incomplete code or conducting A/B experiments without impacting the user base.
- **Debt Register:** A documented record of technical debt, including the reason, impact, and resolution plan, to prevent uncontrolled accumulation of tasks and required refactoring over time.
- **Git Flow:** A versioning strategy with main branches such as `main`, `develop`, `feature/`, `release/`, and `hotfix/*` to manage predictable releases and collaboration among teams.
- **Trunk-Based Development:** A strategy of frequent commits to the main branch, with intensive use of feature flags to control feature exposure and minimize regression risks.
- **Pull Request (PR):** A code merge request reviewed by other team members to ensure quality, consistency, and adherence to project standards.
- **Code Review Checklist:** A list of mandatory criteria (such as tests, linting, and documentation) to be verified before a PR is approved, ensuring the quality of the code delivered.
- **Linting/Formatting:** Tools (`ESLint`, `Prettier`) that automate coding standards, ensuring consistency and preventing common errors before code execution.
- **Husky / lint-staged:** Git hooks that perform automated checks (lint, tests, build) before commits, preventing invalid code from entering the repository.
- **Architecture Decision Record (ADR):** A document that records significant architectural decisions, their context, evaluated alternatives, and justifications, promoting traceability and transparency in technical choices.
- **RFC (Request for Comments):** A formal proposal for a significant change, open for review and discussion by the team before implementation, allowing a collaborative approach in framework development.
- **Daily Stand-up:** A brief meeting for daily alignment on progress, blockers, and priorities, essential for agile teams and maintaining smooth communication during project development.
- **Retrospective:** A recurring meeting to evaluate what went well, what needs improvement, and to define actions for team evolution, promoting continuous improvement within the team.

- **CI/CD Pipeline:** An automated flow that compiles, tests, and distributes the application, ensuring frequent and secure releases, essential for production environments in constant evolution.
- **End-to-End Testing (E2E):** Tests that simulate real application use, covering multiple layers (UI, logic, API) to validate the complete flow and ensure system stability.
- **Observability:** The ability to monitor and understand the behavior of a system in production through logs, metrics, and distributed tracing, ensuring that problems are quickly identified.
- **Crash Reporting:** Real-time automated monitoring of application failures (including Sentry, Firebase Crashlytics) to detect, prioritize, and fix issues effectively, improving the user experience.
- **User Feedback Loop:** A continuous process of capturing user feedback, prioritizing improvements, implementing changes, and communicating results, essential to maintaining the relevance of the app in the market.
- **Roadmap:** A living document that organizes future features, fixes, and strategic objectives, aligning teams, products, and users over time, providing a clear view of project progress.
- **Feature Prioritization:** Techniques (RICE, ICE, MoSCoW) for classifying features and fixes based on impact and effort, ensuring team resources are efficiently allocated.
- **Staged Rollout / Canary Release:** Gradual release of a new version to a subset of users, validating stability before full release, minimizing the risk of production failures.
- **Rollback:** Reverting to a previous stable version in case of critical failures in production, essential to ensure service continuity and avoid impacts on end-users.
- **Dependency Management:** Practices to keep libraries and frameworks updated securely (like Renovate, Dependabot), minimizing risks of vulnerabilities and avoiding breaks in the code.
- **Upgrade Helper:** A tool or guide (such as React Native Upgrade Helper) to migrate projects between framework versions, facilitating maintenance of updated versions without compromising stability.
- **Static Analysis:** Automated checking of the code before execution, covering style, typing, and security, preventing errors and improving overall code quality.
- **Onboarding Guide:** Documentation describing environment setup, standards, and processes to quickly integrate new team members, promoting a smoother and more agile learning curve.
- **Design System:** A set of components, visual standards, and UX guidelines that ensure consistency and efficiency in development, making it easier to create cohesive and accessible interfaces.
- **Team Retention:** Practices and culture that maintain motivation, productivity, and low turnover within the development team, creating a healthy and sustainable work environment.

These terms serve as a working glossary to anchor your implementations and discussions around the publication, evolution, and maintenance of React Native mobile applications. They not only help consolidate your understanding of the discussed practices but also provide a solid foundation for optimizing collaboration and executing long-term strategies.

Index

D

E